D1524610

Behind Barbed Wire

Behind Barbed Wire

An Encyclopedia of Concentration and Prisoner-of-War Camps

Alexander Mikaberidze, Editor

ABC-CLIO™

An Imprint of ABC-CLIO, LLC
Santa Barbara, California • Denver, Colorado

Library of Congress Cataloging-in-Publication Data

Names: Mikaberidze, Alexander, editor.
Title: Behind barbed wire : an encyclopedia of concentration and
    prisoner-of-war camps / Alexander Mikaberidze, editor.
Description: Santa Barbara, California : ABC-CLIO, 2019. | Includes
    bibliographical references and index.
Identifiers: LCCN 2018020587 (print) | LCCN 2018026294 (ebook) |
    ISBN 9781440857621 (ebook) | ISBN 9781440857614 (hardcopy : alk. paper)
Subjects: LCSH: Prisoner-of-war camps—Encyclopedias. | Concentration
    camps—Encyclopedias. | Military prisons—Encyclopedias.
Classification: LCC UB800 (ebook) | LCC UB800 .B45 2019 (print) |
    DDC 365/.4503—dc23
LC record available at https://lccn.loc.gov/2018020587

ISBN: 978-1-4408-5761-4 (print)
    978-1-4408-5762-1 (ebook)

23 22 21 20 19   1 2 3 4 5

This book is also available as an eBook.

ABC-CLIO
An Imprint of ABC-CLIO, LLC

ABC-CLIO, LLC
130 Cremona Drive, P.O. Box 1911
Santa Barbara, California 93116-1911
www.abc-clio.com

This book is printed on acid-free paper ∞

Manufactured in the United States of America

In memory of my great-uncle
Giorgi Mikaberidze
who died in German captivity in February 1943

Contents

Primary Documents

Preface

The study of human violence is a difficult subject. It is disheartening to confront horrific acts that human beings are capable of subjecting one another to. Yet the fact remains that, since the beginning of time, conflicts have evoked acts of inhumanity that shocked even hardened souls. One may agree with the famed French writer Gustav Le Bon's assessment that "By the very fact that he forms part of an organized group, a man descends several rungs down the ladder of civilization. Isolated, he may be a cultivated individual, but in a crowd, he is a barbarian."

The past 200 years seem to confirm the validity of Le Bon's statement. Never before has humanity engaged in bloodshed on such a vast scale and with such ferocity. The two world wars of the twentieth century alone claimed tens of millions of lives and left scars that have not yet healed. The industrial era introduced many changes in the nature and conduct of war, not the least of which was practice of setting up special facilities—concentration camps, as they became known—to intern political, ethnic, or other groups to enhance state security, and to punish or exploit the regime's opponents or groups whose loyalties had become suspect. The ideas of population control and forced labor had existed for centuries—American and Spanish treatments of Native Americans are good examples of these—but it was not until the industrial age that technology of sophisticated weapons and barbed wire allowed for a small guard force to impose detention on larger population. The first modern use of concentration camps can be traced back to the 1868–78 Cuban insurrection. To isolate rebels from the civilian population that sometimes fed or sheltered them, Arsenio Martínez Campos, the governor-general of the island, suggested relocation of hundreds of thousands of rural inhabitants into Spanish-held cities behind barbed wire, a strategy he called *reconcentración*. Campos was hesitant to implement such a draconian measure and was soon replaced by Spanish general Velariano Weyler. Living up to his moniker "The Butcher," Weyler mobilized hundreds of thousands of civilians who, on penalty of death, were compelled to move into specially set up encampments. Conditions at these camps rapidly worsened, and tens of thousands of Cubans perished within a year. The U.S. newspapers widely reported on Spain's atrocities in Cuba and President William McKinley denounced the policy of *reconcentración* as "not civilized warfare. It was extermination. The only peace it could beget was that of the wilderness and the grave."

Yet the practice of *reconcentración* quickly spread. After defeating Spain in Cuba, the United States seized former Spanish colonies, including the Philippines, where American authorities had resorted to *reconcentración* to suppress ongoing insurgencies. In southern Africa, Britain used the concept of concentration camps to defeat the recalcitrant Boers. In 1900, during the Boer War, the British military began forcibly relocating more than 200,000 civilians behind barbed wire. Conditions at these camps were terrible, and lack of supplies, exposure to elements, polluted water supplies, and infectious diseases ended up killing thousands of detainees. Indeed, far more people perished in these camps than in combat. Just as the Boer War ended in 1902, concentration camps appeared in the neighboring German colony of South West Africa (modern-day Namibia) where Germany carried out the first genocidal killings of the twentieth century as it tried to exterminate the rebellious Herero people. The surviving Herero people were herded into concentration camps where mistreatment, diseases, and lack of food killed most of them before the camps were fully disbanded in 1907.

During World War I (1914–1918), the camps made their appearance in Europe where they marked escalation in the nature of warfare as civilians became proxies in the war; European powers resorted to internment camps in an effort to detain enemy nationals, isolate political opponents or simply to exterminate undesirables. In Britain, Prime Minister Herbert Henry Asquith sanctioned detention of thousands of German and Austro-Hungarian "enemy aliens" and the policy was soon extended across much of the vast British Empire. Germany responded with mass arrests of aliens from enemy nations as well. By 1918, concentration camps bourgeoned in many parts of the world, including France, Russia, the Ottoman Empire, Austria-Hungary, Brazil, and India. In the United States, German Americans found their loyalties openly questioned.

World War II marked an important change in the nature of concentration camps. The earlier camps targeted foreigners for internment and fatalities tended to result from neglect or incompetence. But during World War II, these camps evolved into far more sinister institutions, as they were applied toward establishment of various forms of totalitarian regimes by targeting their own citizens and exterminating the undesirables. In the United States and Canada, shortly after the outbreak of hostilities with Japan, tens of thousands of citizens of Japanese descent were taken into custody and placed in camps in the interior, underscoring the power of a modern state that was willing to ignore civil liberties of its own citizens. In the Soviet Union, the Gulag system was designed to destroy domestic opposition and jumpstart economic modernization through the use of forced labor. Sweden, Finland, France, the Netherlands, Italy, Croatia, and other states have all resorted to internment camps during the war. But the concept reached its apotheosis in Nazi Germany where Vernichtungslager, or extermination camps, specialized in the mass annihilation of individuals the state had designated as unwanted. The names of Auschwitz-Birkenau, Treblinka, Bergen-Belsen, Buchenwald, Dachau, Mauthausen-Gusen and many others will forever serve as symbols of human degradation, inhumanity, and death, and conjure up heart wrenching images of piles of bones and skulls, of emaciated men, women and children.

The post–World War II period witnessed many other examples of use of internment camps, be it in Cambodia under the Khmer Rouge or in Yugoslavia during the Bosnian War. Britain used internment camps or "new villages" during the Malayan Emergency of 1948–1960 and routinely interned Irish nationals during the "Troubles" period (1968–1998) in Northern Ireland. North Korean camps first appeared during the post–World War II period and remain linchpins of the Communist government's repression. Similarly, the Chinese government has sent millions to "reeducation camps" during the Cultural Revolution of 1966–1969 and continues to rely on a vast network of forced labor camps to the present day.

Behind Barbed Wire: An Encyclopedia of Concentration and Prisoner-of-War Camps seeks to serve as an accessible source for information on the history of concentration and prisoner-of-war camps. It has been written with high school and college students in mind, but we hope it will also be of benefit to a general audience interested in the subject, as well as to university and secondary school teachers seeking a better understanding of a concrete event or personality. With this goal in mind, we decided to avoid specialized academic vocabulary and use clear and accessible narrative. Because readers can easily get confused by technical terms and diacritical marks on foreign words, we decided to minimize the use of diacritical marks. This encyclopedia is not a comprehensive resource since it is impossible to cover all concentration, internment, prisoner-of-war and death camps. So this work is, by its very nature, selective, but it does seek to provide coverage of major events, personalities, and locations.

Every book is a result of collective effort and I am grateful to many people for their support. This work would not have been possible without the abiding enthusiasm of my editor at ABC-CLIO, Padraic (Pat) Carlin, and development editor Uma Maheswari who patiently and steadfastly shepherded it through the development. On a personal level, this book could not have been written without the help and support of my family and friends. I extend my love and thanks to all of them.

A

Abu Ghraib

Prison facility located about 20 miles west of the Iraqi capital, Baghdad. Known during the regime of Saddam Hussein as a place of torture and execution, it later drew international attention when photographs of inmate abuse and torture at the hands of coalition troops were made public in 2004.

Abu Ghraib, officially called the Baghdad Central Confinement Facility (BCCF) under the Hussein regime, was built by British contractors hired by the Iraqi government in the 1960s. Covering an area of about one square mile, the prison housed five different types of prisoners during the time of Hussein: those with long sentences, those with short sentences, those imprisoned for capital crimes, those imprisoned for so-called special offenses, and foreign detainees. Cells, which are about 16 square meters, held as many as 40 people each.

Starting especially during the 1980–1988 Iran-Iraq War, the Iraqi Baathist regime used the facility to imprison political dissidents and ethnic/religious groups seen as threats to the central government. In particular, hundreds of Arab and Kurdish Shiites and Iraqis of Iranian heritage were arrested and housed in the BCCF; torture and executions became routine. Among the tactics used by prison guards was the feeding of shredded plastic to inmates, and it has been speculated that prisoners may have been used as guinea pigs for Hussein's biological and chemical weapons. Although the Iraqi government kept its actions within the complex secret from Iraqi citizens and the international community alike, Amnesty International reported several specific incidents, including the 1996 execution of hundreds of political dissidents and the 1998 execution of many people who had been involved in the 1991 Shiite revolt. The prison, which contained thousands of inmates who were completely cut off from outside communication and held without conviction, was also used to house coalition prisoners of war during the 1991 Persian Gulf War.

With the 2003 U.S.-led Iraq War and subsequent fall of the Hussein government in Iraq, coalition troops took control of Abu Ghraib Prison. The U.S. military used the complex for holding Iraqi insurgents and terrorists accused of anti-U.S. attacks, although by 2004 it had released several hundred prisoners and shared use of the facility with the Iraqi government. Because of the disarray of the Iraqi criminal system, many common criminals uninvolved in the war were held at the facility as well. Abu Ghraib became a household name in April 2004, when the television program *60 Minutes II* aired photographs of prisoner abuse at the hands of coalition troops. The photos, which showed prisoners wearing black hoods, attached to wires and threatened with electrocution, and placed in humiliating sexual positions, sparked worldwide outrage and calls for the investigation and conviction of the military personnel involved.

In this undated still photo, an Iraqi detainee at Abu Ghraib Prison is intimidated by a U.S. soldier using a trained dog. (Washington Post via Getty Images)

The abuse was immediately decried by U.S. president George W. Bush and Defense Secretary Donald Rumsfeld, who on May 7, 2004 took responsibility for the acts that had occurred "under his watch." The Pentagon, which had been investigating reports of abuse since 2003, launched a further investigation into the acts documented by the photographs. Previously, detainee abuse had been investigated by U.S. Army major general Antonio Taguba (who had been given digital images by Sergeant Joseph Darby in January 2004), who concluded in his 53-page report that U.S. military personnel had violated international law. More than a dozen U.S. soldiers and officers were removed from the prison as a result of the internal investigation.

More details emerged following the *60 Minutes II* broadcast. Photographs that the U.S. government would not allow to be released earlier were circulated in 2006. Most importantly, it appeared that the senior U.S. military officer, Lieutenant General Ricardo Sanchez, had authorized treatment "close to" torture, such as the use of military dogs, temperature extremes, and sensory and sleep deprivation, thus making it more difficult to locate responsibility for the general environment leading to abuse. However, in addition to charging certain troops and contractors with torture, the United States made an effort to reduce the number of detainees—estimated at 7,000 prior to the scandal's outbreak—by several thousand. However, many argued that the measures taken were not harsh enough to fit the crime, and some demanded Rumsfeld's resignation.

In August 2004, a military panel confirmed 44 cases of prisoner abuse at the facility and identified 23 soldiers as being responsible. The so-called ringleader of the operation, Army Specialist Charles Graner, was convicted and sentenced to 10 years in prison in January 2005. Meanwhile, Abu Ghraib was twice attacked by insurgents, who attempted to undermine U.S. security at the facility and set prisoners free. In September 2006, the United States handed over control of Abu Ghraib to the Iraqi government.

Jessica Britt

See also: Bagram Air Base; Camp Bucca.

Further Reading

Danner, Mark. *Torture and Truth: America, Abu Ghraib, and the War on Terror.* New York: New York Review Books, 2004.

Greenberg, Karen J., and Joshua L. Dratel, eds. *The Torture Papers: The Road to Abu Ghraib.* Cambridge: Cambridge University Press, 2005.

Martin, Michael. *The Iraqi Prisoner Abuse Scandal.* Farmington Hills, MI: Lucent Books, 2005.

Strasser, Steven, ed. *The Abu Ghraib Investigations: The Official Independent Panel and Pentagon Reports on the Shocking Prisoner Abuse in Iraq.* New York: PublicAffairs, 2004.

Afghanistan

During the Soviet invasion of Afghanistan (1979–1989), both the Soviets and the Afghan *mujahideen* fighters had been involved in routine abuse, torture, and execution of prisoners of war, who were held at prisons and detention centers in Afghanistan and the neighboring Pakistan. Prisoners were usually kept in zindans, or underground pits and jails that have been traditionally used in Central Asia, but there were also more formal internment complexes, such as Pul-e-Charkhi and Badaber; in 1985, a group of Soviet and Afghan POWs organized a major uprising at the Badaber prison complex. Prisoner exchanges did occur on rare occasions, but most were released only after the Soviet withdrawal from Afghanistan in 1989. In 1996–2001, the Taliban regime presided over the state of terror that targeted every aspect of life in Afghanistan, as the secret police and special patrols spied on the population. Political opponents, as well as civilians accused of transgressions against the strict Islamic laws instituted by the Taliban, were harshly persecuted, with thousands interned in prisons. Kabul's soccer stadium became infamous for public executions that the Taliban had staged, as prisoners were led onto a huge open ground in the back of open-topped vans and summarily shot at close range.

In 2001, in the wake of the 9/11 terror attacks on the United States, American forces invaded Afghanistan and overthrew the Taliban regime. The ensuing War on Terror revealed many challenges of upholding existing laws on the treatment of captives in a new kind of conflict. The United States has refused to grant a prisoner-of-war status to prisoners captured during the invasion of Afghanistan, arguing that they were terrorists who did not meet the requirements laid down by the Third Geneva Convention of 1949 because they failed to conduct military operations in accordance with the laws and customs of war; the U.S. government did declare, though, that captives would be treated humanely in the spirit of international law. The United States established two major detention facilities in Afghanistan, at Bagram military air base and in Kandahar, where captives were (and still are) held while the suspected terrorists were also transferred to the facility at Guantánamo Bay, Cuba.

Since 2001, all warring sides in Afghanistan have been accused of mistreating prisoners. Both the Taliban and the US-allied Northern Alliance earned notoriety for holding prisoners in primitive conditions and intentionally killing them. Thus, in 2001, over 500 captured Taliban fighters were executed by the Northern Alliance in the city of Mazar-e-Sharif, while hundreds of prisoners died while being transferred from Kunduz to a prison in northern Afghanistan; that same year, the Taliban prisoners launched a major uprising at Qala-i-Jangi, a nineteenth-century fortress that had been converted into a makeshift prison. In 2008, the Taliban successfully carried out an attack on the Sarposa prison and released some 1,200 prisoners; three years later the prison was the site of a major prisoner escape.

The American Civil Liberties Union and other human rights organizations accuse the U.S. military of abusing prisoners at its detention facilities, including the Bagram Air Force base, where prisoner mistreatment was particularly pervasive in 2003–2004 and resulted in the deaths of at least three prisoners; the CIA, meanwhile, had maintained secret prisons across Afghanistan, including a notorious facility known as the Salt Pit, in a factory on the plains north of Kabul. These internment facilities were revealed in a 2014 report published by a U.S. Senate committee, which described prisoners being subjected to waterboarding, sleep deprivation, cold, forced nudity, and other mistreatment. In December 2014, the United States transferred all detention facilities in Afghanistan to the Afghan government. A year later, the UN found that prisoner abuse was widespread at detention facilities run by the Afghan security services (the National Directorate of Security [the Afghan intelligence agency], Afghan National Police, Afghan National Army and local police); the report claimed that more than a third of detainees interviewed by the UN have been subjected to mistreatment, including beatings with pipes, electrical shocks, and near asphyxiation; extrajudicial killings have also taken place, especially in Kandahar, where the provincial police chief has been accused of torturing and killing of detainees suspected of being Taliban militants.

Alexander Mikaberidze

See also: Bagram Air Base; Qala-i-Jangi Revolt.

Further Reading

Doyle, Robert. *The Enemy in Our Hands: America's Treatment of Enemy Prisoners of War from the Revolution to the War on Terror.* Lexington: University Press of Kentucky, 2011.

Forsythe, David P. *The Politics of Prisoner Abuse: The United States and Enemy Prisoners after 9/11.* Cambridge: Cambridge University Press, 2011.

Inquiry into the Treatment of Detainees in U.S. Custody. U.S. Senate Committee on Armed Services. Washington: U.S. G.P.O., 2009.

"In U.S. Report, Brutal Details of 2 Afghan Inmates' Deaths," *New York Times*, 20 May 2005, http://www.nytimes.com/2005/05/20/world/asia/in-us-report-brutal-details -of-2-afghan-inmates-deaths.html

Kakar, M. Hasan. *Afghanistan: The Soviet Invasion and the Afghan Response, 1979–1982.* Berkeley: University of California Press, 1997.

U.S. Senate Select Committee on Intelligence. *The Official Senate Report on CIA Torture. Committee Study of the Central Intelligence Agency's Detention and Interrogation Program.* New York: Skyhorse Publishing, 2015.

American Civil War (1861–1865)

During the U.S. Civil War, more than 674,000 prisoners of war were captured by both sides. Over 400,000 individuals spent time in a prison enclosure, and 56,000 did not survive captivity to return home. The mortality rate, nearly 15 percent for all POWs held captive, was higher than the battlefield mortality rate of the war, demonstrating that, in some fashion, surrender was a more dangerous option than fighting. The high death rates were due chiefly to overcrowding, disease, poor food, substandard sanitation, and a lack of supplies.

When the war commenced in 1861, neither side expected to face a protracted conflict involving millions of soldiers. As such, neither side entered the war with plans to hold, feed, clothe, and sustain tens of thousands of war prisoners. Previous American experience with prisoner affairs was relatively scant, and little institutional memory of detainment operations remained in the U.S. Army. Although Brevet Lieutenant General Winfield Scott, the Union army general-in-chief, had spent time as a prisoner during the War of 1812, he devoted little attention to the subject before relinquishing his post in November 1861.

As the war quickly expanded, so did the number and needs of prisoners, particularly in the Eastern Theater. Union detainees taken by the Confederates were sent to Richmond, quickly filling the local jail there. The provost marshal of Richmond, Brigadier General John H. Winder, quickly ordered the conversion of tobacco warehouses and factories into rudimentary holding facilities. More permanent camps soon appeared on Belle Isle in the James River, where it was assumed that the prisoners could be more easily isolated from the populace. Confederates captured by the Union reported to existing federal fortifications along the East Coast, most commonly Fort Delaware, Fort McHenry, and Point Lookout, Maryland. Colonel William C. Hoffman, himself a prisoner on parole and awaiting exchange, assumed the role of commissary general of prisoners.

Even as the number of prisoners grew, both sides expected to resolve the problem through prisoner exchanges. The Confederacy held a surplus of prisoners in 1861, and believed that an exchange agreement would convey legitimacy to their cause by recognizing their right to negotiate as an equal power. President Abraham Lincoln was loath to provide such recognition, but he understood the need to redeem Union captives. In February 1862, negotiators agreed to a general exchange, using a rank equivalency table from 1813 allowing detainees of different ranks to be exchanged.

In June 1862, exchanges formally commenced, allowing each side to reduce the overcrowded facilities. The system allowed prisoners to be exchanged from all branches of service, including privateers. All captives were to be paroled and forwarded to their own lines within ten days of capture. Surplus prisoners were then held out of service by their own forces to await exchange. Although the system was imperfect, it functioned fairly well, and by the end of the year, the prison compounds had virtually emptied.

At the end of 1862, the Union commenced enlistment of African American soldiers. Confederate president Jefferson Davis, fearing the possibility of a slave revolt, announced that white officers commanding black troops could be tried for inciting a servile insurrection. Lincoln threatened retaliation against Confederate prisoners for the mistreatment of any Union soldiers. The exchange cartel soon collapsed, and the number of detainees rapidly rose.

The Confederate advantage in prisoners captured ended in 1863. When Vicksburg surrendered in July 1863, Major General Ulysses S. Grant paroled its 30,000 defenders and sent them home to await exchange. The South did not possess sufficient captives for exchange, but claimed that the Union had already received a surplus of parolees. After substantial debate, Confederate exchange commissioner Robert Ould unilaterally declared the Vicksburg captives exchanged. His Union counterpart, Major General Benjamin Butler, declared the cartel annulled, ensuring that the remaining and subsequent captives would languish in captivity for the rest of the war.

The horrors of captivity associated with Civil War prison camps did not become manifest until 1864, when prison compounds became dangerously overcrowded and exchanges ceased. New facilities could not be completed before detainees began arriving, and supplies of food, clothing, and medicine were inadequate. On both sides, the detainment camps became disease ridden and filthy, with some of the locations, such as Camp Sumter (Andersonville), Georgia, and Elmira, New York, suffering mortality rates of more than 30 percent. The largest contributor to prisoners' misery was not a deliberate policy of mistreatment, but rather a military and political system overwhelmed by the demands of the conflict. Detainees remained a low priority for each government, with both struggling to keep field armies supplied and functional. The needs of prisoners simply faded in the face of more pressing concerns. By the time the plight of captives had become well-known, the war had nearly ended.

Paul J. Springer

See also: Andersonville Prison; American Revolutionary War; Confederate States of America; Elmira Prison (New York).

Further Reading

Sanders, Charles W. *While in the Hands of the Enemy: Military Prisons of the Civil War.* Baton Rouge: Louisiana State University Press, 2005.

Speer, Lonnie R. *Portals to Hell: Military Prisons of the Civil War.* Mechanicsburg, PA: Stackpole Books, 1997.

Springer, Paul J. *America's Captives: Treatment of POWs from the Revolutionary War to the War on Terror.* Lawrence: University Press of Kansas, 2010.

American Revolutionary War (1775–1783)

Soldiers and seamen captured during the Revolutionary War faced very difficult conditions. This was not so much a matter of design, but rather because neither side had given any particular attention to the matter at the onset of fighting, nor anticipated the length and intensity of the struggle and the large number of men who would be captured and must then be housed and fed. Generally speaking, however, British and German troops taken by the Patriot side fared better than Americans in the hands of the British or the Loyalists taken by the Patriots.

The first American soldiers captured by the British may have been the 39 Patriots taken in the Battle of Bunker Hill on June 17, 1775. Normal jail cells were soon crowded past capacity and the numbers swelled dramatically with the commencement of the British New York Campaign in 1776. In the capture of Fort Washington in Manhattan on November 16, alone, the British took 230 officers and 2,607 soldiers, and General Sir William Howe, commander of British forces, reported to London on December 13, 1776, that his army then held at least 4,430 American officers and enlisted men.

The Americans returned the favor at the culmination of the Saratoga Campaign (June 14–October 17, 1777) when 5,895 British and Germans surrendered. The biggest British haul of the war in terms of numbers of prisoners came with the surrender of Charles Town (Charleston), South Carolina, following the siege there of March 29–May 12, 1780, when the British captured 5,466 officers and men. Although British commander Lieutenant General Sir Henry Clinton paroled the militiamen, the Continental Army troops passed into captivity. Following their successful siege of Yorktown (September 28–October 19, 1781), the Americans and French netted the largest prisoner haul of the war: 8,077 British—840 seamen, 80 camp followers, and 7,157 soldiers.

Both sides also captured ships of the other at sea. These included warships, troop transports, supply ships, privateers, and merchantmen and fishing vessels. Their crewmen passed into captivity. On September 30, 1780, American diplomat Henry Laurens was among those taken at sea, along with most of his papers. Among the latter was a draft of a Dutch American treaty of alliance, which helped produce a British declaration of war against the Dutch in December 1780. Laurens spent nearly 15 months in the Tower of London until he was released at the end of December 1781.

Accurate statistics are entirely lacking on the total number of prisoners taken by each side in the war, although what evidence there is suggests that the numbers were about even. With the Patriot side in particular lacking secure facilities to house the numbers taken, many prisoners simply escaped after a short period. Germans in particular were encouraged to do so. When the "Convention Army"—those British and German troops and camp followers who had surrendered at Saratoga in 1777—were transferred from Boston to Charlottesville, Virginia, in the winter of 1778–1779, the route of march selected wound through farming territory settled largely by German immigrants, and many of the German prisoners escaped then. The Americans knew that they were likely to end up as farm hands, replacing many Patriot men who gone off to fight, and that the escaped prisoners were unlikely to return to the British army, or for that matter, to Germany.

Ultimately, some 4,000 British and German prisoners reached Charlottesville and there began erecting Albemarle Barracks, which, at twice the population of the capital of Williamsburg, immediately became the largest city in Virginia. Conditions for the prisoners at Charlottesville were at first very difficult, as the men had to erect their own shelters in winter and those built at first proved largely inadequate. With the Continental Congress unable to provide funds for food, the prisoners soon set about growing their own. Certainly, there were a boon to the local economy, and by spring—thanks largely to their own efforts—the prisoners had improved quarters and Albemarle Barracks boasted gardens, livestock, a store, coffeehouse, church, a tavern with a billiard table, and a theater with a sign reading "Who would have expected all this here?" Here also a number of the German prisoners were paroled to work on local farms. A number simply departed, many of them marrying local women.

The officers of the Convention Army, of course, had better conditions. The top ranking among them, including British army major general William Phillips and commander of Brunswick troops fighting with the British, Major General Friedrich von Riedesel, rented some of the finest homes in Charlottesville. With the state open to British invasion, Virginia governor Thomas Jefferson closed Albemarle Barracks in the fall of 1780, and the remaining prisoners were marching north to Fort Frederick, Maryland, where they were held until the end of the war. In April 1783, when the last were released, fewer than 2,400 remained.

Conditions were much more difficult for most American prisoners of war, who were packed into jails or held aboard prison ships. The British had a difficult time finding sufficient housing for the prisoners taken in the 1776 New York Campaign, especially with the subsequent great fire that destroyed much of the city. The solution was found in utilizing former sugar warehouses, that trade being largely cut off. Prisons in New York City itself included Van Cortland's Sugar House (the northwestern corner of the Trinity churchyard), Rhinelander's (corner of William and Duane streets), the Liberty Street Sugar House (numbers 34 and 36 Liberty Street), and the Provost Jail. The last two were the most feared. In addition to other sugar warehouses, places of imprisonment in the city included dissenters' churches, King's College (Columbia University), and city hall. Subsequent British prisons were established as a consequence of other campaigns, in Philadelphia, Pennsylvania; Savannah, Georgia; and Charles Town (Charleston), South Carolina.

Housing their American prisoners aboard hulks—older ships that were essentially hulls stripped of armament, but also rigging and masts, and thus incapable of going to sea—seemed to the British at the time an ideal solution to the lack of housing. The sailors originally incarcerated below decks were soon joined there by soldiers. The first of these was apparently the *Whitby*, which was in 1776 anchored near Remsen's Mill on the western end of Long Island and converted into a floating prison, but the most notorious was the *Jersey*, a third-rate 64-gun ship that had been dismasted as unfit for service and that held 1,000 or more men in Wallabout Bay on the western end of Long Island just across the East River from New York City. Before the end of the war, there were 26 British prison ships in Wallabout Bay, the East River, and the Hudson. Other prison ships in Wallabout Bay included the *Hunter* and *Stromboli*. Another prison ship, the *Scorpion*, was moored off Paulus Hook.

Conditions were appalling. Overcrowding, inadequate and spoiled food, poor sanitation, and lack of fresh air and light turned them into death traps. The British standard for prisoners was two-thirds the daily ration for a British soldier or sailor, but this was hardly generous, and in point of fact the prisoner standard was seldom met and, when it was, the food was often spoiled and hardly edible. Clothing, bedding, and other necessities were always in very short supply. The floating prisons became vectors of disease, including typhoid, yellow fever, and smallpox. As many as 11,000 prisoners may have died while being held on these ships between 1776 and 1783.

A prison ship was also anchored at St. Lucia in the West Indies to serve as a drop-off point for Americans captured at sea in the vicinity. After the British took Charles Town in May 1780, they also employed prison ships there. Many of the large number of Continental Army prisoners were also held at nearby Haddrell's Point, where the difficult conditions prompted a number to volunteer for service in the British army under a guarantee that it would be in the West Indies and not against their former comrades. Other Americans captured in British, Loyalist, and Indian frontier raids were imprisoned in Canada. Prisoners held by the British there generally received the best treatment, thanks to the humane policies of governor of Quebec, Major General Sir Guy Carleton.

Patriot prisoners were also held at Halifax, Nova Scotia, and in prisons in England itself. Among Americans transported to England and held there was early Revolutionary War Patriot hero, Colonel Ethan Allen, who was captured in a futile effort to seize Montreal in Canada. Many of the Americans taken at sea ended up in Britain. Among the English prisons where Americans were kept during the war were Dartmoor, Old Mill Prison at Plymouth, Forton Prison at Portsmouth, and the Tower of London. The number of American seamen held rose steadily as privateering increased. By 1780, the number of seamen prisoners probably numbered about 5,300.

Conditions in the prisons in England were harsh, but were mitigated by the relief efforts of English Whigs who supported the revolutionaries. American emissary to France, Benjamin Franklin, also raised money to help mitigate the conditions of their confinement. A number of prisoners also escaped and managed to make their way across the English Channel to safety in France.

There is little evidence of Patriot mistreatment of British and German prisoners. The exception to this is that accorded some Loyalist prisoners, a number of whom had a difficult time of it in captivity. Their numbers were relatively few in proportion to those of the soldiers, however. New-Gate Prison in East Granby, Connecticut, was perhaps the most notorious. It was located in a financially failed copper mine purchased by the Connecticut General Assembly in 1773 as a facility for prisoners where escape would be impossible. It initially consisted of a 12×15-foot underground room at the bottom of a mine shaft with an iron gate on the top. The prisoners held at what became known as New-Gate Prison, were those condemned to hard labor and they continued the mining of ore.

During the Revolutionary War, a number of Loyalists and court-martialed Continental Army soldiers were held at New-Gate, and many suffered and died there in its conditions of dampness, constant 50°C temperature, vermin, insects, and darkness. As more prisoners were incarcerated at New-Gate during the war, it was expanded to include the manufacture of hand-wrought nails. Workhouses and guardhouses were added above ground, with the prisoners brought to the surface at 4:00 a.m. to begin their daily toil in the workhouse.

Early in the war, Elias Boudinot was appointed American commissary general of prisoners and commissioned a lieutenant colonel in the Continental Army. Joshua Loring was his counterpart for the British army, while David Sproat held the same position for the Royal Navy. Loring became notorious among Americans and symbolic to them of their enemy's mistreatment of prisoners, although this was more by neglect than design. Sproat enjoyed the same reputation, with Americans believing him to be particularly vindictive.

Boudinot was able to persuade the British to let him keep an agent in New York City on a permanent basis to treat with the British on prisoner issues. Lewis Pintard, who had been a merchant in New York City before the war, accepted this post and was able to arrange some shipments of food and clothing to the prisoners held by the British. John Beatty eventually succeeded Boudinot, while John Franklin replaced Pintard.

Continental Army commander general George Washington attempted early in the war to set up a formal arrangement regarding the exchange of prisoners but, given the disparity in numbers held, the British were not much interested. This changed in the fall of 1777 with the large number of British and German prisoners taken at Saratoga. Although throughout the war the British were not interested in entering into a formal arrangement for the exchange of captives, they were prepared to continue a program of partial exchanges, a number of which occurred. In all the two sides held eight different conferences between 1777 and 1783 regarding the exchange of prisoners but the Americans were only able to secure partial exchanges until 1783.

Exchanges were usually rank for rank. Higher ranking officers might be paroled, that is give their word that they would not fight again until properly exchanged. Thus, General Riedesel was paroled from Albemarle Barracks to New York City, where he spent a year before being formally exchanged in October 1780, and allowed to return to military duty, exchanged for Continental army major general Benjamin Lincoln, who had been taken prisoner in the British capture of Charles Town in May 1780. The need to secure an officer of equivalent rank for the exchange of Continental army major general Charles Lee led Patriot forces to carry out a rather spectacular night raid in July 1777 that netted British brigadier general and commander of British troops at Rhode Island Richard Prescott.

Finally, on May 6, 1783, Washington and British commander lieutenant general Sir Guy Carleton met at Tappan, New York, and there resolved all remaining issues regarding the release of prisoners. Washington informed Secretary of War Benjamin Lincoln in early July 1783 that virtually all prisoners held by the American side had been released.

Although not intended to be deliberately cruel and while it improved somewhat in the course of the war, the British treatment of their prisoners did not serve them well. In fact, it turned many Americans against all things English and hardened Patriot resolve to fight through to final independence.

Spencer C. Tucker

See also: American Civil War.

Further Reading
Abell, Francis. *Prisoners of War in Britain, 1756–1815*. Oxford: Oxford University Press, 1914.

Bolton, Charles Knowles. *The Private Soldier under Washington.* New York: Barnes & Noble, 2011.

Bowman, Larry G. *Captive Americans: Prisoners during the American Revolution.* Athens: Ohio University Press, 1976.

Commager, Henry Steele, and Richard B. Morris. *The Spirit of 'Seventy-Six.* New York: Harper & Row, 1967.

Dabney, William. *After Saratoga: The Story of the Convention Army.* Albuquerque: University of New Mexico Press, 1954.

Dandridge, Danske. *American Prisoners of the Revolution.* Baltimore, MD: Genealogical Publishing Co., 1967.

Lossing, Benson J. *The Pictorial Field Book of the Revolution; or, Illustrations, by Pen and Pencil of the History, Biography, Scenes, Relics, and Traditions of the War for Independence.* 2 vols. New York: Harper & Bros., 1851–1852.

Neimeyer, Charles P. *American Soldiers' Lives: The Revolutionary War.* Westport, CT: Greenwood Press, 2007.

Onderdonk, Henry. *Revolutionary Incidents of Suffolk and Kings Counties: With an Account of the Battle of Long Island and the British Prisons and Prison-Ships.* Reprint, 1846. Port Washington, NY: Kennikat Press, 1970.

Peckham, Howard H., ed. *The Toll of Independence: Engagements & Battle Casualties of the American Revolution.* Chicago: University of Chicago Press, 1974.

Prelinger, Catherine M. "Benjamin Franklin and the American Prisoners of War in England during the American Revolution." *William and Mary Quarterly* 33 (1975): 261–294.

Andersonville Prison

Infamous Confederate facility that housed Union prisoners of war in 1864 and 1865, Andersonville Prison was situated just outside the tiny hamlet of Andersonville, Georgia, in Sumter County, in the southwestern part of the state. Many Confederates referred to it as Camp Sumter. The site was chosen primarily because it was isolated from population centers, was situated along the Southwestern Railroad line, and was surrounded by fertile lands that allegedly could help produce food for the prisoners. In reality, however, the rail line was of no use after Union major general William T. Sherman's march through Georgia, which severed it. And the abundant agricultural lands nearby were planted mainly with cotton, rather than food crops. As a result, the Confederate army was hard-pressed to provide adequate supplies and nutrition to Andersonville's inmates. Conditions at the camp deteriorated badly, and by war's end thousands of prisoners there had died from disease, malnutrition, or abuse.

By late 1863, Confederate officials were growing increasingly concerned with the burgeoning prison population at Libby Prison in Richmond, Virginia, which was straining the city's supplies. By early 1864, the decision had been made to erect a facility near Andersonville to accept Union prisoners being held in Richmond and elsewhere. By then, construction had already begun on a wooden stockade that was to enclose some 16.5 acres of land. Eventually, the stockade would enclose 26 acres as the prison's population swelled. In February 1864, about 500 prisoners arrived at Andersonville, and a Swiss-born immigrant, Major Heinrich (Henry) Wirz, became the camp's first—and only—commandant. Between February and

July 1864, Andersonville's population exploded, reaching some 32,000 prisoners. The huge influx in part was due to the breakdown of the prisoner-exchange cartel in the spring of 1864.

The exponential increase in detainees being held at Andersonville made an already desperate situation even worse. Medicine, clothing, and food were all in very short supply. Overcrowding was perhaps the most serious affliction of the prison, with facilities designed to hold 8,000–9,000 men jammed with four or more times that number at any given time. The stockade was enlarged on several occasions, and many small wooden huts were constructed using prison labor, but there was never adequate shelter for all of the prisoners. Worse still, the once-clear stream that flowed through the stockade became quickly polluted by latrines that were located too close to it. Diseases such as cholera and dysentery became epidemic in the camp, and thousands of detainees died as a result.

Many prisoners complained bitterly about the hard discipline and lax administrative policies meted out by Wirz, who many Northerners categorized as a "fiend." After the war, he was tried for "impairing the health and destroying the lives of prisoners," and was found guilty and hanged in November 1865. Many historians, however, claim that he was made a scapegoat and had not systematically abused internees. Indeed, the daily rations he set for his guards and other prison workers were the same as those for the prisoners. To be sure, while Wirz's reputation may have been exaggerated, there is no doubt that he was a strict and uncompromising disciplinarian.

The worst violence at Andersonville was not instigated by the guards or administration; rather, it came from the prisoners themselves. Prisoners who preyed on the weak and the sick, called "raiders," oftentimes stole from and physically abused and intimidated other prisoners, many of them too ill to fend for themselves. The raiders set up an elaborate bartering system whereby they sold or bartered away food of their fellow inmates. A group of detainees who vowed to protect fellow inmates from the depredations of the raiders soon formed. They were known as the "regulators." When the regulators held six raiders hostage, the prison's administration allowed them to be tried for their crimes. They were found guilty and hanged in the stockade before the prison population. After that, new distribution methods made it much more difficult to steal or barter food within the prison. The regulators also caught other raiders, many of whom were disciplined by forcing them to run the gauntlet, placing them in a stock, or compelling them to move about with a heavy iron ball chained to an ankle.

Andersonville Prison was closed soon after the cessation of hostilities in April 1865, and the last prisoners left its confines in May 1865. A cemetery next to the prison site, containing 12,912 graves and almost 1,000 more unmarked graves, serves as a grim testimonial to the hellish conditions inside the Confederacy's largest prison camp. In all, the prison processed about 45,000 prisoners during its short existence. The site of the camp is now a National Historic Site, honoring American prisoners of war in all of the nation's armed conflicts.

Paul G. Pierpaoli, Jr.

See also: American Civil War; Confederate States of America; Elmira Prison (New York); Libby Prison.

Further Reading

Brown, Daniel P. *The Tragedy of Libby and Andersonville Prison Camps.* Ventura, CA: Golden West Historical Publications, 1991.

Futch, Ovid L. *History of Andersonville Prison.* Gainesville: University of Florida Press, 1977.

Apache Wars (1861–1886)

The Apaches were a Native American population that resided in between present-day Texas and Arizona. They fiercely resisted American expansion and fought a long conflict against the United States starting in 1861 when General James H. Carleton and Colonel Christopher (Kit) Carson received orders to move thousands of Mescalero Apaches to Bosque Redondo, a barren reservation along the Pecos River. After two years of skirmishing with the Apaches, Carleton lured Mangas Coloradas, the Apache chief, under a flag of truce and had him killed. Infuriated Apaches then raided settlements throughout Arizona and New Mexico.

After a decade of fighting, Eskiminzin, chief of the Pinal and Aravaipa Apaches, negotiated a peace with the Americans and, in 1871, he agreed to have his tribesmen settle at Camp Grant, near Tucson. The agreement collapsed after American colonists attacked the Apache settlement and murdered over 140 Native Americans. American authorities then insisted on Apaches moving to reservations. After two years of campaigning, the Apaches were defeated and forced to relocate to the San Carlos Agency, an internment camp on a barren tract of land along Arizona's Gila River, which soon became known known as "Hell's Forty Acres" because of deplorable sanitary and environmental conditions.

Some Apache leaders resisted resettlement—Victorio, Geronimo, and other Apache chiefs fought against the Americans throughout the late 1870s, but were ultimately defeated in 1886. The Apaches were interned at the San Carlos Agency; some Apaches were loaded onto trains and sent to internment camps in Florida, while the most defiant ones were detained at Fort Pickens, a hard labor camp. After public protests condemning the treatment of the Apache prisoners, the American government moved over 350 Apache detainees to an abandoned army barracks in Mount Vernon, Alabama, in 1887.

In later years some Apaches were allowed to return to San Carlos, but American settlers refused to allow their settlement. Thus, Geronimo and hundreds of surviving Apaches had to move to a reservation at Fort Sill, Indian Territory. The U.S. Congress released the last of the Apache detainees in 1913.

Alexander Mikaberidze

See also: Indian Removal Act (1830); Trail of Tears.

Further Reading

Ball, Eve. *In the Days of Victorio.* Tucson: University of Arizona Press, 1970.

Moorhead, Max L. *The Apache Frontier.* Norman: University of Oklahoma Press, 1968.

Thrapp, Dan L. *The Conquest of Apacheria.* Norman: University of Oklahoma Press, 1967.

Utley, Robert M. *The Indian Frontier of the American West, 1846–1890.* Albuquerque: University of New Mexico Press, 1984.

Arbeitslager

In Nazi Germany, *arbeitslager* was a labor camp. Many of these labor camps were established after World War I, when some German organizations pointed out militarist potential of national labor service and perceived them as a tool to instill self-discipline, community spirit, and national pride.

The nature of arbeitslager changed with the rise of the German National Socialist (Nazi) party to power. Labor camps increasingly became *zwangsarbeitslager*, or forced labor camps, where the Nazi regime forcibly employed political dissidents and "undesirable elements" (*unzuverlässige Elemente*) such as the homeless, homosexuals, criminals, political dissidents, communists, Jews, etc. Prisoners were frequently worked to death, given short rations or killed if they became unable to work.

During World War II, these inmates were compelled to provide labor to the German war industry, as well as build and repair German infrastructure damaged by the Allied bombings; the Mittelbau-Dora labor camp complex, for example, played an important role in the production of the V-2 rocket. Furthermore, German industrial conglomerates and corporations used millions of Jews, Slavs, and other peoples residing in German conquered territories as slave laborers. Among these companies were Thyssen, Krupp, Bosch, Daimler-Benz, Demag, Henschel, Junkers, Messerschmitt, Siemens, Volkswagen, etc.; overall, more than 2,000 German companies profited from slave labor during the Nazi era. The German chemical and pharmaceutical industry conglomerate I.G. Farben, for example, established several facilities next to concentration camps and relied on prisoner labor to produce many of its commodities; I.G. Farben's Buna Chemical Plant at Dwory had a contractual relationship with I.G. Farbenindustrie AG Auschwitz, which supplied it with tens of thousands of slave laborers in 1942–1944.

Slave laborers (*zwangsarbeiter*) were grouped into several broad categories. The first, *militärinternierte* (military internees) comprised of prisoners of wars, who, under the Geneva Convention, could be used for work within established restrictions. By 1944, some 2 million POWs were employed as forced laborers in Germany, with the Nazi authorities routinely disregarding the Geneva Convention and treated POWs, especially the Soviet ones, with utter callousness. The second category, *zivilarbeiter* (civilian workers), included civilian population from the territories that Nazi German had occupied. *Ostarbeiter* (eastern workers) represented the third category of forced laborers and included civilians from Polish and Soviet regions that had been forcibly moved to labor camps. It is estimated that as many as 15 million people from twenty European countries had been forced laborers during World War II.

Within labor camps, work parties (*Arbeitskommandos*) were usually clothed in striped pajama-style uniforms; colored patches were used to distinguish types of prisoners: red for political opponents, violet for Jehovah's Witnesses, green for criminals, yellow for Jews, black for "asocials" (*Asoziale*), brown for Romanis, and pink for homosexuals. Inmates were given a number that was tattooed on the arm. Their daily routine began with a lengthy roll call (*appell*), after which those assigned to a work parties would leave for their stations. They worked for the rest of the day (with a brief lunch break), oftentimes performing heavy labor in bad weather and dangerous conditions; the corpses of those who died during the day had to be carried back to the compound.

Alexander Mikaberidze

See also: Concentration Camps; Gulag; Sevvostlag; Slave Labor (World War II).

Further Reading

Allen, Michael Thad. *The Business of Genocide: The SS, Slave Labor, and the Concentration Camps.* Chapel Hill: University of North Carolina Press, 2005.

Campbell, Joan. *Joy in Work, German Work: The National Debate, 1800–1945.* Princeton: Princeton University Press, 2014.

Herbert, Ulrich, and William Templer. *Hitler's Foreign Workers: Enforced Foreign Labor in Germany under the Third Reich.* Cambridge: Cambridge University Press, 2006.

Argentina

Between 1974 and 1983, Argentina was ravaged by the struggles between a military dictatorship and its political opponents. The roots of what became known as the Dirty War (*Guerra Sucia*) stretch back to the early 1930s, when the military became active in Argentine politics. Ultraconservative elements within the Argentine Army argued that the political process was beyond redemption and that elections and political pluralism threatened to move Argentina in the wrong direction.

The Mothers of the Plaza de Mayo gather in Buenos Aires, April 1982. They are women whose children disappeared during the Dirty War of 1976–1983 in Argentina. (Michael Brennan/Getty Images)

General José Félix Uriburu's dictatorship (1930–1932), which openly embraced such antidemocratic viewpoints, appears to have foreshadowed the Dirty War. The Perónist movement, led by President Juan Perón, emerged out of a military dictatorship beginning in 1946 and helped polarize Argentine politics and society. After a military coup forced Perón from power in 1955, his supporters fought successfully to limit the ability of any party, group, or force to rule effectively in Argentina. Anti-Perónist factions within the military became increasingly frustrated with decades of struggle against the Perónist forces, which dominated labor unions. As the military became more involved in Argentine politics, the political scene became increasingly violent and unstable. Student groups, Catholic reform groups connected to working-class and rural communities, and factions within the Perónist movement became radicalized.

Influenced by successful guerrilla strategies in other settings—most notably the 1959 Cuban Revolution—opponents of the Argentine military armed themselves and trained for battle in the 1960s. With the political process wholly discredited, groups on the Right and Left clashed violently beginning in 1969. On the Left, a number of groups, led by the Montoneros and the Ejercito Revolucionario del Pueblo (Revolutionary Army of the People), kidnapped business leaders and government officials, robbed banks and businesses, attacked government sites, and challenged the authority of the military and its civilian allies. On the Right, groups such as the Argentine Anti-Communist Alliance, with ties to the military, police force, and conservative factions within the Perónist movement, also emerged.

The political chaos and violence had reached a crucial point by 1972. Pressure from all sides forced government authorities to allow Perón's return from exile, as activists across the political spectrum had fought to bring the ex-president back to power. The polarization of the political process had frustrated anti-Perónist elements in the military. Having failed at their attempts to rule without the Perónists, they accepted his return and inevitable election in 1973. Yet Perón's return brought no solution. Political and economic mayhem continued as rival factions fought for positions within the Perónist movement after 1973. Perón's 1974 death only added to the volatile environment. Behind the scenes, the military once again moved to take control of the country.

The Dirty War began in earnest with military-sponsored campaigns against guerrilla operations in northwestern Argentina in 1974. Combining political and security operations, military commanders seized authority across provinces and systematically detained, interrogated, and killed thousands of "subversives," whom its officers had identified as "enemies of order." By 1975, using clandestine operations against real and suspected terrorist cells, the military had neutralized guerrilla forces throughout the country.

At this juncture, a second phase of the Dirty War began. Commanders of the armed forces deposed María Estela Martínez de Perón's government in 1976. The army, navy, air force, and police throughout the country then deployed anti-subversive units that targeted enemies of the state for detention. Over 300 internment camps and detention centers were established across the country, with the Escuela Superior de Mecánica de la Armada (ESMA; Higher School of Mechanics of the Navy) becoming one of the most notorious detention centers. The ensuing kidnappings, tortures, and murders launched a wave of state-sponsored terrorism that aimed at "disciplining" the population. It is estimated that as many as 40,000 Argentineans may have been detained at these sites and murdered in the Dirty War during 1974–1983.

Working with military officials in Brazil, Chile, Uruguay, and Paraguay, the Argentine military dictatorship shared intelligence and coordinated actions against targeted enemies who had fled across borders to avoid capture. The military junta speciously justified its abhorrent actions as a broad and just campaign against international communism and in support of Christian civilization. Understandably, the Dirty War generated significant domestic and international opposition. Although many of the dictatorship's officers had received training at the U.S.- backed School of the Americas, U.S. president Jimmy Carter cited human rights violations as justification for limiting aid to Argentina. The Mothers of the Plaza de Mayo, an organization of mothers of victims of the regime's policies that held silent marches near the presidential palace, led a growing domestic opposition that pressured the dictatorship. Ultimately, economic mismanagement and military blunders during the Falklands War forced the dictatorship from power and ended its campaign of political violence in 1982.

Daniel Lewis

See also: Chile.

Further Reading
Lewis, Paul. *Guerrillas and Generals*. Westport, CT: Praeger, 2002.
Rock, David. *Authoritarian Argentina*. Berkeley: University of California Press, 1993

Armenian Genocide

Although invoking the term "concentration camp" today conjures up images from the Holocaust, historical scholarship points to the actions of the Spanish in Cuba (1896–1897), the British in South Africa (1899–1902), the Americans in the Philippines (1901–1902), and Germans in South West Africa (1904–1907) as the earliest cases of the use of concentration camps to control, suppress, exploit, or destroy civilians.

Concentration camps were also employed during the Armenian Genocide of 1915–1923, committed by the Young Turks in the dying days of the Ottoman Empire, as World War I raged on. Close to 2 million Armenians were deported from their homes. Many died from massacres, hunger, disease, and exposure to harsh conditions. Hundreds of thousands of deportees who survived the initial wave of deprivation and brutalities arrived in the South East of the Ottoman Empire (in what is now Syria) beginning in May 1915. They were incarcerated in concentration sites, from the initial "resting camps" and transit camps north of Aleppo, like Islahiye, Bozanti, and Mamoura, to the eventual camps along the Euphrates River and in Ras ul-Ayn. Some of the camps were in operation briefly, while others, like Islahiye, operated from the summer of 1915 to the spring of 1916. Tens of thousands of deportees met their death from disease, starvation, and attacks by brigands on these camps.

Deportees were then pushed further east along the Euphrates River and "settled" in camps in Meskene, Dipsi, Abuharar, Sebka, and Deir ez Zor, under harsh conditions. In Meskene for example, the number of deportees rose from 20,000 to 100,000 in early 1916, up to 60,000 of whom would die of starvation and disease. The authorities designated a Turkish director for each camp who oversaw major operations, while the internal affairs of camps were run by an Armenian supervisor selected from the deportees. Corruption and embezzlement, as well as abduction of women and children, were commonplace as camp directors, local officials, guards, and others in position of power preyed upon the civilian Armenians who were essentially pronounced fair game. Some Armenians engaged in humanitarian resistance through underground networks that connected the camps and provided relief to the deportees.

In early 1916, most camps along the Euphrates line were closed and the deportees were pushed farther along the river to Deir ez Zor. Concomitantly, in March–April 1916, 40,000 Armenians interned in the Ras ul-Ayn camp were massacred. These measures signaled the beginning of a second phase in the Armenian Genocide, which would culminate in the destruction of the overwhelming majority of the surviving deportees in this area.

The influx of deportees to Deir ez Zor raised their number in the camps there to 200,000. A series of sackings and new appointments in the Zor region guaranteed that the ruling Ottoman party Committee of Union and Progress' massacre plans could be swiftly implemented on the ground. Salih Zeki, who had proven his credentials as a ruthless murderer in Everek (in the Kayseri region), took over the position of governor general of Zor. Realizing the impossibility of killing tens of thousands with the men he had at his disposal, Zeki recruited locals who had committed massacres in Ras-ul Ayn, and embarked on the destruction of the Armenians in Deir ez Zor.

For the perpetrators, killing had become a profitable enterprise, as clothing and valuables were invariably taken from the victims. As a result, many locals left their jobs to take part in the massacres. Large convoys of Armenians were divided into groups of a few thousand, taken out of the camps, and massacred on nearby hills or burnt alive in caves. When the victorious British forces entered Syria in October 1918, there were, in all, only about a thousand Armenians still alive in Deir ez Zor.

Khatchig Mouradian

See also: Deir ez Zor.

Further Reading

Akcam, Taner. *The Young Turks' Crime against Humanity: The Armenian Genocide and Ethnic Cleansing in the Ottoman Empire*. Princeton, NJ: Princeton University Press, 2012.

Dundar, Fuat. *Crime of Numbers: The Role of Statistics in the Armenian Question, 1878–1918*. New Brunswick: Transaction Publishers, 2010.

Kevorkian, Raymond. *The Armenian Genocide: A Complete History*. London: I. B. Tauris, 2011.

Auschwitz

German concentration camp complex near Auschwitz (Oswiecim in Polish) in eastern Poland that served as one of the epicenters of the Holocaust. More Jews were killed in Auschwitz during the war than in any other single location. Since the victims came from every part of Europe, and because Auschwitz operated longer than any other death camp, it has come to symbolize the Nazi determination to destroy the Jews.

Understanding the history of Auschwitz is a challenge because of the complexity of its story. Initially, Auschwitz was established as a concentration camp for Polish soldiers and political prisoners. After June 1941, Soviet prisoners of war were added to the prison population. During the first two years of its operation, little distinguished Auschwitz from any other Nazi camp, or indeed could predict the role it would play in the Holocaust. It must also be remembered that there was not a single Auschwitz, but rather three main camps—Auschwitz I, Auschwitz II (Birkenau), and Auschwitz III (Monowitz)—along with approximately 50 satellite camps located over a wide geographical region. Thus, even at the height of the killings, Auschwitz concentration and work camps continued to exist next to the Auschwitz death camp of Birkenau.

In the winter of 1940–1941, the German industrial conglomerate I.G. Farben, taking advantage of governmental tax breaks for industrialist building in the newly conquered territories, chose the Auschwitz area as the site for the construction of a new plant. The availability of a railroad junction and raw material, along with the chance to utilize cheap concentration camp labor, added to the allure of the area. An arrangement was made between I.G. Farben and the SS, whereby the latter would provide slave labor (drawn from Auschwitz inmates) and I.G. Farben would pay the SS for the use of the workers. At the same time, SS chief Heinrich Himmler ordered the camp system expanded to accommodate over 100,000 inmates, probably in expectation of a massive number of Soviet prisoners.

In the fall of 1941, a local Nazi official, ordered to kill a number of Soviet POWs, decided to experiment with the use of Zyklon B (a hydrogen cyanide gas compound manufactured by I.G. Farben commercially for delousing). A small farmhouse was sealed off and the first tests involving the gassing of prisoners were carried out.

In accordance with Nazi anti-Semitic ideology, the character of Auschwitz underwent a change in late 1941. It maintained its original features—political, industrial, agricultural, and penal—but now, through the murder installation at Birkenau, it also became an elaborate and gigantic factory of death created for the purpose of methodically and efficiently murdering millions of people, specifically Jews. These mass murders took place in specially-designed gas chambers utilizing Zyklon B gas. Auschwitz seemed a logical place as a site for the implementation of the Holocaust because it was remote from major population centers. Moreover, the presence of the rail lines and junctions referred to earlier ensured that access was not subject to unreliable roads. When high-ranking Nazi officials learned of the effectiveness of Zyklon B in killing Jews, they adopted it as the method of choice, thereby merging industrial production with mass slaughter.

While the first killings took place at Auschwitz I, Auschwitz II (Birkenau) became the focal point for the gassing of Jews brought from all over Europe. Initially, two converted farmhouses were employed in this task. By the middle of 1942, however, specially built gas chambers and crematoria were in use, enabling the Germans to gas and then incinerate several thousand people per day.

To clean the bodies out of the chamber and sort the clothes and valuables of those who were murdered, the Nazis created several groups of *Sonderkommando* (special squads) of prisoners, who were in turn murdered every two to three months. The SS (and I.G. Farben) intended that by replacing weak and ailing prisoners with slightly healthier inmates, they would be able to maintain production levels. On October 7, 1944, members of the Sonderkommando revolted, not in any expectation of escape, but in order to destroy as much of the gas chambers and crematoria as possible. They were also hoping to buy time to bury manuscripts, evidence of the horrible work they were forced to carry out. Over 400 Sonderkommando men were killed, along with approximately 15 SS guards. The manuscripts they hid were not discovered for more than a decade.

As the Soviet armies continued their advance toward Germany throughout the latter half of 1944, the position of Auschwitz seemed uncertain. In September, Heinrich Himmler ordered the Auschwitz commandant, Rudolf Hoess, to oversee the camp's liquidation. When delay threatened and the Soviets drew nearer, on November 26, 1944, Himmler issued another order concerning the destruction of Auschwitz. On January 6, 1945, four Jewish women who had smuggled gunpowder to the Sonderkommando for their revolt were executed in Auschwitz. They were among the last prisoners killed in the camp.

After considerable administrative difficulties—and much debate concerning the method of withdrawal—the complete evacuation of the complex was ordered for January 17, 1945. One day later, some 22 thousand men and women left the camp; the next day a further 3.5 thousand were evacuated. They were about all that was left of a camp complex, which at one time could boast a population of possibly 200 thousand. The earliest date of free contact with Soviet forces was January 22, 1945. When the camp was formally occupied two days later, there were only 2,819 survivors left in the camp.

Much of the Auschwitz complex has been preserved, and serves today as a grim reminder of the Nazi attempt at destroying the Jewish people. It has become the symbol par excellence of the Holocaust, a place where over a million Jews and countless numbers of others were murdered.

Fred Krome

See also: Bełżec; Bergen-Belsen; Birkenau; Chełmno; Concentration Camps; Extermination Centers; Gas Chambers; Hoess, Rudolf; Holocaust, The; I.G. Farben Case (1947); J.A. Topf & Söhne; Zyklon B Case (1946).

Further Reading

Gutman, Yisrael, and Michael Berenbaum, eds. *Anatomy of the Auschwitz Death Camp.* Bloomington: Indiana University Press, 1994.
Van Pelt, Robert Jan. *The Case for Auschwitz: Evidence from the Irving Trial.* Bloomington: Indiana University Press, 2002.

Australia

Soon after the start of World War I, Australia passed the War Precautions Act that authorized local authorities to intern "enemy subjects with whose conduct they were not satisfied"; in 1916, the authorities announced that anyone whose father or grandfather was foreign would himself be considered a foreigner and therefore subject to internment. Australian government then followed the precedent set by the British government during the Boer War (1899–1902) and had set up internment camps for enemy aliens. Several camps were ultimately established, including at Berrima, Holsworthy, Trial Bay, Bourke, Molonglo, Torrens Island, and in Canberra; by 1915, they held almost 3,000 people of German and Austro-Hungarian origin. The existing Holsworthy Army camp in New South Wales was expanded to house the internees and turned into "German Concentration Camp" that was the largest internment camp in Australia. Internees lived in open-sided canvas huts and suffered from summer heat and winter cold, as well as mistreatment from guards. The internees were released at the end of the war, but the Australian government deported over 6,000 prisoners to their countries of origin or descent.

Australia again revived internment camps during World War II, when the National Security Act of 1939 called for enemy aliens to be interned; in addition, Australia received prisoners of war captured by the Allied powers. New camps were established across much of Australia. In New South Wales, the authorities formed three Hay Internment and POW camps in 1940; the first internes arrived in September 1940 and included over two thousand refugees from Nazi Germany and Austria (most of whom were Jewish) who had first fled to Britain and were interned there; The British government later decided to forcibly transport these refugees to Australia on the HMT *Dunera*; known as "the Dunera Boys," these refugees had suffered from cruel and inhumane treatment during transportation, forcing the British government to later apologize for its actions and pay compensation to the victims. The Dunera Boys were soon joined in internment at Hay by a second, smaller contingent of internees: German and Austrian Jewish refugee families evacuated from Singapore on the *Queen Mary* in September 1940, to escape the Japanese threat. In November 1940, the Hay Camp 6 received Italian civilian internees, while Camps 7 and 8, which were vacated in May 1941 when the *Dunera* internees had been evacuated, were turned into prisoner of war camps for Italian POWs. In December 1941, Japanese internees were conveyed to Hay Camp 6, while over 2,200 Japanese POWs were sent to a separate camp near Cowra in New South Wales, which also held over 14,000 Italian and 1,500 German POWs. In August 1944, in the largest prison escape of World War II, over 1,000 Japanese POWs attempted to escape the Cowra Camp, leading to clashes with Australian forces, which claimed the lives of 4 Australian soldiers and 231 Japanese prisoners; although over 350 POWs escaped, most of them were recaptured within next few days while others committed suicide to avoid recapture.

In Queensland, the Australian authorities maintained major POW and internment camps at Gaythorne and Enoggera, while smaller facilities operated at North Ward POW Compound, Stuart Prison (Stuart, Townsville), and Thompson's Point POW camp. The province of Victoria also featured several internment facilities, the most important of which was Dhurringile Internment and POW camp, a Victorian era prison that was turned into an internment camp for alien civilians and prisoners of war. Several Loveday camps functioned in South Australia, with Camps 9 and 10 holding some 2,000 Italian internees and POWs while, Camp 14 comprised of several compounds for Italian, German, and Japanese POWs. In addition, Moorook West, Woolenook and Katarapko wood camps, also in South Australia, employed Italian prisoners of war as wood cutters for the Allied war effort.

As World War II ended in September 1945, Australia began to release internees and prisoners of war, and gradually dismantled most of the camp complexes.

More recently, Australia has come under intense international scrutiny for its harsh policy on asylum seekers. In 2011–2016, Australia saw a vast increase in the number of refugees reaching its shores; many of these asylum seekers were refugees from conflicts in the Middle East who attempted to reach Australia on boats from Indonesia. At its peak, 18,000 people arrived in Australia illegally by sea, and hundreds have died making the dangerous sea crossing. To stem the tide of immigrants, Australian government supported tough asylum policies, including intercepting migrant boats and towing them back to Indonesia. Most crucially, to deal with some 1,700 detainees, Australia set up offshore processing centers that, critics argue, represent modern internment camps. Currently, one such center exists on the Pacific island nation of Nauru, and another on Manus Island in Papua New Guinea. Human rights groups say that conditions in these camps are inadequate and internees suffer from poor hygiene, cramped conditions, unrelenting heat, and a lack of facilities.

Alexander Mikaberidze

See also: Britain; Torrens Island.

Further Reading

Carr-Gregg, Charlotte. *Japanese Prisoners of War in Revolt: The Outbreaks at Featherston and Cowra during World War II*. New York: St. Martin's Press, 1978.

Fischer, Gerhard, *Enemy Aliens: Internment and the Homefront Experience in Australia, 1914–1920*. St. Lucia, Qld: University of Queensland Press, 1989

Gordon, Harry. *Die like the Carp: The Story of the Greatest Prison Escape Ever*. Melbourne: Transworld, 1980.

Moore, Bob, and Kent Fedorovich. *The British Empire and Its Italian Prisoners of War, 1940–1947*. New York: Palgrave Macmillan, 2002.

Tampke, Jurgen, and Colin Doxford. *Australia, Willkommen: A History of Germans in Australia*. Kensington, N.S.W.: New South Wales University Press, 1990.

Winter, Jay, ed. *The Cambridge History of the First World War. Volume III: Civil Society*. Cambridge: Cambridge University Press, 2014.

B

Badaber Revolt (1985)

An uprising by Soviet and Afghan prisoners of war at the Badaber fortress. Badaber (Badhaber) is a village in Peshawar District of Khyber Pukhtunkhwa province in northwestern Pakistan. Between 1958 and 1970, it was a secret intelligence listening post for the U.S. Air Force and played an important role in directing Gary Powers's infamous reconnaissance flight in 1961. Following the Soviet invasion of Afghanistan in 1979, the village became not only a refugee camp, but also an important staging grounds for the Afghan *mujahideen* who opposed the Soviet presence in Afghanistan. The local fortress was turned into a training facility where the *mujahideen* received training from Pakistani and Egyptian military instructors, as well the U.S. Central Intelligence Agency, which maintained Operation Cyclone to arm and finance the *mujahideen*. Furthermore, the fortress was also used as a detention facility where the Afghan *mujahideen* of the Jamiat-e Islami party had held the captured Soviet and Democratic Republic of Afghanistan (DRA) soldiers, who endured primitive conditions, were denied of bare essentials and were forced to perform hard labor.

On April 26, 1985, at least 14 Soviet and some 40 Afghan POWs overpowered their guards, seized weapons, and unsuccessfully attempted to escape. Fierce fighting ensued as the Jamiat-e Islami troops gathered reinforcements, including tanks and Pakistani helicopters, to suppress the revolt; during brief negotiations, the POWs requested (but were denied) meeting with the Soviet or Afghan ambassadors to Pakistan or representatives from the International Red Cross and Red Crescent Movement. On November 27, a massive explosion in the armory, probably caused by a direct artillery strike to the armory—though some say the insurgents blew it themselves—destroyed the prison and killed its defenders; the *mujahideen* and Pakistani forces lost over 120 men while the Badaber base was almost completely destroyed. While the Pakistani government confirmed that an uprising had occurred at Badaber, it was extremely concerned about international fallout and quickly moved to suppress all further details until 1992, when names of some Soviet POWs involved in the uprising were revealed.

Alexander Mikaberidze

See also: Afghanistan.

Further Reading

Braithwaite, Rodric. *Afgantsy: The Russians in Afghanistan, 1979–89.* New York: Oxford University Press, 2013.

Elistratov, Igor. "Vosstanie v Badabere: V poiskakh istiny," *Smolensk*, July 2007, http://www.journalsmolensk.ru/07-07/14/14.PHP

Kudoyarov, Radik. *Taina lagerya Badaber. Afganskii kapkan.* Documentary film, http://russia.tv/brand/show/brand_id/10507/

Bagram Air Base

Former Afghan and Soviet air force facility that became the major military base for the U.S.-led coalition forces after the U.S. invasion of Afghanistan in 2001. Located in Parwan Province, approximately 47 km (27 miles) north of Kabul, the base was constructed in the 1950s, but was expanded during the Soviet invasion of Afghanistan (1979–1989), when it served as the key hub for Soviet operations. After the Soviet withdrawal, the provincial Afghan government took control of the base before the Taliban took over in 1999. During the U.S.-led invasion of Afghanistan (Operation Enduring Freedom), British special forces units captured the air base, which was quickly modernized and expanded; by 2003–2004, the base comprised of over 1,200 structures and two major runways, capable of launching some 140,000 air missions annually; it was from Bagram Air Base that the operation that killed al Qaeda leader Osama bin Laden had been launched in 2011.

Bagram Air Base has also served as a major prisoner camp—the Bagram Theater Internment Facility or Bagram Collection Point (BCP)—that many humanitarian groups and organizations criticized for prisoner abuse. In 2004, the *New York Times* investigation revealed many other instances of mistreatment of prisoners, including being deprived of sleep, forced nudity, chained to the ceiling, beaten, or subjected to the so-called peroneal strikes, which involved severe blows to the side of the leg above the knee; detainees were mistreated so badly that two died from abuse in 2002, one of them a taxi driver who interrogators later admitted was an innocent man caught up in the wrong place at the wrong time.

The U.S. Army Criminal Investigation Command placed over two dozen U.S. servicemen under investigation and eventually charged 15 of them. In response to this scandal, the United States helped build a new detention facility at Parwan in 2009 and transferred its management to the Afghan authorities three years later. In December 2014, the United States closed all detention facilities in Afghanistan and no longer officially maintains custody of any detainees.

Alexander Mikaberidze

See also: Abu Ghraib; Camp Bucca; Sarposa.

Further Reading

"Afghans 'Abused at Secret Prison' at Bagram Airbase," *BBC News*, April 15, 2010, http://news.bbc.co.uk/2/hi/south_asia/8621973.stm

Forsythe, David P. *Politics of Prisoner Abuse: The United States and Enemy Prisoners after 9/11.* Cambridge: Cambridge University Press, 2011.

"U.S. Finally Closes Detention Facility at Bagram airbase in Afghanistan," *The Guardian*, December 11, 2014, https://www.theguardian.com/world/2014/dec/11/afghanistan-us-bagram-torture-prison

Banjica Concentration Camp

A German concentration camp in Serbia during World War II. Established in the Banjica neighborhood of Belgrade, the camp interned over 23,000 Serbs, Jews, Romanis, political dissidents and others between 1941 and 1944. Detainees were arrested by either the Gestapo, the German Feldgendarmerie (military police), or by *Specijalna policija Uprave grada Beograda* (SP UGB), a Serbian collaborationist political police organization. The camp was under the command of the German Gestapo official Willy Friedrich, but *Srpska državna straža* (the Serbian State Guard), the military arm of the collaborationist Government of National Salvation led by Milan Nedić, supplied the prison staff. The camp was notorious for its harshness and inmates were subjected to cruel and inhuman treatment, with thousands of prisoners summarily executed at the firing ranges at Jajinci, Marinkova Bara, and the Jewish cemetery. In late 1944, as their war effort was collapsing, the Germans attempted to conceal their crimes at Banjica by forcing the surviving prisoners to disinter and incinerate the remains of those killed at the camps. A special unit, consisting of 100 Jewish and Serbian prisoners and about 50 members of the *Sicherheitspolizei* (Security Police) and German military police undertook this gruesome task until the German departure from the camp in early October.

In 1969, the Yugoslav government opened the Museum of the Banjica Concentration Camp at the site.

Alexander Mikaberidze

See also: Yugoslavia.

Further Reading

Mojzes, Paul. *Balkan Genocides: Holocaust and Ethnic Cleansing in the 20th Century.* Lanham, MD: Rowman & Littlefield, 2011.

Tomasevich, Jozo. *War and Revolution in Yugoslavia, 1941–1945: Occupation and Collaboration.* Stanford, CA: Stanford University Press, 2001.

Bataan Death March (1942)

A forced march of 12,000 U.S. soldiers and 64,000 Filipino troops after the Japanese captured the Bataan Peninsula in the Philippines in April 1942. On April 3, 1942, Japanese general Masaharu Homma launched a new offensive against the Bataan defenders. The U.S. Far Eastern commander, General Douglas MacArthur, had ordered the troops to continue to fight, but six days later, with his men worn down by the strain of constant combat, disease, and starvation, Major General Edward P. King, commander of the forces on Bataan, ordered them to surrender. The troops had been on half rations since January.

Homma had decided that he would hold the prisoners at Camp O'Donnell, 100 miles away. The Japanese forced the prisoners to march 52 miles from Mariveles to San Fernando, Pampanga, in order to be transported by rail to Capas, Tarlac. They would then walk another 8 miles to Camp O'Donnell. King expressed concern about his men being able to make this trip and asked that trucks transport them to their final location. Homma rejected the request.

The trek began on April 10, 1942 and lasted for over a week. The march is remembered for its sheer brutality, but before it even began, each prisoner was searched, and anyone found to possess a Japanese souvenir was executed on the spot.

Allied soldiers were, for the most part, denied food and water by their guards until the completion of their journey. The only food that some received was a bit of rancid rice. The prisoners of war were given only a few hours of rest each night in crowded conditions. One of the worst forms of punishment inflicted on the captives was known as the sun treatment, in which the prisoner, denied any water, was forced

Thousands of American and Filipino prisoners were forced by their Japanese captors to walk over 60 miles in a brutally savage trek that would later be known as the Bataan Death March. Some 70,000 men were marched along this route, but cruel treatment and starvation killed 7,000–10,000 before the march reached its destination. (Corbis via Getty Images)

to sit in the scalding Philippine sun without the protection of a helmet. Prisoners were beaten, kicked, and killed for falling behind or violating the smallest rule.

Between 7,000 and 10,000 of the prisoners died before reaching Camp O'Donnell. The Japanese had failed to take into consideration both the poor health of their captives and their numbers. Although a few of the prisoners escaped into the jungle, most were physically unable even to make the attempt. A number were murdered at random by their guards.

Many who survived the march died in the overcrowded, suffocating boxcars on the rail trip to Capas. In the two months after reaching the camp, 1,600 Americans and 16,000 Filipinos died of starvation, disease, and maltreatment. The cruelty of the march became well known, and U.S. commanders used the story of the Bataan Death March to motivate their troops in subsequent fighting against the Japanese.

T. Jason Soderstrum

See also: Camp O'Donnell; Japan; Sandakan Death Marches; World War II Prisoners of War.

Further Reading
Berry, William A. *Prisoner of the Rising Sun.* Norman: University of Oklahoma Press, 1993.

Falk, Stanley Lawrence. *Bataan: The March of Death*. New York: Norton, 1962.

Hubbard, Preston. *Apocalypse Undone: My Survival of Japanese Imprisonment during World War II*. Nashville, TN: Vanderbilt University Press, 1990.

Batu Lintang Camp

A Japanese internment camp at Kuching, Sarawak on the island of Borneo during World War II. The camp was established in 1942 to house both Allied prisoners of war and civilian internees. The camp, commanded by Lieutenant Colonel Tatsuji Suga, comprised of about ten compounds surrounded by a five-mile perimeter of barbed wire fence. Over the next three years, it held about 3,000 British, Australian, Dutch, and Indonesian prisoners and civilian internees who were segregated into categories and assigned separate compounds. Prisoners suffered from food shortages, lack of adequate living quarters, disease, forced labor, and brutal treatment; hundreds of prisoners died at the camp. The camp was liberated on September 11, 1945, by the Australian 9th Division.

Alexander Mikaberidze

See also: Japan.

Further Reading

Ooi, Keat Gin, ed. *Japanese Empire in the Tropics: Selected Documents and Reports of the Japanese Period in Sarawak, Northwest Borneo, 1941–1945*. Athens: Ohio University Center for International Studies, 1998.

Belene Camp

Situated on Persin Island in the Danube in the neighborhood of the village of Belene, the Belene camp, also referred to as the Belene Concentration Camp, was the most notorious Communist-era forced labor camp in Bulgaria. Opened in 1949, it operated until the end of the 1980s, but reached its highest capacity at the beginning of the 1950s when, during the purges of the Bulgarian Communist leader Vaiko Chervenkov, thousands of prisoners had been interned there. Prisoners suffered from inhuman conditions, deprived of food, tortured, and otherwise mistreated, resulting in hundreds perishing. Although Belene was formally closed in 1959, it continued to hold political opponents of the Communist regime while, in the 1980s, it served as an internment camp for hundreds of Bulgarian Turks who had opposed assimilation policies of the Bulgarian authorities. After the collapse of the Communist regime in Bulgaria, Belene became a site for remembrance of the victims of the prison camps and an annual remembrance service is held since 2015.

Alexander Mikaberidze

See also: Bulgaria, Internment and Labor Camps.

Further Reading

Baev, Jordan. "De-Stalinisation and Political Rehabilitations in Bulgaria," in Kevin McDermott and Matthew Stibbe, eds. *De-Stalinising Eastern Europe: The Rehabilitation of Stalin's Victims after 1953,* 150–169. New York: Palgrave Macmillan, 2015.

"The Belene Concentration Camp in Bulgaria," Declassified Memo, Central Intelligence Agency, October 1951, https://www.cia.gov/library/readingroom/docs/CIA-RDP80 -00809A000700050030-1.pdf

Geshev, Nedyalko. *Belene. Ostrovut na zabravenie. Spomeni.* Sofia, BG: DF Robinzon, 1991.

Belomorkanal

A major ship canal constructed by forced labor of Gulag inmates. As part of its first five-year plan, the Soviet government, led by Joseph Stalin, envisioned rapid modernization of industry and vast improvements in existing infrastructure. The Belomorkanal was one of the approved projects and it was designed to connect the White Sea to the Baltic Sea. The canal was envisioned as a visible symbol of the rapid development of the Soviet Union that would facilitate movement of cargos and goods and promote Soviet commerce and industry. The canal was the first major project constructed in the Soviet Union using forced labor, and was often trumpeted as an example of reforming "class enemies" through "corrective labor." The canal was constructed by prisoners supplied by the Belbaltlag camp directorate (White Sea–Baltic Corrective Labor Camp Directorate) of the Gulag. As many as 100,000 prisoners were employed in digging (by hand) the canal in rocky terrain; conditions were brutal and as many as 25,000 inmates perished during the construction. The 140-mile canal was completed in 20 months between 1931 and 1933, but it never played any significant role in Soviet commerce or industry.

Alexander Mikaberidze

See also: Gulag; Sevvostlag; Stalin, Joseph.

Further Reading

Khlevniuk, Oleg V. *The History of the Gulag. From Collectivization to the Great Terror.* New Haven, CT: Yale University Press, 2004.

Ruder, Cynthia A. *Making History for Stalin: The Story of the Belomor Canal.* Gainesville: University Press of Florida, 1998.

Bełżec

In early 1940, German officials built a number of forced labor camps along the Bug River. Just outside the village of Bełżec, in southeastern Poland, the Germans erected a labor camp, which also served as the headquarters for all of the regional labor camps. Administered by the SS, the camp at Bełżec interned Jews from the Lublin district, where they were compelled to build various military facilities on the Bug River. By year's end, the labor camp was deactivated; its laborers were either shot or deported to other detention facilities. In November 1941, the SS and local police officials began erecting an extermination camp at the site of the old labor camp. It was to be the Nazis' first dedicated extermination facility. The new camp commenced operations in March 1942, when Jews deported from Lublin, Lvov, and Kraków began arriving by rail cars. Bełżec quickly became a death camp, where several hundred thousand people were murdered.

Bełżec was ideally suited as an extermination camp because it was situated less than one-quarter of a mile from a major rail line. The camp, which measured 886 feet per side, was supervised by 20–30 SS and police officers along with an auxiliary police unit of 90–120 men. This group was multiethnic, constituting Ukrainian and Polish civilians, as well as former Soviet prisoners of war. Commanding the facility were SS major Christian Wirth (March–June 1942) and SS first lieutenant Gottlieb Hering (June 1942–June 1943). The Nazis went to considerable trouble to conceal the activities inside the facility in an effort to keep the local population in the dark about the mass killings there.

The Germans had the deportations and killing down to a science: trains of 40–60 boxcars with 80–100 people per car arrived at the Bełżec station. The prisoners were brought into the facility, stripped of their possessions, and usually separated by gender (men were kept separate from women and children). Deportees were then forced to disrobe and told to walk through the "tube," a narrow, concealed walkway that led to the gas chambers. The unsuspecting prisoners were told they were going to communal showers. Once a chamber was full, the doors were sealed and carbon monoxide gas was pumped into the room via a large machine. This process was repeated until all deportees were killed (a few, however, were temporarily spared to work as slave laborers in the camp). These prisoners were compelled to work in the killing areas, separating newly-arrived prisoners' possessions, removing bodies from the gas chambers, and burying them in mass graves adjacent to the facility.

Fearful that their nefarious activities might be discovered, German officials ordered the mass graves exhumed in October 1942. The remains were incinerated in open-air furnaces, while machines were employed to crush any surviving bone fragments. Meanwhile, between March and December 1942 alone, at least 435,500 Jews, Poles, and Romanis were murdered at Bełżec. Most had come from southern Poland, but there were also Jews from Austria, Germany, and Czechoslovakia. Meanwhile, by June 1943, conscript laborers had finished the task of exhuming bodies and burning them. The workers were subsequently shot or deported to other facilities. To mask their activities, German officials bulldozed the entire site, constructed a large home, and planted crops and trees. The Soviets uncovered the horrors of Bełżec when they occupied the area in July 1944.

Paul G. Pierpaoli, Jr.

See also: Bergen-Belsen; Birkenau; Chełmno; Concentration Camps; Extermination Centers; Gas Chambers; Holocaust, The; J. A. Topf & Söhne; Zyklon B Case (1946).

Further Reading
Arad, Yitzhak. *Belzec, Sobibor, Treblinka: The Operation Reinhard Death Camps.* Bloomington: Indiana University Press, 1987.

Bauer, Yehuda. *A History of the Holocaust.* New York: Franklin Watts, 2001.

Bergen-Belsen

German concentration camp during World War II, situated near the village of Bergen in northwestern Germany. It was originally designated a camp for political prisoners, and was not equipped with gas chambers or crematoria. Prisoners were subjected to a very limited diet, and most deaths at the camp resulted from starvation, malnutrition, or diseases like typhus and dysentery, resulting from unsanitary water. The guards at Bergen-Belsen were notoriously brutal, especially the female contingent, and the camp was considered an especially tough place to be imprisoned.

In December 1944, Joseph Kramer was transferred to Bergen-Belsen from Birkenau as camp commander, and the regime of brutalization intensified dramatically. Kramer, who the British called "The Beast of Belsen," created at Bergen-Belsen perhaps the most brutal of the concentration camps. Beatings, torture, random shootings, and senseless cruelty were the order of the day. The incompetence of Kramer's administration was magnified as prisoners from other camps were sent to Bergen-Belsen beginning in the late winter of 1945.

Bergen-Belsen's regular prisoner muster was about 10,000. As Allied armies threatened to capture various concentration camps on the Eastern and Western fronts, however, prisoners were moved to camps deeper in Germany, and by April 1945, Belsen held almost 80,000 prisoners in a space designed to hold barely one-tenth that number. The acute shortage of food, together with the poor water quality and next to no medical care, saw prisoner welfare transformed into a catastrophe, and Kramer lost control of the situation. The camp guards stopped keeping track of prisoners and decided to refrain from contact with them because they were afraid of catching typhus. Any semblance of order simply disappeared. No one disposed of the growing number of dead, and some prisoners reportedly resorted to cannibalism.

The British captured Bergen-Belsen in April 1945, and Kramer was taken into immediate custody. Upon touring the camp, British soldiers found about 30,000 starving and diseased survivors, and about 35,000 corpses lying in various parts of the camp, including entire barracks blocks. It was one of the most horrifying scenes of the entire war, and film footage from the time became an iconic testament to the brutality of the Nazi regime. Kramer, for his part, was sentenced to death by a British military court on November 17, 1945, and hanged a few days later.

Lee Baker

See also: Auschwitz; Bełżec; Birkenau; Chełmno; Concentration Camps; Extermination Centers; Gas Chambers; Hoess, Rudolf; I.G. Farben Case (1947); J.A. Topf & Söhne; Kramer, Josef; Zyklon B Case (1946).

Further Reading

Herzberg, Abel Jacob. *Between Two Streams: A Diary from Bergen-Belsen.* London: Tauris Parke, 2009.

Reilly, Joanne. *Belsen: The Liberation of a Concentration Camp.* New York: Routledge, 1998.

Berger, Gottlob (1896–1975)

German general who commanded the entire German prison camp organization in the concluding stages of World War II. Born at Gerstetten, near Ulm, he served in the German Army during World War I and awarded the Iron Cross First Class. After the war, he led the Einwohnerwehr militia (formed by former German soldiers) and joined the National Socialist (Nazi) Party in 1922. By 1940, he rose through the Nazi ranks, serving in the paramilitary *Sturmabteilung* (SA) before becoming head of the *Schutzstaffel* (SS) Main Office (SS-HA). In this position, he played an important role in the formation of the infamous Waffen-SS, the armed wing of the Nazi Party's SS organization.

During World War II, Berger took part in the work of the Reich Ministry for the Occupied Eastern Territories and was one of the architects of the Heuaktion Operation (1944) that kidnapped some 50,000 Polish children (aged 10 to 14) in the German-occupied Polish territories and transported them to Germany proper as slave laborers. In July 1944, Berger became chief of the German prisoner-of-war camps system. He did show some concern for the plight of POWs, clashing with senior Nazi officials over the rate of distribution of Red Cross parcels and directly disobeying some orders related to POWs. He surrendered to U.S. troops near Berchtesgaden in May 1945 and was promptly arrested.

At the Nuremberg Military Tribunals for war crimes, Berger was sentenced to 25 years imprisonment, but his sentence was later reduced to 10 years, partly due to testimonials from high-ranking Allied officers in appreciation for his efforts on behalf of the prisoners; he was eventually released after serving six-and-a-half years.

Alexander Mikaberidze

See also: Concentration Camps; Holocaust, The; Nuremberg Trials.

Further Reading

Phillips Nuremberg Trials Collection: Trial 11 - Ministries Case, http://libguides.law.uga .edu/c.php?g=177170&p=1164760

Weale, Adrian. *The SS: A New History*. London: Little, Brown, 2010.

Beria, Lavrenty (1899–1953)

Beria oversaw the vast system of forced labor camps in the Soviet Union as head of the NKVD (Soviet secret police) from November 1938 to January 1946. The NKVD served as the Soviet Union's police force for political security. Among its other duties, it ran the Gulag (Main Administration of Camps) with its expansive network of corrective labor camps, corrective labor colonies, and special settlements. It also administered a parallel structure of internment camps for prisoners of war and foreign civilian internees that was known as GUPVI (*Glavnoe upravlenie po delam voennoplennykh i internirovannykh*, Main Administration for the Affairs of Prisoners of War and Internees). These two camp systems employed millions of forced laborers during Beria's tenure as head of the NKVD.

In particular, Beria oversaw the expansion and transformation of the special settlement regime into a system that would not only socially isolate certain ethnic groups, but would also economically integrate them into regions far from their homelands. Beria organized the deportation of over 3 million people to remote locations in the Soviet Union during the 1940s. More than 2 million of these people

Lavrenty Beria headed the Soviet Union's secret police and supervised the notorious Gulag prison system under Joseph Stalin. (Library of Congress)

came from eight nationalities that were deported in their entirety— the Russian Germans, Karachais, Kalmyks, Chechens, Ingush, Balkars, Crimean Tatars, and Meskhetian Turks. Confined to internal exile in Siberia, Kazakhstan, Central Asia, and the Urals, these deportees received the legal status of special settlers. As such, they could not leave their assigned settlements without written permission from special NKVD commandants. They also lacked the freedom to choose their employment. The Stalin regime used them as a captive labor force to develop the agriculture, fisheries, industry, mining, and forestry of sparsely inhabited regions of the Soviet Union.

During World War II (1939–1945), the Stalin regime mobilized nearly 400,000 of these and earlier deportees belonging to suspect nationalities and placed them into forced labor battalions. This system of forced labor garnered the name *trudarmiia* (labor army) from the Soviet citizens conscripted into it. Beria's NKVD sent 220,000 of these men and women to work in gulag camps under conditions similar to those of convicts. The remaining 180,000 worked for civilian commissariats under NKVD supervision and lived in NKVD-guarded barracks. The ethnic composition of these forced laborers consisted of more than 315,000 Russian Germans, 14,000 Russian Koreans, 15,000 Kalmyks, and 5,000 Crimean Tatars, as well as Russian Finns, Russian Greeks, and others. They built factories, erected dams, laid railways, felled timber, mined coal, extracted oil, and manufactured munitions in Siberia, Kazakhstan, and the Urals during the 1940s. The mass induction of Russian Germans and other stigmatized nationalities into forced labor brigades mitigated the loss of labor from the reduction of gulag prisoners during World War II, due to releases into the Red Army and increased mortality. Labor army conscripts also suffered a high rate of excess mortality during this time due to malnutrition, disease, exposure, and other causes. More than 100,000 Russian Germans may have perished as a result of their service in the labor army.

J. Otto Pohl

See also: Gulag; NKVD; Stalin, Joseph; Soviet Union, Deportations in.

Further Reading

Knight, Amy. *Beria: Stalin's First Lieutenant*. Princeton, NJ: Princeton University Press, 1993.

Pohl, J. Otto. *Ethnic Cleansing in the USSR, 1937–1949.* Westport, CT: Greenwood, 1999.

Pohl, J. Otto. *The Stalinist Penal System.* Jefferson, NC: McFarland, 1997.

Polian, Pavel. *Against Their Will: The History and Geography of Forced Migrations in the USSR.* Budapest: Central European Press, 2004.

Berman, Matvei (1898–1939)

Soviet intelligence officer and head of the Gulag prison camp system from 1932 to 1937. Born into a Jewish family in the Chita district of the Zabaikalskaya (Transbaikal) province, Berman graduated from a military school in Irkutsk and joined the Russian army. He soon became politically active, supported the radical socialist-revolutionary group Bolsheviks and participated in the October Revolution of 1917. In 1918, Berman joined the newly established Russian secret police, Cheka, and took part in the Russian Civil War, serving as chief of state security in the town of Glazov; in later years he was People's Commissar for State Security in the Buryat-Mongol Autonomous Soviet Socialist Republic and head of the Joint State Political Directorate (OGPU, Soviet secret police) in the Uzbek Soviet Socialist Republic.

Starting in 1929, Berman played an important role in the creation of the Soviet prison camp system, serving as its head in 1932–1937. During his tenure, the Gulag emerged as the largest penal system in the world, holding more inmates than prisons and camps in the rest of the world. Berman was involved in dozens of major constructions projects that mercilessly exploited prisoners' labor, including the infamous White Sea–Baltic Canal, which alone employed some 200,000 prisoners (thousands of whom had perished), and the Moscow-Volga Canal. In 1938, during Joseph Stalin's purges, Berman was arrested on charges of belonging to a "terrorist and sabotage organization" and was executed the following year. In 1957, he was legally rehabilitated.

Alexander Mikaberidze

See also: Gulag; NKVD.

Further Reading
Applebaum, Anne. *Gulag: A History of the Soviet Camps.* London: Allen Lane, 2003.

Jakobson, Michael. *Origins of the Gulag: The Soviet Prison Camp System, 1917–1934.* Lexington: The University Press of Kentucky, 2015.

Bicycle Camp

A Japanese prisoner of war camp on Java during World War II; it derived its name from the 10th Battalion of the Dutch colonial army, which utilized bicycles. Bicycle Camp was located in Koenigplein, a suburb of Batavia (modern-day Jakarta, Indonesia), and comprised of a rectangular area (approximately 700 by 900 feet) surrounded by a high brick wall and featuring several large barrack buildings. Unlike most Japanese POW camps, Bicycle Camp had adequate sanitation. Prisoners were segregated by nationality into groups and included Indian, British, Dutch, American, and Australian soldiers; by 1943, some 4,000 POWs were held at the camp, although their number fluctuated as the Japanese moved prisoners to other camps. The camp continued to operate until the war's end in 1945.

Alexander Mikaberidze

See also: Japan.

Further Reading

Fujita, Frank. *Foo: A Japanese-American Prisoner of the Rising Sun.* Denton: University of North Texas Press, 1993.

Rivett, Rohan D. *Behind Bamboo: An Inside Story of the Japanese Prison Camps.* Sydney: Angus and Robertson, 1946.

Birkenau

One of three Nazi extermination camps in southern Poland, situated some 37 miles west of Krakow. There were three separate concentration camps at the site—Auschwitz I, Birkenau (Auschwitz II), and Monowitz (Auschwitz III). The largest of the three, Birkenau was built to alleviate overcrowding at Auschwitz I; construction commenced in October 1941. Birkenau's "provisional" gas chamber, in which prisoners were herded and killed, was operational by early 1942. It was known as the "little red house" because the Germans had converted a small brick house into a makeshift gas chamber. A second, larger gas chamber was constructed and became operational by June 1943; it remained Birkenau's primary killing facility and was nicknamed the "little white house" because it was a converted brick house painted white. Prisoners were killed with a gas derived from prussic acid, but known by its brand name, Zyklon B. It was far faster and more efficient than carbon monoxide, which had initially been used to murder detainees in Nazi death camps. It is believed that as many as 1 million people were exterminated at Birkenau between 1942 and late 1944, when the Germans suspended operations there.

The process of mass killing at Birkenau was virtually identical to that in other extermination facilities. Prisoners typically arrived by rail—in overcrowded boxcars—and were separated by gender upon arrival. They were then ordered to surrender all personal possessions, disrobe, and move toward "communal showers," a cruel euphemism for the gas chamber. After the detainees were killed by the poison gas, prison workers emptied the chamber of bodies and deposited them in large crematoria. By June 1943, Birkenau had four large crematoria, which operated almost around the clock. The vast majority of prisoners were Jews from Central and Eastern Europe, although there were also a large number of Romanis as well.

Like most of the Nazi death camps, Birkenau was staffed by SS officials, along with locally recruited police forces. Prisoners also helped run the facility. Prisoner functionaries known as *Kapos* helped maintain order and discipline in the barracks, while crematoria personnel Sonderkommandos were drafted to process newly arrived prisoners and readied them for the gas chambers. They also gathered detainees' personal possessions, removed any gold that murdered victims might have had in their teeth, and moved the corpses into the crematoria. Including prisoners, Birkenau may have had as many as 2,000–3,000 slave workers. For security reasons, to ensure the truth about Birkenau would not be disclosed to the outside world, these prisoners were also killed on a regular basis, to be replaced by newly arrived Jewish slave laborers.

Paul G. Pierpaoli, Jr.

See also: Auschwitz; Extermination Centers; Gas Chambers; Holocaust, The; J.A. Topf & Söhne; Zyklon B Case (1946).

Further Reading

Dwork, Debórah, and Robert Jan van Pelt. *Auschwitz: 1270 to the Present.* New York: Norton, 1996.

Gutman, Yisrael, and Michael Berenbaum, eds. *Anatomy of the Auschwitz Death Camp.* Bloomington: Indiana University Press, 1994.

Levi, Primo. *Survival in Auschwitz: The Nazi Assault on Humanity.* Austin, TX: Touchstone, 1995.

Bloemfontein Concentration Camp

The first significant concentration camp to be established by the British authorities in South Africa during the Boer War in 1899–1902. To overcome the Boer resistance, the British government pursued a dual policy: prosecuting war and sending the Boer prisoners of war to the prisoner-of-war camps overseas (i.e. at St Helena, Bermuda, India, and Ceylon); and of targeting the civilian population, burning the Boer property and moving women and children into the newly established concentration camps.

Bloemfontein camp was established in September 1900 on the outskirts of a small town of Bloemfontein; it was designed to intern women, children, and men who were not of commando age, those under 16 or over 60. Its size quickly increased from some 500 people in November 1900 to over 2,000 in January 1901; by March 1901, there were already over 3,000 people at the camps and in August the camp housed 7,500, double the size of the neighboring town itself. Much of existing information about Bloemfontein camp comes from the writings of Emily Hobhouse, who arrived there in January 1901. Overcrowding, meager water supply, lack of basic necessities, and disease were a never-ending struggle in the camp, which the British military administration was unable to overcome; Hobhouse observed that even the military brass considered "the whole thing . . . a grievous and gigantic blunder and . . . an almost insoluble problem." Camp conditions contributed to the spread of measles, typhoid, dysentery, and other diseases, which, in light of insufficient medical care, claimed hundreds of lives. Probably the most famous inmate of the Bloemfontein camp was a little girl, Lizzie van Zyl, who died in May 1901. Her photograph—a skeletal child clutching her precious doll—became the symbol of the inhumanity of the camp system. By the end of 1901, as the result of publicity that Hobhouse and others brought to Bloemfontein, conditions in the camp improved, and a number of charitable volunteer groups delivered the much needed provisions and supplies.

When the Boer War ended, the detainees were allowed to gradually leave the camp before it was finally closed on January 3, 1903.

Alexander Mikaberidze

See also: Boer War (1899–1902); Britain.

Further Reading

Heyningen, E. van. "Women and Disease. The Clash of Medical Cultures in the Concentration Camps of the South African War" in *Writing a Wider War. Rethinking Gender, Race, and Identity in the South African War, 1899–1902.* Edited by G. Cuthbertson et al., 186–212. Athens: Ohio University Press, 2002.

Hobhouse, Emily. *The Brunt of the War and Where It Fell.* London: Methuen, 1902.

Webb, Simon. *British Concentration Camps: A Brief History from 1900–1975.* London: Pen & Sword Books, 2016.

Boer War (1899–1902)

The British took increasingly harsh measures beginning in 1900 to try to defeat Boer guerrilla fighters in South Africa during the Second Anglo-Boer War (1899–1902). In June, the British warned the Boers that farms near sabotaged railroad lines, or from which British troops were fired on, would be burned. A few months later, it was announced that farms hiding and protecting combatant Boers would also be razed. Shortly thereafter, selected farms were designated for destruction, and the so-called land clearance policy was implemented near the end of the year. These actions were intended to punish the Boers, individually and collectively, and to deprive the fighting Boers of food and shelter. Within weeks, numerous Boer

Boer families in a British concentration camp at Eshowe, Zululand, Second Boer War, 1900. This represented one of the first uses of the internment of civilians in camps in wartime. The objective of the British was to hamper the Boer insurgents by removing civilians from the land, thereby restricting the fighters' food supplies. Diet and sanitary conditions in the camps were poor and some 28,000 internees died from disease and malnutrition. (Print Collector/Getty Images)

families were homeless, and many other refugees sought British protection from possible Boer reprisals. The British solution was to concentrate the displaced Boers in protected camps near the railways.

The British establishment of concentration camps for the Boer refugees was well intentioned, although there was an initial lack of command interest in the issue. Moreover, the British did not anticipate the large numbers of homeless Boers, nor did they allocate adequate resources for the camps.

Conditions in the camps varied considerably. A superintendent—assisted by a storekeeper, clerks, a medical officer, a dispenser, a matron, and nurses—ran each one. At first, the refugees were housed in prefabricated wooden huts, but the supply of those was soon exhausted. Large tents, and later bell tents, were then used to house the internees. Extra medical care was frequently provided by camp inmates, who were paid for their assistance. Food was rationed, based on guidelines issued

Table 1   Major British Camps

Region	Location	
Transvaal	Balmoral	Meintjes Kop
	Barbeton	Middelburg
	Belfast	Nylstroom
	Heidelberg	Pietersburg
	Irene	Potchefstroom
	Johannesburg	Standerton
	Klerksdorp	Van der Hoven's Drift
	Krugersdorp	Vereeniging
		Volksrust
Orange Free State	Bethulie	Kroonstad
	Bloemfontein	Norvals Pont
	Brandfort	Springfontein
	Harrismith	Vredefort Road
	Heilbron	Winburg
Natal	Colenso	Ladysmith
	Eshowe	Merebank
	Howick	Pietermaritzburg
	Jacobs Siding	Pinetown
		Wentworth
Cape Colony	Aliwal North	Orange River
	East London	Port Elizabeth
	Kabusie	Uitenhage
	Kimberley	Vryburg
	Mafeking	

by medical authorities for the maintenance of health, and generally consisted of a pound of meal and about a half pound of meat per day, plus coffee and sugar. Additional food, clothing, and supplies were sold in camp shops at regulated prices. Attempts were made to find employment for as many of the refugees as possible, with many families being paid up to £20 a month for their work. Boers who surrendered voluntarily were generally allowed to keep their livestock. Schools were set up in the camps for children.

Administrative difficulties soon arose, and conditions in some of the camps became very bad. Health issues were a primary concern. While the living conditions and food in the camps were supervised carefully, medical authorities were still unaware of a number of issues, including the possible vitamin deficiency of the diet due to lack of fresh vegetables. Moreover, the Boers had normally lived on isolated farms or in widely separated villages, and were unfamiliar with the hygiene requirements of community living. The crowded conditions of the camps facilitated the exposure to and spread of contagious diseases to such a degree that simple illnesses became fatal. In addition, the winter of 1901–1902 was extremely severe, which exacerbated the situation.

Critical accounts of the conditions in the camps began to reach Britain early in 1901. Emily Hobhouse, a British social worker who had established the South African Women and Children Distress Fund, arrived in South Africa on December 27, 1900, to deliver supplies to the camps. She was shocked by the living conditions she saw, and on her return to London, she produced a report that exposed the worst aspects of the refugee camps. Newspapers and public officials demanded inquiries, which helped lead to improvements.

Separate concentration camps were established for white and black refugees. There were reportedly 27,927 deaths in the white camps during the war, of which 26,251 were women and children. Of the 115,700 people who were interned in black camps (which numbered at least 66, with perhaps as many as 80), there were 14,154 deaths recorded, of which about 8 percent were children.

The concentration camps of the Second Anglo-Boer War must not be confused or equated with the German camps of World War II, although the former tainted the reputation of the British. For the most part, given the level of knowledge at the time and availability of resources, many British camp administrators had performed their duty the best they could. Many South Africans considered the operations of the camps a crime—although Boer commandant-general Louis Botha admitted during the war that "one is only too thankful nowadays to know that our wives are under English protection" (Pakenham, 1979)—and this has left an indelible impression on their memory.

Harold E. Raugh, Jr.

See also: Bloemfontein Concentration Camp; Britain.

Further Reading

Barthorp, Michael. *The Anglo-Boer Wars: The British and the Afrikaners, 1815–1902.* Poole, UK: Blandford, 1987.
Heyningen, Elizabeth van. *British Concentration Camps of the South African War, 1900–1902.* Boer Concentration Camp Project, http://www2.lib.uct.ac.za/mss/bccd/

Lee, Emanoel. *To the Bitter End: A Photographic History of the Boer War, 1899–1902*. New York: Viking, 1985.

Pakenham, Thomas. *The Boer War*. New York: Random House, 1979.

Bosnian War

One of the defining characteristics of the war in Bosnia-Herzegovina has been the use of the chilling phrase *etnicko ciscenje*, or ethnic cleansing. The reality of this policy as an aim of the conflict has come to public attention most strongly in the establishment of detention camps. Media images of the suffering experienced by thousands of Bosnia's inhabitants served to isolate the Serbs in world opinion and led to the widespread view that only the "traditional" Balkan propensity to violence could explain the cause and nature of the conflict. The camps have thus assumed a symbolic importance that is probably greater than their real significance, and have played a substantial role in the propaganda war in the international media.

The overriding impression created by media treatment of the issue is that the camps were operated solely by Bosnian Serbs and run along the lines of the death camps of Nazi Germany. However, there is evidence that all sides in the conflict operated such camps, and that there was considerable variation in their management, even among different camps operated by the same side. Thus, a myth has been created that will no doubt play an important role long into the future. There has already been an attempt to rewrite Yugoslav history from that period, with Croatian president Franjo Tudjman's challenge of the previously accepted accounts of the Croatian Ustache camps such as Jasenovac. We can expect to see further rewriting of history given the paucity of information about the camps of the Bosnian conflict.

According to the incomplete figures available, only a minority of people actually died within the camps. Many more were killed when they were shipped out of the camps to other locations to meet their deaths or when their villages were overrun. What is certain is that the Nazi camps' industrialized, conveyor-belt approach to killing was not a feature of the Bosnian War. Instead, the deaths that occurred were from poor hygiene, starvation, sustained beating, and "sport" deaths, in which the victims' tormentors practiced sadistic, "imaginative," individualized killings. Furthermore, these camps were not purpose-built, but were frequently located in former industrial units, probably the only sites available in most areas. Of the camps featured most often in media coverage, Manjača was farm owned and operated by the Yugoslav People's Army, Keraterm was a former ceramics factory, and Omarska was an abandoned iron mine. There is evidence that in the Serb-run camps organization and management were chaotic, with different authorities responsible for different camps (Manjača was controlled by the Bosnian Serb Army and Omarska by the Commune of Prijedor) which led to difficulties and delays when aid agencies and other organizations such as United Nations High Commissioner for Refugees (UNHCR) attempted to gain access. These delays inevitably led to the impression that the Bosnian Serbs were deliberately restricting access.

The existence of the camps, although known to various international agencies, did not become public knowledge and thus an issue of concern until the summer of 1992. The first person to break the news of their existence was Roy Gutman of

New York's *Newsday*, closely followed by *The Guardian*'s Maggie O'Kane and ITN. ITN's coverage of Manjača flashed around the world and is generally considered to be the reason for the camp's appearance on the international political agenda.

There is considerable evidence that many camps were established, although some were of a very temporary nature. By August 1993, for example, the International Committee of the Red Cross estimated that there were 6,474 inmates in 51 camps. These numbers probably represent only a portion of the total number of inmates and camps at that time, and the complete figures may never be known. The Bosnian Serbs certainly conceived of the camps as fulfilling one of their war aims: the creation of ethnically pure areas. Most of the inmates were civilians, as Croat and Muslim community leaders and soldiers were generally isolated and taken away (the evidence suggests for execution) when Bosnian Serb forces arrived in an area. Imprisoning civilians achieved several aims: ethnic cleansing, hostages for exchange (in one instance 400 Croats for diesel fuel), and the creation of fear, which further enabled ethnic cleansing by encouraging civilians to flee before advancing military forces.

The camps had varying impacts on the various sides and across socioeconomic classes. In the early stages of the war, when the Bosnian Serbs were securing large areas of territory, most of the camps, including Manjača and Omarska, were run by them. Under intense international pressure, camps that were known to the media and international agencies were gradually closed and the inmates transferred to holding centers in Croatia. Later stages of the war saw the creation of camps by the Muslims and Croats, and relatively little is known of these, as by then media attention had shifted to Sarajevo and the various Muslim enclaves. One Croat-run camp, Mostar, is known to have had conditions as bad or even worse than those of the Serb camps. Mostar was established by the Ustache-inclined Croatian Party of Rights at the former Yugoslav People's Army heliport near the town, and inmates were kept in fuel tanks. Many died from the fumes, and a considerable number of people were murdered for sport by guards (including women) stationed there.

Finally, evidence suggests that among the Serbs, captured non-Serb civilians were screened to determine their fate. Those who were highly literate (such as teachers) or who occupied relatively high socioeconomic positions in the area seem to have disappeared (presumably executed), and very few from these groups ever made it to the camps. One inmate of Trnopolje camp told Red Cross officials, "Only the working class lived."

Little is really known about the camps of the Bosnian War, and what is known is distorted by often sensationalist media reporting. Much investigative work needs to be done to obtain a more accurate picture of their purposes, roles, and consequences.

Robert Jiggins

See also: Manjača; Omarska.

Further Reading

Gutman, Roy. *A Witness to Genocide: The 1993 Pulitzer Prize-Winning Dispatches on the "Ethnic Cleansing" of Bosnia.* New York: Macmillan, 1993.

Vulliamy, Ed. *Seasons in Hell: Understanding Bosnia's War.* London: Simon & Schuster, 1994.

Brändström, Elsa (1888–1948)

A Swedish Red Cross nurse and philanthropist, renowned for her efforts to assist prisoners of war during World War I. Born in St. Petersburg, Russia, into the family of a Swedish diplomat, Brändström studied in Stockholm and, at the outbreak of World War I, she volunteered as a nurse for the Swedish Red Cross. Witnessing cold, hunger, and diseases at the POW camps, she organized and supervised the distribution of relief to hundreds of thousands of Austro-Hungarian and German prisoners of war who had been interned in Russia during World War I. Despite military and political upheaval in Russia, she established a Swedish Aid organization and made several trips to Siberia to deliver supplies to POWs. Her tireless efforts to save prisoners earned her the nickname "Engel von Sibirien" or "The Angel of Siberia."

Brändström continued her work even after the Bolshevik Revolution and the start of the Russian Civil War. She was arrested as a suspected spy in 1918; several of her colleagues had been executed while she remained in captivity until 1920. Returning to Sweden, she continued fund-raising efforts on behalf of the former prisoners of war. In the 1920s she published her memoirs, opened a home for the orphans of dead prisoners of war, and established sanatoriums to help the reintegration of prisoners into civilian society. When Hitler assumed power in 1933, she moved with her husband to the United States, where she continued to help war refugees from Europe. After World War II, she raised funds to assist civilians impacted by the war and played an important role in establishing aid organizations CARE International (Co-operative for American Relief in Europe) and CRALOG (Council of Relief Agencies Licensed for Operation in Germany). She died of bone cancer in 1948.

Alexander Mikaberidze

See also: Cavell, Edith Louisa; World War I Prisoners of War.

Further Reading

Brändström, Elsa. *Among the Prisoners of War in Russia and Siberia.* London: Hutchinson, 1929.

Jones, Heather. *Violence against Prisoners of War in the First World War: Britain, France and Germany, 1914–1920.* Cambridge: Cambridge University Press, 2011.

Juhl, Eduard, Herta Epstein, and Margarete Klante. *Elsa Brändström: Weg und Werk einer großen Frau in Schweden, Sibirien, Deutschland, Amerika.* Stuttgart, DE: Quell-Verl., 1963.

Britain

The United Kingdom of Great Britain and Northern Ireland was one of the first states to resort to concentration camps. During the Boer War, British authorities set up over thirty concentration camps in South Africa where tens of thousands of civilians had been detained in an effort to break the Boer resistance; in addition, islands in Bermuda's Great Sound were used as sites for internment camps where over 4,000 Boers were confined.

During World War I, British interned citizens of Germany, Austria-Hungary, and the Ottoman Empire on the Isle of Man, where they were held in internment camps at Knockaloe and Douglas. Meanwhile, British colonial forces invaded German South West Africa, where they rounded up Germans and sent them to concentration camps in Pretoria and Pietermaritzburg; detainees from German East Africa were moved to internment facilities in India, where large camps existed at Ahmednagar, Belgaum, and Kataphar, while a separate internment camp operated at Diyatalawa on the island of Ceylon (modern Sri Lanka). The British government also imprisoned Irish Republicans in internment camps in Shrewsbury, Bromyard, and Frongoch. The latter camp, located in Merionethshire in Wales, was initially a prisoner-of-war camp where German POWs were held in an abandoned distillery but, following the Irish Easter Rising in 1916, almost 2,000 Irish political prisoners were interned here; the Frongoch camp, thus, played an important role as forging ground for the Irish revolutionary cause and, under the leadership of Irish republican leaders Michael Collins and Richard Mulcahy, became the University of Revolution.

World War II witnessed expansion of the British internment and concentration camps. The Isle of Man, once again, served as the primary site for the internment of civilian enemy aliens, and major camps were set up at Ramsay (Mooragh Camp) and Douglas (Metropole Camp and Hutchinson Camp). British Nazi sympathizers, detained under the provisions of Defence Regulation 18B, were kept in internment camps or shipped overseas. German nationals and other suspect individuals were arrested and interned in British-held India, where central internment camp existed at Ahmednagar and small camps operated at Deolali, Dehradun, Calcutta, Bihar, and other locations.

Britain also interned refugees from war-ravaged Europe; in case of Jewish refugees who sought to emigrate to the British-held Palestine, the British government decided to detain them in internment camps in Cyprus where up to 30,000 Holocaust survivors were held to prevent their entry into Palestine. It must be noted also that the British government allowed the Polish Government in exile to establish its own internment camps in Scotland, where Polish camps existed at Rothesay (for political crimes) on the Isle of Bute and at Tighnabruaich (for criminals on the Scottish mainland).

After World War II, Britain continued to use concentration camps to protect its colonial possession. During the 1952–1960 Mau Mau Uprising in Kenya, the British established a 'detention and rehabilitation' program that led to arrests of tens of thousands of individuals who were suspected of revolutionary agitation. The Pipeline, as the program was labeled, categorized prisoners into one of three groups: "whites" who were cooperative and therefore worthy of repatriation; "greys" who were reasonably compliant, and were released after spending some time at labor camps; and "blacks" who were die-hard Mau Mau rebels and subject to indefinite detention at camps. Internment facilities were overcrowded and prisoners suffered from mistreatment and lack of bare essentials. A similar situation was also in the Malay Peninsula during the Malayan Emergency (1948–1960) when the British authorities used internment camps to detain thousands of Malayans and suppress the Malayan revolt. Under the plan developed by the British Army's director of operations General Sir Harold Briggs, the British launched forced relocation of some 500,000 Malayans into "New Villages," internment camps surrounded by barbed wire, police posts, and floodlit areas that were designed to keep the inhabitants in and the guerrillas out.

During the period of "Troubles" (1968–1998) in Northern Ireland, the British security and military detained hundreds of Irish nationalists and Republicans and were held in internment facilities (i.e. Long Kesh Detention Centre). This internment policy proved to be counter productive and the plight of detainees, many of whom when on hunger strikes (including the 1981 Irish hunger strike) only further galvanized the Irish nationalist cause and increased support for the Irish Republican Army. The incarceration of people under anti-terrorism laws specific to Northern Ireland continued until the Good Friday Agreement of 1998.

Alexander Mikaberidze

See also: Boer War (1899–1902); Defence Regulation 18B.

Further Reading

Benlow, Colin. *Boer Prisoners of War in Bermuda*. Bermuda: Island Press, 1994.

Brennan-Whitmore, W. J. *With the Irish in Frongoch*. Cork, IE: Mercier Press, 2013.

Webb, Simon. *British Concentration Camps: A Brief History from 1900–1975*. London: Pen & Sword Books, 2016.

British Army Aid Group

A British organization established to support and assist the Allied soldiers in Japanese captivity in China during World War II. Established in 1942 by Lieutenant Colonel Lindsay Ride, the BAAG operated for over three years and had assisted over 200 Allied soldiers in escaping from the Japanese captivity. It played a crucial in maintaining communications with and providing clandestine supplies to the prisoners in the Japanese camps.

Alexander Mikaberidze

See also: Japan; World War II Prisoners of War.

Further Reading

Ride, Edwin. *BAAG: Hong Kong Resistance, 1942–1945*. Hong Kong: Oxford University Press, 1981.

Brussels, Declaration of (1874)

The Declaration of Brussels was a project of an international declaration concerning the laws and customs of war attached to the final protocol of the Brussels Conference, signed at Brussels on August 27, 1874, by the representatives of fifteen states, which included, amongst others, Austria-Hungary, France, Germany, Great Britain, Italy, Russia, and Turkey, but not the United States of America.

After the end of the American Civil War in 1865 and the Franco-Prussian War in 1871, many legal experts were concerned about the way in which the laws and customs of war had been upheld in these wars. The International Committee of the Red Cross called for the creation of an international criminal tribunal to judge violations of the Geneva Convention, but the idea failed to garner sufficient support. Then, in 1874, on the initiative of Emperor Alexander II of Russia, the delegates of European powers gathered in Brussels to create an international framework of laws and customs of war.

The Conference approved the draft submitted by the Russian government. The declaration comprised of 56 articles that defined who should be recognized as belligerents, means of injuring the enemy, sieges and bombardments, spies, prisoners of war, the sick and wounded, treatment of private persons, taxes and requisitions, capitulations, and armistices, as well as interned belligerents and wounded cared for by neutrals.

It proved impossible to obtain the ratifications required to make the Declaration effective, since some governments (especially Germany and Britain) were unwilling to accept it as a binding convention.

The Brussel Declaration marked an important step in the process of codification of the laws of war. During the Balkan Wars of 1875–1878, a group of European international law experts formed a committee to re-examine the Brussels Declaration and to submit supplementary proposals on the subject. The efforts led to the adoption of the Manual of the Laws and Customs of War at Oxford in 1880. Better known as the Oxford Manual, it was designed to be more suitable as the basis for national legislation within each power, rather to create a wider international framework. Unlike the Brussel Declaration, the Manual also contained provisions for sanction for any party that violated its rules. Thus, both the Brussels Declaration and the Oxford Manual served as the basis of the two Hague Conventions on land warfare and the Regulations annexed to them, adopted in 1899 and 1907.

Alexander Mikaberidze

See also: Geneva Convention Relating to Prisoners of War (1929); Geneva Convention Protocol I (1977); Lieber Code.

Further Reading

Best, Geoffrey. *Humanity in Warfare: The Modern History of the International Law of Armed Conflict.* London: Weidenfeld and Nicolson, 1980.

Ferencz, Benjamin B. *Enforcing International Law—A Way to World Peace: A Documentary History and Analysis.* London: Oceana Publications, 1983.

"Project of an International Declaration concerning the Laws and Customs of War. Brussels, August 27, 1874," The International Committee of the Red Cross, https://ihl -databases.icrc.org/ihl/INTRO/135

Buchenwald

Buchenwald, located outside Weimar, south of Berlin, was the largest Nazi concentration camp on German soil. The irony of the location is that the city of Weimar was long the center of German democratic thought.

An emaciated survivor of Buchenwald concentration camp, April 23, 1945.

Buchenwald was established in 1937, and from then until the end of World War II in 1945, it held 239,000 Jews, Romanis, homosexuals, and political prisoners. By 1938, the majority were Jews, although at first German policy was to pressure Jewish prisoners into leaving Germany by 15-hour days of forced labor in Buchenwald's quarries. In such circumstances, about 10,000 Jews were freed when their families arranged emigration. After 1942, when the Nazis had decided on the "Final Solution"—the total destruction of Europe's Jews—all Jewish prisoners were either shipped to their deaths in the east or placed in permanent slave labor, often worked to death. Some 1,000 children were also kept at Buchenwald in special barracks, and most of them survived the war. As the war progressed, several hundred captured British, Canadian, and American prisoners of war were also kept at Buchenwald. They were deemed spies by the Nazis because they had crashed their planes in France and tried to return to the Allied lines, aided by the French Resistance.

Buchenwald was not an extermination camp like Auschwitz. It was a concentration and forced labor camp, where the slave laborers were exploited as thoroughly as possible. Most worked in stone quarries or at an armaments factory operated by the camp; some were shipped out from Buchenwald to 130 "factory camps" to aid the German war effort. Arrivals were greeted by an iron sign, *Jedem das Seine*—"To each his own,"—or, more accurately, "You get what you deserve."

Prisoners at camps such as Buchenwald were often beaten to death, and many died from malnutrition and exhaustion. Ten thousand died at Buchenwald of neglect and disease; they are remembered with a simple memorial. Thousands of Soviet prisoners of war were summarily executed. More than 1,000 women prisoners were brought to Buchenwald to serve in the camp brothel for staff members.

Some prisoners were subjected to gruesome medical experiments aimed at improving Nazi medical treatment for its own troops. Prisoners were subjected to poison experiments, burned with phosphorus, and infected with diseases. The evil of Buchenwald has often been symbolized by the camp commandant's wife, Ilse Koch, who made lampshades from the skin of Jewish victims, particularly those with tattoos. In April 1945, as the Allied armies advanced toward Weimar, the Nazis began evacuating Jewish prisoners. In the forced march to the west that followed, one-third of the prisoners died.

In 1945, Buchenwald became the first Nazi concentration camp to be liberated by American troops, a day after the prisoners rose up against their captors and killed most of the guards. At liberation, Buchenwald still held 25,000 prisoners, 4,000 of whom were Jews. A total of about 56,000 people perished at Buchenwald. Most died from being worked to death under harsh conditions and inadequate food, but gallows were built at the very start of the camp, and arbitrary executions were common. More than 1,000 victims died by hanging.

From 1945 to 1950, occupying Soviet forces ran an internment camp at Buchenwald for 32,000 Germans; at first it was for suspected war criminals, but it soon turned into a prison for opponents of the communists. More than 7,000 prisoners died during this period.

As at the site of every former Nazi concentration camp, debate rages over the meaning of the site and how it should be presented. One position considers all Holocaust sites hallowed ground to be left untouched as memorials to those who died there. Others see the moral and educational value of showing the details of the Holocaust to future generations; they want the camps preserved and restored to the state they were in as part of the Nazi attempt to destroy the Jewish people. Both sides agree that as the remaining survivors age and die, the camps are the most important tangible reminder of the Holocaust.

At Buchenwald, this conflict is especially acute. For 40 years, Buchenwald was part of communist East Germany. The communists denied any responsibility for the Holocaust, blaming it on the Nazis, whom they identified with the West Germans. With the unification of Germany in 1990, Buchenwald generated furious argument until communist administrators were removed from their jobs. The site is gradually being restored.

The present-day camp reflects the ambiguities of modern German attitudes toward the Holocaust. Most of the original buildings were destroyed shortly after 1945. The current administration uses the former SS officers' rooms, and a backpackers' youth hostel has been placed in the camp guards' barracks. A museum recounts in pictures and artifacts the stark realities of camp life, and shows a documentary film. The film, a relic of the communist past, tells more about communist political prisoners than about Jewish victims. In a recent about-face that still manages to avoid the full horror of Buchenwald's place in the Holocaust, the present German authorities have focused on Buchenwald's history after the liberation. There is a memorial at the site of the children's barracks.

Norbert C. Brockman

See also: Auschwitz; Bełżec; Bergen-Belsen; Birkenau; Chełmno; Concentration Camps; Extermination Centers; Gas Chambers; Holocaust, The; I.G. Farben Case (1947); J.A. Topf & Söhne; Zyklon B Case (1946).

Further Reading
Hackett, David A. *The Buchenwald Report*. Boulder, CO: Westview Press, 1997.
Young, James. *The Texture of Memory: Holocaust Memorials and Meaning*. New Haven, CT: Yale University Press, 1994.

Bulgaria, Internment and Labor Camps

In 1944, as the German forces suffered defeat and retreated from the Soviet Union, the Red Army invaded Bulgaria and helped set up a Communist regime. In early October 1944, the Communist authorities called for prosecution of "collaborators" and "counterrevolutionaries," which soon came to encompass not only actual Nazi sympathizers and collaborators, but also non-communist intellectuals and civilians suspected of "bourgeois sensibilities." Over the next year, thousands (over 11,000 by some estimates) of people's courts had been held and more than 2,100 individuals had been executed.

In 1945, the Bulgarian authorities established, under the supervision of the Ministry of Internal Affairs, the so-called educational labor hostels (*trudovovûzpitatelni obshtezhitiya*) in agrarian and industrial areas, and heavily relied on forced labor to both revamp its economy and get rid of political opponents. The most notorious of these labor camps was located in Belene, on the island of Persin in the Danube, where some 7,000 people were interned in 1952.

After the death of Soviet dictator Joseph Stalin in 1953, Bulgaria experienced a period of de-Stalinization when the number of prisoners in labor camps declined. However, the spread of political turmoil in 1956—most notably in Hungary, but also in some Bulgarian cities—caused the Bulgarian communist authorities to resort to political repression, and the labor camp population rapidly rebounded. In addition to Belene, a labor camp for women opened in Skravena (near Lovech) and a separate camp, sardonically christened "Sunny Beach" after the well-known seaside resort, was established in Lovech, where prisoners were forced to do hard labor in a nearby quarry; overall, between 1944 and 1962, the Bulgarian communist regime operated about 100 labor camps that interned over 15,000 people. In the 1960s, the labor camps were turned into formal prisons, where political dissidents were held as common criminals.

In the 1970s and 1980s, many members of the Pomak and Turkish communities, who opposed assimilating policies of the Bulgarian government, were held at Belene and other complexes; about 18,000 people were killed without trial, more than 2,500 were executed after mass trials, and nearly 200,000 suffered from repressions. While some details on the Bulgarian camp system leaked in early 1950s, the full picture emerged only after the fall of the Communist regime.

In March 1990, the Ministry of Internal Affairs set up a commission to investigate the living conditions in the labor camps. Some labor camp guards and officials, including Georgi Tsankov, Minister of the Interior from 1951 to 1962 and

General Mircho Spasov, who was directly in charge of the labor camps system, were arrested and held responsible.

Alexander Mikaberidze

See also: Belene Camp.

Further Reading

Baev, Jordan. "De-Stalinisation and Political Rehabilitations in Bulgaria," in Kevin McDermott and Matthew Stibbe, eds. *De-Stalinising Eastern Europe: The Rehabilitation of Stalin's Victims after 1953, 150–169.* New York: Palgrave Macmillan, 2015.

"The Belene Concentration Camp in Bulgaria," Declassified Memo, Central Intelligence Agency, October 1951, https://www.cia.gov/library/readingroom/docs/CIA-RDP80 -00809A000700050030-1.pdf

Geshev, Nedyalko. *Belene. Ostrovut na zabravenie. Spomeni.* Sofia, BG: DF Robinzon, 1991.

Luleva, Ana, ed. *Prinuditelniyat trud v Bulgariya (1941–1962): spomeni na svideteli.* Sofia, BG: Marin Drinov, 2012.

Todorov, Tzvetan. *Voices from the Gulag: Life and Death in Communist Bulgaria.* University Park: Pennsylvania State University Press, 1999.

Bullet Decree (1944)

The Bullet Decree (Kugel-Erlass) was a secret directive issued by the Nazi authorities on March 4, 1944. Under its provisions (and in direct contravention of the Geneva Conventions), recaptured escaped officer and noncommissioned officer prisoners of war were to be sent to concentration camps to be worked to death or executed. The recaptured POWs were to be handed over to the Sicherheitsdienst, the intelligence agency of the SS and the Nazi Party, and transferred to the Mauthausen-Gusen concentration camp; although POWs from the British Commonwealth and United States were initially exempt from the order, the Nazi authorities soon extended its provisions. Thus, in March 1944, 50 officers of the British Royal Air Force, who escaped from the camp at Sagan, were shot on recapture, on the direct orders of Adolf Hitler. The number of escaped prisoners of war executed under the provisions of the Bullet Decree varies, but it is estimated that as many 5,300 may have been killed, the vast majority of them being Soviet prisoners of war.

Alexander Mikaberidze

See also: Geneva Convention Relating to Prisoners of War (1929); Hitler, Adolf; World War II Prisoners of War.

Further Reading

Overmans, Rüdiger. "German Policy on Prisoners of War, 1939–1945," in Jörg Echternhamp, ed. *Germany and the Second World War. Volume IX/II: German Wartime Society 1939–1945*, 733–881. Oxford: Clarendon Press, 2014.

Burma-Thailand Railway

Military railroad that the Imperial Japanese Army (IJA) constructed between Nong Pladuk in Thailand and Thanbyuzayat in Burma. The total length of the railroad was approximately 415 kilometers. The assignment to undertake the railroad construction was announced by the IJA Headquarters in June 1942. Construction started the following month, and the railway was completed in October of the following year.

According to Japanese source materials, the purpose for its construction was to secure an alternate land route to Burma, and to build new links of trade and communication between Thailand and Burma. The railway also had the important role of intercepting and cutting off aid to Chiang Kaishek (Jiang Jieshi) through Burma and of facilitating the IJA's "Imphal Campaign."

The route of the railway is characterized by some of the world's soggiest weather, traversing an area of dense jungles and steep mountains, which was moreover a hotbed of tropical diseases. To expedite the completion of its construction, the IJA mobilized 62,000 Allied prisoners of war, as well as an estimated 300,000 Asian workers. The IJA did not properly provide the prisoners with facilities and daily necessities. During the period from the beginning to the completion, approximately 12,000 Allied prisoners who worked on its construction died of sickness and mistreatment caused by their captors. The exact death rate of Asian construction workers is unknown, but it is estimated that more than 90,000 of the Asians died. That of the IJA is also around 7 percent.

In December of 1945, the Japanese Army Ministry presented to the Supreme Commander of the Allied Forces an accounting which said, "The Japanese Army shared the same pains and pleasures together with the prisoners and the general laborers," and alleged that, "the construction supervisors, in keeping with a policy guideline that considered the prisoners and laborers as 'divine spirits of construction,' worked incessantly to improve the prisoners' treatment." The expression that they were treated like "divine spirits of construction" actually meant that in the camps, railway construction was given absolute priority, while their humanity was denied.

Due to the brutalities and the violation of the war rules, many related personnel were indicted and brought to trial after the war. For example, just at the Singapore Tribunal, there were 24 cases of related indictments; 111 persons were judged guilty, of which 32 received death sentences. The majority of those judged guilty were primarily associated with the POW camps along the railway rather than supervising the railway construction as technicians. As a result, 33 among the judged guilty and 9 among the death sentences were Koreans whose country was at the time under Japan's colonial rule.

Nobuko Margaret Kosuge

See also: Japan; World War II Prisoners of War.

Further Reading
Chalker, Jack. *Burma Railway: Images of War, the Original War Drawings of Japanese POW Jack Chalker.* London: Macer Books, 2007.

Kinvig, Clifford. *River Kwai Railway: The Story of the Burma-Siam Railroad.* London: Brasseys, 1998

McCormack, Gavan, and Hank Nelson, eds. *The Burma-Thailand Railway: Memory and History.* Crows Nest, NSW: Allen & Unwin, 1993.

Bushell, Roger Joyce (1910–1944)

British officer and pilot, who, as a German prisoner of war, organized the famed escape from Stalag Luft III. Born in South Africa in 1910, Bushell was educated at Cambridge and joined the Royal Air Force in 1932. By the start of World War II, he commanded the 92nd Squadron; in May 1940 he was credited with damaging two German fighter aircrafts before being shot down over the German-occupied territory in northwestern France. He was captured and conveyed to the Dulag Luft camp near Frankfurt before being sent to the Stalag Luft III, near Sagan (now Żagań, Poland).

Bushell quickly established relations with British and American prisoners and plotted several escape attempts in 1941–1942. He persevered despite early setbacks and, in 1943, masterminded what became the most famous POW escape of the entire war. Under his leadership, over 600 prisoners took part in digging secret tunnels. German authorities discovered some of the tunnels, but prisoners were able to complete one tunnel, codenamed "Harry." On March 24, 1944 the prisoners attempted to escape but things did not go as planned and only 76 officers succeeded in getting out of the camp.

Bushell and his colleagues escaped on a train that they boarded at Sagan railway station but were recaptured the following day at Saarbrücken. Fifty of the recaptured 76 prisoners were tried under the provisions of the Bullet Decree and sentenced to death. Bushell was one of the victims of the Stalag Luft III murders. He was buried at the Poznan Old Garrison Cemetery in Poznan, Poland. The escape that he organized and led served as the basis for the famous 1963 movie *The Great Escape*; the character played by Richard Attenborough, Roger Bartlett, was modeled on Roger Bushell.

Alexander Mikaberidze

See also: Great Escape; World War II Prisoners of War.

Further Reading
Brickhill, Paul. *The Great Escape*. London: Cassell, 2000.
Walters, Guy. *The Real Great Escape*. London: Bantam, 2013.

Butovo Firing Range

Site of mass executions by Soviet secret police and a key location of the Great Terror of 1937 and 1938. Located near the village of Drozhzhino, south of Moscow, Butovo was a private estate before the Bolshevik revolution of 1917. Starting in the 1920s, the estate was under control of the Soviet secret police (first OGPU, then NKVD) that turned parts of it into a firing range. During Joseph Stalin's Great Purges, thousands of prisoners were brought to the newly designated "Special Location" and summarily executed; it is estimated that over 20,000 people were shot at the range between August 1937 and October 1938, while 562 individuals were executed in a single day on February 28, 1938. Prisoners were delivered to the range in trucks ostensibly carrying supplies. Once inside the range, they were kept in a large barrack where they were checked, taken in groups to the pits and shot. The firing range remained secret until the collapse of the Soviet Union in 1991. The Russian Orthodox Church took over the ownership of the lot in 1995 and had a memorial church built there.

Alexander Mikaberidze

See also: Beria, Lavrenty; Bykivnia Mass Grave Site; Gulag; Serpantinka.

Further Reading

Bakirov, E., and V. Shantsev. *Butovskii polygon, 1937–1938*. Moscow: Panorama, 2002.

Schlogel, Karl. *Moscow, 1937*. New York: John Wiley & Sons, 2014, chapter 33.

Bykivnia Mass Grave Site

A National Historic Memorial on the site of the former village of Bykivnia (Russian: Bykovnia) where the Soviet secret police executed tens of thousands of Soviet prisoners. Starting in the 1920s, the Soviet government arrested, imprisoned, abused, and executed thousands of Soviets citizens who were accused of a whole range of crimes against the Soviet state and the Communist Party; surviving evidence suggests that among the Bykivnia victims were some 3,400 Polish POWs. One of Bykivnia's last intakes was a group of Red Army officers and soldiers who broke through the German encirclement only to be executed by the Soviet secret police, NKVD, three weeks before the fall of Kiev in September 1941.

The Bykivnia victims were taken from prisons and camps ran by the Soviet secret police, interrogated, tortured, and executed. The NKVD then disposed of the bodies of the killed by burying them in mass graves in the pine woods on the outskirts of the village of Bykivnia; in 1936, a special zone for secret burials was designated and built. In 1941, when the Red Army was forced to abandon Ukraine, the Soviet authorities sought to destroy the site, but was it was still discovered by the German military, which conducted some preliminary excavations. In 1943, after the Soviet recaptured Ukraine, Bykivnia became a secret NKVD site once more.

The number of victims buried at Bykivnia remains unknown, but is estimated at over 120,000 individuals. After the war, the Soviet authorities claimed that the mass graves contained victims of the German executions and erected a special obelisk to the memory of "Soviet soldiers, partisans, members of the underground and peaceful citizens killed by the Fascist occupying forces from 1941 to 1943." However, new investigations in the late 1980s and 1990s revealed the Soviet culpability in the Bykivnia murders. Following its independence, Ukraine designated Bykivnia as a National Historic Memorial.

Alexander Mikaberidze

See also: Beria, Lavrenty; Gulag; Serpantinka.

Further Reading

Berkhoff, Karel. "Bykivnia: How Grave Robbers, Activists, and Foreigners Ended Official Silence about Stalin's Mass Graves Near Kiev," in Elizabeth Anstett and Jean-Marc Dreyfus, eds., *Human Remains and Identification: Mass Violence, Genocide and the "Forensic Turn,"* 59–82. Manchester: Manchester University Press, 2015.

Keller, Bill. "Behind Stalin's Green Fence: Who Filled the Mass Graves?" *New York Times*, March 6, 1989.

Kuromiya, Hiroaki. *The Voices of the Dead: Stalin's Great Terror in the 1930s*. New Haven, CT: Yale University Press, 2007.

C

Cabanatuan

A Japanese prisoner-of-war camp near Cabanatuan City in the Philippines. Prior to World War II, this facility was used as an American Department of Agriculture station and a training grounds for the Filipino army. After the fall of the Philippines in 1942, thousands of American prisoners of war had been forced to embark on the infamous Bataan Death March that claimed hundreds of lives. The survivors were then sent to the Cabanatuan complex that comprised of some 100 acres wide rectangular-shaped camp, which was surrounded by eight foot tall barbed wire fences and multiple pillbox bunkers and guard towers. The POWs, who had been subjected to routine mistreatment, malnourishment, and torture, nicknamed the camp "Zero Ward" for a low probability of getting out of it alive. At the height of

American prisoners rescued in the daring raid staged by U.S. Rangers on Cabanatuan prison camp, 1945. (Bettmann/Getty Images)

World War II, the camp held about 8,000 prisoners of war (from the United States, Britain, Norway, and the Netherlands), making it the largest POW camp in the Philippines. As the tide of war turned in American favor, the number of POWs held at Cabanatuan steadily declined, as able-bodied prisoners were evacuated to other areas in the Philippines, Japan, and Japanese-occupied territories, where they were employed in labor camps. POWs made multiple escape attempts, but most of them had failed; after one of the failed attempts, the Japanese guards forced the prisoners to watch as the four recaptured prisoners were abused, forced to dig their own graves, and then executed. To prevent future escapes, the Japanese authorities warned that ten prisoners would be executed for every escapee.

In late January 1945, American intelligence reports had indicated that the Japanese were planning to kill the remaining prisoners at Cabanatuan as they withdrew toward Manila. A quick plan was developed by Sixth Army leaders and Filipino guerrillas to send a small rescue force to the camp. On January 30, 1945, in the Cabanatuan raid—led by Lt. Colonel Henry Mucci of the 6th Ranger Battalion—American troops struck 30 miles behind Japanese lines to rescue 489 emaciated and sickly POWs (and 33 civilians). The rangers, aided by Filipino guerrillas, killed more than 200 members of the Japanese garrison, evaded two Japanese regiments, and reached the safety of American lines the following day. The Raid at Cabanatuan remains of the most successful of its kind in U.S. military history.

Alexander Mikaberidze

See also: Japan; World War II Prisoners of War.

Further Reading

Breuer, William B. *The Great Raid on Cabanatuan: Rescuing the Doomed Ghosts of Bataan and Corregidor.* New York: John Wiley & Sons, Inc., 1994.

Carson, Andrew D. *My Time in Hell: Memoir of an American Soldier Imprisoned by the Japanese in World War II.* New York: McFarland & Company, 1997

Rottman, Gordon. *The Cabanatuan Prison Raid—The Philippines 1945.* London: Osprey Publishing, 2009.

Cabrera

Island in the Mediterranean Sea and site of the notorious camp for the French prisoners of war during the Napoleonic Wars. The small island of Cabrera is part of the Balearic Islands and is just the south of the island Mallorca (Majorca). At the start of nineteenth century, it was a desolate and uninhabited place.

In 1808, Emperor Napoleon of the French invaded Spain but faced unexpected challenges. On July 21, 1808, French general Pierre Dupont de l'Etang came across a Spanish army and fought an inconclusive battle at Bailén. Finding himself isolated, Dupont chose to surrender his corps of nearly 22,000 French, Swiss, Polish, and Italian troops. Although the terms of the capitulation specified that the French would be repatriated home, the Spanish government (the Junta of Seville) refused to approve the terms. Instead, the French prisoners were interned in prison ships in Cádiz harbor where hundreds died of disease and neglect. In 1809, some 9,000 prisoners were transported to the island of Cabrera, where they were abandoned with just scant supplies and tents. The prisoners slowly starved for the next five years and out of 11,800 prisoners brought to Cabrera in 1809–1814, only 3,700 survived by the end of the Napoleonic Wars in April 1814.

Alexander Mikaberidze

See also: French Revolutionary and Napoleonic Era.

Further Reading
Smith, Denis. *The Prisoners of Cabrera: Napoleon's Forgotten Soldiers, 1809–1814.* New York: Four Walls, Eight Windows. 2001.

Cambodian Killing Fields

A term describing a vast complex of prisons, killing sites, and mass graves in Cambodia where hundreds of thousands of people had been killed by the Khmer Rouge regime between 1975 and 1979. The term was coined by Cambodian journalist and interpreter Dith Pran—who had witnessed the killings and managed to escape from the country—but it became part of wider public consciousness in 1984, when the movie *The Killing Fields*, chronicling the Cambodian genocide, was released to critical and popular acclaim.

In its broadest meaning, the Cambodian Killing Fields refer to a state-sponsored terror campaign that the Khmer Rouge waged in the 1970s. Some 20,000 mass grave sites have been identified over the last two decades and estimates of the total number of deaths resulting from Khmer Rouge terrors range from 1.7 to 2.5 million (out of population of about 8 million). More narrowly, the term refers to a system of prisons and killing sites that the Khmer Rouge established to persecute and exterminate their political opponents. Thus, at the Tuol Sleng prison, at least 16,000 prisoners were incarcerated and methodically killed between 1975 and 1979, while another 9,000 individuals were executed at Choeung Ek, 11 miles south of Phnom Penh.

In 1997, 18 years after Vietnam invaded Cambodia and toppled the Khmer Rouge regime, the Cambodian government agreed to prosecute those responsible for the genocide. Starting in 2006, Extraordinary Chambers in the Courts of Cambodia, a special court set up with the help of the United Nations, examined crimes against humanity in Cambodia and prosecuted the most senior responsible members of the Khmer Rouge, including Kang Kek Iew, who supervised the Khmer prison system and Nuon Chea, who was the right-hand man to the Khmer leader Pol Pot; they were convicted and sentenced to life imprisonment.

Alexander Mikaberidze

See also: Choeung Ek; Kang Kek Iew.

Further Reading
Case 001 (Trial of Kang Kek Iew), Extraordinary Chambers in the Courts of Cambodia, https://www.eccc.gov.kh/en/case/topic/1

Dunlop, Nic. *The Lost Executioner: A Journey into the Heart of the Killing Fields.* New York: Walker and Company, 2005.

Kiernan, Ben. *The Pol Pot Regime: Race, Power and Genocide in Cambodia under the Khmer Rouge, 1975–1979.* New Haven, CT: Yale University Press, 2008.

Camp Bucca

A U.S. detention camp near Umm Qasr, Iraq. After the U.S. invasion of Iraq in 2003, the British military established a camp to house Iraqi prisoners of war. The Camp Freddy, as this British installation became known, was eventually transferred to American control and renamed Camp Bucca after New York City fire marshal Ronald Bucca, who died in the terrorist attacks of September 11, 2001.

During the early stages of the U.S. involvement in Iraq, there were reports of detainee abuse at Camp Bucca, including physical violence during interrogation. After the Abu Ghraib prisoner abuse scandal, the U.S. Army moved many detainees from Abu Ghraib to Camp Bucca and sought to introduce key changes to turn the camp into an example of a model detention facility. The detainees were interned in 10 climate-controlled housing compounds and provided with access to healthcare, education, and entertainment; prisoners could also participate in a family visitation allowance program. Each compound held up to 800 prisoners, who chose their own leader to both maintain order within a compound and serve as a liaison with the camp authorities.

In 2007–2008, Camp Bucca was the largest detention facility in the world, with a prisoner population of over 20,000 men. In 2009 the camp authorities gradually released or transferred detainees before shutting down the camp. A year later the U.S. military handed the base to the government of Iraq.

Alexander Mikaberidze

See also: Abu Ghraib; Bagram Air Base; Sarposa.

Further Reading

Angell, Ami. *Terrorist Rehabilitation: The U.S. Experience in Iraq.* Boca Raton, FL; CRC Press, 2012.

Khalil, Ashraf. "Camp Bucca Turns 180 Degrees from Abu Ghraib," *Los Angeles Times*, Jan 10, 2005.

Pryer, Douglas. *The Fight For The High Ground: The U.S. Army and Interrogation during Operation Iraqi Freedom I, May 2003–April 2004*, MA in Military Art and Science thesis, U.S. Army Command and General Staff College, 2009 www.dtic.mil/get-tr-doc/pdf?AD=ADA502354

Camp Chase

Union mustering and prisoner of war facility in Columbus, Ohio. First established in May 1861, Camp Chase was named for former Ohio governor and Secretary of the Treasury Salmon P. Chase. As many as 150,000 Union soldiers passed through Camp Chase between 1861 and 1865, mustering into or out of the volunteer army, while some 25,000 Confederate prisoners were housed there or passed through the facility. Most of the Confederate detainees were from western military campaigns. Early on, Confederate officers and parolees were allowed to venture into Columbus, eat in restaurants, and register in hotels. Camp Chase also became a popular tourist attraction, and state officials even permitted group tours of the facility. By early 1863, however, such lax discipline resulted in the assumption of control by federal authorities, who quickly transferred officers interned at Camp Chase to

Johnson's Island Prison on Lake Erie. Rules were significantly tightened for the prisoners, all mail was censored, and public visitation was forbidden.

Conditions for prisoners housed at Camp Chase were far from ideal—barracks designed for 4,000 men were jammed with as many as 7,000; food was meager and poor; and the poorly-drained, muddy ground caused all sorts of health problems, as did contaminated water supplies and open latrines. Prisoners were often badly treated by ill-trained guards.

Toward the end of the war, some improvements were made to Camp Chase, many of them by the prisoners themselves. Barracks facilities were expanded to accommodate 7,000 men, but influxes of new prisoners resulted in more overcrowding; by early 1865, the expanded barracks were housing as many as 9,400 men.

The precise number of detainees who died at Camp Chase is not known, but the adjacent cemetery, with 2,260 Confederate graves, is a grim testimonial to the high rate of deaths there from disease, malnutrition, and exposure. At least one smallpox outbreak ravaged the camp during the war.

Camp Chase was closed shortly after the war ended, and it was dismantled entirely in 1867. All that remains of the facility today is the Confederate cemetery, with 2,260 white headstones.

Paul G. Pierpaoli, Jr.

See also: American Civil War; Andersonville Prison; Camp Douglas; Camp Ford; Confederate States of America.

Further Reading

McCormick, Robert W. "About Six Acres of Land: Camp Chase, Civil War Prison," *Timeline* 11, 5 (September-October 1994): 34–43.

Smith, Robin. *Columbus Ghosts*. Worthington, OH: Emuses, Inc., 2002.

Camp Douglas

Located near Chicago, Illinois, Camp Douglas was one of the largest Union prison camps for captured Confederate soldiers. Of the more than 26,000 Confederate detainees held at Camp Douglas, more than 4,400 died, making it the deadliest of all Union camps. The camp was initially established as a recruitment and training center in 1861, but was converted into a prison after Brigadier General Ulysses S. Grant captured Fort Donelson, Tennessee, on February 15, 1862, along with some 15,000 Confederate defenders. More than 3,000 of these captives had reached Camp Douglas by February 21, 1862.

The camp had several advantages, including existing barracks and its location on a major rail line. However, it had little provision for securing prisoners, forcing the emergency construction of a stockade wall. The section of camp for the detainees, called Prison Square, held 64 barracks 24 by 90 feet in size, each with its own kitchen and bunks for 95 men.

The prison easily accommodated its first captives, but within a few months it was well above its planned capacity of 6,000 men. Overcrowding soon overwhelmed the logistical system of the camp. The location, on low ground, was subject to regular flooding, and the sewage system proved insufficient, causing disease and mortality rates to climb. Officials of the U.S. Sanitary Commission recommended abandoning the site, but instead, Union leaders added to the number of captives. In the winter of 1862–1863, the camp's monthly mortality rate reached 10 percent. The camp hospital contained only 120 beds, forcing hundreds of sick prisoners to remain in the barracks. Camp authorities did little to heat the barracks, which added to the deteriorating conditions. By late 1864, more than 12,000 prisoners had been crammed into Prison Square.

Camp Douglas also witnessed more successful escapes than any other Union prison, with 343 reported. Camp commandants devoted much time and considerable resources attempting to improve security, but could not always stop the desperate captives. In the fall of 1864, rumors circulated of a Confederate plot to attack the camp and free the prisoners, although no assault occurred. After General Robert E. Lee's surrender in April 1865, Union officials reduced the camp's population by allowing prisoners to swear the oath of allegiance to the United States and leave for home. Those who refused the oath were released by the end of July 1865, and the camp was decommissioned and demolished that fall.

Paul J. Springer

See also: American Civil War; Andersonville Prison; Camp Ford; Confederate States of America.

Further Reading

Levy, George. *To Die in Chicago: Confederate Prisoners at Camp Douglas, 1862–1865.* Gretna, LA: Pelican, 1994.

Pucci, Kelly. *Camp Douglas: Chicago's Civil War Prison.* Charleston, SC: Arcadia Publishing, 2007.

Camp Ford

Located near Tyler, Texas, Camp Ford was the largest Confederate Army prisoner camp west of the Mississippi River. More than 5,000 Union prisoners were sent to Camp Ford, with approximately 300 dying there of all causes. The camp was built in the spring of 1862 for recruitment and training purposes. It was converted to a prison in the fall of 1863, with detainees initially held on open ground. Rumors of a planned mass escape prompted the construction of a crude stockade.

In the spring of 1864, battles in Louisiana and Arkansas had swelled the prison's population to more than 5,000. Prisoners continued to be held in an open stockade with little shelter, but guards did allow detainees to construct their own living quarters using wood from local forests. Despite the rough-hewn conditions, the mortality rate remained relatively low, thanks mostly to ample food supplies in the area. Union control of the Mississippi River had prevented the shipment of beef and grain to the rest of the Confederacy, leaving plenty for the captives. Prisoners also tended garden plots to supplement their rations, minimizing diet-related sickness. Detainees at Camp Ford spent much of their time on handicrafts, which could be traded to the guards for luxuries. They made furniture, musical instruments, flatware, pottery, and chess sets.

Camp Ford's eventual overcrowding caused illness to spread beyond the capabilities of the small camp hospital by late 1864. When word of General Robert E. Lee's April 9, 1865, surrender reached Camp Ford, the guards simply walked away, leaving the prisoners to fend for themselves. Some managed to walk the 300 miles to Fort Smith, Arkansas, to obtain assistance for their comrades who were unable to travel. The camp has been restored, and is now a public historic park owned by Smith County, Texas.

Paul J. Springer

See also: American Civil War; Andersonville Prison; Camp Douglas; Confederate States of America.

Further Reading

Lawrence, F. Lee, and Robert W. Glover. *Camp Ford CSA: The Story of Union Prisoners in Texas.* Austin: Texas Civil War Centennial Advisory Committee, 1964.

Sanders, Charles W. *While in the Hands of the Enemy: Military Prisons of the Civil War.* Baton Rouge: Louisiana State University Press, 2005.

Camp O'Donnell

Japanese prisoner-of-war camp, located near the village of Capas, the province of Tarlac, Philippines. Camp O'Donnell was originally a training base of the Philippine Army's 71st Division. In 1942, following the Japanese conquest of the Philippines, the base was turned into a prisoner-of-war camp where some 60,000 Filipino and 9,000 Americans POWs, the survivors of the brutal Bataan Death March, were brought.

The camp was not yet complete when the first prisoners arrived in mid-April 1942; the complex covered over 600 acres and housed prisoners in segregated sections, one for the Filipinos and the other for the Americans. The camp became infamous for brutal conditions and mistreatment of prisoners, who arrived at the camp in already poor physical condition. The Japanese authorities had declined to treat the POWs in accordance with the Geneva Convention of 1929, and made little provision for the treatment of prisoners who found little adequate food, shelter, and medical treatment at the camp; In just several months, some 29,000 Filipinos and over 1,500 American POWs perished due to disease, malnutrition, and abuse; the camp thus became synonymous with brutal and dehumanizing conditions.

By summer of 1942, the Japanese authorities, overwhelmed by the size of POW population, began to transfer prisoners to Cabanatuan, Palawan, and other camps, where conditions turned out to be even worse. Camp O'Donnell was ultimately liberated by the American and Filipino forces in January 1945. It figured prominently in the post-war prosecution of Japanese war criminals: General Masaharu Homma, commander of the Japanese 14th Army, was charged with responsibility for thousands of deaths at this camp, tried by the Tokyo War Crimes Tribunal, found guilty, and executed.

Alexander Mikaberidze

See also: Cabanatuan; Far East, British Military Trials; Geneva Convention Relating to Prisoners of War (1929); Japan.

Further Reading

Alexander, Irvin, and Dominic J. Caraccilo. *Surviving Bataan and Beyond: Colonel Irvin Alexander's Odyssey as a Japanese Prisoner of War.* London: Greenhill, 2005.

Hardee, David L., and Frank A. Blazich. *Bataan Survivor: A POW's Account of Japanese Captivity in World War II.* Columbia: University of Missouri Press, 2016.

Kenneth B Murphy, and James T. Murphy. *When Men Must Live: An Inspirational True Story of Courage, Hope, and Freedom.* Los Gatos, CA: MG2, 2009.

Olson, John E. *O'Donnell, Andersonville of the Pacific* [n.p.], 1985.

Camp 22

A notorious prison camp in North Korea, reportedly closed in 2012. Located in the North Hamgyong province of North Korea, close to its border with China, the Camp No. 22 was a maximum security area that was established in the 1960s to intern victims of the North Korean Communist government's political repressions; the camp was significantly expanded in the 1980s and the 1990s, and came to cover a vast area in a mountain valley. Based on existing scant information, the camp may have interned as many as 50,000 prisoners who had been charged with a wide array of crimes against the state and the Communist party. Prisoners were assigned to one of prison labor colonies, where they worked at either factories, farms, or mines. Testimonies of former guards reveal extremely harsh conditions at the camp, where malnutrition, disease, and abuse was widespread, resulting in high mortality rates; some prisoners had been subjected to experimentation and placed in a gas chamber. Prisoners were routinely forced to do hard physical labor and attend ideological reeducation classes, with recalcitrant individuals subjected to torture and abuse. In 2012, there were unverified reports that the camp was closed, but satellite images indicate that the camp continues its operation.

Alexander Mikaberidze

See also: North Korea.

Further Reading

Hawk, David. *The Hidden Gulag—Exposing Crimes against Humanity in North Korea's Vast Prison System.* U.S. Committee for Human Rights in North Korea, 2012.

Political Prison Camps in North Korea Today. Jongno-gu, Seoul: Database Center for North Korean Human Rights, 2011.

"The Testimony of An Myong-chol, an Ex-guard at a Political Prisoners' Camp in North Korea," *Monthly Chosun Ilbo,* March 1995, archived version at https://web.archive.org/web/20131022224821/http://monthly.chosun.com/client/dataroom/databoard read.asp?idx=9&cPage=5&table=dataroom

Canada

After the start of World War I, Canadian authorities moved quickly to intern and isolate "aliens of enemy nationality." Under the terms of the War Measures Act, civil liberties were suspended and tens of thousands of Germans and Austro-Hungarians were required to register with the authorities. Over 8,000 Austro-Hungarians, including ethnic Ukrainians, Croats, and Serbs, had been placed in internment camps for the duration of war. Conditions at these camps varied, with the Castle Mountain Internment Camp, located in remote part of the Canadian Rockies, considered the harshest. The internment lasted not only for the duration of the war, but also for several years after the war ended; by 1920, the vast majority of internees were released, but a small number of them, considered to be too radical, were deported to Europe.

With the start of World War II, Canada revived the practice of internment camps. The Defence of Canada Regulations of 1939 sanctioned detaining thousands of people of German, Italian, and Japanese ancestry, as well as individuals considered a danger to national security. Most German and Italian Canadians were interned in Camp Petawawa situated in the Ottawa River Valley.

Table 1   **Major Internment Camps in Canada during World War I, 1914–1920**

Camp Location	Date of opening	Date of closing
Montreal, Quebec	August 13, 1914	November 30, 1918
Kingston, Ontario	August 18, 1914	November 3, 1917
Winnipeg, Manitoba	September 1, 1914	July 20, 1916
Halifax, Nova Scotia	September 8, 1914	October 3, 1918
Vernon, British Columbia	September 18, 1914	February 20, 1920
Nanaimo, British Columbia	September 20, 1914	September 17, 1915
Brandon, Manitoba	September 22, 1914	July 29, 1916
Lethbridge, Alberta	September 30, 1914	November 7, 1916
Petawawa, Ontario	December 10, 1914	May 8, 1916
Toronto, Ontario	December 14, 1914	October 2, 1916
Kapuskasing, Ontario	December 14, 1914	February 24, 1920
Niagara Falls, Ontario	December 15, 1915	August 31, 1918
Beauport, Quebec	December 28, 1914	June 22, 1916
Spirit Lake, Quebec	January 13, 1915	January 28, 1917
Sault Ste. Marie, Ontario	January 13, 1915	January 29, 1918
Amherst, Nova Scotia	April 17, 1915	September 27, 1919
Monashee-Mara Lake, British Columbia	June 2, 1915	July 29, 1917
Fernie-Morrissey, British Columbia	June 9, 1915	October 21, 1918
Banff-Castle Mountain and Cave & Basin, Alberta	July 14, 1915	July 15, 1917
Edgewood, British Columbia	August 19, 1915	September 23, 1916
Revelstoke-Field-Otter, British Columbia	September 6, 1915	October 23, 1916
Jasper, Alberta	February 8, 1916	August 31, 1916
Munson, Alberta-Eaton, Saskatchewan	October 13, 1918	March 21, 1919
Valcartier, Quebec	April 24, 1915	October 23, 1915

After the Japanese attack on the U.S. naval base at Pearl Harbor, Hawaii, and on the British-held Hong Kong (where Canadian troops were stationed) in December 1941, the Canadian government feared a Japanese invasion in its western provinces. Consequently, it declared much of the Pacific coastline a protected area and began forcible removal of the Japanese citizens from British Columbia. Special trains carried detainees into the Canadian interior, with able-bodied men sent to labor camps, while women, children, and seniors were placed in internment camps in various parts of Canada. Japanese homes, businesses, and fishing boats were confiscated and sold in order to cover their detention expenses. Those who resisted were dispatched to prisoner-of-war camps in Petawawa, Ontario, or to Camp 101 on the northern shore of Lake Superior. Although the Japanese internment ended after the war, Canada's prime minister William Lyon Mackenzie King (1935–1948) discouraged the Japanese Canadians from returning to their homes. As many as

Table 2   Major POW Camps in Canada during World War II, 1939–1945

Location	Province	Period
Chatham	Ontario	1944–1946
Fingal	Ontario	1945–1946
Gravenhurst	Ontario	1940–1946
Espanola	Ontario	1940–1943
Mimico	Ontario	1940–1944
Monteith	Ontario	1940–1946
Bowmanville	Ontario	1941–1945
Kingston	Ontario	1940–1943
Hull	Quebec	1941
Petawawa	Ontario	1942–1946
Farnham	Quebec	1940–1946
Newington (Sherbrooke)	Quebec	1942–1946
Feller College / Grande Ligne	Quebec	1943–1946
Sorel	Quebec	1945–1946
Fredericton (Ripples)	New Brunswick	1941–1945
Neys	Ontario	1943–1946
Angler	Ontario	1941–1946
Seebe	Alberta	1939–1946
Medicine Hat	Alberta	1943–1945
Ozada	Alberta	1942
Lethbridge	Alberta	1942–1946
Wainwright	Alberta	1945–1946
Red Rock	Ontario	1940–1941
Whitewater	Manitoba	1943–1945
Wainfleet	Ontario	1943–1945

4,000 Japanese Canadians chose to move to Japan, while the remaining chose to stay in the interior of the country; very few of them regained confiscated property and businesses. In 1988, Prime Minister Brian Mulroney issued a formal apology on behalf of the Canadian government for the wrongs it had done against Japanese Canadians during wartime.

In addition to internment camps, Canada also established over two dozen prisoner of war camps—the largest of them at Lethbridge and Medicine Hat—where some over 34,000 prisoners, mostly German, were interned and employed in various tasks. Conditions in Canadian camps tended to be better than average; prisoners enjoyed protections under the terms of the Geneva Convention, were adequately provisioned and housed, and had a variety of recreational activities. They were often sent to farms and factories to help alleviate the labor shortages. Some POWs tried to escape from the camps. In January 1941, Franz von Werra, a German pilot captured by the British in 1940, managed to escape from a train transporting him to a camp and, crossing the St. Lawrence River into the United States, he returned to Germany via Central and South America. Upon his return to Germany in April 1941, he received a hero's welcome and Adolf Hitler awarded him the Iron Cross (Germany's highest military award). Werra died later that year when his plane crashed into the North Sea off the Netherlands.

Alexander Mikaberidze

See also: Britain; Internment of Japanese Americans.

Further Reading

Carter, David. *Behind Canadian Barbed Wire: Alien, Refugee and Prisoner of War Camps in Canada, 1914–1946*. Elkwater, AB: Eagle Butte Press, 1998.

Farney, James, and Bohdan S. Kordan. "The Predicament of Belonging: The Status of Enemy Aliens in Canada, 1914." *Journal of Canadian Studies* 39.1 (2005): 74–89.

Hickman, Pamela, and Masako Fukawa. *Righting Canada's Wrongs: Japanese Canadian Internment in the Second World War*. Toronto: James Lorimer & Company, 2011.

Kordan, Bohdan, and Peter Melnycky. *In the Shadow of the Rockies: Diary of the Castle Mountain Internment Camp*. Edmonton, AB: CIUS Press, 1991.

Kordan, Bohdan. *Enemy Aliens: Prisoners of War: Internment in Canada during the Great War*. Kingston, ON: McGill-Queen's University Press, 2002.

Luciuk, Lubomyr. *In Fear of the Barbed Wire Fence: Canada's First National Internment Operations and the Ukrainian Canadians, 1914–1920*. Kingston, ON: Kashtan Press, 2001.

Cavell, Edith Louisa (1865–1915)

A British nurse celebrated for saving the lives of prisoners of war during World War I. Born and raised in England, Cavell moved to Belgium in 1890s and worked at the nursing school in Brussels. During World War I, as the German forces occupied Belgium, Cavell managed a medical facility and offered care of the wounded soldiers and civilians. She also sheltered and cared for Allied soldiers who had been cut off behind German lines or who had escaped from captivity; she assisted at least two hundred Allied prisoners of war in escaping to the neutral Netherlands.

Edith Louisa Cavell, ca. 1910. Cavell was executed by the Germans for assisting Allied soldiers in German-occupied Belgium during Word War I. (Library of Congress)

In August 1915, Cavell was betrayed to the German authorities and arrested for harboring the Allied soldiers. She was accused of treason, found guilty by a court-martial and shot by a German firing squad on October 12, 1915. Her execution received worldwide condemnation and extensive press coverage.

Alexander Mikaberidze

See also: Brändström, Elsa; World War I Prisoners of War.

Further Reading

Beck, James Montgomery. *The Case of Edith Cavell: A Study of the Rights of Noncombatants.* New York: G.P. Putnam's Sons, 1915

Ryder, Rowland. *Edith Cavell.* London: Hamish Hamilton, 1975.

Čelebići Camp

A notorious prison camp maintained by the Bosniak and Bosnian Croat forces during the Bosnian War (1992–1995). Established in the spring of 1992 at the village of Čelebići, Konjic municipality, the camp was used by the Bosnian Ministry of the Interior, Croatian Defence Council and, in later years, the Bosnian Territorial Defence Forces, to intern Bosnian Serb prisoners of war and civilians detained during military operations. Detainees were subjected to cruel and inhuman treatment, including torture, sexual assaults, and beatings; dozens of prisoners were summarily shot or beaten to death. After the war, the International Criminal Tribunal for the former Yugoslavia (ICTY) charged four individuals, including the camp commander Zdravko Mucić, for their roles in the crimes committed at the camp; in 1998, all but one of them were found guilty. The Čelebići trial is noteworthy for a landmark judgement made by the ICTY, which for the first time qualified rape as a form of torture.

Alexander Mikaberidze

See also: Bosnian War.

Further Reading

"The Čelebići Case" (IT-96-21), International Criminal Tribunal for the Former Yugoslavia, http://www.icty.org/case/mucic/4

Stover, Eric. *The Witnesses War Crimes and the Promise of Justice in The Hague.* Philadelphia: University of Pennsylvania Press, 2005.

Central Agency for Prisoners of War

For over a century, the Central Agency for Prisoners of War served as the clearing-house for information on POWs and civilians interned by all belligerent nations.

In October 1914, as the World War I was underway, the International Committee of the Red Cross (ICRC) established a special agency designed to collect and process information about prisoners of war so that respective governments and families could be informed and contact established. This institution has its roots in the International Agency for Aid to Sick and Wounded Military Personnel, also known as the Basle Agency, that performed a similar function during the Franco-Prussian War of 1870–1871; similarly, the Belgrade Agency of the ICRC collected and shared information on POWs during the Balkan Wars of 1912–1913. Building upon these experiences, the Central Agency for Prisoners of War played a crucial role in collecting and disseminating information on the captured soldiers from both Allies and the Central Powers; the agency coordinated transmission of correspondence between POWs and their families, receiving and processing thousands of letters and parcels each day. More crucially, the agency maintained lists of the prisoners held by all combatant sides; by 1923, when the agency concluded it work, its database held over 7 million index cards on individual prisoners.

During World War II the agency was revived and performed functions similar to those done during World War I; however, reflecting a different nature of the new conflict, the agency also dealt with Jewish refugees and a far greater number of internally displaced individuals and refugees. With a staff of almost 4,000 individuals, the agency processed a prodigious volume of material, including tens of millions of parcels and letters, and developed a database with some 36 million index cards. It formally completed its work in June 1947, but continued to perform some of its functions as the Central Tracing Agency of the ICRC, which still played an important role in gathering and sharing information on prisoners in conflicts around the world.

Alexander Mikaberidze

See also: World War I Prisoners of War.

Further Reading

Gradimir Djurovic, *The Central Tracing Agency of the International Committee of the Red Cross: Activities of the ICRC for the Alleviation of the Mental Suffering of War Victims.* Geneva: Henry Dunant Institute, 1986.

International Committee of the Red Cross. *Report of the International Committee of the Red Cross on its Activities during the Second World War, September 1, 1939–June 30, 1945. Vol. 2: "The Central Agency for Prisoner of War,"* Geneva, 1948.

"The International Prisoners-of-War Agency in WWI," International Committee of the Red Cross, https://www.icrc.org/eng/resources/documents/misc/57jqgr.htm

Changi

A prison complex, first built by the British and then administered by the Japanese, in the eastern part of Singapore. The prison was initially constructed in 1936 by the British administration of the Straits Settlements as a civilian prison, modeled after the infamous Sing Sing Prison in the U.S. state of New York. After the

Japanese occupation of Singapore in 1942, the prison was transformed into a major internment camp where the Japanese interned most of the European civilians (about 3,000 people in a complex designed for some 600 prisoners) while the neighboring Changi military barracks (part of a heavily fortified coastal defense that the British had built) were turned into a POW camp, where some 20,000 Allied soldiers (majority of them British and Australian) were ultimately kept in squalor, hunger, and abuse. In May 1944, the civilian internees were moved to a separate camp at Sime Road, while the POWs remained at Changi. In 1944, the British and Australian prisoners built a small chapel inside the camp, where Stanley Warren of the 15th Regiment, Royal Regiment of Artillery, painted a series of murals while Sgt. Harry Stodgen built a Christian cross out of a used artillery shell. In 1942, a revolt of British and Australian prisoners at the Selarang Barracks resulted in the executions of several prisoners, for which Japanese commander general Shimpei Fukuye was later tried and convicted of a war crime.

After the war, the Changi complex was used to hold Japanese (and a few German) prisoners, including the *kempeitai* (military police) and guards from concentration camps. The Allied-built chapel was dismantled and shipped to Australia, where it was reconstructed at the Royal Military College (Duntroon, Canberra), while the cross was sent to Britain. The Changi complex continued to serve as a prison for decades after the war. In 2000, much of it was demolished and its inmates were relocated to a new consolidated prison complex.

Alexander Mikaberidze

See also: Japan; Far East, British Military Trials.

Further Reading

Bose, Romen. *The End of the War. Singapore's Liberation and the Aftermath of the Second World War.* Singapore: Marshall Cavendish, 2010.

Cook, Haruko Taya, and Theodore Failor Cook. *Japan at War: An Oral History.* New York: New Press, 1992.

Havers, R.P.W. *Reassessing the Japanese Prisoner of War Experience: The Changi POW Camp, Singapore, 1942–1945.* London: Routledge, 2012.

Chełmno

Nazi death camp administered by the SS, established on December 8, 1941, near Chełmno (Kulmhof in German), 30 miles to the northwest of the Polish city of Łodz, along the Ner River, in modern-day west-central Poland. The camp was located in the Wartheland administrative district, which the Germans established after they began their occupation of Poland. Chełmno has the dubious distinction of being the first dedicated death camp built by the Germans, and was the first stationary camp that employed poison gas to kill its internees. Most of the victims at Chełmno were Polish Jews, although there were also Romanis interned there, as well as Polish political prisoners and Soviet prisoners of war. Many of Chełmno's Jewish victims—especially during the early stages of the camp's operations— came from the large ghetto in Łodz, which the SS and local police began to liquidate on January 16, 1942. Chełmno operated as a killing center from December 8, 1941, until March 1943, and again during June and July 1944.

The SS perfected the system of mass killing at Chełmno, which operated with factory-like precision. Most of the exterminations occurred at the *Schloss* (castle), where internees were sent a short distance from the main camp, usually by truck or rail. They were told that they were being transported to a forced labor camp. Once the prisoners entered the *Schloss*, they were stripped of their clothing and any personal possessions. They were then led into a cellar and through a short ramp, which emptied into a large truck-like van with no windows. Once the van had reached capacity (which was 50–70 people), the doors were closed and locked, and camp personnel attached a tube to the truck's exhaust pipe and directed it into the truck's interior. The engine was started, and usually within 10 minutes all of the internees had died from carbon monoxide poisoning. Any prisoners still found alive were shot dead.

The van full of corpses was then driven to an outlying series of mass graves, where the bodies were dumped and buried. Later, several crematoria were constructed adjacent to the mass graves, and most of victims' bodies were thereafter incinerated. In the latter stage of the camp's operations, Jews from Austria, Bohemia, Germany, Hungary, Luxemburg, and Moravia were also deported to Chełmno and killed.

It is estimated that at least 152,000 people were killed at Chełmno, including at least 5,000 Romanis from the surrounding areas in Poland. After July 1944, SS officials deported the remaining prisoners at Chełmno; most were sent to Auschwitz-Birkenau. In September 1944, fearing that the Allies would uncover their despicable deeds at the camp, German authorities ordered Chełmno's mass graves to be exhumed. The remains were then incinerated in crematoria. By the end of the year, the extermination vans were sent to Berlin. The camp was permanently decommissioned on January 17, 1945, as Soviet forces approached the area. Thirteen individuals were tried and convicted of war crimes in connection with Chełmno. Nine were tried at Łodz in 1945, right after World War II ended; the remaining four were tried between 1962 and 1965 in Germany.

Paul G. Pierpaoli, Jr.

See also: Auschwitz; Bełżec; Bergen-Belsen; Birkenau; Concentration Camps; Extermination Centers; Gas Chambers; Holocaust, The; I.G. Farben Case (1947); J.A. Topf & Söhne; Zyklon B Case (1946).

Further Reading

Hilberg, Raul. *The Destruction of the European Jews.* New York: Holmes and Meier, 1962.

Kogon, Eugen. *The Theory and Practice of Hell: The German Concentration Camps and the System behind Them.* New York: Farrar, Straus and Giroux, 2006.

Wachsmann, Nikolaus. *KL: A History of the Nazi Concentration Camps.* New York: Farrar, Straus and Giroux, 2015.

Chieti

An Italian prisoner-of-war camp on the Adriatic coast of Italy during World War II. Located near Pescara, the camp was set up to hold Allied officers captured in North Africa, with most prisoners being British and Commonwealth troops. Conditions in the Chieti camp, which held some 1,600 prisoners, were onerous, but not appalling as in many camps kept by the Axis powers; the prisoners did suffer the lack of adequate shelter, food, and clothing, but were allowed to set up music bands, stage theatrical plays, and hold film screenings. After Italy capitulated in September 1943, Germany took control of the camps and evacuated prisoners to German POW camps.

Alexander Mikaberidze

See also: World War II Prisoners of War.

Further Reading

Lett, Brian. *An Extraordinary Italian Imprisonment: The Brutal Truth of Campo 21, 1942–1943.* Barnsley, South Yorkshire: Pen & Sword Military, 2014.

Chile

During Augusto Pinochet's dictatorship in the 1970s and 1980s, the Chilean government relied on a wide network of detention centers and internment camps to prosecute and, in many cases, liquidate its political opponents; as many as 80 detention centers existed in the Chilean capital of Santiago alone. Pinochet's regime murdered thousands of political opponents and interned almost 100,000 Chilean civilians. The Estadio Nacional Julio Martínez Prádanos, the national stadium of Chile, was the most visible symbol of the regime's repression, as it was converted into an internment camp where thousands of people were imprisoned and abused. Major internment camps existed at Pisagua and Chacabuco (in the Atacama desert of northern Chile), while a secret detention center operated at Villa Grimaldi (in Santiago) where more than 5,000 Chileans were held and over 200 people were killed.

Alexander Mikaberidze

See also: Argentina.

Further Reading

Frazier, Lessie Jo. *Salt in the Sand: Memory, Violence, and the Nation-State in Chile, 1890 to the Present.* Durham, NC: Duke University Press, 2007.

China

Following the Communist Revolution in 1949, the Chinese government developed a vast system of prisons and camps where opponents of the regime detained for "reeducation" and "rehabilitation." In 1957, Chinese Communist leader Mao Zedong commenced the Anti-Rightist Movement targeting Chinese intellectuals who resisted the Communist policies; over 500,000 journalists, writers, and educators were labeled as "rightists," removed from their jobs, and sent to labor camps.

Mao's next project, The Great Leap Forward (1958–1962), sought to jumpstart China's industrialization and catch up to the Western powers by mobilizing resources of the entire nation. In order to acquire capital and free up the labor necessary for the Great Leap, Mao established thousands of agricultural communes, where millions of Chinese were forcibly sent to work. The Great Leap Forward had devastating impact on China. Agricultural and industrial productivity plummeted while government officials, fearful of retribution, concealed the truth and inflated the production numbers. The resulting famine is believed that have claimed some 20 million lives between 1959 and 1962.

Just as the nation was reeling from the Great Leap, the Chinese government launched the Cultural Revolution (1966–1969), during which the Communist authorities targeted the Four Olds: old ideas, old culture, old customs, and old habits. In the process, they detained, imprisoned, brutalized, and killed an estimated 100 million individuals whose devotion to the party and state had been questioned. Millions of Chinese citizens were sent to laogai, or labor camps, that were established to reeducate the detainees through penal labor. In the words of one prisoner, "Every morning we would all get up and line up, with the guards at the camp pointing guns at us. They would divide us up into groups and assign us to plots of land. Within that plot of land we would pick grapes, tea leaves, cotton, and other things. We couldn't go beyond our assigned space—there was an invisible line. Cross that line, and you're shot" (Funakoshi 2013).

In 1994, the Chinese government officially abolished the term laogai, only to rename it *jianyu*, or prison. The system still survives to the present day, and is utilized to suppress dissent and root out potential sources of opposition, whether political, economic, or religious in nature; at the same time, the system allows for exploitation of prisoners as a source of free labor. It is estimated to have between 1,000 and 1,500 facilities, and a prison population of over 1.5 million.

China's internment policy is particularly nefarious toward minorities in Xinjiang (a province in western China). Recent reports suggest that some 1,000,000 Uighurs—the largest ethnic group in Xinjiang—has been interned without any criminal charges and subjected to torturous conditions.

Alexander Mikaberidze

See also: Mao Zedong.

Further Reading

Bachman, David. *Bureaucracy, Economy, and Leadership in China: The Institutional Origins of the Great Leap Forward.* Cambridge: Cambridge University Press, 1991.

Becker, Jasper. *Hungry Ghosts: Mao's Secret Famine.* New York: The Free Press, 1996.

Funakoshi, Minami. "China's 'Re-Education through Labor' System: The View from Within," *The Atlantic*, February 6, 2013.

Muhlhahn, Klaus. *Criminal Justice in China: A History.* Cambridge, MA: Harvard University Press, 2009.

Robinson, Thomas, ed. *The Cultural Revolution in China.* Berkeley: University of California Press, 1971.

Seymour, James D., Richard Anderson, and Sidong Fan. *New Ghosts, Old Ghosts: Prisons and Labor Reform Camps in China.* New York: Routledge, 2015.

Williams, Philip F., and Yenna Wu. *The Great Wall of Confinement: The Chinese Prison Camp through Contemporary Fiction and Reportage.* Berkeley: University of California Press, 2004.

Wu, Hongda Harry. *Laogai—The Chinese Gulag.* Boulder, CO: Westview Press, 1992

Choeung Ek

The most well-known of the "killing fields" in Cambodia. During its state-sponsored terror campaign in the 1970s, the Khmer Rouge regime killed over 2 million people (out of population of about 8 million). Many victims perished at a vast system of prisons and killing sites that the Khmer Rouge established to persecute and exterminate their political opponents. One such site existed in the former orchard at Choeung Ek, 11 miles south of Phnom Penh, where 8,895 human bodies have been discovered in mass graves; the final number of victims would be much higher since much of the 2.4 hectare site has not been excavated. Many victims were former political prisoners who were imprisoned at the Tuol Sleng complex and trucked to Choeung Ek for executions.

Today, Choeung Ek serves as a memorial to the victims of the Cambodian genocide; a Buddhist *stupa* (shrine) has been built at the location, with its acrylic glass sides filled with more than 5,000 human skulls. The Choeung Ek Center for Genocide Crimes is also located here.

Alexander Mikaberidze

See also: Cambodian Killing Fields; Tuol Sleng Prison.

Further Reading

Dunlop, Nic. *The Lost Executioner: A Journey into the Heart of the Killing Fields.* New York: Walker and Company, 2005.

Kiernan, Ben. *The Pol Pot Regime: Race, Power and Genocide in Cambodia under the Khmer Rouge, 1975–1979.* New Haven, CT: Yale University Press, 2008.

Colditz

A Renaissance castle in the town of Colditz near Leipzig, Dresden, which served as the prisoner-of-war camp during World War II.

The town of Colditz traces its origins back to medieval period but the castle itself dates to the sixteenth century. In the nineteenth century, the castle served as a resort for the affluent Germans and was converted into a sanatorium for tuberculosis patients during the World War I (1914–1918). In the 1930s, the Nazi government of Germany converted the Colditz Castle into a prison for political opponents.

When World War II began in 1939, the castle, which is located on a rocky outcrop overlooking the Mulde River, was turned into a high security prison for captured Allied officers who were considered particularly dangerous or prone to escape. Oflag IV-C, as the castle was officially designated, received its first prisoners in late 1939, when over 100 Polish officers were briefly kept there. The first British prisoners arrived the following year, while some several hundred French and Dutch officers joined them in 1941; in August 1941, Dutch officer Machiel van den Heuvel led the first successful prisoner escape from the castle. In 1943, the German authorities moved all Dutch, Polish, Belgian, and French prisoners to other POW camps and used the Colditz Castle to hold the American and British officers. The first American prisoners—Colonel Florimund Duke and Captains Guy Nunn and Alfred Suarez, who were captured in Hungary—arrived at the castle in August 1944.

Colditz was a unique facility because it was controlled by the Wehrmacht and upheld provisions of the Geneva Convention; thus, prisoners who tried to escape were not summarily executed as it often happened at other camps, but were punished with solitary confinement. Overall, conditions at Colditz were better than in other German prisoner-of-war camps—the Allied prisoners frequently received food parcels from the Red Cross, could send and receive letters, partake in sports and entertainment, and even produce moonshine alcohol.

Despite its seemingly impregnable location, Oflag IV-C was the site of numerous escape attempts, with prisoners devising the ever more ingenuous ways to get away, including concealing themselves inside a tea chest and a mattress. Probably the most famous (and certainly most ambitious) attempt was dreamt up by British prisoners Jack Best and Bill Goldfinch, who built a fully functional glider in the attic of the castle chapel. The glider, with a wingspan of 32 feet, was built out of discarded pieces of wood and sleeping bags, but it never took into air because the war ended before it was ready for a flight. These escape attempts provided the inspiration for many novels, television shows, and feature films, including *The Colditz Story* (1955), *Escape of the Birdmen* (1971), and the *Colditz* mini-series (2005).

Because of such prominence in print, on film, and through television, Colditz played a major role in shaping perceptions of the prisoner-of-war experience in Nazi Germany, and contributed to the development of what some describe as the "Colditz myth"—popular perception of being a German POW as a boy's frolic, of high-spirited Allied officers outsmarting humorless German guards and completing daring escape attempts that took the heroes to Switzerland and freedom. The reality was far starker.

Alexander Mikaberidze

See also: Stalag; World War II Prisoners of War.

Further Reading

Chancellor, Henry. *Colditz: The Definitive History: The Untold Story of World War II's Great Escapes*. London: Hodder & Stoughton, 2001.

Eggers, Reinhold. *Colditz: The German Story*. Translated and edited by Howard Gee. Barnsley, UK: Pen & Sword Military, 2007.

Mackenzie, S.P. *The Colditz Myth: British and Commonwealth Prisoners of War in Nazi Germany*. Oxford: Oxford University Press, 2006.

McNally, Michael. *Colditz: Oflag IV-C*. Oxford: Osprey, 2010.

Concentration Camps

Concentration camps are most often associated with Nazi Germany, but the modern concentration camp is generally thought to have originated with Spanish general Valeriano Weyler y Nicolau in 1896 during the Cuban insurrection against Spain. Weyler sought to concentrate the civilian population near army installations, isolating these reconcentrados from the guerrillas. In Cuba at that time—and also in the Philippines during the 1899–1902 Philippine-American War and in South Africa under the British during the 1899–1902 Boer War—large numbers of civilians died in such camps as a consequence of overcrowding, disease, and inadequate supplies.

During the period of the Third Reich, Nazi Germany established a number of different types of concentration camps. These began as penal institutions employed for the incarceration of real and perceived opponents of the Nazi regime. Initially, the Nazis held these opponents in "protective custody quarters," of which the first was a camp established on March 20, 1933 at a compound about nine miles northwest of Munich, on the outskirts of the town of Dachau. Other camp establishments soon followed, among them Oranienburg, Papenburg, Esterwegen, Kemna, Lichtenburg, Borgermoor, and Columbia Haus, the SS "special" prison at Berlin.

For the most part, these were rapidly established, highly improvised affairs. Little regard was paid to administration, discipline, or utilization. Some were run by SS officers; many were staffed by SA men, often locals who knew or were known by those they were guarding. Nicknamed *"Wilde-KZ"* ("wild concentration camps"), they frequently operated without any apparent system or direction, and little in the way of planning or procedure. Often, their very location was impromptu. Dachau was a former gunpowder factory; Oranienburg was originally a brewery (and later, a foundry); and Borgermoor and Esterwegen were initially simply rows of barracks set down on open expanses of marshy heathland. Elsewhere, prisoners had to build their own habitations, and started their camp life living in tents.

It is important to emphasize that these camps were originally places of political imprisonment. They had political aims and selected their captives using political criteria, removing political opposition from the midst of the community, and in so doing intimidating the population so they would accept the Nazi regime.

In mid-1934 an Inspectorate of Concentration Camps was created to coordinate these diverse camps, with Theodor Eicke as the first Inspector. He selected Dachau as the model by which all concentration camps were to be run, resulting in many of the more haphazardly built camps being closed down.

Despite these closures, by the middle of the 1930s the range of those who could be sent to the concentration camps had been broadened considerably. By now the Nazis were arresting not only political prisoners, but also Jehovah's Witnesses, those who they termed antisocials, homosexuals, and common criminals, some of whom had the added "distinction" of also being Jewish.

Despite this growth, by early 1938 only three camps were operating: Dachau, Buchenwald, and Sachsenhausen. After the Anschluss (union) of Germany with Austria in March 1938, a camp for Austria, Mauthausen, was added, and a camp exclusively for women was established at Ravensbrück in 1939.

The onset of war in September 1939, however, saw the expansion of the concentration camp system to levels hitherto not contemplated. Originally, the Nazis intended their system to be a device that worked to suppress political dissents, but as the Third Reich expanded, the rationale was broadened to include religious prisoners of conscience (Roman Catholic priests, Protestant clergy, Jehovah's Witnesses), racial prisoners (Jews, Romanis, and Sinti), antisocial elements (vagrants, itinerant merchants, and "work-shy individuals"), prisoners based on sexual preference (male homosexuals), foreign opponents of the Nazis (resistance fighters, political opponents), and prisoners of war (in particular, prisoners from the Soviet Union). In almost all cases, the Nazis exploited the labor of their prisoners, often working them to death in conditions of utmost privation. In many of the camps, a separate compound for women was also built, to complement that at Ravensbrück.

More camps were an obvious necessity to accommodate these new prisoners. Accordingly, late in 1939, the Inspectorate of Concentration Camps was authorized to examine the possibility of setting up new camps that could begin operation as soon as possible. One of the first of these, located in southwestern Poland near the confluence of the Vistula and Sola Rivers, was to be built just outside the town of Oswiecim. In German the name was Auschwitz.

Auschwitz was not constructed on the Dachau model. The region in which it was located was a source of raw materials that could be exploited, and accordingly the camp eventually grew to become a vast complex covering 15 square miles. As a result, several sub-camps were also established in which prisoner slave-workers would be housed. Few of these sub-camps served any other purpose than that of industrial or agricultural production.

In March 1942, concentration camp administration was transferred to the SS Economic and Administrative Department (the SS-Wirschafts- und Verwaltung-shauptamt, or WVHA), which saw a transformation of the camps' original, political character to one of economic exploitation, as well as political torture.

This was paralleled by the development of camps outside the Old Reich. Many new centers were built in the Nazi-occupied countries, as it was not always practicable to transport the prisoners to Germany or Poland. A vast array of new types of camps also evolved, with forty-three different categories of camps existing at the height of the Nazis' power. The camp system lost its purely German content and became a continental phenomenon, spreading throughout Europe for the multiple tasks of exploitation of slave labor, extending the network of terror over occupied populations, and mass annihilation of those targeted for this purpose by the SS.

While not all fitted into the Dachau model, they nonetheless fell under the general jurisdiction of the Inspectorate of Concentration Camps, and were thus differentiated from ghettos or military prisoner-of-war camps. These included *Schutzhaftlager* (protective custody camps), *Aussiedlungslager* (resettlement camps), *Durchgangslager* (transit camps), *Straflager* (punishment camps), *Arbeitslager* (labor camps), *Judenarbeitslager* (Jewish labor camps), *Zivilgefangenenlager* (camps for civilian prisoners), *Sonderlager* (special camps), *Zwangsarbeitslager* (forced labor camps), *Arbeitserziehungslager* (labor education camps), *Judendurchgangslager* (Jewish transit camps), *Polizeihaftlager* (police detention camps), *Umerziehungslager* (reeducation camps), and *Isolationslager* (isolation camps). To all these, of course, could be added the colloquially termed *Vernichtungslager*, the extermination camps.

The range of the camps, in purpose, method, size, and duration, was thus extremely wide. Together, they blanketed Nazi-occupied Europe in a terror system as comprehensive as it was effective. The concentration camp, regardless of the form it took, came to symbolize the true essence of the Nazi regime.

Six of the Vernichtungslager located in Poland—Auschwitz-Birkenau, Bełżec, Chełmno, Majdanek, Sobibór, and Treblinka—altered the nature and course of concentration camp development. They were a departure from anything previously visualized, in both their design and character. Auschwitz has already been referred to. Bełżec, near Lvov, was established at the end of 1941, as was Chełmno. Majdanek, located at Lublin, had already been formed by the end of 1940, while Treblinka, near the village of Malkinia Gorna, was set up during the course of

1941. Sobibór, a camp built near Włodawa, was established in March 1942. With the sole exception of Auschwitz, these camps were different from all the others in that they did not perform any of the functions—political, industrial, agricultural, or penal—attributed to those further west or north.

Because of the existence of these Vernichtungslager, the image of the Nazi concentration camps was irrevocably transformed, such that all are now mainly viewed as elaborate and gigantic factories created for the purpose of destroying human lives en masse. Until the creation of the extermination camps, however, this was not always the case, with the system performing numerous other functions besides killing. The death camps, on the other hand, were institutions designed to methodically and efficiently murder millions of people, specifically Jews.

The nature of the eastern camps is well understood now, but the people of Europe at the time could not even imagine the truth. Prisoners elsewhere, particularly in the transit camps awaiting transportation to the east, certainly had no idea what awaited them in Poland. Once transported, they still had little notion of the true character of the eastern camps, often finding out only after the doors to the gas chambers had slammed shut behind them.

Overall, the concentration camp system underwent huge transformations over the twelve-year course of the Third Reich, until the camps were liberated by British, American, Canadian, and Soviet forces during 1944 and 1945. Literally millions had been incarcerated, with untold numbers murdered as a result of their existence.

By 1943, the concentration camps could be seen to function in the following ways: as the means of removing real or potential opposition from the mainstream of German politics; as penal institutions for German criminals; as unofficial prisoner-of-war camps, generally for Soviet soldiers; as huge reservoirs of slave labor; as centers of agriculture, mining, and industry; as collection and transit points for so-called racial prisoners; and as extermination installations. The singular political aims originally envisaged for the camps had become almost completely submerged within ten years.

Throughout the war, the camps remained detention centers for political prisoners, but their essentially political nature had almost disappeared by 1943. The character which replaced it—forced labor and economic exploitation—was reflected not only in the part Auschwitz played in the German war effort, but also in the important roles of camps such as Dora (for rocket and missile research), Ravensbrück (for the manufacture of armaments), and Westerbork (for the development of electronic instruments). Thousands of camps and sub-camps played their part in producing something of benefit to the German war effort, an activity which intensified with the deteriorating fortunes of the war from 1944 onward.

The concentration camps established in Germany and throughout Europe thus underwent massive changes of role and function during their twelve-year existence. From originally being a practical response to the challenges arising from the Nazi accession to power, they moved into other fields of operation and justification, while still containing the political nucleus that gave them birth—a nucleus that contained all the elements of a repressive and anti-human ideology which rejected the most fundamental ideals and freedoms fought for since Europe had emerged from the Dark Ages. From being "wild" institutions, the camps became massive cities housing tens of thousands of people, all of whom the Nazis identified as some sort of political criminal. Anybody who fell within the orbit of "enemy" did so because they had committed a "political" offence, even if that was only to have been born into an ethnic or religious group the Nazis had proscribed. The camps' very raison d'être changed, from being compounds for political prisoners to huge economic concerns comprised of giant industrial plants whose sole design was to exploit the abundant slave labor they possessed for the greater good of the German Reich. That itself changed with the establishment of a third strain of camps which served as extermination centers for those the Nazis deemed racially undesirable.

Paul R. Bartrop

See also: Auschwitz; Bełżec; Bergen-Belsen; Boer War (1899–1902); Chełmno; Dachau; Majdanek; Omarska; Sobibór; Spanish-American War; Treblinka.

Further Reading

Bartrop, Paul R. *Surviving the Camps: Unity in Adversity during the Holocaust.* Lanham, MD: University Press of American, 2000.

Kogon, Eugen. *The Theory and Practice of Hell: The German Concentration Camps and the System Behind Them.* New York: Berkley Windhover Books, 1975.

Wachsmann, Nikolaus. *KL: A History of the Nazi Concentration Camps.* New York: Farrar, Straus and Giroux, 2015.

Confederate States of America

During the Civil War, Confederate troops captured more than 211,000 Union prisoners of war. Fewer than 17,000 were paroled on the battlefield, leaving nearly 195,000 in captivity. More than 30,000 perished in Confederate prison facilities, for a mortality rate of more than 15.5 percent, compared to the Federal mortality rate for Confederate prisoners of 12 percent.

Confederate leaders believed that the rebellion would require only a few skirmishes to demonstrate the seriousness of secession, and thus they did not foresee the capture and custody of so many enemy troops. The need to create a government from scratch; recruit, train, and supply an army; and prepare to defend an enormous geographic region soon overwhelmed the fledgling Confederacy. It is thus unsurprising that the need to prepare for captives remained a low priority at the outset of the conflict.

Although the first battles created an influx of prisoners, they were easily housed in the vicinity of the capital at Richmond. The Confederate provost marshal of Richmond, Brigadier General John H. Winder, became the de facto commissary general of prisoners, although he was not formally appointed to the post until late 1864. Winder initially ordered tobacco warehouses converted to prison compounds in the belief that the Union troops would soon be exchanged. However, exchange negotiations took longer than expected, and Winder began ordering detainees sent into captivity in other locations throughout the Southern states. Even when the prisoner exchange system began to function in 1862, Union prisoners sent for exchange were all routed through Richmond, ensuring that the city's detention facilities would remain almost constantly at or above capacity.

In 1863, the exchange system effectively collapsed, largely due to accusations by each side that the other was attempting to cheat the system. Richmond's prison compounds, already too full, could not hold all of the incoming prisoners, and so Winder sought permission to construct new facilities well behind the front lines. He believed that the supply situation for prisons would be mitigated if prisoners lived near supplies of food. Construction of compounds commenced slowly, allowing Winder to relieve some of the pressure on the Richmond facilities.

Many of the new sites were poor locations, however, distant from rail lines and away from useful resources, including potable water. Many of the camps were opened before shelters could be constructed, thus prisoners were often placed into empty stockades with poor water supplies and no construction materials. Department commanders began forwarding thousands of prisoners to these makeshift facilities, packing the stockades with new detainees. Disease and malnutrition soon spread throughout the camps. The most notorious Confederate facility, Andersonville Prison (Camp Sumter), opened in February 1864 in west-central Georgia. Its compound, designed for up to 10,000 detainees, soon held more than 30,000. More than 100 prisoners died daily in the torrid summer months, resulting in nearly 13,000 dead at the camp in less than 11 months of operation.

After the war, contemporary politicians and later historians alleged that Confederate authorities had deliberately mistreated their captives. The commandant of Andersonville, Major Heinrich (Henry) Wirz, was tried, convicted, and executed for the deaths of prisoners in his charge in what is regarded as the first modern war crimes trial. In reality, the Confederate system, as awful as it was, reflected the general inability of the political and military leaders to create a supply system capable of maintaining their own forces, much less Union captives. The unfortunate Union prisoners were more victims of circumstance than a planned policy of torment.

Paul J. Springer

See also: Andersonville Prison; U.S. POW Camps, 1861–1865.

Further Reading

Hesseltine, William B. *Civil War Prisons: A Study in War Psychology.* New York: F. Ungar, 1964.

Sanders, Charles W. *While in the Hands of the Enemy: Military Prisons of the Civil War.* Baton Rouge: Louisiana State University Press, 2005.

Speer, Lonnie R. *Portals to Hell: Military Prisons of the Civil War.* Mechanicsburg, PA: Stackpole Books, 1997.

Convention against Torture and Other Cruel, Inhuman or Degrading Treatment or Punishment (1984)

The Convention against Torture and Other Cruel, Inhuman or Degrading Treatment or Punishment is one in a series of United Nations (UN) agreements with the purpose of protecting human rights around the world, and specifically seeks to prevent torture around the world. The Convention against Torture, which was adopted and opened for signature by the UN General Assembly on December 10, 1984, requires member nations to take serious legislative, administrative, and judicial measures in preventing torture within their nations' borders and in territories under their jurisdiction. In addition, it also forbids participating governments from returning individuals to their home nations if it is believed that the home nation practices any form of torture method. The convention consists of 33 articles. Articles 17 through 33 establish the Committee against Torture (CAT), a body of ten individuals who serve to enforce the regulations set forth by the convention.

Article one defines torture as any act by which severe pain or suffering, whether physical or mental, is intentionally inflicted on a person for such purposes as obtaining information from him or another person for a confession; punishing him for an act he or another person committed or is suspected of having committed; intimidating or coercing him or another person; or for any reason based on discrimination of any kind when such pain or suffering is inflicted by or at the instigation of or with the consent or at the command of a public official or other person acting in an official capacity. The convention does not include in its definition of torture pain or suffering arising only from or incidental to lawful sanctions.

Article two specifically addresses how member nations must take legislative, administrative, and judicial measures to prevent acts of torture in its boundaries and in its territories. In addition, it states that there are no exceptions where torture will be allowed, including time of war, threat of war, political instability, or any other public emergency. The text of the convention also states that never may an order from a superior officer or a public authority be a justification of torture. If a nation has signed the treaty without any reservations, then there are no exceptions where it can use torture without breaking its treaty obligations.

Article three details how no member government may expel or extradite a person to a state where there are substantial grounds for believing that the person would be subjected to torture. In order to determine whether or not there are torture methods practiced, or chances of torture in the person's native state, the member nation's government must appoint competent authorities who are to take into account all relevant information and take into consideration, if applicable, the existence of a consistent pattern of human rights violations.

The other articles detail how member governments should judicially and administratively enforce the regulations set forth by the convention, including making all acts of torture criminal offenses under the signatory nation's criminal law, outlining the procedure that should be followed if a person is suspected of having committed torture, and establishing a way for torture victims to be fairly and adequately compensated. In addition, the convention's text explains that each member nation must ensure that information regarding the prohibition of torture be included in the formal training of all law enforcement personnel, military personnel, medical personnel, public officials, and others who may be involved in the custody, interrogation, or treatment of any person subjected to any form of arrest, detention, or imprisonment. To prevent torture, article eleven states that each government must systematically review interrogation rules, instructions, methods, and practices, in addition to arrangements for the custody and treatment of persons subjected to any form of arrest, detention, or imprisonment in any territory under its jurisdiction.

The Optional Protocol to the Convention against Torture and other Cruel, Inhuman or Degrading Treatment or Punishment (OPCAT), which was created and opened for signatures on January 9, 2003 by the UN General Assembly, is an addition to the UN Convention against Torture. It establishes a system that provides for regular visits by independent international and national appointees to places where people are deprived of their liberty, and also establishes an international inspection system for places of detention. The Optional Protocol was created because the UN Committee against Torture was limited in its power because it was only able to analyze and discuss the self-written reports of the respective governments. The committee lacked the power to visit countries or inspect detention facilities without the respective country's permission. The Optional Protocol was ratified on June 22, 2006.

Following ratification by the 20th member government, the Convention against Torture and Other Cruel, Inhuman or Degrading Treatment or Punishment came into force on June 26, 1987. June 26th is now recognized as the International Day in Support of Torture Victims.

Charlene T. Overturf

See also: Geneva Convention Relating to Prisoners of War (1929).

Further Reading

Convention against Torture and Other Cruel, Inhuman or Degrading Treatment or Punishment, http://untreaty.un.org/cod/avl/ha/catcidtp/catcidtp.html

Burgers, Herman, and Hans Danelius. *UN Convention against Torture: A Handbook on the Convention against Torture and Other Cruel, Inhuman, or Degrading Treatment or Punishment.* Frederick, MD: Aspen Publishers Inc., 1988.

Levinson, Sanford. *Torture: A Collection.* New York: Oxford University Press, 2004.

Cowra Incident

A mass escape by Japanese prisoners of war from an Australian camp. During World War II, Australia set up several internment facilities for the capture Japanese soldiers. Over 2,000 Japanese POWs were a camp near Cowra in New South Wales, which also held several thousand Italian and German POWs. The camp was divided into four separate compounds, with each containing about 20 barracks and enclosed by barbed wire fences. Japanese noncommissioned officers and other ranks were interned in B Compound (the northeast quarter) while officers were in D Compound (the southeast quarter). The Japanese POWs were treated well and in accordance with the 1929 Geneva Convention, but relations between the guards and prisoners remained tense, partly due to significant cultural differences.

On Friday, August 4, Australian camp authorities, acting in accordance with international law, issued a notice that all non-officer Japanese prisoners would be relocated to the Hay Prisoner of War Camp on August 7. Yet during the night of August 5, over 1,000 Japanese POWs attempted to escape the Cowra Camp, in what became the largest prison escape of World War II. Armed with an assortment of improvised weapons and wearing a few sets of clothing, the prisoners stormed the barbed wire fence and broke out of the compound. The ensuing clashes with

Australian forces claimed the lives of 4 Australian soldiers and 231 Japanese prisoners; although over 350 POWs escaped, most of them were recaptured within next 10 days, while others committed suicide to avoid recapture.

Alexander Mikaberidze

See also: Australia; Featherston Camp (New Zealand).

Further Reading

Asada, Teruhiko. *Night of a Thousand Suicides: The Japanese Outbreak at Cowra*, Translated and edited by Ray Cowan. Sydney: Angus and Robertson, 1970.

Carr-Gregg, Charlotte. *Japanese Prisoners of War in Revolt: The Outbreaks at Featherston and Cowra during World War II*. New York: St. Martin's Press, 1978.

Cuba. See Spanish-American War

D

Dachau

In Dachau, a pleasant suburb outside Munich, Germany, the first Nazi concentration camp was built in 1933, just two months after Adolf Hitler and the Nazis took power. Dachau was used as a training camp for SS camp personnel, instilling in them the attitude that prisoners were *Untermenschen*, or subhumans, and creating a climate of fear through intimidation and violence.

During its 12 years of existence, Dachau was a camp for political prisoners, and its population was largely made up of dissidents and members of groups considered inferior. The former included Socialists, Christian leaders, and some Jehovah's Witnesses; the latter was largely made up of Romanis, Jews, homosexuals, criminals, and Polish intellectuals. Dachau was an important camp for religious dissidents. More than 3,000 clergy, mostly Catholic, were imprisoned there, including bishops and one cardinal. The Vatican has since beatified six of these priests as martyrs, while the Orthodox Church recognizes a Serbian bishop as a saint.

Dachau was not an extermination camp, so German Jewish prisoners were often shipped to the death camps in Poland. However, Hungarian and other Jews were brought to Dachau in 1944 to work as slave laborers in munitions factories. By the time of the liberation in April 1945, about 30 percent of the camp population was Jewish. The "politicals" were made up of prominent leaders from every country invaded by the Nazis. In all camps, the prisoners formed an internal government, but at Dachau the prisoners' experience in leadership made it possible to control the criminal element that preyed upon the weak in many other camps.

Among the 206,206 prisoners registered at Dachau during its existence, 31,591 deaths were recorded, though the number is certainly higher. This figure does not include the mass executions of Soviet and French prisoners of war, who were dispatched by firing squads shortly after arrival. It also does not include invalids shipped away and executed elsewhere. Most of the Dachau prisoners were used as slave labor, with upwards of 37,000 working in armament factories in 36 subsidiary camps. Both work and living conditions were harsh, with insufficient food, regular beatings, and unsanitary crowding. Each barracks housed some 1,500 people in unheated wooden buildings built for 200. By the end in 1945, typhus was rampant in the camp, and the Red Cross tried to keep the prisoners from being freed before the American army arrived, for fear of spreading the disease through the countryside.

Many prisoners suffered from medical experiments performed on the living. Some were kept in freezing water to see how long they could survive and still be revived. More than a thousand were infected with malaria, including numbers of

Survivors of the Dachau concentration camp cheer the arrival of their American liberators on April 30, 1945. More than 32,000 prisoners were liberated, many of whom were British, Canadian, and American. (Bettmann/Getty Images)

Polish priests, and some with tuberculosis. Experiments with pressurization left victims permanently deaf and disfigured.

The camp, with more than 30,000 prisoners (almost 10,000 had been marched off three days earlier), was liberated by the American Seventh Army. Some American soldiers were so traumatized by what they saw that a number of Nazi guards were shot even after they had surrendered. The troops were never prosecuted. The shocked and infuriated American commanding officer ordered the citizens of Dachau to march through the camp to see its devastation so that they could never deny the evil that had existed among them. Forty camp staff members were tried for war crimes, and 36 were sentenced to death.

Dachau is probably the most visited of the Nazi concentration camps. One barracks has been reconstructed to show the living conditions, and an introductory film and display convey the horror of the place. The gas chamber (never used), the gallows, and the crematorium have been maintained. Where the ashes of the dead were thrown is now a park marked with a Star of David and a cross. Three memorials—a Protestant chapel, the Catholic Christ in Agony church, and a Jewish memorial—honor the dead. In the field used for roll call each day is a sculptured memorial to the dead. Behind the camp is a Carmelite convent of nuns who offer prayers for reparation.

A Russian Orthodox chapel commemorates the celebration of the Orthodox Easter that took place a week after the camp fell to the Americans. Using makeshift vestments pinned together from Nazi towels, the Russian, Greek, and Serb prisoners chanted the entire liturgy from memory, including the traditional commentary of Saint John Chrysostom, recited by a monk from Mount Athos. The main feature of the chapel is an icon of Christ leading the prisoners out of the camp gates.

Norbert C. Brockman

See also: Auschwitz; Bełżec; Bergen-Belsen; Birkenau; Chełmno; Concentration Camps; Extermination Centers; Gas Chambers; Holocaust, The; I.G. Farben Case (1947); J.A. Topf & Söhne; Zyklon B Case (1946).

Further Reading

Bauer, Yehuda. *A History of the Holocaust.* New York: Franklin Watts, 2001.

Berben, Paul. *Dachau, 1933–1945: The Official History.* San Francisco: Norfolk Press, 1975.

Marcuse, Harold. *Legacies of Dachau.* Cambridge: Cambridge University Press, 2008.

Ryback, Timothy W. *The Last Survivor: In Search of Martin Zaidenstadt.* New York: Pantheon, 1999.

Dartmoor Massacre (1815)

British massacre of American prisoners of war at Dartmoor Prison, located in Princetown, near Devonshire, England on April 6, 1815.

Shortly after the start of the War of 1812 between Britain and the United States, hundreds of American prisoners arrived in England. They were initially interned in the hulks off Plymouth but, as their numbers increased, the decision was made to move them to the Dartmoor Depot and house them in Number 4 War Prison. Dartmoor Prison was dark, damp, and rife with disease. The discipline meted out by the guards was harsh, and most of the prisoners received only enough food to avoid starvation. The prison became increasingly crowded as prisoner exchange cartels broke down, and by the end of the war, Dartmoor had received 5,542 American POWs. Of that number, 252 died while in captivity.

Representatives of the United States and Great Britain signed the Treaty of Ghent on December 24, 1814, formally ending the war. The treaty was formally ratified and went into effect on February 18, 1814. It included a provision for the immediate repatriation of all prisoners, but their release was delayed by a diplomatic argument over which nation should bear the costs for their sustenance. According to the Prisoner of War Exchange Cartel of May 12, 1813, each nation bore the responsibility of paying the costs of its own citizens held by the enemy. The British argued that because they had issued hammocks, blankets, horse rugs, jackets, pants, vests, caps, and shoes to each prisoner, the prisoners should be held back from repatriation until the debt was paid. American commissioners presented similar bills to the British, and the financial negotiations stretched on for months.

American POWs in Dartmoor Prison knew that the war had ended, and were aware of the repatriation clause of the treaty. They also reported that the amount of food issued in the prison decreased after the cessation of hostilities. Rumors of repatriation swept through the prison population, fueling the prisoners' anger about their continued confinement. After repeated written protests failed to move British authorities, the prisoners decided to stage a protest within the prison.

The protest took place on April 6, 1815. Seeing thousands of furious, shouting prisoners, the poorly trained guards panicked and opened fire. The protest erupted into chaos as the prisoners attempted to escape the bullets. Seven were killed and 31 others were wounded by musket fire. The prisoners continued to be held in confinement until the end of the month, when the survivors were allowed to board ships and return to the United States. When word of the killings reached the United States, it provoked a major outpouring of rage. Eventually, the British government agreed to pay restitution to the families of the dead and wounded prisoners, but the incident remained as a legacy of the poor treatment afforded American prisoners held by the British during the conflict.

Paul J. Springer

See also: American Revolutionary War; Cabrera; French Revolutionary and Napoleonic Era; Norman Cross.

Further Reading

Allen, Phineas. *Dartmoor Massacre*. Pittsfield, MA: Phineas Allen, 1815.

Andrews, Charles McLean. *The Prisoner's Memoirs, or, Dartmoor Prison*. New York: Charles Andrews, 1815.

Hickey, Donald. *The War of 1812: A Forgotten Conflict*. Urbana: University of Illinois Press, 1989.

Davao Prison and Penal Farm

Established in 1932, Davao was initially a large prison facility near Panabo City, Davao del Norte, Philippines; it is sometimes referred to as DAPECOL, Davao Penal Colony. After the conquest of the Philippines during World War II, the Japanese turned it into a prison and penal camp where some two thousand American prisoners were held.

In the spring of 1943, William Edwin Dyess and nine other Americans POWs (and two Filipinos convicts), who had been captured during the Japanese conquest of the Philippines and survived the brutal Bataan Death March, managed to escape from Davao. This was the only large-scale escape of Allied POWs from the Japanese in the Pacific Theater during World War II. Dyess and his group spent several weeks evading Japanese forces, and then served with a local guerrilla group. In retaliation for their escape, the Japanese beheaded 25 prisoners of war.

The camp was closed June 6, 1944, as the American forces proceeded with the liberation of the Philippines. The Japanese evacuated the POWs first to Cebu and to Manila, but the ship carrying the POWs was sunk by an American submarine, whose crew was unaware that American POWs were onboard; only 83 prisoners survived and reached the shore and were rescued by guerrillas.

Alexander Mikaberidze

See also: Bataan Death March (1942); Japan; World War II Prisoners of War.

Further Reading

Gladwin, Lee A. "American POWs on Japanese Ships Take a Voyage into Hell," *The Prologue Magazine* (The U.S. National Archives), 35/4(Winter 2003), https://www.archives.gov/publications/prologue/2003/winter/hell-ships-1.html

Lawton, Manny. *Some Survived: An Eyewitness Account of the Bataan Death March and the Men Who Lived Through It*. Chapel Hill, NC: Algonquin Books, 1984.

Lukacs, John D. *Escape from Davao: The Forgotten Story of the Most Daring Prison Escape of the Pacific War.* New York: NAL Caliber, 2010.

Nordin, Carl. S. *We Were Next to Nothing: An American POW's Account of Japanese Prison Camps and Deliverance in World War II.* London: McFarland, 1997.

Death Camps

Death camps, sometimes referred to as extermination camps, were killing factories established by the Germans in order to carry out the so-called Final Solution, or the eradication of European Jews. Although Jews were the principal victims of the death camps, the Nazis also used the facilities to engage in the mass murder of Romanis, Soviet prisoners of war, and other groups deemed to be "subversive" or "undesirable." Historically, Holocaust scholars usually categorize six Nazi-run camps located in Poland as strictly death camps. They included: Chełmno (the first of the dedicated death camps, which began operations on December 8, 1941); Auschwitz-Birkenau; Bełżec; Majdanek; Sobibór; and Treblinka. Hundreds of thousands of other Jews and those targeted for persecution died in various concentration and forced labor camps throughout Europe, but the main mission of those camps was not mass extermination as such. In the death camps, immediate extermination was the only reason for their existence.

By 1943, the death camps were engaged in a system of mass killing that resembled a finely tuned and managed factory. Some have termed the system an "assembly line of death." At places like Auschwitz, where the killing was on a truly frightening scale, as many as 1,000 people at a time could be killed in a single gas chamber using Zyklon B gas, which led to a slow and agonizing death. Once the victims had been killed, Sonderkommandos, prisoners who worked for the camp administration, removed gold teeth or fillings from the corpses and took them to mass graves or crematoria for disposal. Most of the victims' bodies were incinerated. At Auschwitz, the crematoria worked virtually 24 hours a day.

In the latter stages of World War II, the death camps were either decommissioned or relocated as Soviet troops advanced from east to west. In some cases, German officials ordered bodies in mass graves exhumed and incinerated so that Allied troops would not find them. They also attempted to disguise or cover up the activities that occurred at some of the camps. In the winter and spring of 1945, as Germany was close to collapse and Allied troops converged on Germany and Poland from both the east and west, the liberators found unmistakable evidence of the atrocities that had been perpetrated there. Among some of the most haunting photos of World War II were the pictures of victims' corpses stacked like cordwood outside gas chambers and crematoria.

Paul G. Pierpaoli, Jr.

See also: Concentration Camps; Extermination Centers.

Further Reading

Hilberg, Raul. *The Destruction of the European Jews.* New York: Holmes & Meier, 1962.

Kogon, Eugen. *The Theory and Practice of Hell: The German Concentration Camps and the System behind Them.* New York: Farrar, Straus and Giroux, 2006.

Defence Regulation 18B

One of the British Defence Regulations that suspended the right of affected individuals to habeas corpus and sanctioned the detention of people perceived to be threats to national security.

On the eve of World War II, the British government enacted a number of laws and regulations to fight subversion and sabotage by "any person [believed] to be of hostile origin or associations or to have been recently concerned in acts prejudicial to the public safety or the defence of the realm." On August 24, 1939, the British Parliament approved the Emergency Powers (Defence) Act that granted the British government emergency powers to prosecute the war effectively, including creating Defence Regulations that came to control almost every aspect of everyday life in Britain.

In 1940, after the German victories over Denmark and Norway where local Nazi sympathizers supported the German invasion, the British government became concerned about the far right groups potentially attempting to topple it and felt compelled to amend the 1939 act, significantly extending the its powers under the Defence Regulations to require persons "to place themselves, their services, and their property at the disposal of His Majesty." Furthermore, the new regulations enabled the creation of special courts to administer criminal justice in war zones and to prosecute offenders for violating the Defence Regulations. Thus, an Order-in-Council amended the Defence Regulation 18B on May 22, 1940, and granted the British government the power to detain any person who posed a threat to national security by being a leader or a member of any organization that was presumed to be under foreign influence or control.

During World War II, the British government used the Defence Regulation to intern over 1,800 people, including hundreds of members of the British Union of Fascists (including its leader, Sir Oswald Ernald Mosley). The Detainees were initially kept at HM Prison Wandsworth for men and HM Prison Holloway for women, but the men were later moved to HM Prison Brixton. As the number of detainees increased, the British authorities established internment camps, initially at Ascot Racecourse and Huyton, but later on the Isle of Man. The number of the 18B internees declined once the fears of the German invasion subsided after the Battle of Britain and, by 1944, most detainees were in fact released. The Defence Regulation ceased to have effect with the end of the war in May 1945.

Alexander Mikaberidze

See also: Britain; Canada; Australia.

Further Reading

Goldman, A. L. "Defence Regulation 18B: Emergency Internment of Aliens and Political Dissenters in Great Britain during World War II," *Journal of British Studies* 12 (1973): 120–136.

Simpson, A. W. Brian. *In the Highest Degree Odious: Detention without Trial in Wartime Britain.* Oxford: Clarendon Press, 1992.

Deir ez Zor

A city in the Ottoman Empire (nowadays in Syria) that served as one of the main terminus points of Armenians who were forcibly deported from across the Ottoman

Empire. Located about 280 miles northeast of Damascus along the Euphrates River, Deir ez Zor lies amid the hot, dusty, and arid desert. When the Young Turks commenced the Armenian massacres in 1915, the surviving Armenians were detained and forced to march into the wilderness of southeastern Anatolia, with thousands dying en route due to abuse, rape, starvation, exposure, and sickness. By late 1916, Deir ez Zor had emerged as focal point for refugees, with tens of thousands of Armenians residing in various camps outside the town; as many as 200,000 Armenians perished of starvation, illness, and abuse in the Deir ez Zor area.

In 1989–1991, the Armenian Apostolic Church in Syria built a monument and church in Deir ez Zor as a memorial to the victims of the Armenian genocide in eastern Syria; the complex was largely destroyed in 2014 when Islamic fundamentalists seized the area.

Alexander Mikaberidze

See also: Armenian Genocide.

Further Reading

Balakian, Grigoris. *Armenian Golgotha: A Memoir of the Armenian Genocide, 1915–1918.* New York: Alfred A. Knopf, 2009.

Kevorkian, Raymond. *The Armenian Genocide: A Complete History.* London: I.B. Tauris, 2011.

Miller, Donald Earl, and Lorna Touryan Miller. *Survivors: An Oral History of the Armenian Genocide.* Berkeley: University of California Press, 1999.

Denmark

During World War II, the Danish government established an internment camp to detain political radicals (i.e. Communists) and to avoid deportation of Danish citizens to German concentration camps. The Horserød internment camp (Danish: Horserødlejren) was located near Helsingør in North Zealand, in a former prison installation that was expanded in 1940–1941 to accommodate increase number of inmates, many of whom were detainees under the Anti-Communist Act that the Danish government adopted in August 1941. In 1943, when Germany invaded Denmark, the camp fell into the German hands and the inmates were deported to the German concentration camp at Stutthof. In 1943–1944, the German authorities used Horserød as a concentration camp for the Danish Jews and members of Danish resistance; hundreds of inmates were brought here before transportation to the German concentration camps at Ravensbrück and Sachsenhausen. After the end of World War II, Horserød briefly served as an internment camp for Danes accused of Nazi collaboration, and was reorganized into a prison facility in 1947.

The German occupation of Denmark also witnessed the establishment of the second internment camp. When the German military authorities began deporting Danish citizens to concentration camps in Germany, the Danish government protested and suggested building an internment camp on the Danish territory. In March 1944, the Germans accepted the deal and the "Police Prison Camp Fröslee" (German: Polizeigefangenenlager Fröslee; Danish: Frøslevlejren) was established in the community of the same name just across the border in Danish territory. The camp was intended for political prisoners and Danish resistance fighters, and not for the detention or deportation of Jews.

In mid-August 1944, the camp received the first group of prisoners and, by March 1945, its population increased to over 3,000 inmates. With the end of the war, the camp saw an influx of the Danish collaborators and Nordic prisoners of war from Germany. By 1949, most inmates had served their sentences and the camp was converted to army barracks under the name of Padborg Camp (Padborglejren). In 1969, the Frøslev Prison Camp Museum (Frøslevlejrens Museum) was opened and, in 2001, a national memorial park was established on the former campgrounds.

Alexander Mikaberidze

See also: Concentration Camps; Finland; Holocaust, The; Sweden; World War II Prisoners of War.

Further Reading

The Frøslevlejren, https://natmus.dk/museer-og-slotte/froeslevlejrens-museum/

Jensen, Steven, and Mette Bastholm Jensen. *Denmark and the Holocaust.* Copenhagen: Danish Center for Holocaust and Genocide Studies, 2003

Dmitrovlag/Dmitlag

The Dmitrov Corrective Labor Camp was one of the largest internment camps maintained by the Joint State Political Directorate, the Soviet secret police, in the 1930s. Established in September 1932, the camp was located near the town of Dmitrov, north of Moscow, and was formally part of the Gulag system. The camp was established to provide forced labor for the massive infrastructure projects needed to supply Moscow with drinking water, and to improve navigation on the Moscow and Volga rivers. During the camp's six-year existence, almost 200,000 prisoners were employed in digging canals and building infrastructure to supply the Soviet capital with clean water. By 1936, the prisoners dug six massive water reservoirs and constructed a waterway that was 80 miles long and featured over 200 structures, including 11 locks and 14 dams. The Moscow Canal, which formally opened in July 1937, reduced the travel distance between Moscow and St. Petersburg by over 600 miles. Yet this achievement came at a terrible price—mistreatment, malnutrition, and hard work claimed at least 22,000 lives, but it is widely thought that the death toll was significantly higher.

The Soviet authorities used Dmitrovlag for propaganda purposes. Celebrating the construction of the Moscow Canal, they declared that "at the initiative of the great Stalin, the city of Moscow, which was formerly far removed from 'big water' [i.e. ocean], has thus been transformed into a port of three seas: the White Sea, the Baltic, and the Caspian Sea" (Ruder: 178) The Dmitrovlag was often portrayed as an 'ideal' camp where a special Cultural-Educational Division was set up and a theater and an orchestra, staffed with prisoners, were maintained; imprisoned artists were employed in producing propaganda posters and banners while writers helped publish several newspapers that carried articles with instructive headlines such as "Learn to Relax" and "Drown Your Past on the Bottom of the Canal." The camp was officially dissolved on January 31, 1938.

Alexander Mikaberidze

See also: Belomorkanal; Gulag; Sevvostlag; Vorkuta Camps.

Further Reading

Ruder, Cynthia. "Water and Power; The Moscow Canal and 'The port of Five Seas,' " in Jane Costlow and Arja Rosenholm, ed. *Meanings and Values of Water in Russian Culture* (London: Routledge, 2017), 175–188.
Schlögel, Karl. *Moscow, 1937.* Cambridge: Polity Press, 2012.

Dora-Mittelbau

Nazi forced labor and concentration camp situated in central Germany, north of the town of Nordhausen. Known also as Dora-Nordhausen or Nordhausen, the facility was also close to the Harz Mountains. It began as a sub-camp of the Buchenwald concentration camp and became an autonomous facility in October 1944. The year before, prisoners from Buchenwald were forced to start construction on a sprawling industrial complex and prison, which eventually became Dora-Mittelbau. Prisoners at Dora-Mittelbau were forced to work in the factories and quarries nearby. Most of the prisoners were Jews, but there were also some Romanis, criminals, and "asocials" (mainly homosexuals). Eventually, Dora-Mittelbau would have more than 30 sub-camps and a permanent prisoner population of 12,000–13,000.

Most prisoners worked and lived underground, where they slaved on weapons development projects and labored in various war-related industries. The Germans had placed much of this activity underground after Allied air raids had destroyed above-ground facilities. The conditions in which the prisoners lived and worked were appalling; they saw no daylight and breathed no fresh air for weeks at a time, which increased sickness and disease. Indeed, the death rate at Dora-Mittelbau was higher than at most other concentration camps because of these circumstances. Food was scarce and bad, and medical care was virtually nonexistent. When prisoners became too ill or exhausted from work, they were shipped out to Mauthausen or Birkenau, where most were killed. Discipline, which was harsh and arbitrary, was meted out under the supervision of the SS, which ran the camp.

As more war production was relocated to the area, prisoners built a vast array of sub-camps, linked by tunnels, and were often built into the sides of mountains. The more important sub-camps included Nordhausen, Niedersachswerfen, and Neusollstedt. In addition to working in munitions plants, prisoners also labored at a nearby ammonia works and stone quarry. Dora-Mittelbau had an active underground resistance movement, through which some prisoners purposely sabotaged items or slowed production. Individuals suspected of such activities were summarily killed. It is estimated that at least 200 detainees were put to death because of their resistance activity.

As Allied forces pressed into Germany from the east and west in the spring of 1945, the Germans sought to liquidate Dora-Mittelbau. Many detainees were sent to Bergen-Belsen, but many died on the forced march to northern Germany.

When U.S. troops liberated the camp in April 1945, only a few critically ill prisoners remained there. In all, as many as 60,000 prisoners worked at or transited through Dora-Mittelbau. About 9,000 alone died from overwork; several thousand more died from starvation and disease.

Paul G. Pierpaoli, Jr.

See also: Auschwitz; Bełżec; Bergen-Belsen; Birkenau; Chełmno; Concentration Camps; Extermination Centers; Gas Chambers; Holocaust, The; I.G. Farben Case (1947); J.A. Topf & Söhne; Zyklon B Case (1946).

Further Reading

Arich-Gerz, Bruno. *Mittelbau-Dora: American and German Representations of a Nazi Concentration Camp. Literature, Visual Media and the Culture of Memory from 1945 to the Present*. New Brunswick, NJ: Transaction Publishers. 2009.

Kogon, Eugen. *The Theory and Practice of Hell: The German Concentration Camps and the System behind Them*. New York: Farrar, Straus and Giroux, 2006.

Schaft, Gretchen, and Gerhard Zeidler. *Commemorating Hell: The Public Memory of Mittelbau-Dora*. Urbana: University of Illinois Press, 2011.

Drancy

The Drancy internment and transit camp, located just outside of Paris, was used as an assembly center for arrested Jews who were later deported to extermination camps during the German Military Administration of Occupied France during World War II. Over 65,000 French, Polish, and German Jews, including approximately 11,000 children, were exported from Drancy on 64 rail transports from June 1942 to July 1944. The overwhelming majority of the prisoners that passed through the Drancy camp were Jews, however a small percentage of the prisoners at the camp included members of the French Resistance. The camp at Drancy was liberated on August 17, 1944.

The Drancy camp was located to the northeast of Paris in the suburb of Drancy. Prior to World War II, architects Marcel Lods and Eugéne Beaudouin conceived the facility as a modern urban community. The building was noteworthy for its integration of high-rise residential apartments, making it one of the first structures of its kind in France. The complex was named La Cité de la Muette, meaning "The Silent City," when it was built, as it stood for peaceful ideals. The multi-story U-shaped building was confiscated by Nazi authorities shortly after the occupation of France in 1940, and was initially used as police barracks before becoming the primary detention center for Jews (and other individuals labeled as "undesirable") who were arrested in the Paris region. The facility was designed to accommodate 700 people, yet at the height of its use it housed more than 7,000 prisoners.

In August of 1941, the Drancy camp was created by the Vichy government of Philippe Pétain, in cooperation with the Nazi occupation authorities. The facility was established as an internment camp for foreign Jews in France after the arrest and roundup of over 4,000 Jews in Paris in August 1941. Drancy later became the major transit camp for deporting Jews out of France. French police initially staffed the camp under the supervision of the German Security Police, and several thousand prisoners managed to obtain release in the first year of the camp's existence. Documented testimonies exist of brutality by the French guards, including the execution of 40 Jewish prisoners in retaliation for a French attack on German personnel.

The conditions in the camp were very harsh due to a neglect of basic human needs. The Jews at Drancy suffered from a lack of personal needs, inadequate food, unsanitary conditions, and overcrowding. In addition to the brutal conditions inside the camp, small children, upon arrival, were immediately separated from their parents. Evidence exists that over 3,000 Jews died in French camps including Drancy; others, such as Noe, Gurs, and Recebedou, also saw many deaths due to starvation and lack of medical needs.

Beginning in the summer of 1942, Germans began the systematic deportation of Jews from Drancy to killing centers located in occupied Poland. Sixty-four railway transports left Drancy carrying Jews on rail cars designed for cattle. The first was June 22, 1942; the last on July 31, 1944. In total, over 65,000 Jews were deported from Drancy to Auschwitz-Birkenau and the Sobibór killing centers. One-third of the Jews who had been deported from Drancy were French citizens, the others were foreign Jews who had immigrated from Poland, Germany, Austria, and elsewhere. A number of distinguished French Jewish intellectuals and artists were held in Drancy, including René Blum, a famous choreographer and younger brother of Prime Minister Léon Blum; Tristan Bernard, a philosopher; and poet Max Jacob, who died while imprisoned at Drancy.

Beginning in the early hours of the morning July 16, 1942, and lasting through the next day, an event occurred known as The Great Raid of the Vel' d'Hiv, where nearly 13,000 Jews were arrested in Paris. The adult men were sent directly to Drancy, while many of the women and children were held for five days without food or medical care inside the Vélodrome d'Hiver, an indoor cycling stadium, before being transferred to Drancy. The adults were then transported to Auschwitz and gassed; the children remained in Drancy for weeks without proper care or adequate food. Several babies and young children died due to neglect and the uncaring treatment of the French guards. Eventually all of the children were also transported to Auschwitz, to be gassed upon arrival.

In July 1943, Nazi Germany took direct control of the Drancy camp under the leadership of SS officer Alois Brunner, an Austrian who worked as Adolf Eichmann's assistant. The Germans taking over the day-to-day operations at Drancy was part of an intensification of all facilities for the mass exterminations of all Jews throughout Nazi-occupied Europe.

On April 6, 1944, SS-Hauptsturmführer and Gestapo member Klaus Barbie, known as the "Butcher of Lyon," captured Jewish children on a raid in a children's home in Izieu, where the children had been hidden. He arrested all 44 children and 7 adults. The children were shipped directly to Drancy, and then put on the first available train toward the death camps in the east. Of the 44 children of Izieu, not a single one survived.

As Allied forces neared Drancy on August 15 and 16, 1944, the German authorities there burned all the camp documents prior to fleeing. On August 17, 1944, the Swedish consul-general, Raoul Nordling, took control of the camp. He found 1,542 surviving Jews at the camp, and asked the French Red Cross to care for them. Of the 65,000 Jews that were exported from the Drancy camp to killing centers between June 22, 1942 and July 31, 1944, fewer than 2,000 survived the Holocaust.

For more than 40 years, the government of France did not admit responsibility for the Vichy government of Philippe Pétain and French police arrest, detainment, and exportation of French Jews during World War II. It was on July 16, 1995 that, in a historic speech, then-president Jacques Chirac recognized the responsibility of the French State in seconding the "criminal folly of the occupying country," and in particular, the role the French police had in organizing the 1942 Vel' d'Hiv Roundup.

In 1973, a memorial sculpture entitled, "The Gates of Hell" was created by Shelomo Selinger, the French-Israeli sculptor, to commemorate the French Jews who had passed through Drancy. In 2012, the French president, François Hollande, opened a Holocaust memorial museum. The museum provides details about the persecution of the Jews in France and includes many personal mementoes of the inmates. Some of the items include personal belongings left by inmates (some of which are inscribed with their owner's name), aluminum drinking mugs, messages written on the walls, and an archive of cards and letters written by prisoners to their relatives prior to deportation.

Jessica Evers

See also: Auschwitz; Concentration Camps; France; Holocaust, The; Sobibór.

Further Reading

Butler, Hubert. *The Children of Drancy.* Mullingar, IE: Lilliput Press, 1988.

Rajsfus, Maurice. *Drancy: Un camp de concentration tres ordinaire, 1941–1944.* Paris: Le Cherche Midi, 1996.

Wellers, Georges. *From Drancy to Auschwitz.* Boston: M-Graphics Publishing, 2011.

Dulag Luft

Abbreviated from Durchgangslager der Luftwaffe (Transit Camp of the Air Force), Dulag Luft was a prisoner-of-war camp where most Allied airmen caught in Nazi occupied Europe were sent. There were several camps set up across Germany and German-occupied territories, but the main center was at Oberursel, near Frankfurt. A former experimental agricultural center on the outskirts of the small town, the Oberursel camp comprised of ramshackle brick buildings lightly guarded by barbed wire fencing, with a satellite camp at Wetzlar set up later in the war to help cope with the large numbers of prisoners. From December 1939 onward, this camp served as the first point of call for the captured Allied airmen before they were sent to a permanent prisoner-of-war camp. In 1941, a group of British prisoners, led by Wing Commander Harry Day, dug a tunnel and escaped from the Oberursel Camp, only to be recaptured within a week.

Alexander Mikaberidze

See also: Colditz; Germany; Great Escape; Stalag.

Further Reading

Clutton-Brock, Oliver. *RAF Bomber Command Prisoners of War in Germany, 1939–1945.* London: Grub Street, 2003.

Miller, Donald L. *Masters of the Air: America's Bomber Boys Who Fought the Air War against Nazi Germany.* New York: Simon & Schuster, 2006.

E

Eichmann, Adolf (1906–1962)

German Schutzstaffel (SS) lieutenant colonel and key figure in the destruction of European Jewry during World War II. Born on March 19, 1906, in Solingen in the Rhineland, Germany, Karl Adolf Eichmann moved with his family to Linz, Austria, in 1914. He left the Linz Higher Institute for Electro-Technical Studies after two years and became a salesman. In 1932, he joined the Austrian National Socialist movement, but he fled to Germany in 1934 when it was outlawed. Sent to Berlin, he joined the SS Sicherheitsdienst (Security Service, SD) and was assigned to its Jewish Office. There, he became the Nazi expert on Jewish affairs and handled negotiations concerning the emigration of German Jews to Palestine, which he visited briefly in 1937. Following the *Anschluss* (union) with Austria and absorption of Bohemia and Moravia, he headed the Office for Jewish Emigration.

With the beginning of World War II, Eichmann transferred to the Gestapo and created the Reich Central Emigration Office to handle the relocation of European Jews to Poland. That office was then combined with the Jewish Affairs Office to form Department IV-A-4B, known as the Dienststelle Eichmann (Eichmann Authority). He helped organize the Wannsee Conference of January 1942 that developed the mechanics of the Final Solution and was put in charge of the transportation of Jews to the death camps of Poland. Eichmann later told an associate that he would "die happily with the certainty of having killed almost 6 million Jews."

Adolf Eichmann, pictured here in a Jerusalem courtroom, was a principal player in the Nazi's "final solution," the murder of millions of Jews and other people the Third Reich considered undesirable. He was tried and executed in Israel in 1962. (Library of Congress)

After the war, Eichmann lived in various places under aliases until he escaped to Argentina, where he lived and worked near Buenos Aires in obscurity under the name Ricardo Klement. On May 11, 1960, Israeli Secret Services captured him and smuggled him from the country illegally to stand trial in Israel. Eichmann claimed he was only following orders and, in any case, could be accused only "of aiding and abetting" the annihilation of the Jews, not killing them. Found guilty by an Israeli court on December 15, 1961, he was sentenced to death. Unrepentant, he was hanged at Ramleh Prison on May 31, 1962. His body was then cremated, and the ashes scattered.

Douglas B. Warner

See also: Holocaust, The.

Further Reading

Arendt, Hannah. *Eichmann in Jerusalem: A Report on the Banality of Evil.* New York: Viking, 1963.
Donovan, John. *Eichmann: Man of Slaughter.* New York: Avon Book Division, Hearst, 1960.
Malkin, Peter Z., and Harry Stein. *Eichmann in My Hands.* New York: Warner, 1990.
Reynolds, Quentin. *Minister of Death: The Adolf Eichmann Story.* New York: Viking, 1960.

Eichmans, Fyodor (1897–1938)

Soviet intelligence officer and the first head of the Gulag system. Born in the Courland province of the Russian empire, Eichmans studied at a technical college before pursuing a military education in Riga. In 1916 he joined the Latvian Riflemen and participated in the final two years of World War I. At the same time, he was active in radical circles and joined the Russian Social Democratic Worker's Party in 1917.

After the Bolshevik coup in October 1917, Eichmans served in the Petrograd branch of the notorious Cheka, the first of a succession of Soviet secret police institutions. He took part in the Russian Civil War (1918–1921), fought in Central Asia and, after 1922, led the 2nd Division of the Eastern Department of the newly established State Political Directorate (Gosudarstvennoe politichieskoe upravlenie, GPU) that was responsible for combatting political subversion in Central Asia and the Far East. In 1923, he was appointed head of the notorious Solovki (Solovetskii) Special Camp, where thousands of opponents of the Soviet regiment were detained and abused. In this capacity, Eichmans emerged as a key figure in the development of the Soviet prison camp system since Solovki served as a prototype for detention and labor camps that eventually constituted Gulag. In 1929, he became head of the 3rd Division of Special Directorate of the reorganized Soviet secret police, Joint State Political Directorate (OGPU).

In 1930, Eichmans became the first head of Ulag (The Directorate of Camps), a predecessor to the Gulag, and supervised the formation of its core components: the Solovetskii, Visherskii, Severnyi, Kazakhstanskii, Dalnevostochnyi (the Far East), Sibirskii, and Sredneaziatskii camps. That same year he led the notorious Waigatsch expedition of the OGPU, which had the goal of developing zinc and lead deposits on the remote Arctic island of Waigatsch with the help of the forced labor of Gulag prisoners. In 1932, he was recalled to the head office of the OGPU, where he directed various directorates, In 1937, during Joseph Stalin's Great Purges, Eichmans was accused of participating in an alleged Trotskyist plot and executed the following year. He was legally rehabilitated after Stalin's death in 1956.

Alexander Mikaberidze

See also: Gulag; NKVD.

Further Reading

Solzhenitsyn, Aleksandr. *The Gulag Archipelago.* Translated by Thomas Whitney. New York: HarperPerennial, 1975, three volumes.

Volkhard Knigge, Irina Scherbakowa. *Gulag. Spuren und Zeugnisse 1929–1956.* Göttingen, DE: Wallstein, 2012

Elmira Prison (New York)

Union prisoner-of-war camp located in Elmira, New York. The Elmira Prison was formed by using part of old Fort Rathburn, which had fallen into disuse and disrepair. On July 6, 1864, its surviving barracks building, known as Barracks #3, was pressed into service as a prison. When the building was filled, additional prisoners were held in its environs, both in tents and crude temporary structures. Elmira, New York, was chosen as a prison site chiefly because it was close to several important rail lines, including the Northern Central and Erie Railways.

Life at Elmira Prison proved to be a thoroughly miserable experience for the 12,122 Confederate prisoners who were housed there until the summer of 1865. Elmira's inmates, who dubbed the place "Hellmira," suffered from high levels of disease, malnutrition, inadequate water supplies, deplorable hygiene, poor drainage, and frequent exposure and death during the bitter winter months. The last prisoner was released on September 27, 1865. Union records indicated that an astounding 2,917 inmates died in the camp. The prison camp was soon demolished and became farm land. Later, in the early twentieth century, the site was converted into a residential area; there are currently no traces of Elmira Prison, although Woodlawn Cemetery, about two miles from the Elmira site, remains a grim testimonial to the several thousand Confederates who died at the prison during 1864 and 1865.

Paul G. Pierpaoli, Jr.

See also: U.S. POW Camps, 1861–1865.

Further Reading

Hesseltine, William B., ed. *Civil War Prisons.* Kent, OH: Kent State University Press, 1972.

Horigan, Michael. *Death Camp of the North: The Elmira Civil War Prison Camp.* Mechanicsburg, PA: Stackpole Books, 2002.

Engerau Trials (1945–1954)

A small village near the frontier area Slovakia-Hungary-Austria (today: town district Petrzalka of the Slovakian capital Bratislava), Engerau became a site of a forced labor camp for Hungarian Jews during World War II. Engerau was the northern most point of the Reich Defense Line ("South East Rampart", Südostwall), a system of trenches and ramparts erected by the Nazis in the last months of the war against the advancing Red Army. From December 1944 until March 1945, more than 2,000 Hungarian Jews had dug up entrenchments there, more than 400 out of them died of exhaustion, diseases, or were beaten to death by their guards, the Viennese SA men ("storm troopers"). When the Soviet troops approached, the camp was evacuated on March 29, 1945, but not before a special detachment shot those who were sick or unfit to march, while many others were killed during the ensuing march to Bad Deutsch Altenburg (Lower Austria). The surviving Jews were shipped upstream to Mauthausen, where many more prisoners died of exhaustion.

These abominable crimes, partly committed on the "doorstep" of the Austrian population, caused a series of legal proceedings in post-war Austria against some 70 accused. In five main trials between 1945 and 1954 against 21 defendants, the Vienna "People's Court" imposed nine death sentences and one life imprisonment.

The first case before an Austrian "People's Court" was an Engerau Trial: On July 31, 1945, the First State Attorney of Vienna had completed the indictment against four members of the SA guards who were charged with murder, assault and battery, as well as violation of human dignity. The trial took place on August 14–16, 1945, becoming the first Nazi war crimes trial in Austria. Three defendants were sentenced to death while the fourth defendant was imprisoned for eight years. On November 20, 1945, two of the sentenced to death were hanged in the Viennese District Court, and the third one was executed on the December 2, 1945.

The second Engerau trial took place only three months later in November 1945. Five more members of the SA guard were indicted. The verdicts were two sentences to death and three imprisonments from six months up to two years. The death sentences were carried out on February 2, 1946.

The third trial, taking placed in October–November 1946, was probably the most important, since it included nine criminals, including two camp commandants, the head of the northern sub-section of the South East Rampart and his deputy. The other five defendants were members of the SA camp guards. Both camp commandants and two camp guards were sentenced to death and executed on July 25, 1947. The sub-section commander was sentenced to a 19-year imprisonment, while one defendant was acquitted.

The fourth Engerau proceeding was not actually a court case, but rather constituted investigations by police and magistrate against the SA sub-section commander, who had been the head of the SA camp guards in Engerau. He was sentenced to 10 years imprisonment for different crimes in a separate trial.

By early 1950s, the number of trials before the People's Courts decreased and the Austrian government considered suspending the courts' special jurisdiction over Nazi crimes. The Allies, especially the United States, however, insisted on further prosecution of Nazi perpetrators. In 1954, two more defendants were found guilty of war crimes and given lengthy prison sentences.

Claudia Kuretsidis-Haider

See also: Holocaust, The; Mauthausen-Gusen.

Further Reading

Klarsfeld, Beate. *Wherever They May Be!* New York: Vanguard, 1975.

Manvell, Roger. *S.S. and Gestapo.* New York: Ballantine, 1969.

Extermination Centers

This term distinguishes the Nazi death camps, whose primary purpose was the systematic murder of mainly Jews by gassing, from other concentration camps where thousands died through overwork, starvation, and abuse, but whose intended focus was not on the industrialized mass murder of Jews.

In the autumn of 1941, the decision was made by Hitler to begin the physical extermination of European Jews. The Reich Main Security Office (RSHA) of the SS and SS general Odilo Globocnik directed Operation Reinhard, a plan to begin the murder of European Jews. He was responsible for building camps, organizing deportations, and collecting the financial assets of Jews killed. Though it began in 1941, this piece of the Final Solution would be named after Reinhard Heydrich, head of the RSHA, who was assassinated by partisans in June 1942. Aktion Reinhard incorporated three camps: Bełżec (operational March 1941), Sobibór (operational May 1942), and Treblinka II (new killing center addition operational July 1942). To these Aktion Reinhard camps, we must also add Chełmno (operational December 1941). Lastly, though not *solely* an extermination camp, Auschwitz contained a dedicated killing center, Auschwitz II-Birkenau, which began gassing Jews in January 1942. Demonstrating an important continuity in the development of decision-making regarding the Final Solution, these extermination camps were often staffed by specialists who had already practiced mass killing in the context of the "euthanasia" program (Aktion T-4), often via gassing. A small group of SS officers and men were responsible for the operation of these killing centers, often along with a larger guard force made up of Ukrainian or other foreign volunteers.

With the exception of Auschwitz, these camps were fundamentally different from other Nazi concentration camps, such as Dachau or Mauthausen, in that they were centered around the sole task of the mass murder of Jews on arrival. The majority of Jews murdered in these centers had previously been confined in ghettos in eastern Europe or in holding camps in western Europe. The extermination centers maintained only a small force of slave laborers, who existed solely to support the machinery of murder, not to perform any other kinds of forced labor. Upon arrival in these camps, Jews were subjected to a selection in which a very small number were chosen to augment the camp labor force. The remainder were segregated by sex, separated from their property, shaved, and then forced into a gas chamber where they were murdered, either by carbon monoxide gas (in Bełżec, Chełmno, Treblinka, and Sobibór) or by Zyklon B, a de-lousing agent (in Auschwitz). In many camps, this process was accompanied by an attempt by the Germans to conceal the true nature of the facility, as at Treblinka, where commandant Franz Stangl had a fake train station created, complete with flowerbeds. Members of a special squad, or *Sonderkommando,* would then remove the bodies, search them for hidden valuables or gold teeth, and then burn them using a variety of methods, including crematorium and open pits.

The Operation Reinhard camps were all closed by August 1943, with Chełmno and Auschwitz remaining in operation until the arrival of Soviet forces in 1945. Together, these three extermination centers were responsible for the murders of 1.7 million people, mainly Jews, but also Sinti/Romani and Soviet POWs. At least 1.1 million more were murdered at Auschwitz.

Beyond the inhumanity and the massive scale of the loss of human life, the extermination centers represent for many the deadly potential of the combination of racism, modern bureaucracies, and technology. Moreover, the operation of these camps required far more participants than simply those staffing them. It required experts in deportation such as Adolf Eichmann, along with many other so-called desk murderers, who were responsible for coordinating train schedules and resources for the camps, as well as more hands-on killers who acted as guards and camp administrators. In addition, one can see in the extermination camps many of the varied collaborators in the Nazi genocidal project. Doctors, such as Josef Mengele, performed experiments on inmates. Businesses, such as Topf, were contracted to build and maintain crematoria. Finally, the looted valuables and property of the murdered Jews were funneled back into the larger German economy.

Waitman W. Beorn

See also: Auschwitz; Bełżec; Bergen-Belsen; Birkenau; Chełmno; Concentration Camps; Dachau; Gas Chambers; Holocaust, The; I.G. Farben Case (1947); J.A. Topf & Söhne; Mauthausen-Gusen; Medical Experimentation during World War II; Sobibór; Sonderkommando; Treblinka; Zyklon B Case (1946).

Further Reading

Arad, Yitzhak. *Belzec, Sobibor, Treblinka: The Operation Reinhard Death Camps.* Bloomington: Indiana University Press, 1987.

Breitman, Richard. *The Architect of Genocide: Himmler and the Final Solution.* New York: Knopf, 1991.

Hilberg, Raul. *The Destruction of the European Jews.* New York: Holmes & Meier, 1985.

F

Far East, British Military Trials

In the aftermath of World War II, the newly created United Nations established two international military tribunals to deal with war crimes; one at Nuremburg, dealing with Nazi Germany, and the other at Tokyo, Japan. In the latter case, major figures in both defeated regimes, the so-called class A, were put on trial under the auspices of the International Military Tribunal for the Far East (IMTFE). In addition to this, the United Nations allowed a number of smaller hearings in Asia, the B and C classes accused of conventional war crimes and crimes against humanity. Seven countries, including the United Kingdom, set up courts to prosecute Japanese officials in these categories.

Allied discussions about war crimes trials were held during wartime meetings, such as the Quebec Conference of August 1943. The genesis of British war crimes tribunals came in November 1944, when the War Cabinet decided that military courts would be established to deal with suspected criminals. Authority over them was given to the Secretary of War. In June 1945, regulations for trying war crimes cases were set forth, although they were not completed by the time Japan surrendered that September. The South East Asia Command (SEAC), commanded by Admiral Lord Louis Mountbatten, was given total authority over British military courts. Individual tribunals were established within its command structure on a largely geographical basis. Investigations until the end of the war were conducted by units of E Group, Force 136, which was attached to the Special Operations Executive (SOE). Nearly 36,000 personal statements were collected from British military personnel and civilians who witnessed or endured Japanese atrocities. Further evidence was mounted through newspaper reports, interviews with local citizens, and official documentation. By December 1945, there were seventeen separate investigatory bodies established under E Group. The British government finally decided in October of that year to proceed with the trials, and nearly 500 were scheduled to be heard by the summer of 1946.

Military courts were set up in 25 cities across British possessions in Malaya, Northern Borneo, and Burma, as well as in Hong Kong and Singapore. The first three regions dealt with cases exclusively from the area, while Hong Kong and Singapore handled trials dealing not only with those cities, but also events in China, Taiwan, and on the high seas. Of the 918 cases eventually brought to trial before British military courts, 168 involved atrocities in Malaya, 132 in Burma, and 123 in Singapore. By far, Singapore, as the center of proceedings for incidents in Indonesia, Thailand, Indochina, and the South Pacific, was the scene of the most trials, with 464.

The first trials got underway in January 1946 in Singapore. By May, there were nearly 9,000 accused under British arrest throughout Asia, but only 175 had actually been prosecuted. The main problem was a lack of staff. With the Japanese surrender came the rush to demobilize and send the soldiers home. As a result, the work of investigators and military courts was extremely slow. By the end of 1946, the majority of cases remained unfinished, prompting the British government to extend the deadline for all trials. Another problem was the political circumstances that accompanied the establishment and operations of the courts. Burma was in the throes of decolonization, finally earning its independence in January 1948. Cases in Malaya and Singapore unfolded against the backdrop of nationalism, growing anti-British sentiment, and the threat of communist insurgency. In many areas, some of the accused were non-Japanese who had joined with the conquerors during the war. In pursuing their political goals after the war, many Asian nationalists advocated reconciliation, and opposed some of the trials. Equally important was the fact that everywhere in the Far East, British power and authority had been fundamentally undermined by Japanese victories in World War II. In this light, the courts were seen as a re-imposition of declining imperial rule rather than an attempt at justice. In short, there were many other political considerations which complicated the prosecution of those accused of war crimes.

Several top Japanese officials were convicted and sentenced to death by British military courts. Admiral Kumakichi Harada, the Japanese commander in Java, was found guilty of crimes against civilians and prisoners of war at his trial in Singapore in October 1946. Admiral Teczo Hara was tried in April 1946 for the execution of natives on the Andaman Islands. Lieutenant General Fufuye Shimpei, prison camp commander in Malaya, was sentenced to death in February 1946. Major General Sato Tamenori was found guilty of killing Burmese civilians and sentenced to hang in March 1946. However, several major cases remained unresolved. Colonel Tsuji Masanobu, implicated in massacres of Chinese in Singapore and Malaya, had escaped and remained at large, ironically aided by Chinese Nationalists who wanted his expertise in their war against Communists. In addition, still outstanding was the case of the *Suzu Maru*, a Japanese cargo ship used in transporting British prisoners of war for slave labor among the Indonesian islands, which was sunk by an American submarine in November 1943, with the loss of nearly 400 men. Nonetheless, in April 1949, the British agreed with the joint Allied Far Eastern Commission that all proceedings should be ended by that September. In December 1948, the last trials in Hong Kong finished, and in October 1949, in conjunction with the United States, the British government closed its war crimes tribunals.

Suggestions that the trials were racially fixated on British victims, and especially prisoners of war, are not borne out by evidence. It has been estimated that as much as 27 percent of Allied prisoners of war, many of them British, died in Japanese camps during the war, whereas only 4 percent died under German control. Still, in total, 550 of the 918 cases brought before British courts dealt with Japanese crimes against civilians. The vast majority of these involved Asians. Only 227 cases dealt with prisoners of war, and many of those were Indian, Chinese, and Burmese. Of the 218 found guilty and sentenced to death, 188 were charged with acts against civilians, compared to just 66 who acted against soldiers. Moreover, there is little evidence that the trials were rigged or compromised innocent officials. Of the 918 convicted, 355 were members of the dreaded *Kempeitai*, the Japanese secret police, renowned for their ruthlessness and cruelty in occupied territories. Of the 218 executed, 112 worked for the *Kempeitai*.

On the whole, British military courts were fair. In some instances, they even exonerated Japanese soldiers who carried out orders on pain of death. The British trials also avoided the controversy that accompanied American tribunals. Rather, the British contended with bureaucratic shortcomings, and the realities of their declining influence in Asia.

Arne Kislenko

See also: Japan; Nuremberg Trials; Yokohama Trials.

Further Reading

Hirofumi, Hayashi. "British War Crimes Trials of Japanese," *Nature, People, Society: Science and the Humanities* July 31, 2001, http://www32.ocn.ne.jp/~modernh/eng08.htm

Law Reports of Trials of War Criminals, selected and prepared by the United Nations War Crimes Commission, Volume VI (London: Her Majesty's Stationary Officer, 1948), www.ess.uwe.ac.uk/WCC/warcrimfe.htm#HIGHER

Piccigallo, P.R. *The Japanese on Trial: Allied War Crimes Operations in the Far East 1945–1951*. Austin: University of Texas Press, 1979.

Rees, Laurence. *Horrors in the East: Japan and the Atrocities of World War II*. New York: Da Capo Press, 2001.

Featherston Camp (New Zealand)

Prisoner-of-war camp for Japanese soldiers at Featherston, New Zealand, notorious for a 1943 rioting. The camp was originally established a military training ground during World War I, and processed some 60,000 troops during the war; it was also used an internment camp for German civilians in the concluding years of the war. During World War II, the defunct Featherston military camp was re-established and turned into a prisoner-of-war camp to house Japanese soldiers captured by the American forces in the Pacific theater of war. The camp comprised of a small hospital and four rectangular compounds, surrounded by barbed wire and dotted with small shelters that housed prisoners (eight men to a hut); originally intended to house about 500, the camp held over 800 prisoners by 1943. They were guarded by 122 New Zealand guards, most drawn from reservists, that received no special training for dealing with POWs.

Conditions at the camp were tolerable and the prisoners were somewhat surprised by comparatively kind treatment they had been shown at the camp. Camp administration allowed prisoners to elect their representatives, and each compound had its own leader who supervised order and cleanliness; prisoners received medical care and ample food supplies, were free to maintain small gardens, and engage in recreational activities. Yet the camp became infamous for events of February 1943, when almost 300 POWs in the second compound refused to work. The trouble started with the arrival of 250 new POWs, who were military veterans captured during the Guadalcanal Campaign. They were thoroughly imbibed with the spirit of the Japanese military code (*Senjinkun*) that exalted loyalty, esprit de corps, filial piety, and devotion to the cause, while forbidding retreat or surrender. Tensions between guards and the new POWs increased as the Japanese officers told their subordinates not to work for the enemy. The camp commandant, Lt. Col. Donald Donaldson, decided to punish this disobedience by imposing forced labor on the prisoners. On February 25, the situation in Compound No. 2 quickly escalated as the Japanese refused to work and the camp authorities became determined to make them. In an ensuing fracas, the guards opened fire at some 240 defiant prisoners, killing 48 and wounding almost 100; 10 guards were injured and 1 died by friendly fire. A military court of enquiry assigned most of the responsibility for the incident to the prisoners, who were unaware that the 1929 Geneva Convention on Prisoners of War did sanction compulsory work; the report also acknowledged vast cultural differences that contributed to the incident.

The remaining Japanese prisoners were repatriated after the end of World War II.

Alexander Mikaberidze

See also: Australia; Cowra Incident.

Further Reading

Carr-Gregg, Charlotte. *Japanese Prisoners of War in Revolt: The Outbreaks at Featherston and Cowra during World War II.* St. Lucia.: University of Queensland Press, 1978.

Michiharu Shinya, and Eric Thompson. *Beyond Death and Dishonour: One Japanese at War in New Zealand.* Auckland, NZ: Castle Pub., 2001.

Nicolaidi, Mike, and Eric Thompson. *The Featherston Chronicles: A Legacy of War.* Auckland, NZ: HarperCollins, 1999.

Filtration Camps in Chechnya

During its two wars in Chechnya in 1994–1996 and 1999–2003, the Russian government resorted to mass internment centers to "filter" local population, detain suspect rebel fighters, and suppress insurgency. The term "filtration camp" can be traced back to World War II, when the Soviet secret police established special camps to check Soviet citizens who had been captured by the Germans during World War II. More than 4 million former prisoners of war and civilian internees went through such filtration camps in 1945–1949.

During the wars in Chechnya, the Russian security services once again resorted to filtration camps and detained tens of thousands of civilians. In theory, the camps should have served as sites for a quick check of identity and permanent residence registration papers of the detainees in order to determine their status as civilians or combatants. But in practice, the camps turned into internment camps where ethnic Chechens were interrogated and detained for long periods and subjected to beatings, torture, and, in some cases, summary executions; the civilians were detained arbitrarily without any evidence of wrongdoing.

The Russian security forces' attitude toward the detainees could be summed up in the statement that the Russian chief of the general staff M. Kolesnikov made: "the prisoners [are] treated normally, though from the formal point of view they should [be] shot by firing squad as bandits." Probably the most infamous of these camps was located at the village of Chernokozovo where an existing penitentiary facility was turned into four filtration camps, where detainees were abused, tortured, and killed. In 2000–2010, human rights groups publicized numerous evidence of abuses the Russian security services has perpetrated at the filtration camps.

Alexander Mikaberidze

See also: Concentration Camps.

Further Reading

Case of Bitiyeva and X vs Russia, European Court of Human Rights, June 2007

Gall, Carlotta, and Thomas de Waal. *Chechnya: Calamity in the Caucasus.* New York: New York University Press, 1998.

Quénivet, Noëlle. "The Rule of Law in the Russian Federation. Case Study; Filtration Camps in Chechnya," *Central Asia & Central Caucasus Press AB*, http://www.ca-c.org/dataeng/quenivet.shtml

'Welcome to Hell:' Arbitrary Detention, Torture, and Extortion in Chechnya, Human Rights Watch Report, New York, 2000.

Finland

As World War I led to the collapse of the Russian Empire in 1917, Finland emerged as an independent state, but deeply torn by political and social schisms. Tensions between the Reds (radicals of Social Democratic Party who represented urban poor and industrial and agrarian workers) and the Whites (conservatives with strong support from middle-class and rural population) quickly escalated into a civil war. Supported by their Bolshevik brethren from Russia, the Reds launched a major offensive to seize power, but suffered decisive defeats at Tampere and Vyborg. The Whites, supported by Germany, then counterattacked and won at Helsinki and Lahti, bringing the war to conclusion in May 1918.

During the war, the Whites captured some 80,000 Red prisoners of war who were interned in over a dozen major prisoner-of-war camps. Conditions in the camps were terrible, with prisoners suffering from lack of food and essentials. These factors, combined with a flu epidemic and mentality of indifference and retribution on the part of the victors, led to high mortality rates. It is estimated that over 12,000 prisoners died of malnutrition and various diseases. At the Tammisaari camp in Ekenäs, probably the most notorious of the Finnish camps, an average of 30 prisoners died every day. The majority of the prisoners were paroled or pardoned in 1919; it must be noted that in 1973, the Finnish government agreed to pay reparations to the camp survivors.

During World War II, Finland sided with Germany and launched a major offensive into Soviet Union's East Karelia, subsequently occupying this region. The Finnish authorities established concentration camps for the Russian populace of East Karelia, ostensibly to secure the area behind the front lines against sabotage and partisan attacks. The first of these camps appeared at Petrozavodsk in late 1941; eventually nine major camps—at Petrozavodsk, Medvezhyegorsk, Olonets, the

Ilyinskoye State Farm, etc.—interned over 20,000 Russian detainees, including children. Because of malnourishment, disease, and mistreatment, the mortality was quite high in camps, especially during the summer of 1942. In October 1943, the Finish military administration in East Karelia dropped the use of the term "concentration camp" and renamed the camps to "transit camps" (*siirtoleiri*). The camps continued to operate until June 1944, when the Finnish troops were forced to leave the region. In September, Finland and the Soviet Union signed an armistice, which stipulated the release of any Soviet (or Allied) prisoners of war and interned Soviet citizens; by 1945, over 42,000 Soviet prisoners and 1,600 civilian internees were repatriated. In addition, the Soviets demanded the handing over of the German prisoners of war who remained in Finnish custody and, between 1945 and 1946, Finland transferred over 2,500 German POWs.

Alexander Mikaberidze

See also: Concentration Camps; Sweden.

Further Reading

Kinnunen, Tiina, and Ville Kivimaki, ed. *Finland in World War II: History, Memory, Interpretations.* Leiden, ZH, NL: Brill, 2012.

Tepora, Tuomas, and Aapo Roselius, ed. *The Finnish Civil War 1918: History, Memory, Legacy.* Leiden, ZH, NL: Brill, 2014.

Flick Case (1947)

Five members of the Flick Concern, a group of German industrial enterprises that included coal mines and steel plants, were charged with using slave labor and POWs, deporting persons for labor in German-occupied territories, and plundering private property—the Aryanization of Jewish properties—in the first trial of German industrialists after World War II.

On February 8, 1947, the U.S. Military Government indicted Friedrich Flick, the largest private German iron and steel manufacturer (and also Germany's wealthiest man) and four associates, charging them with war crimes and crimes against humanity. Indicted along with Flick were SS brigadier general Otto Steinbrinck, Flick's chief deputy until 1939, when he became head of a government-owned company; Konrad Kaletsch, Flick's cousin and the financial director of the Flick Concern; Bernhard Weiss, Flick's nephew and one of the three principal executives operating the Concern; and Dr. Herman Terberger, a member of the board of directors.

According to the indictment, all five defendants took part in and profited from the slave labor program; they were held to be responsible for the death or suffering of over 10,000 French, Poles, and Russians, and as well as workers of other nationalities, who had been forced to work at their maximum ability while food and shelter were held to a minimum. Four of the men were charged with taking part in the plunder of occupied territories and of planning such plunder in advance of military operations; Terberger was not charged with this count. Documents captured by the Allies in their occupation of Germany showed that Flick and his associates, along with six other steel companies, tried to push the German government into confiscating mills from French owners after the Germans invaded France; the company gained possession of the Rombach ore mines in France and a railroad car plant in Riga, Latvia, using this tactic.

Flick, Steinbrinck, and Kaletsch were also charged with profiting from the process of Aryanization of Jewish property, including the acquisition of the brown coal mines belonging to Julius and Ignatz Petschek of Czechoslovakia. The prosecution included this charge as a crime against humanity because the Flick Concern would pressure Jewish owners to sell their property at less than fair value; in a maneuver to make the transactions appear more legal, the German government took possession of property before passing it on to the Flick Concern. In a document obtained by the prosecution, Flick wrote in November 1939, "I said these transactions could later on become the subject of the inquiry of an international court."

The fourth count of the indictment charged Flick and Steinbrinck with supporting the criminal activities of the SS by contributing large sums to and being members of Heinrich Himmler's "Circle of Friends." Flick and his associates were not charged with crimes against the peace due to the challenges of gathering evidence across the four zones of occupation in Germany. Steinbrinck was charged alone on the fifth count of being a member of the SS from 1933 until the end of the war.

Judge Charles B. Sears from the Court of Appeals of the State of New York presided over the trial held in Nuremberg, Germany. On December 22, 1947, the tribunal announced its verdict. Flick was convicted of all charges except the charge involving Aryanization of Jewish property; the tribunal dismissed this charge against all defendants on grounds that it was not a "crime against humanity." Steinbrinck was pronounced guilty on two of the five counts; he was convicted for being a member of the SS and funding Himmler's Circle of Friends. Weiss also was convicted on two counts. The other defendants were acquitted.

In delivering the verdicts, the judges made a number of statements about the legality of the trial, as well as expressing some compassion for the defendants. Judge Sears stated that "the court was not a tribunal of the United States" or a court-martial or military commission, but instead an international tribunal established by the International Control Council under Control Council Law 10. The verdict also appeared to be critical of the prosecution. The judges noted that Flick knew about the 1944 attempt on Adolf Hitler's life and had sheltered one of the conspirators, and that Steinbrinck, as a U-boat commander, had risked his life and his crew to rescue survivors from a ship he had sunk. The tribunal pointed out that Flick and his associates had risked clashes with Nazi leaders to provide better food, shelter, and clothing to the Concern's laborers. The defendants' most deplorable act, according to the verdict, was that some of the profits gained through the work of slave laborers went to fund Himmler's SS.

At the reading of the verdict, Flick announced that he had committed no crimes. He explained his relationship with the German government: "After the [Nazi] seizure of power, every industrialist in the long run had to get into some sort of relationship with the new holders of power." He argued that he had either to work with the Nazis or risk financial ruin or death. Sentenced to seven years in prison, dating from his original capture on June 13, 1945, Flick was released from

Landsberg prison in 1950, his sentence reduced for good behavior. After his release, he worked to build another financial empire. At his death in 1972, Friedrich Flick was again Germany's richest man.

John David Rausch, Jr.

See also: Holocaust, The; Nuremberg Trials.

Further Reading

Stallboumer, L.M. "Big Business and the Persecution of the Jews: The Flick Concern and the 'Aryanization' of Jewish Property Before the War," *Holocaust and Genocide Studies* (1999). 13:1–27.

Stokes, Raymond. *Divide and Prosper: The Heirs of I.G. Farben under Allied Authority, 1945–1951.* Berkeley: University of California Press, 1989.

Trials of War Criminals before the Nuremberg Military Tribunals under Control Council Law. "The Flick Case." Washington, DC: Government Printing Office, 1952, No. 10., vol. 6

Flossenbürg

Nazi concentration and forced labor camp system first built in the spring of 1938. It was situated outside the village of Flossenbürg in northeastern Bavaria, not far from the Czech border. The area had large deposits of granite, which the Germans hoped they could quarry using forced labor from the camp. Flossenbürg's main camp received its first prisoners—100 individuals from the Dachau concentration camp—on May 3, 1938. Administered by the SS, the camp was first designed to be a prison for German men who were considered "asocial," as well as for repeat criminal offenders. By the end of the year, the prison population had grown to 1,500. Prior to 1944, few Jews were sent to Flossenbürg.

In early 1940, Czech and Polish prisoners began arriving at the camp, including resistance fighters. By the end of 1941, Flossenbürg had 3,150 detainees; an additional 1,750 Soviet prisoners of war were housed in a separate facility within the camp grounds. More political prisoners and resistance operatives arrived during 1942 and 1943, including those from France, Germany, the Soviet Union, and the Netherlands. Detainees worked in the nearby quarries, but as the war progressed, more were put to work in German aircraft factories and an SS-operated weaving shop. Nearly 100 sub-camps were erected to accommodate these workers, all under the Flossenbürg umbrella.

Beginning in August 1944, when perhaps only 100 Jews had been imprisoned at Flossenbürg, there was a mass concentration of mainly Polish and Hungarian Jews at the camp, who would number at least 10,000 by January 1945. In the winter of 1945, another 13,000 Jews flooded Flossenbürg and its sub-camps. Many had been forcibly moved from camps in the east as Soviet troops pushed German forces toward the west. The camp's population had now swelled to nearly 40,000, including some 11,000 women, and peaked at 53,000 (with 14,500 in the main camp) in March 1945.

Conditions were horrific. Meager food rations, lack of proper sanitary facilities, and virtually no medical care doomed thousands to death from starvation, disease,

Flossenbürg concentration camp. Established in the spring of 1938, the camp rapidly grew in size. At its high point in March 1945, nearly 53,000 prisoners were in the Flossenbürg camp system, including about 14,500 in the main camp. (Bettmann/ Getty Images)

or overwork. Beatings and harsh punishments killed hundreds of others, and the more senior inmates, most of them habitual criminals who had been locked up for years, preyed on newer detainees. Rape and sexual exploitation were commonplace, and the corrupt camp administration did nothing to stop such activities.

The mortality rate at Flossenbürg, while never reaching the levels seen at death camps, was nonetheless shocking. In 1941, more than 1,000 Soviet prisoners of war were executed there. That same year, 500 Poles were shot dead, and in March 1945, 13 Allied prisoners of war were hanged, including 1 American. These deaths did not include the thousands who died in other ways; the total number who died at Flossenbürg and its sub-camps is estimated to be about 30,000 (of whom 3,515 were Jews), out of a total of 97,000 who had been in the camp at one time or another.

In April 1945, as U.S. troops closed in on Flossenbürg, the Nazis ordered an immediate evacuation. All able-bodied prisoners were sent on a forced march toward Dachau; those unable to undertake the journey were shot or left for dead. At least 7,000 detainees died in this process, principally by starvation and exhaustion. When Flossenbürg was finally liberated on April 23, U.S. troops found just 1,500 people—many of them wracked by hunger and disease.

Paul G. Pierpaoli, Jr.

See also: Concentration Camps; Germany; World War II Prisoners of War.

Further Reading

Abzug, Robert. *Inside the Vicious Heart: Americans and the Liberation of Nazi Concentration Camps.* New York: Oxford University Press, 1985.

Kogon, Eugen. *The Theory and Practice of Hell: The German Concentration Camps and the System behind Them.* New York: Farrar, Straus and Giroux, 2006.

Wachsmann, Nikolaus. *KL: A History of the Nazi Concentration Camps.* New York: Farrar, Straus and Giroux, 2015.

Foca Camp

During the 1992–1995 Bosnian War, Montenegrin and Serbian forces committed many atrocities in and around the ancient city of Foca. Among them was the establishment of "rape camps," where Muslim women were systematically raped or sexually abused. Foca is situated on the Drina River in eastern Bosnia, an area which the Serbs hoped to "ethnically cleanse" of Muslims. The Serbs not only established rape and killing camps, but they also destroyed virtually all vestiges of Muslim culture, including museums, schools, mosques, and libraries. In the summer of 1992, Roy Gutman, an American journalist, and British journalist Ed Vulliamy, first reported on the existence of the Serbian rape camps.

Gutman's and Vulliamy's reporting on the atrocities in eastern Bosnia quickly garnered international attention. The Serbians and Montenegrins in turn worked feverishly to cover up or destroy all evidence of the camps, fearing that they could be accused of war crimes and crimes against humanity. At the same time, press coverage of these nefarious activities led many human-rights groups, including Human Rights Watch, to include sexual violence as an international war crime. The use of mass rape by Serbian and Montenegrin forces was a clever calculation on their part, as the act of rape was considered to be particularly vile by Muslims. The sexual violence was thus designed to force out any Muslims who had not otherwise been killed or deported earlier.

Eventually, some 14 Serbian leaders were tried and convicted for their participation in the Foca atrocities, including Dragan Gagovic, Gojko Jankovic, Janko Janjic, Radomir Kovac, Zoran Vukovic, Dragan Zelenovic, Dragoljub Kunarac, Radovan Stankovic, Savo Todovic, Milorad Krnojelac, and Mitar Rasevic. Some of the defendants were tried by the International Criminal Tribunal for the Former Yugoslavia (ICTY), and others by the Court of Bosnia and Herzegovina. Radovan Karadzic was also arrested and tried for his part in the Foca calamity, but his trial is ongoing.

In the fall of 2004, the Association of Women-Victims of War, headquartered in Sarajevo, attempted to put up a small commemorative plaque in Foca to remember the female victims of rape during the Bosnian War. That effort was met with stiff resistance from Foca's non-Muslims, and the plaque was never erected. Of the 22,000 or so Muslims who lived in Foca prior to the war, only about 2,000 were left after the conflict ended. During the early 2000s, some dislocated Muslims returned, but they are still a very small minority in Foca.

Paul G. Pierpaoli, Jr.

See also: Bosnian War; Yugoslavia.

Further Reading

Allen, Beverly. *Rape Warfare: The Hidden Genocide in Bosnia-Hercegovina and Croa-tia.* Minneapolis: University of Minnesota Press, 1996.

Zinsstag, Estelle. "Sexual Violence against Women in Armed Conflicts: Standard Responses and New Ideas," *Social Policy & Society* 5:1 (2005), 137–148.

Fort Cass

A fort maintained by the U.S. Army to facilitate the removal of the Cherokee on what became known as the Trail of Tears. Located on the Hiwassee River, near the present-day Charleston, Tennessee, the fort served as a focal point in a vast complex of internment camps where the Cherokee were kept in 1838, before forced to march west to Indian Territory.

The long-simmering tensions between the state of Georgia and the Cherokee Nation were exacerbated by the discovery of gold near Dahlonega, Georgia, in 1829, resulting in the Georgia Gold Rush. As speculators began trespassing on Cherokee lands, pressure mounted on the U.S. Government to implement the Compact of 1802 that sought to extinguish Indian land claims in Georgia. The Indian Removal Act of 1830 sanctioned forcible removal of the Native American population from the land that was highly desirable to the white settlers. In 1835, in an effort to intimidate the local population, the U.S. Army built Fort Cass; three years later, Brigadier General Winfield Scott arrived here to take command of the "Army of the Cherokee Nation," which was tasked with forced deportation of the Cherokee people. Despite opposition from the Cherokee Nation, the U.S. government recognized the bogus Treaty of New Echota as ceding the Cherokee land to the colonist, and forged ahead with plans to cleanse the Southern states of the native population. The treaty had specified May 23, 1838, as the deadline for all voluntary removal of the Cherokee people. As the deadline passed, the U.S. army launched military operations to drive Cherokees from their homes; by mid-summer, thousands of the Cherokees were brought to Fort Cass, where they were kept in internment camps for several months as the U.S. authorities made preparations for further deportation; many Cherokees died in these camps due to lack of basic necessities and disease that spread rapidly because of bad sanitary conditions. The last of the Cherokee left Fort Cass in December 1838.

Alexander Mikaberidze

See also: Apache Wars; Indian Removal Act (1830); Trail of Tears (1838); Seminole Wars.

Further Reading

Ehle, John. *Trail of Tears: The Rise and Fall of the Cherokee Nation.* New York: Anchor Books, 1988.

Perdue, Theda, and Michael D. Green. *The Cherokee Nation and the Trail of Tears.* New York: Viking, 2007.

Fossoli di Carpi

During World War II, the Italian fascist government of Benito Mussolini constructed a network of camps and prisons to house enemy soldiers captured during warfare in Europe and North Africa. An ally of Nazi Germany, Italian camps held many Allied prisoners of war sent from the North African campaign.

Six kilometers outside the small northern Italian city of Carpi, fascist authorities erected a camp on former farmland in May 1942 to house British soldiers captured in North Africa. From May 1942 to September 1943, Italian fascist forces interned some 5,000 enemy soldiers at Fossoli.

During Fossoli's use as a prisoner-of-war camp, Italy had operated as an autonomous ally to Germany. However, following the Allied invasion of southern Italy in September 1943, and Mussolini's subsequent overthrow, the Italian government abandoned its German partnership and, on September 8, 1943, declared allegiance to the Allies. Germany responded by invading Italy and occupying all of northern Italy as far south as Rome. This included a German takeover of Fossoli. The German arrival heralded the mass deportation of some 5,000 prisoners of war to forced labor camps in eastern Europe. After deporting all of the POWs, the Germans left Fossoli and instructed local government officials in Carpi to clean and prepare the camp for the arrival of Jewish prisoners.

The first Jews arrived at Fossoli on December 5, 1943. In addition to Jews, Italians arrested for their opposition to fascist and Nazi policies were also sent to Fossoli. The Jews and political prisoners were separated into different sections of the camp. Italian fascist authorities (those still loyal to Mussolini and Nazi causes) monitored and guarded prisoners from December 5, 1944, to March 15, 1945. During this period, four deportations of Jewish prisoners occurred. The first convoy of 83 prisoners departed Fossoli for Bergen-Belsen on January 26, 1944, and was followed by another transport of 69 Jews to Bergen-Belsen on February 19. The first deportation to Auschwitz of 517 Jews left the Carpi train station on February 22, 1944. The final deportation during the Italian-run period of Fossoli departed on March 12, carrying 71 individuals to an unknown destination.

The Germans took over control of Fossoli from the Italians on March 15, 1944. Under German command, an additional 2,032 Jews were deported to the Nazi camps of Auschwitz (1,821), Bergen-Belsen (171), Buchenwald (21), and Ravensbrück (19). German and Italian forces also deported an unknown number of political and civilian prisoners prior to the camp's closure in August 1944. The camp functioned briefly thereafter, from August to November 1944, as a transit camp for forced labor to German occupied territories.

Alexis Herr

See also: Auschwitz; Buchenwald; Bergen-Belsen; Holocaust, The; Ravensbrück; World War II Prisoners of War.

Further Reading

Lamb, Richard. *War in Italy, 1943–1945: A Brutal Story*. New York: Da Capo Press, 1996.

Ori, Anna Maria. *Il Campo di Fossoli: Da campo di prigionia e deportazione a lugo di memoria 1942–2004*. Carpi, IT: Stampa Nuovagrafica, 2008.

Weinberg, Gerhard L. *Germany, Hitler, and World War II*. Cambridge: Cambridge University Press, 1995.

France

With the start of World War I in 1914, France resorted to internment camps to isolate German, Austrian, and Ottoman nationals. Some of the detainees were kept at Pontmain in the department of Mayenne, others at Fort-Barreaux in Isère, or Graveson and Frigolet in Bouches-du-Rhône. During the Spanish Civil War, the French government interned Spanish Republican refugees and military personnel at the Rieucros Camp, Camp de Rivesaltes, Camp Gurs, and Camp Vernet; some detainees were allowed to stay in France, but those involved in the Republican paramilitary brigades were oftentimes turned over to the Franco government of Spain. After the Nazi occupation of France and establishment of the Vichy regime in 1940, the Spanish detainees were deported to Nazi Germany, with some 5,000 Spaniards perishing at the Mauthausen concentration camp.

The Vichy regime expanded the scale and scope of the internment camps, which played an important role in its policy of assimilating ethnic minorities into the French mainstream and deporting thousands of French Jews to Nazi Germany. Thus, thousands of Romanis were detained on the charges of "nomadism" and placed at camps where they were deprived of adequate amounts of food and necessities. At the same time the Vichy regime broadened its efforts to detain the Jews, who were incarcerated in over a dozen concentration camps, including at Gurs, Le Milles, Rivesaltes, and St. Cyprien; by 1941 some 40,000 Jews had already been arrested, while thousands more were sent to labor camps (*Compagnies de Travail*). A concentration camp at Drancy (a suburb of Paris) served as a key assembly and detention camp for Jews who were transported to the extermination camps in Germany; in 1942–1944, almost 70,000 individuals passed through this camp on their way to a certain death. The Vichy French also maintained internment and labor camps in North and West Africa, with major facilities at Conakry, Timbuctoo, and Kankan (West Africa).

After the end of World War II, tens of thousands of German prisoners of war were detained at POW camps, including at Rennes and Camp de Rivesaltes.

During the Algerian War (1954–1962) the French colonial authorities resorted to internment camps as part of their counterinsurgency measures, with hundreds of thousands of Algerians forced to move to *villages de regroupement* (resettlement camps) in an effort to deny the National Liberation Front its support base; by 1961, some 3 million Algerians were affected by this policy.

Alexander Mikaberidze

See also: Drancy; Holocaust, The.

Further Reading

Fogg, Shannon L. *The Politics of Everyday Life in Vichy France: Foreigners, Undesirables and Strangers*. Cambridge: Cambridge University Press, 2009.

Marrus, Michael, and Robert Paxton. *Vichy France and the Jews*. Stanford, CA: Stanford University Press, 1981

McDougall, James. *A History of Algeria*. Cambridge: Cambridge University Press, 2017.

Franz, Kurt (1914–1998)

Born in Düsseldorf on January 17, 1914, Kurt Hubert Franz became infamous for his cruelty in Nazi extermination camps, especially Treblinka, where he served as the camp's third commandant.

For a German citizen who never joined the National Socialist German Workers' Party or any of its affiliated organizations, Franz rose quickly after joining the army in 1935, serving initially as a cook, and then volunteering for the Death's Head Unit (the SS-Totenkopfverbände) in 1937. He served in several capacities during his career. He was a guard at Buchenwald, took part, beginning in 1939, in Aktion T-4, the so-called Nazi euthanasia program, and, in the spring of 1942, served at Bełżec as commander of the Ukrainian guard unit. Later in 1942, he was sent to Treblinka.

At Treblinka, as he had at Bełżec, he commanded the Ukrainian guard unit. He soon became deputy commandant of the camp, serving under Franz Stangl. On August 2, 1943, a revolt of prisoners at Treblinka proved to be unsuccessful, but it resulted in significant destruction to the camp. When Stangl was transferred after the revolt, Franz replaced him as camp commandant. By that time, his primary responsibility was to dismantle the camp and cover up any signs of the mass murders that were committed there.

Franz displayed a level of day-to-day cruelty that he clearly enjoyed, and he was able to exercise it in Treblinka at will. His methods were varied but they all terrified the prisoners. He beat and shot prisoners without hesitation, often on an arbitrary basis, as if for sport. One of the many ways he made himself the most feared man in the camp was to sic his 150 pound St. Bernard dog, Barry, on any prisoner— for any reason, or for no reason at all. The dog was trained to bite the buttocks and genitals of the selected prisoner. Its strength and viciousness were well known throughout the camp.

The pure evil of his actions was seen in acts like shooting prisoners who had not yet detrained from the cattle car that brought them to Treblinka. He often killed children and babies, sometimes by kicking them to death, and he perfected the use of a whip to maximize the suffering of the victim. His appearance, however, belied his actions. He was nicknamed Lalke, meaning "the doll" in Yiddish, because of his soft baby face.

After leaving Treblinka, Franz spent some time in northern Italy where he continued in his role as a sadistic murderer of Jews. After the war, he hid in plain sight in Germany, first working on bridges, and then, for the next decade, working as a cook, the skill that he brought with him when he first joined the German army. In December 1959, Franz was arrested in his home town of Düsseldorf.

He was then brought to trial, along with 10 other camp officials, in what is known as the First Treblinka Trial, held in Düsseldorf between October 1964 and August 1965. He was sentenced to life in prison, and served 28 years before being released in 1993 for health reasons. He died in 1998.

There is a coda to Franz's life. In 1959, upon Franz's arrest, his home was searched. Discovered there was a private photo album with pictures of Treblinka, this despite the fact that cameras and photographs were forbidden in the camp. The original album is now housed at Yad Vashem in Jerusalem. The title Franz gave to the album is revelatory. The German "Schone Zeiten" has been translated as "Good Times," or "Beautiful Times."

Michael Dickerman

See also: Holocaust, The; Treblinka.

Further Reading

Arad, Yitzhak. *Belzec, Sobibor, Treblinka: The Operation Reinhard Death Camps.* Bloomington: Indiana University Press, 1987.

Klee, Ernst, Willi Dressen, and Volker Riess, eds. *"The Good Old Days": The Holocaust as Seen by Its Perpetrators and Bystanders.* New York: Free Press, 1988.

French Revolutionary and Napoleonic Era

The French Revolution marked a break with the past. The French revolutionary government invoked principles upon which POWs had to be treated. Thus, a decree of the French National Assembly of May 4, 1792, placed prisoners of war under the safeguard and protection of the nation and declared that the POW should be treated based on the principles of justice, humanity, and equality. The decree further specified that prisoners were to be interned away from the frontlines and were to be paid on the same scale as French soldiers; they could gain limited freedom of parole by pledging not to fight again and parolees were to enjoy the same rights under the French common law as any other citizen. The Decree of August 3, 1792, proclaimed the principle of reciprocity and stated that exchanges of prisoners were to be negotiated on a man-to-man basis, irrespective of rank.

Despite these intentions, the Revolutionary armies did mistreat prisoners, and the ideological and national hatred that the revolutionary turmoil introduced into the war made things particularly intolerable. In September 1793 and May 1794, the National Convention, dominated by radical revolutionaries, prohibited exchanging of prisoners and demanded all émigré prisoners, and later British, Hanoverian, and Spanish prisoners as well, to be executed as an "example of the vengeance of an outraged nation." The Convention thought better of these odious decrees and, on December 30, 1794, revoked them as contrary to existing laws of the war. Still, military necessity was often used to justify mistreatment of prisoners, whether by denying them sufficient provisions or actually massacring them. In 1798, General Napoleon Bonaparte had over 2,000 Ottoman prisoners shot, claiming they had violated an earlier parole, had shown a clear intent to fight him, and had shown no mercy to the wounded/captured French troops; most crucially, Napoleon argued he lacked resources to intern the prisoners. In 1800, French general Andre Massena, whose garrison was starving during the bitter siege of Genoa, had no choice but to leave hundreds of Austrian prisoners without supplies on hulks in the harbor after the Austrians and British refused to feed them.

The Treaty of Amiens, signed by France and Britain in 1802, prohibited the practice of demanding ransom for the release of prisoners and called for speedy repatriation of troops upon the end of hostilities. In general, these provisions were upheld during the subsequent Napoleonic Wars. The British transported the French army, with its weapons and baggage, from Egypt to France in 1801–1802 and from Portugal in 1808. But the French troops that surrendered to the Spanish at Bailen in 1808 were subjected to a far harsher treatment. The Franco-Spanish agreement called for repatriation of the French prisoners, but the terms were not honored and, apart from senior officers, thousands of French, Polish, Swiss, and Italian soldiers were transported and abandoned on the deserted island of Cabrera (off the coast of Majorca) for five years; out of 11,800 sent to Cabrera, only 3,700 survived.

During the Peninsular War, the Spanish guerrillas took few prisoners, and bloody atrocities that they committed were followed by equally horrendous reprisals by the French. In 1812, when Napoleon invaded Russia, over 200,000 French troops fell into Russian captivity and, despite Russian efforts to place these prisoners in internment facilities, thousands of prisoners died due to cold weather, poor conditions, and violence. On campaign, the British usually treated their prisoners of war well, and often protected them from being massacred by the Spanish or Portuguese irregulars. Back in England, prisoners were confined to prison hulks (i.e. at Chatham, Portsmouth, and Plymouth), and there were numerous complaints about conditions at these floating ships, especially at Chatham, where several thousand prisoners were reported to have died. At the same time, the influx of large numbers of prisoners—between 1793 and 1815, over 100,000 prisoners were brought to Britain and remained in captivity for the duration of war—caused British prisons and hulks to fill up rapidly and forced British government to come up with new ways of coping with prisoners. As the result, Britain constructed their first purpose-built prisoner-of-war camps at Norman Cross and Dartmoor.

Alexander Mikaberidze

See also: American Revolutionary War; Cabrera; Dartmoor Massacre (1815); Norman Cross.

Further Reading

Abell, Francis. *Prisoners of War in Britain 1756 to 1815: A Record of Their Lives, Their Romance and Their Sufferings.* Oxford: Oxford University Press, 1914.

Chamberlain, Paul. *Hell Upon Water: Prisoners of War in Britain, 1793–1815.* Stroud, UK: The History Press, 2016.

Mikaberidze, Alexander, and François Houdecek, eds. *Special Issue Devoted to Prisoners of War, Napoleonic. La Revue.* 2014/3 (21) https://www.cairn.info/revue -napoleonica-la-revue-2014-3.htm

G

Gas Chambers

The use of gas chambers to kill large numbers of people in a short period of time was pioneered by the Germans during the Holocaust. It is estimated that at least 1 million Jews, Romanis and Sinti people were executed in gas chambers between roughly 1940 and 1945. The use of gas chambers in concentration and death camps essentially systematized mass killing, turning these facilities into factories of death. The gas chambers were usually made to look like communal showers, in order to fool detainees into thinking that they would be engaging in an innocuous activity such as showering or delousing. Nearly all the victims of Nazi gas chambers were cremated in large, on-site crematoria.

Early on, and especially in camps like Bełżec and Treblinka, the Nazis used carbon monoxide to kill prisoners. However, by 1941, in camps like Auschwitz and Stutthof, Zyklon B (hydrogen cyanide) became the preferred method of extermination. Gassing people with Zyklon B was more efficient and required less gas than methods employing carbon monoxide. It also permitted camp personnel to have less contact with the internees as they were gassed, sparing them the ghastly sight of people choking and gasping for air as their bodies leaked fluids.

By 1941, all concentration and death camps in Poland were employing Zyklon B gas chambers, which were built by the German firm of J.A. Topf & Söhne. The company made a tidy fortune building such horrific devices. By 1942–1943, Auschwitz had become the largest death camp in the east, and camp officials used Zyklon B as the gas of choice while they engaged in the wholesale extermination of most of the camp's internees.

Paul G. Pierpaoli, Jr.

See also: Auschwitz; Chełmno; Death Camps; J.A. Topf & Söhne; Sobibór; Stutthof; Treblinka; Zyklon B Case (1946).

Further Reading

Bauer, Yehuda. *A History of the Holocaust*. Rev. ed. New York: Franklin Watts, 2001.

Schleunes, Karl A. *The Twisted Road to Auschwitz: Nazi Policy toward German Jews, 1933–1939*. Urbana: University of Illinois Press, 1970

Wachsmann, Nikolaus. *KL: A History of the Nazi Concentration Camps*. New York: Farrar, Straus and Giroux, 2015.

Geneva Convention Protocol I (1977)

Additional Protocol I to the Geneva Conventions of 1949, which applies to international armed conflicts and the protection of war victims, was adopted in 1977, following a four-year negotiating process. As of June 2017, 174 states were party to Protocol I, with the United States, Israel, Iran, India, and Turkey being notable exceptions.

Protocol I was negotiated during and in the immediate aftermath of the Vietnam Conflict and constituted an attempt to update both the Geneva Convention of 1949, concerning the protection of victims, and the 1907 Hague Convention, concerning methods and means of war. The 102 articles are divided into six parts: part 1 (Art. 1–7) general provisions; part 2 (Art. 8–34) wounded sick and shipwrecked; part 3 (Art. 35–47) methods and means of warfare—combatant and prisoner of war status; part 4 (Art. 48–79) civilian population; part 5 (Art. 80–91) execution of the conventions; and, the protocol, part 6 (Art. 92–102) final provisions.

One particularly contentious issue during the negotiating process was the scope of application of the protocol, in particular whether it should apply exclusively to traditional interstate armed conflicts or if it should also apply to some or all conflicts involving liberation movements of various types. Indeed, some delegations favored the development of a uniform body of law applicable to all conflicts. In the end, the diplomatic conference adopted Art. 1 (4), whereby Protocol I was regarded as applicable to traditional interstate armed conflicts, and also to "armed conflicts in which peoples are fighting against colonial domination and alien occupation and against racist regimes in the exercise of their right of self-determination." The adoption of this pejorative provision probably ensured some countries did not immediately ratify the protocol, but does not appear to have had a substantial long term effect.

Combatant and prisoner-of-war status was another contentious issue during the negotiation process, and the issue continues to be regarded as contentious in some circles. Under the older law, as embodied in Art. 4 of the 1949 Geneva Prisoner of War Convention, members of organized resistance movements had to meet several criteria, including requirements to wear some kind of uniform and to carry their arms openly, in order to be regarded as prisoners of war on capture; members of resistance movements found it difficult to both meet these criteria and remain effective. Art. 44 of Protocol I eliminates the requirement that resistance fighters wear some kind of uniform; it also modifies the arms obligation, so that arms are now required to be carried openly only during each military engagement and while the fighter is visible to an adversary when engaged in a military deployment prior to an attack.

Parts 3 and 4 of the protocol substantially update the old body of law concerning the conduct of hostilities; many of the provisions in these parts are regarding stating current customary law. In brief, the protocol defines the expression "military objective," and then states that military commanders are required not only to direct their operations against military objectives, but also to ensure that the losses to the civilian population and the damage to civilian property are not disproportionate to the concrete and direct military advantage anticipated. Attacks which are not directed against military objectives, particularly attacks directed against the civilian population, and attacks which cause disproportionate civilian casualties or civilian property damage, may constitute the offence of unlawful attack. In determining whether or not such an offence has been committed, the following duties of commanders must be considered; military commanders must: a) do everything practicable to verify that the objectives to be attacked are military objectives; b) take all practicable precautions in the choice of methods and means of warfare with a view to avoiding or, in any event, to minimizing incidental civilian casualties or civilian property damage; and c) refrain from launching attacks which may be expected to cause disproportionate civilian casualties or civilian property damage.

The protocol imposes obligations on defenders as well as attackers; in particular, defenders are obligated to take precautions to protect civilians under their control against dangers resulting from military operations and, to the extent practicable, to avoid placing military objectives, civilians, and civilian objects in the same location.

W.J. Fenrick

See also: Brussels, Declaration of (1874); Geneva Convention Relating to Prisoners of War (1929).

Further Reading

Bothe, M., Karl Josef Partsch, and Waldemar A. Solf, *New Rules for Victims of Armed Conflicts.* The Hague: Martinus Nijhoff Publishers, 1982.

Sandoz, Yves, Christophe Swinarski, and Bruno Zimmerman, eds., *Commentary on the Additional Protocols of 8 June 1977 to the Geneva Conventions of 12 August 1949.* International Committee of the Red Cross, The Hague: Martinus Nijhoff Publishers, 1987.

Geneva Convention Relating to Prisoners of War (1929)

The 1929 Geneva Convention, which sets out the legal rights of prisoners of war, was signed on July 27, 1929. It was the third of the four Geneva Conventions that enshrine humanitarian principles in international law. The first Geneva Convention of 1864 was intended to regulate the evacuation and treatment of wounded on a battlefield, and to offer protection for medical teams assisting them.

The 1929 Geneva Convention was compiled at an international conference convened by the Swiss Federal Council at Geneva from July 1 to July 27, 1929. This conference was called to revise the Geneva Convention of 1906 on the treatment of the sick and wounded, and to debate a new convention on the treatment of prisoners of war, based upon two draft conventions approved by the 10th and 11th International Conferences of the Red Cross. The conference was divided into two commissions. Paul Dinichert, the Swiss delegate presiding over the conference, took charge of the commission entrusted with the revision of the 1906 Convention. The second commission, headed by Harald Scavenius, was charged with producing the convention on prisoners of war. The American delegate at the conference was Hugh R. Wilson and the British, Sir Horace Rumbold.

The second Geneva Convention of 1906 extended the 1864 regulations to war at sea. While both these conventions offered a measure of protection to those who were captured wounded, they did not otherwise affect the treatment of prisoners of war. The major international law concerning the treatment of prisoners of war, prior to 1929, was the Hague Convention on Land Warfare of 1907.

The third Geneva Convention came about as a result of World War I, when the harsh treatment of some prisoners of war, particularly Italians, Russians, and Romanians in Germany and Austro-Hungarians in Russia, led to the realization that the 1907 Hague Convention did not provide enough safeguards for combatants taken prisoner. For example, the 1907 Hague Convention did not outlaw states carrying out reprisals upon prisoners of war. There was also no prohibition of the use of prisoner labor near battlefronts. The 1929 Convention set out to rectify these omissions. However, it was also intended to add proactive measures to protect prisoners. During World War I, various ad hoc systems, such as neutral inspection, the exchange of badly wounded prisoners, and the internment of certain categories of deserving prisoners in neutral countries, had developed to provide prisoners of war with a greater level of protection. The Geneva Convention of 1929 gave neutral inspection, internment, and prisoner exchange a basis in international law.

Although it incorporated much of the 1907 Hague Convention relating to prisoners of war, the 1929 Geneva Convention was much more comprehensive. Consisting of 97 articles, it included stipulations to protect prisoners from public curiosity and from insults, and stated that prisoners should have medical inspections once monthly. In Article 3, it stipulated that women should be treated with all the regard due to their sex, and that prisoners retained their full civil status. Article 16 stated that prisoners of war should be allowed complete liberty in the exercise of their religion, and that ministers of any religion who were prisoners of war should be allowed to minister fully to members of the same religion. Concerning interrogations, the 1929 Convention stipulated in Article 5 that "every prisoner of war is bound to give, if he is questioned on the subject, his true name and rank, or else his regimental number" and that no coercion was to be used on prisoners to secure information as to "the condition of their army or country. Prisoners who refuse to answer may not be threatened, insulted or exposed to unpleasant or disadvantageous treatment of any kind whatever." The definition of who constituted a prisoner of war in the 1929 Geneva Convention was taken from The Hague Convention of 1907.

The Geneva Convention was the major international legislation governing the treatment of prisoners of war during World War II. This was problematic, as the U.S.S.R. was a non-signatory, and therefore Germany argued that its Soviet prisoners of war were not entitled to the rights codified in 1929. This argument was used to justify Germany's treatment of Soviet prisoners of war, which led to horrific death rates among Soviet prisoners of war in Germany. Other countries, such as Japan, also gained notoriety during World War II for not abiding by the standards set out in the 1929 Convention. Perhaps the greatest failing of the 1929 Geneva Convention was that it provided no adequate protection for civilian prisoners in wartime.

Heather Jones

See also: Brussels, Declaration of (1874); Convention against Torture and Other Cruel, Inhuman or Degrading Treatment or Punishment (1984); Geneva Convention Protocol I (1977); Lieber Code.

Further Reading

Cochet, François. *Soldats sans armes. La captivité de guerre: une approche culturelle.* Brussels: Bruydant, 1998.

Convention relative to the Treatment of Prisoners of War, http://www.icrc.org/ihl.nsf /INTRO/305

Djurović Gradimir. *L'Agence Centrale de Recherches du Comité International de la Croix-Rouge. Activité du CICR en vue du soulagement des souffrances morales des victimes de guerre.* Geneva: Institut Henry Dunant, 1981.

Germany

Germany made extensive use of internment, concentration, and death camps in the twentieth century. At the start of the century, following the German suppression of the Herero and Nama peoples in German South West Africa (now Namibia), the German colonial official set up a network of concentration camps—Shark Island, Windhoek, Okahandja, Karibib, Swakopmund, Omaruru, Luderitz—to intern survivors. During World War I, thousands of Allied citizens caught by the outbreak of war on the territory of Germany were detained at internment camps (*internierungslager*) at Ruhleben, Holzminden, Havelberg, Celle Castle, and Rastatt.

During World War II, Germany established a number of different types of concentration camps (*konzentrationslager*). These may be grouped as penal, transit, labor, or extermination centers. Most served more than one purpose; that is, they were typically both penal and labor. But all of the camps saw brutality and the merciless loss of lives, whether as the result of disease, starvation, torture, exposure to the elements, forced labor, medical experiments, or outright execution. All major camps had sub-camps that were sources of slave labor. Collectively, the camps numbered in the thousands.

The Nazis opened their first concentration camp at Dachau, near Munich, in March 1933, only two months after Adolf Hitler came to power. This camp was the model for the many others to follow. It operated continuously until April 1945, when the U.S. Army liberated the inmates. Originally intended for the temporary detention of political prisoners, the camps became permanent institutions manned by the Schutzstaffel (SS) Totenkopfverbände (Death's Head detachments). In these camps, the more sadistic guards, of whom there was no shortage in the SS, were more or less free to inflict indescribable cruelties on the inmates without fear of disciplinary action.

The camp system gradually evolved from penal camps to the infamous death mills of Auschwitz, Bełżec, Chełmno, Majdanek, Sobibór, and Treblinka. At first, the camps housed political enemies. Foremost were the communists and social democrats. Jews were initially targeted insofar as they belonged to these other groups, but they were considered spoilers of German blood and quickly became the primary victims. In time, Romanis, Jehovah's Witnesses, homosexuals, and the mentally ill all fell prey to the Nazis and their collaborators. By 1939, seven large camps existed, with numerous sub-camps. These seven large camps were Dachau, Sachsenhausen, Buchenwald, Neuengamme, Flossenbürg, Mauthausen, and Ravensbrück. As the war spread, forced labor became more and more a part of war production, and prisoner exploitation expanded. In the end, the camps stretched from the Pyrenees to eastern Europe, and literally millions of people had perished in them. Some camps, notably Drancy in France and Westerbork in the Netherlands, were primarily transit facilities, where Jews were herded together for onward shipment via railroad to the dreadful death mills.

No one will ever know just how much the people in the surrounding communities knew about the internal workings of the camps, but the Nazis had accomplices wherever camps existed. There were penal, work, or transit camps in all the countries occupied by or allied with Germany. In western and eastern Europe, including in the Baltic states, indigenous troops augmented the SS in the camps. In southern Europe, local forces operated their own camps or executed their victims rather than ship them to the death mills of eastern Europe. One glaring case was the Jasenovac camp operated by the Nazi puppet of Croatia. There, the Croatian Fascists, the Ustaşe, killed tens of thousands of Serbs, Jews, Romanis, and political enemies.

All the camps were very much alike. In them, the guards did whatever they could to strip every bit of human dignity from the inmates. Those who could do so were forced to work at hard manual labor 11 to 12 hours a day. Those who could not were encouraged to die. The sign over the camp gate reading *Arbeit macht Frei* (Work Brings Freedom) meant the work of slave labor, and freedom only in the release of death.

On arrival at a concentration camp, men and women were segregated and taken off for medical inspection. There, they were forced to strip naked and were deloused. Heads were shorn, the hair retained to use for manufacturing mattresses and upholstering furniture. Following a cursory medical inspection, those pronounced fit to work were given clothes, had numbers tattooed on their arms, and were assigned to barracks where they would exist until they became too weak to work any longer. Those judged unfit to work were taken off in another direction to be executed. For those who passed the medical inspection, life in the camp was defined by deliberate degradation, with every effort expended to break them physically, mentally, and morally. Barracks were so overcrowded that there was often not enough room for everyone to lie down at once. Buckets were frequently the only sanitary facilities provided, and there were never enough of these. Barracks were unheated, and in many, there was no cover provided, even in winter.

At dawn each morning, men and women lined up in front of their respective barracks for roll call, standing in their thin rags, even in winter. This dreaded *zahlappell* (roll call) occurred at 3:00 a.m. and was repeated at 5:00 p.m. It lasted for hours each time, until the guards could make an official and complete count. Every form of disease was present in the camps, with little or no medical treatment provided. Nourishment was completely inadequate. Breakfast usually consisted of a cup of ersatz coffee and a small portion of stale or moldy bread, lunch was typically a cup of poorly fortified soup, and dinner routinely consisted of a small serving of bread, perhaps some potatoes or cabbage, and putrid tea.

Punishment in the camps was frequent and brutal, and it often occurred without justification. It had to be especially horrific if it was to exceed the brutality of daily life in the camps. Regulations in some camps required that beating with an axe handle was to be restricted to 25 blows at a time and that a week had to pass before a second beating could be given, but the guards seem not to have paid much attention to such rules. Often, the inmates were assembled to witness punishments and executions, and prisoners were sometimes placed in solitary confinement in total darkness, in cells where they could not stand, sit, or lie down for days or weeks.

At Buchenwald, Bergen-Belsen, and elsewhere, medical experiments were carried out on unwilling victims, who, if they survived, were often maimed for life. Such experiments investigated, among other things, the effects of rapid compression and decompression, how much cold and exposure a person could stand before dying, and how best to revive a victim of freezing. A number of German industries, such as I.G. Farben, the giant chemical firm that also manufactured the Zyklon B gas employed in the death camps, were attracted to Auschwitz and other camps with the promise of cheap slave labor. At Auschwitz, I.G. Farben built an enormous factory to process synthetic oil and rubber in order to take advantage of the slave labor available. This facility was the largest plant in the entire I.G. system, and it was built largely by slave labor. Work was physically exhausting, and beatings for any breach of the rules were common. I.G. claimed it provided a special diet for its workers, which nonetheless resulted in a weight loss of six to nine pounds a week for the prisoners. Death usually came after three months. As an I.G. physician's report noted, "The prisoners were condemned to burn up their own body weight while working and, providing no infection occurred, finally died of exhaustion." Slave labor became a consumable raw material. At least 25,000 people were worked to death at I.G. Auschwitz.

All inmates had to wear insignia (colored triangles) revealing the reason for their incarceration. There were variations, but typically, the Jews wore two superimposed triangles that formed a yellow star. Common criminals wore green. Political prisoners had red. Persons considered asocial (e.g., Romanis and vagrants) wore black. Homosexuals wore pink and Jehovah's Witnesses purple. Prisoners had to observe a definite hierarchy of prisoner officials, as well as the SS guards. The average prisoner had to answer to fellow prisoners at work or in the barracks. The most despised fellow prisoner was the Kapo, typically a heavy-handed supervisor willing to beat prisoners for the slightest infraction. The prisoners' work assignments and records were in the hands of other prisoners known as scribes and elders. These prisoner officials could make an inmate's life miserable, or even end it. Likewise, they could make life somewhat easier, and it often behooved ordinary prisoners to make note of this situation. Prisoner officials received better treatment in exchange for their cooperation, but comforts were rare indeed for the victims of this brutal process.

The Nazi concentration camp system took the lives of millions and was the principal instrument of the Holocaust.

Dewey A. Browder

See also: Arbeitslager; Auschwitz; Bełżec; Bergen-Belsen; Birkenau; Buchenwald; Bullet Decree (1944); Chełmno; Colditz; Concentration Camps; Dachau; Death Camps; Dora-Mittelbau; Eichmann, Adolf; Extermination Centers; Flick Case (1947); Gas Chambers; Gestapo; Gross-Rosen; Herero Genocide, Concentration Camps and; Hitler, Adolf; Hoess, Rudolf; Holocaust, The; I.G. Farben Case (1947); J.A. Topf & Söhne; Kinderblock 66;

Koch Trial (1951); Kramer, Josef; Krupp Case (1948); Lamsdorf; Mauthausen-Gusen; Medical Experimentation during World War II; Mengele, Josef; Monowitz; Natzweiler-Struthof; Neuengamme; Niederhagen; Nuremberg Trials; Okahandja; Ravensbrück; Sachsenhausen; Shark Island; Concentration Camps; Slave Labor (World War II); Sobibór; Sonderkommando; Stalag; Stutthof; Swakopmund; Treblinka; Trostinets; Windhoek; Zyklon B Case (1946).

Further Reading

Bauer, Yehuda. *A History of the Holocaust.* New York: Franklin Watts, 1982.

Sofsky, Wolfgang. *The Order of Terror: The Concentration Camp.* Translated by William Templer. Princeton, NJ: Princeton University Press, 1997.

U.S. Holocaust Memorial Museum. *Historical Atlas of the Holocaust.* New York: Macmillan, 1996.

Gestapo

The Geheime Staatspolizei (Gestapo) was the Nazi regime's secret state police that existed in German-held European territory during 1933–1945. The Gestapo was responsible for the elimination of all political opposition to the National Socialist German Workers' Party (Nazi Party), which entailed the deportation of thousands of Jews and other so-called undesirables to concentration camps before and during World War II.

When the Nazis first rose to power in 1933, Hermann Göring (who was then serving as minister of the interior and was one of Adolf Hitler's top lieutenants),

Gestapo officials recording data on incoming prisoners at a German concentration camp. Those waiting to be questioned are seated on the ground (left) under guard. (Library of Congress)

reorganized the Prussian police force. He separated the political spy unit from the regular police forces and placed the new grouping, the Gestapo, under his own direct command. In 1934, Heinrich Himmler, who headed the paramilitary units known as the Schutzstaffel (SS), took command of the Gestapo.

Two years later, Himmler was appointed chief of all police forces, and he eventually placed the Gestapo under Heinrich Muller. As the Nazis' bureaucratic network expanded, the Gestapo was shuffled under various security organizations, and it operated alongside many other police groupings, all of whose duties overlapped. Concentration camps were technically under the authority of the Gestapo, although in reality it was the SS that kept them running. Nonetheless, it was Gestapo commander Adolf Eichmann who oversaw the transport of millions of European Jews to concentration camps, like Auschwitz, in Poland.

There were no civil restraints that the Gestapo had to observe in carrying out its duties. Not only could police arrest suspects, but they also could make "preventative" arrests. Anyone who could possibly oppose or be perceived to oppose the Nazis could be arrested, tortured, killed, or released—all without any oversight by an judicial body. Tens of thousands of Jews, political intellectuals, clergy, homosexuals, Catholics, Romanis, and other "undesirables" simply disappeared. Gestapo police were also part of the death squads that followed behind the German Army as it invaded Poland and Russia. Those mobile units were responsible for the on-site killing of Jews and other targeted groups.

When Germany surrendered and World War II came to an end, the Gestapo was officially designated a criminal agency and disbanded.

Kellie Searle

See also: Auschwitz; Eichmann, Adolf; Germany; Hitler, Adolf.

Further Reading

Butler, Rupert. *The Gestapo. A History of Hitler's Secret Police, 1933–1945*. Havertown, PA: Casemate, 2004.

Cranckshaw, Edward. *Gestapo*. London: Bloomsbury, 2013.

Kahn, David. *Hitler's Spies: German Military Intelligence in World War II*. New York: Da Capo Press, 2001.

Gospić

A concentration camp set up by the Ustaše government of the Independent State of Croatia during World War II. The Ustaše adopted many of the Nazi German policies, including forming concentration camps and persecuting ethnic minorities and political opponents. The Gospić concentration camp was established in May 1941 as part of a larger complex of camps, with other branches located at Jadovno, Ovčara, and Pag. The first group of inmates—most of them Serbs, but also Jews and Romanis—arrived here on June 30, 1941, and the camp population steadily increased in size. Prisoners were subjected to extreme violence and abuse, with over 42,000 of them perishing before the war ended.

Alexander Mikaberidze

See also: Jasenovac; Sisak; Ustaše.

Further Reading

Israeli, Raphael. *The Death Camps of Croatia. Visions and Revisions, 1941–1945*. London: Routledge, 2017.

West, Richard. *Tito and the Rise and Fall of Yugoslavia*. London: Faber & Faber, 2012.

Great Escape

An escape by the British prisoners of war from the German Stalag Luft III camp during World War II. Stalag Luft III was established in March 1942 near the town of Sagan (now Żagań, Poland), about 100 miles southeast of Berlin. The camp was managed by the German air force (Luftwaffe) and was designated to hold any Allied pilots and crew taken prisoner.

The first prisoners at the Stalag were British officers, who arrived there in April 1942. By the end of the year, they were joined by the captured American pilots. The German authorities kept the Allied prisoners segregated, with the North Compound holding British airmen, while the South Compound was for Americans. Each compound consisted of 15 single-story huts, which housed 15 to 20 men. Overall, the camps held about 2,500 British officers, about 7,500 Americans, and some 900 prisoners from other Allied air forces.

In March 1943, Royal Air Force squadron leader Roger Bushell developed a plan for a mass escape from the North Compound. More than 600 prisoners were involved in the construction of tunnels. The digging was rather difficult because the barracks housing the prisoners were raised above the ground, while the camp itself was located on a sandy subsoil that could weaken the structural integrity of tunnels. Nevertheless, the prisoners persevered in constructing three tunnels that were designated as "Tom," "Dick" and "Harry." The Germans discovered and destroyed "Tom" while the prisoners had to abandon "Dick" when it became clear that the German plans for camp expansion would have prevented the prisoner escape. "Harry" was dug from the Hut 104, and the prisoners had to devise ingenious methods to overcome technical challenges of constructing a 300-foot-long tunnel that was 30 feet underground. One of the greatest challenges lay in disposing of the dug up sand without the prison guards noticing. The prisoners resorted to small pouches attached inside their trousers, which allowed them to scatter sand discreetly as they walked around the camp. In March 1944, the tunnel was completed. During the night of March 24, several hundred prisoners attempted to escape, but faced several unexpected problems that prevented most of them from escaping; ultimately only 76 prisoners managed to crawl to freedom. Upon learning of the escape, the German authorities conducted extensive search for the prisoners and recaptured 73 escapees. Adolf Hitler demanded severe penalties as an example for other prisoners, and 50 prisoners were executed by the Gestapo. Of the three successful escapees, Norwegians Per Bergsland and Jens Müller made it safely to Sweden by boat, while the Dutch Bram van der Stok snuck through France to a British consulate in Spain.

After the end of World War II, the British escape from the Stalag III Luft entered public conscience through the writings of Paul Brichill, whose book, titled *The*

Great Escape, gave the very name to the event. A heavily fictionalized version of the escape was then depicted in the film *The Great Escape* (1963).

Alexander Mikaberidze

See also: Bushell, Roger Joyce; Stalag.

Further Reading

Barris, Ted. *The Great Escape: A Canadian Story.* Thomas Allen, 2013.

Brickhill, Paul. *The Great Escape.* New York: Norton, 1950.

Walther, Guy. *The Real Great Escape.* London: Bantam Press, 2013.

Gross-Rosen

Nazi-administered concentration and forced labor camp located near the village of Gross-Rosen (now Rogoznica, Poland), about 40 miles southwest of Wrocław in modern-day western Poland. The facility was built in 1940 as a sub-camp of the Sachsenhausen concentration camp; the following year, it became autonomous, in an arrangement which would eventually encompass some 97 sub-camps. Upon its inception, most prisoners were put to work in a nearby granite quarry, where many died from accidents and overwork. At that time, most detainees were political prisoners, resistance fighters, or those deemed "socially unacceptable" (gay men and Romanis, for example). Not until late 1943 and early 1944 did Jews begin arriving at Gross-Rosen and its sub-camps in large numbers. The facility was administered by the SS, which also owned the adjacent quarry.

Conditions at Gross-Rosen were similar to other concentration camps. Food was meager and poor, sanitation was primitive, and medical care was virtually nonexistent. Thousands fell victim to starvation and diseases of various kinds, and large numbers of others were killed arbitrarily by guards during beatings and cruel punishments or from overwork.

As the war progressed and the Germans began relying more and more on forced labor, Gross-Rosen (with its sub-camps) became one of the largest concentration camp complexes in all of Europe. Eventually, prisoners worked throughout eastern Germany and western Poland for companies like I.G. Farben, Daimler-Benz, and Krupp. Brünnlitz, a sub-camp, later became famous when German industrialist Oskar Schindler relocated his factory there, shielding some 1,100 Polish Jews from Nazi depredations and likely death.

It is estimated that at least 125,000 prisoners were detained at or passed through Gross-Rosen between 1941 and 1945. By January 1945, Gross-Rosen and its sub-camps held 76,728 prisoners, the majority of whom, by that time, were Jewish. The camp's January 1945 census indicated that almost 26,000 women were interned there, one of the largest groupings of female prisoners in all of the vast German concentration camp system. Most of the Jews at Gross-Rosen had been relocated there from camps in Poland and Hungary.

When Soviet troops began approaching the complex in January 1945, camp officials ordered a mass evacuation. Some 40,000 prisoners endured a brutal forced march to the west in bitterly cold weather, during which several thousand died. The survivors were eventually sent to other concentration camps within Germany. Soviet forces liberated Gross-Rosen in February 1945. By then a total of about 40,000 prisoners had died in camp or during the forced evacuation march.

Paul G. Pierpaoli, Jr.

See also: Arbeitslager; Auschwitz; Bełżec; Bergen-Belsen; Birkenau; Buchenwald; Bullet Decree (1944); Chełmno; Colditz; Concentration Camps; Dachau; Death Camps; Dora-Mittelbau; Eichmann, Adolf; Extermination Centers; Gas Chambers; Gestapo; Hitler, Adolf; Holocaust, The; I.G. Farben Case (1947); J.A. Topf & Söhne; Kinderblock 66; Koch Trial (1951); Kramer, Josef; Krupp Case (1948); Lamsdorf; Mauthausen-Gusen; Medical Experimentation during World War II; Monowitz; Natzweiler-Struthof; Neuengamme; Niederhagen; Nuremberg Trials; Ravensbrück; Sachsenhausen; Slave Labor (World War II); Sobibór; Sonderkommando; Stalag; Stutthof; Treblinka; Trostinets; Zyklon B Case (1946).

Further Reading

Hilberg, Raul. *The Destruction of the European Jews.* New York: Holmes and Meier, 1962.

Kogon, Eugen. *The Theory and Practice of Hell: The German Concentration Camps and the System behind Them.* New York: Farrar, Straus and Giroux, 2006.

Wachsmann, Nikolaus. *KL: A History of the Nazi Concentration Camps.* New York: Farrar, Straus and Giroux, 2015.

Guantanamo Bay Detention Camp

American military prison at Guantanamo Bay in Cuba. In one of the most controversial aspects of what has been termed the U.S. war on terrorism, prisoners held at the camp have been stripped of legal protections afforded to citizens of any nationality under U.S. and international law. Legally classified as enemy combatants, prisoners may be detained indefinitely and without access to counsel. Hundreds of such detainees from more than 35 nations have been kept prisoner at the camp since 2002 without formal charges, and beyond the legal protection of the Geneva Conventions.

The U.S. military acquired Guantanamo Bay as a naval base as a consequence of the Spanish-American War of 1898. It has maintained the facility, despite tensions with the communist regime in Cuba, led by Fidel Castro. Until the terrorist attacks of September 11, 2001, against the United States, the U.S. military had used the base primarily as a detention center for Cuban and Haitian refugees. Despite being only 45 square miles in size, more than 9,000 U.S. personnel are stationed at the facility.

Guantanamo has come under intense international scrutiny. The U.S. military moved its first detainees of the war on terrorism in Afghanistan there on January 11, 2002, and by early 2014, 779 individuals from more than 35 nations had been held there (some were later released or transferred) without formal charges and with no access to lawyers or contact with their families, diplomats, or national government officials. The Guantanamo Bay detainees have also been denied the rights accorded to prisoners of war under the Geneva Conventions. In short, detention of these prisoners at Guantanamo Bay violates the rights accorded prisoners as understood by most scholars of international law.

The administration of President George W. Bush refused to change its policies regarding the detainees, however. The Bush administration contended that detainees at Guantanamo Bay fell into a new legal category of enemy combatants and, as such, must be assumed to be guilty until proven innocent, though precisely what evidentiary or legal avenues remained open to detainees is unclear. Bush's successor, President Barack Obama, vowed to close the facility when he took office in 2009, but as of April 2014, the facility was still open.

Human rights organizations such as Amnesty International and the International Committee of the Red Cross (ICRC), as well as former military officials working at Guantanamo Bay, have described the conditions of prison life there. Prisoners are alleged to have been kept in isolation cells for many days at a time; beaten and otherwise physically harmed; exposed to aggressive dogs, loud music, and strobe lights; and kept caged but exposed in outdoor cells during violent tropical weather. Prisoners are also alleged to have been subjected to extremely hot and cold temperatures, chained in uncomfortable or strenuous positions, denied food and water, and been forced to defecate and urinate upon themselves. Other allegations claim that prisoners have been sexually harassed and abused, and have had their religious beliefs ridiculed. The U.S. government refuses to grant the ICRC access to prisoners.

One of the most controversial allegations is that foreign nationals have in recent years been abducted by U.S. forces, tortured in their native countries with U.S. assistance and instruction, and then sent to Guantanamo Bay for further persecution and detention. Evidence has been presented to Amnesty International, the Red Cross, and the British government that nationals of Pakistani, Chinese, Afghan, Egyptian, Syrian, Canadian, and Iraqi descent, among others, have been detained in this way. A handful of missing people throughout the world have become "ghost detainees"; that is, they are believed by many to have been abducted in such fashion and then completely disappeared. In 2004, the ICRC prepared a confidential report on conditions at Guantanamo Bay, accusing the U.S. military of resorting to "humiliating acts, solitary confinement, temperature extremes, and use of forced positions" against prisoners. The report concluded that "the construction of such a system, whose stated purpose is the production of intelligence, cannot be considered other than an intentional system of cruel, unusual and degrading treatment and a form of torture." The U.S., government rejected the Red Cross findings, but subsequent reports by the *New York Times* and the *Washington Post* described interrogation techniques approved for use at Guantánamo Bay that would constitute a cruel and inhumane treatment and be considered illegal under the U.S. Constitution.

Those known to be held at Guantanamo Bay have been routinely denied access to lawyers, and non-U.S. detainees are not given the rights to have any levied charges tried in courts where appeals are possible. A variety of legal rulings by U.S. courts, including by the Supreme Court, have asserted that Guantanamo Bay detainees have the right to military tribunals as prisoners of war, and even to U.S. military or criminal courts in some cases. Nevertheless, the Bush administration unilaterally declared that any trials of camp detainees would be conducted by a new body formed in June 2004 and known as the Combatant Status Review Board (CSRB). That board was directly responsible only to the executive branch of the government and there was no appeals process. Moreover, its tribunals accept coerced testimony or admissions as evidence. Defense lawyers, if they are consulted at all, are not given access to any evidence presented in the government. Because of this, the CSRB violates both international law and generally accepted human rights law.

On January 22, 2009, two days after taking office, President Obama signed an executive order that mandated a suspension of criminal proceedings at Guantanamo Bay and the closure of the facility by year's end. This drew the immediate ire and suspicion of a number of Americans, who believed such a move would imperil national security. In May 2009, the U.S. Senate voted to deny funds that might be used for the transfer or release of Guantanamo Bay detainees. Nevertheless, in December Obama signed another executive order that would have transferred all prisoners to an Illinois prison. That move caused outrage in Illinois, Obama's adoptive home state. Early the next year, the Guantanamo Review Task Force concluded that 126 detainees were eligible for transfer, but that 40 others were deemed too dangerous to move. Meanwhile, many U.S. states flatly refused to take any of the prisoners, and so Guantanamo Bay remained open. Realizing that he was losing the battle to close the facility, in 2011 Obama signed an order forbidding the transfer of certain prisoners to the mainland United States or foreign nations, effectively ensuring that Guantanamo Bay would remain open for the foreseeable future. Attempts to try some of the suspects held there in U.S. civilian courts have likewise been stymied.

As of April 2016, there were 80 detainees still incarcerated at Guantanamo Bay; this represented a 45 percent reduction of the prisoner population since 2014. In 2013, after his reelection, Obama vowed to renew his push to close the prison, but there was little support for this in Congress. Nevertheless, his administration began to gradually release prisoners deemed less dangerous to their home nations or third-party nations willing to take them in under condition that they be closely supervised. In February 2016, Obama announced a plan to close the facility at Guantanamo for good by transferring the remaining prisoners there to prisons located in the United States. Obama believed that the move was necessary because of the great costs involved in housing prisoners in Cuba; he also stated that America's enemies, including the Islamic State (IS) and Al-Qaeda, were using the Guantanamo facility for propaganda and recruiting purposes. Most Republicans slammed Obama's plan as foolhardy and reckless, however, and several states named as potential new homes for the prisoners indicated that they would fight any attempt to relocate Guantanamo detainees within their borders. With Congress still controlled by the Republicans, it appeared unlikely that Obama's plan would be implemented in the short term. The Obama Administration did succeed in reducing the number of inmates from about 245 to 41, but was unable to transfer the remaining inmates. Following his win in the 2016 presidential elections, President Donald J. Trump vowed to keep the prison open and to use it to detain "bad dudes."

Nancy Stockdale

Further Reading

Bravin, Jess. *Terror Courts: Rough Justice at Guantanamo Bay.* New Haven, CT: Yale University Press, 2014.

Bruck, Connie. "Why Obama Has Failed to Close Guantanamo," *The New Yorker,* August 1, 2016, https://www.newyorker.com/magazine/2016/08/01/why-obama-has-failed-to-close-guantanamo

Hafetz, Jonathan. *Obama's Guantánamo: Stories from an Enduring Prison.* New York: New York University Press, 2016.

Priest, Dana, and Joe Stephens. "Pentagon Approved Tougher Interrogations," *Washington Post,* May 9, 2004, http://www.washingtonpost.com/wp-dyn/content/article/2004/05/09/AR2005040206867.html

Saar, Erik, and Viveca Novak. *Inside the Wire.* New York: Penguin, 2005.

Gulag

Russian acronym for Glavnoye Upravleniye Lagerey (State Director of Camps), an agency of the Soviet secret police, which administered the Soviet system of forced labor camps where political dissenters, dissidents, and other "enemies of the state" were sent.

Labor camps existed in Czarist Russia and continued during the early Soviet era under Vladimir Lenin. However, the labor camp system was thoroughly reorganized and expanded in the 1930s, reaching its zenith in the period of Joseph Stalin's rule. Unlike labor camp system before and after it, people were imprisoned in the Gulag not just for what they had done, but also for who they were, in terms of class, religion, nationality, and race. The gulag was one of the means by which to implement Stalin's political purges, which "cleansed" the Soviet Union of real and imagined enemies.

The first gulag victims were hundreds of thousands of people caught in the collectivization campaigns in the early 1930s. After the Red Army's invasion of the Baltic States and Poland in 1939–1941, the secret police incarcerated potential resisters. When Adolf Hitler sent German armies into the Soviet Union in June 1941, people of German ancestry in eastern Europe were incarcerated as well. Following the German defeat at Stalingrad, the Red Army advanced west, capturing and imprisoning enemy soldiers. Stalin also incarcerated partisan groups from all over eastern Europe.

Table 1   Administrators of the Gulag System

Name	Years
Fyodor Ivanovich Eichmans	April 25, 1930–June 16, 1930
Lazar Iosifovich Kogan	June 16, 1930–June 9, 1932
Matvei Davidovich Berman	June 9, 1932–August 16, 1937
Izrail Israelevich Pliner	August 16, 1937–November 16, 1938
Gleb Vasilievich Filaretov	November 16, 1938–February 18, 1939
Vasili Vasilievich Chernyshev	February 18, 1939–February 26, 1941
Victor Grigorievich Nasedkin	February 26, 1941–September 2, 1947
Georgy Prokopievich Dobrynin	September 2, 1947–January 31, 1951
Ivan Ilyich Dolgich	January 31, 1951–October 5, 1954
Sergei Yegorovich Yegorov	October 5, 1954–April 4, 1956
Pavel Nikolaevich Bakin	April 4, 1956–May 6, 1958
Mikhail Nikolaevich Kholodkov	May 6, 1958–June 13, 1960

Following World War II, the Allies agreed that all Russian citizens should be returned to the Soviet Union. This naturally included Soviet POWs held by the Germans. The Western Allies also forced anti-Soviet émigrés, many of whom had fought with Hitler, to return to the Soviet Union. The vast majority of these were either shot or simply disappeared into a gulag. In March 1946, the Soviet secret police began incarcerating ethnic minorities, Soviet Jews, and youth groups for allegedly "anti-Stalinist" conspiracies, as well as people who were viewed as a hindrance to Sovietization campaigns in Eastern Europe.

The "juridical" process for sentencing people to a gulag comprised a three-person panel, which could both try and sentence the accused, or simply rely on Article 58 of the Soviet Criminal Code. Article 58 deprived Soviet citizens suspected of "illegal" activity of any rights and permitted the authorities to send anyone to the camps for any reason, justified or not. The Gulag served as an institution to punish people, but also was meant to fulfill an economic function, for Stalin sought to deploy workers in remote parts of Russia in brutal climates but with rich natural resources.

In the early 1950s, Gulag authorities issued reports revealing that the camp system was unprofitable. Stalin, however, commanded further construction projects such as railways, canals, power stations, and tunnels. Thus, thousands of prisoners died and maintenance costs skyrocketed. To an extent, the situation changed in the gulags after the war because the inmates had changed. These "new politicals" were well-organized and experienced fighters who often banded together and dominated the camps. Slowly, authorities lost control.

Immediately following Stalin's death in March 1953, Lavrenty Beria briefly took charge, reorganized the gulags, and abandoned most of Stalin's construction projects. He granted amnesty to all prisoners sentenced to five years or less, pregnant women, and women with children under 18. He also secretly abolished the use of physical force against detainees. In June 1953, he announced his decision to liquidate the gulags altogether. However, Beria was subsequently arrested and executed. The new Soviet leadership under Nikita Khrushchev reversed most of Beria's reforms, although it did not revoke the amnesties.

Because neither Beria nor Khrushchev rehabilitated the political prisoners, they began to fight back with their new and well-organized groups. They killed informers, staged strikes, and fomented rebellions. The biggest of these occurred in Steplag, Kazakhstan, and lasted from spring until late summer 1954. Inmates seized control, but Soviet authorities brutally quashed the revolt. In the aftermath of the Steplag rebellion, the secret police relaxed gulag regulations, implemented an eight-hour day, and gradually began to re-examine individual cases. This process was accelerated by Khrushchev's condemnation of Stalin's rule in February 1956. In the so-called Thaw Era, the gulags were officially dissolved, and the two biggest camp complexes in Norilsk and Dalstroi were dismantled. Despite the Thaw, certain "politicals" were still incarcerated.

Under Leonid Brezhnev, "politicals" were renamed "dissidents." In the wake of the Hungarian Revolution in October 1956, the KGB used two camps in Moldova and Perm to incarcerate dissidents. In contrast to former prisoners, these detainees consciously criticized the government and purposely invited incarceration to gain the attention of Western media. By 1966, Brezhnev, and later Yuri Andropov, then chairman of the KGB, declared these dissidents insane and imprisoned them in psychiatric hospitals. When Mikhail Gorbachev took power in 1985 and embarked on reform, perestroika brought a final end to the gulags in 1987, and glasnost allowed limited access to information about their history.

It is impossible to determine just how many people were imprisoned and how many died in the gulags. Conservative estimates hold that 28.7 million forced laborers passed through the Gulag system, although there were never more than 2.6 million people at a time in the system.

Frank Beyersdorf

See also: Beria, Lavrenty; Berman, Matvei; Eichmans, Fyodor; Kogan, Lazar; NKVD; Sandarmokh; Serpantinka; Sevvostlag; Solovki Special Camp; Solzhenitsyn, Aleksandr; Stalin, Joseph; Vorkuta Camps.

Further Reading

Applebaum, Anne. *Gulag: A History*. New York: Doubleday, 2003.

Ivanova, Galina Mikhailovna, with Donald J. Raleigh. *Labor Camp Socialism: The Gulag in the Soviet Totalitarian System*. Translated from the Russian by Carol Fath. Armonk, NY: M. E. Sharpe, 2000.

Khevniuk, Oleg. *History of the Gulag*. New Haven, CT: Yale University Press, 2003.

Solzhenitsyn, Aleksandr. *The Gulag Archipelago, 1918–1956: An Experiment in Literary Investigation*. 3 vols. New York: Harper and Row, 1974–1978.

H

"Hanoi Hilton." *See Hoa Lo Prison*

Hay Internment Camp. *See Australia*

Heim, Aribert (1914–1992)

Austrian-born Nazi physician whose bizarre and cruel medical experiments on concentration camp internees earned him the sobriquet "Dr. Death." Aribert Heim was born on June 28, 1914, in Radkersburg, Austria. In 1935, he joined the Austrian Nazi Party, and three years later, after the German annexation of Austria, he became a member of the SS. In 1940 he became a member of the Waffen-SS, and in October 1941 was appointed chief doctor at the Mauthausen concentration camp, where he began to engage in outrageous and highly unethical experiments on internees.

Heim's experiments included injecting various substances—including gasoline, phenol, various poisons, and water—directly into prisoners' hearts to see which substance resulted in the quickest death. Others included chemical and surgical castration, performing surgical procedures without anesthesia, removing organs from healthy individuals and leaving them to die in the operating room, and crude attempts at amputation and the reattachment of limbs. Soon camp prisoners began referring to Heim as "Dr. Death."

In February 1942, Heim was transferred to Finland, where he worked for a time in local hospitals. Exactly what he did after that, until the end of the war, is not entirely clear, although he might have been a camp doctor at Buchenwald and Sachsenhausen. On March 15, 1945, he was taken captive by U.S. troops and sent to a prisoner-of-war camp. Unaware at the time of his past activities, occupation authorities released him later that year, and he resumed a medical practice in Baden-Baden, Germany. In 1962, Heim disappeared after being tipped off that he was about to be arrested for war crimes. He eventually settled in Cairo, Egypt, where he allegedly converted to Islam and assumed the name Tarek Hussein Farid. Meanwhile, he became the Simon Weisenthal Center's most-wanted Nazi-at-large. Over the years, there were reports of him being in South America and Europe, but for much of the time he was actually in Egypt.

Heim remained in written communication with family and friends and regularly received money from a sister in Austria. Finally, in 2009, it was determined by several different sources that Heim had died of cancer on August 10, 1992, in Egypt. This information was corroborated by Heim's son, Rudiger, who agreed to be interviewed about his father's whereabouts. Heim's son had been with his father at the time of his death.

Paul G. Pierpaoli, Jr.

See also: Germany; Medical Experimentation during World War II; Mengele, Josef; Oberheuser, Herta; Unit 731.

Further Reading

Lifton, Robert Jay. *The Nazi Doctors: Medical Killing and the Psychology of Genocide.* New York: Basic Books, 2000.

Proctor, Robert. *Racial Hygiene: Medicine under the Nazis.* Cambridge, MA: Harvard University Press, 1988.

Herero Genocide, Concentration Camps and

In December 1904, the German government in Berlin rescinded Lieutenant-General Lothar von Trotha's infamous Extermination Order, which approved on the spot executions of Herero men found inside the German occupied regions in South West Africa. Instead, the government-issued orders for the installation of a network of strategically placed concentration camps in the colony.

The concept of concentration camps was invariably borrowed from South Africa, where British commander-in-chief, Lord Kitchener, had ordered the internment of thousands of Boer women and children, as well as several thousand Africans, in confined camps. In Britain, the Liberal members of Parliament, C. P. Scott and John Ellis, described these as "concentration camps", a term adopted by the German authorities who called them *Konzentrationslager.*

On January 16, 1905, von Trotha ordered the construction of secure camps at military installations in the towns of Windhoek, Okahandja, Karibib, Swakopmund, and Omaruru. Further camps were later added in Luderitz and Keetmanshoop. The concentration camps were typically fenced in by a thick layer of felled thorn-bush trees, or by barbed wire, and patrolled by armed guards from the neighboring fort or garrison. The conditions were exceedingly poor. The food, for example, consisted mostly of rice or flour, which was often rendered useless by a lack of cooking utensils. In missionary correspondence, rice was repeatedly highlighted as a cause of disease in the camps.

The provision of labor was one of the key functions of the concentration camps and as such, the camps fell under the *Etappenkommando,* the supply command of the Rear command. An ordinance passed in June 1905 allowed for the daily, weekly, or monthly rental of prisoners from the military, and individual settlers as well as local businesses, such as the Woermann Company, made ample use of the scheme.

In November 1905, von Trotha departed the colony. Taking over the civilian administration was Governor Friedrich von Lindequist. Having previously served as Deputy Governor in South West Africa, von Lindequist was known by the settlers as a hardliner on the so-called native question. Lindequist was responsible for a further escalating of the concentration camps policy. In partnership with the Rhennish and Catholic missions, Lindequist's collection campaign resulted in the eventual internment of more 12,000 Hereros who had survived von Trotha's campaigns by hiding out in the bush.

At least 70 percent of all prisoners of the concentration camps were women and children who were subjected to the same inhumane conditions as the men, including hard physical labor. Sexual and physical abuse was not uncommon. It is estimated that more than 30,000 Namibians were in the camps, and that close to 70 percent of these people died as a result. The German colonial government was at all times aware of the situation, yet no significant measures were taken at any level to curb the high death rates.

The camps were gradually dismantled between the end of 1907 and mid-1908. The first camp to be closed down permanently was the Shark Island camp in Luderitz, which was unilaterally closed by the new commander of the colonial army in South West Africa, Major Ludwig von Estorff. The last camps were closed by April 1908, when construction on the Keetmanshoop railway line was all but complete.

Casper W. Erichsen

See also: Germany; Okahandja; Shark Island; Swakopmund; Windhoek.

Further Reading

Drechsler, Horst. *"Let Us Die Fighting": The Struggle of the Herero and Nama against German Imperialism (1844–1915).* Berlin: Academie-Verlag, 1996.

Olusoga, David, and Casper W. Erichsen. *The Kaiser's Holocaust: Germany's Forgotten Genocide and the Colonial Roots of Nazism.* London: Faber and Faber, 2010.

Hitler, Adolf (1889–1945)

Supreme leader of the National Socialist German Workers' Party (Nationalsozialistische Deutsche Arbeiterpartei) (NSDAP), also called the Nazi Party. Born in Braunau am Inn, Austria, Hitler had a troubled childhood and saw his aspiration to become an artist dashed in Vienna. It was during this time that Hitler developed his animosity toward Jews, as well to internationalism, capitalism, and socialism. He developed an intense sense of nationalism and expressed pride in being of German descent. He served with distinction in the German army during World War I, suffered from a British gas attack, and earned the Iron Cross First Class for bravery.

After the war, Hitler tapped the growing sense of frustration and disillusionment in Germany to guide the Nazi Party to political prominence and then into power. He was appointed chancellor of Germany in 1933. By 1934, Hitler had consolidated his power to emerge as the dictator of Germany and held virtually absolute power. His ideology and policies made Germany a racially based political state, where only those people considered to be of Aryan biological stock enjoyed the legal status of citizenship. He also pushed Germany into a large-scale and state-sponsored rearmament program, which helped renew Germany's economy and eliminated unemployment.

Eventually, Hitler's grandiose plans influenced him to aggressively threaten and annex neighboring European nations, including Austria, Czechoslovakia, and Poland, which, in turn, commenced World War II in 1939. Hitler briefly conquered most of Europe during the period from 1939 to 1941, and played an instrumental role in the development of the German internment system that was designed to isolate political, social, ethnic, and religious "undesirables." Hitler's policy of lebensraum called for deporting the population of occupied eastern Europe and the Soviet Union to West Siberia, for use as slave labor or to be murdered.

Starting in 1939, Hitler's virulent anti-Semitism sustained German government's sustained effort to exterminate European Jews. Supervised by Heinrich Himmler and administered by Adolf Eichmann, the policy saw development of a vast network of concentration and death camps that resulted in the murder of over 6 million Jews, as well millions of other individuals (Romanis, Poles, Soviet citizens and POWs, political opponents, Jehovah's Witnesses, gays and lesbians). In 1941, Hitler ordered the invasion of the Soviet Union, a decision he soon came to regret. Despite early successes, the German army suffered catastrophic defeats and was forced to retreat back into Germany. By late April 1945, Berlin fell and Hitler committed suicide to elude capture by the Soviet troops.

Alexander Mikaberidze

See also: Arbeitslager; Auschwitz; Bełżec; Bergen-Belsen; Birkenau; Buchenwald; Bullet Decree (1944); Chełmno; Colditz; Concentration Camps; Dachau; Death Camps; Dora-Mittelbau; Eichmann, Adolf; Extermination Centers; Gas Chambers; Gestapo; Gross-Rosen; Holocaust, The; I.G. Farben Case (1947); J.A. Topf & Söhne; Kinderblock 66; Koch Trial (1951); Kramer, Josef; Krupp Case (1948); Lamsdorf; Mauthausen-Gusen; Medical Experimentation during World War II; Monowitz; Natzweiler-Struthof; Neuengamme; Niederhagen; Nuremberg Trials; Ravensbrück; Sachsenhausen; Slave Labor (World War II); Sobibór; Sonderkommando; Stalag; Stutthof; Treblinka; Trostinets; Zyklon B Case (1946).

Further Reading

Fritz, Stephen G. *Ostkrieg: Hitler's War of Extermination in the East.* Lexington: University Press of Kentucky, 2015.

Gordon, Sarah. *Hitler, Germans, and the Jewish Question.* Princeton, NJ: Princeton University Press, 1988.

Hitler, Adolf. *Mein Kampf.* New York: Houghton Mifflin, 1998.

Kershaw, Ian. *Hitler.* 2 vols. New York: W. W. Norton. 1999–2000.

Shirer, William L. *The Rise and Fall of the Third Reich.* New York: Fawcett Crest, 1960.

Ullrich, Volker. *Hitler: Ascent, 1889–1939.* New York: Vintage, 2017.

Hoa Lo Prison (Hanoi Hilton)

The best-known and most notorious of the camps or prisons housing American prisoners of war in the Hanoi area during the Vietnam War. Hoa Lo Prison, dubbed the "Hanoi Hilton" by Robert H. Shumaker, the second U.S. POW there, was a large fortress covering a city block in the heart of Hanoi. Built by the French in 1886, its original name was Prison Centrale; later it was known as the Maison Centrale. Hoa Lo means "fiery furnace" or "fiery crucible," taken from the location of the prison on Hoa Lo Street, where earthen coal stoves were once made and sold. Some called the prison "the Devil's Island of Southeast Asia."

Hoa Lo's 4-foot-thick walls were 20 feet high, but electrified barbed wire extended them an additional 5 feet. The prison was a series of beige, stucco-walled cell blocks and administration buildings. It had glass-embedded walls and red-tiled roofs. Some POWs said it reminded them of the description of the Bastille in Charles Dickens's *A Tale of Two Cities.*

North Vietnamese guards talk to American prisoners of war at the infamous "Hanoi Hilton" during the Vietnam War. The prison, officially known as Hoa Lo, was built by the French at the turn of the twentieth century when Vietnam was still part of French Indochina. (Bettmann/Getty Images)

Formerly a place of incarceration for high-ranking Vietnamese government officials, the Hanoi Hilton was one of a number of prisons located in or near Hanoi, including those known as the Zoo, Alcatraz, the Briarpatch, and Camp Hope (Son Tay). Some 700 American POWs were housed in these camps between August 1964 and February 1973, when Operation HOMECOMING began their release. There are no exact U.S. figures on the total number of POWs who were held in the Hanoi Hilton, but it is estimated that by late 1970, as many as 360 prisoners were housed in "Camp Unity," one of its cellblocks.

This prison of concrete and mortar was a forbidding structure. A dry moat around the prison separated its tall walls. The prison itself was divided into sections, and each of these cell blocks was further divided. The prisoners gave each cell block different names, such as New Guy Village, Heartbreak Hotel, Little Vegas, and Camp Unity. Almost all new prisoners were housed temporarily in New Guy Village.

Sanitation was poor, and the cells were infested with insects and rodents. Much of the food was inedible, and medical treatment was poor to nonexistent. Torture and isolation were commonplace. Benjamin Schemmer, a POW, recalls that prisoners "were crowded 40 to 60 men in each room, some of them only 22 by 45 or 60 feet long."

Most of our knowledge of Hoa Lo Prison and other POW camps comes from prisoner debriefings and numerous published personal accounts. These are testimonials of faith and courage. Robert Reissner, shot down on September 16, 1965, stated, "I guess if there was any one thing that happened to many of us in prison, it was that we were no longer embarrassed talking about God or religion. We gained a lot of faith not only from private prayers but also from sharing our feelings about God with each other."

The North Vietnamese constantly used various means to break captives psychologically, mostly to gain confessions or information for propaganda purposes. Prisoners were isolated and prohibited from communicating, and were tortured in specially-designed interrogation rooms. Other deprivations included beatings, extended darkness, shacklings, and not being permitted to bathe. Despite deplorable conditions and inhumane treatment, prisoners managed to maintain communication with each other and to get news from the outside. The prisoners organized, held regular church services, taught each other foreign languages and math, and reenacted their favorite movies. At one time, Hoa Lo held such notable POWs as Jeremiah A. Denton, Jr., John S. McCain, III, and James B. Stockdale. Some prisoners had been held there since as early as 1967.

Two factors contributed to the increase in the POW population at Hoa Lo. A November 21, 1970, attempt to rescue POWs at Son Tay camp caused the North Vietnamese to move more than 200 American aircrew members there. And in 1972, as bombing raids of Hanoi continued, the North Vietnamese rounded up POWs from camps scattered throughout the North and moved them to downtown Hanoi. The prison was poorly equipped to handle the increasing number of American prisoners, however.

Even before the Son Tay Raid and the bombing of Hanoi, conditions at the Hanoi Hilton improved. Some attribute this to a letter-writing campaign by Americans demanding more humane treatment of the prisoners. Others attribute the change to the death of Ho Chi Minh in September 1969, or to propaganda statements by North Vietnamese that backfired. Whatever the reasons, torture sessions to gain military information abated, and prisoners were even allowed to write and receive letters. Captives were given new clothes, allowed to exercise and bathe regularly, and were given much-needed medical treatment and food.

With the signing of the Paris peace accords on January 23, 1973, the release of the POWs began. The first 116 of the 566 American prisoners of war released landed at Clark Air Force Base in the Philippines on February 12, 1973. The first man off the plane was Navy Captain Jeremiah Denton, who, after seven and a half years in captivity, saluted the American flag.

In 1997, a Singapore company began turning most of what had been the Hanoi Hilton into a block of luxury apartments and stores.

Gary Kerley and Spencer C. Tucker

See also: Vietnam War.

Further Reading

Gargus, John. *The Son Tay Raid: American POWs in Vietnam Were Not Forgotten.* College Station: Texas A&M University Press, 2007.

Risner, Robinson. *The Passing of the Night: My Seven Years as a Prisoner of the North Vietnamese.* New York: Random House, 1973.

Routledge, Howard, and Phyllis Routledge. *In the Presence of Mine Enemies, 1965–1973: A Prisoner at War.* London: Collins, 1974.

Rowan, Stephen A. *They Wouldn't Let Us Die: The Prisoners of War Tell Their Story.* Middle Village, NY: Jonathan David, 1973.

Schemmer, Benjamin F. *The Raid.* New York: Harper & Row, 1976.

Hoess, Rudolf (1900–1947)

Commandant of the Auschwitz concentration camp from 1940 to 1943. Born on November 25, 1900, in Baden-Baden, Germany, Hoess grew up in a strict Roman Catholic household, and his family wanted him to train for the priesthood. During World War I, he was eager to join the army, but instead joined the Red Cross in 1916, since he was too young to volunteer to fight. He quickly tired of this and lied about his age so he could join the army. He was posted to the Middle Eastern Front and served in Turkey and Palestine. Hoess was wounded twice and was awarded the Iron Cross and other decorations. After the war, he visited the Holy Land, where his faith was shaken by the traffic in holy relics.

Hoess returned to Germany and, as with many of his contemporaries, had no idea of what to do with his life. Like many young veterans, he joined a Freikorps group and found himself fighting Poles and Lithuanians in the Baltic lands. Hoess was completely at home in the right wing militaristic milieu in which the Freikorps operated. He was rabidly conservative, racist, and extremely nationalistic. He joined the National Socialist German Workers' Party—the Nazis—in 1922 and plunged into street fighting against communists and "traitors." In June 1923, he was arrested for beating a man to death for turning a "patriot" over to the French for crimes committed during the Ruhr occupation. He was sentenced to prison for 10 years and remained in prison until July 1928.

Hoess married Hedwig Hensel in 1929, and ultimately had five children (they later lived at Auschwitz with him). He emerged from prison a hero to right wing nationalists, but retired to private life and turned away from active politics until Heinrich Himmler asked him to join the SS in 1934, and Hoess's life changed forever when he agreed.

Hoess's first job in the SS was as a noncommissioned officer among the guards at Dachau concentration camp. He was a model guard and worked his way up the ranks. In August 1938, he was transferred to the concentration camp at Sachsenhausen, and was made commandant in December 1939. Hoess paid such close attention to detail and was capable of such concentrated work that when Himmler decided to create a new camp at Auschwitz, Poland, in April 1940, he appointed Hoess as its first commandant.

There were already a few shabby buildings at the site when he arrived, but Hoess built Auschwitz into a large, efficient killing machine. In October 1941, he cleared a huge area around Auschwitz and built a second camp, Auschwitz II, called Birkenau, which became Auschwitz's killing center. Hoess built a third camp, Auschwitz III, or Monowitz, in May 1942 to provide slave labor for German chemical firm I.G. Farben's synthetic rubber works. By 1943, Auschwitz was an enormous complex that at its height housed about 100,000 prisoners. It is estimated that 2.5 million people died in Auschwitz—mostly Jews, but also Romanis, Russian prisoners of war, and many other nationalities and ethnic groups.

Hoess was intimately involved in selecting the best methods for killing large numbers of people. He participated in experiments in which a truck's exhaust fumes were piped back into a sealed cabin to asphyxiate those trapped inside. When it was decided that trucks took too long to kill large numbers of people, Hoess helped with the implementation of the gas chambers. Ultimately, he found a fumigation poison, Zyklon B, which could kill faster and more thoroughly than exhaust fumes. Hoess was efficient at administrative details and keeping to a strict schedule. This clerk-like adherence to routinely horrific matters ingratiated him with Himmler, who also had the mentality of a clerk.

In December 1943, Hoess was rewarded for his work at Auschwitz with a promotion to chief inspector of all concentration camps. He traveled all over Germany inspecting and improving the function of the Nazi camps, whether death or slave labor camps. As the German armies retreated across Europe, he then began to arrange for the dismantling of some of the camps.

When Germany surrendered in May 1945, Hoess knew he was a wanted man and went into hiding. The Allies actively looked for him, and in March 1946, he was discovered and arrested. He was a witness at the trial of the major war criminals at Nuremberg, and then was turned over to the Polish government, who demanded his extradition. He was tried for murder and various war crimes and was found guilty. Hoess never denied what he did, but—like most Nazis on trial—claimed simply to have been following orders and was therefore blameless. He was taken to Auschwitz, the scene of so many of his crimes, and hanged on April 15, 1947.

Lee Baker

See also: Auschwitz; Germany; Nuremberg Trials; Zyklon B Case (1946).

Further Reading

Fest, Joachim C. *The Face of the Third Reich: Portraits of the Nazi Leadership.* New York: Pantheon Books, 1970.

Harding, Thomas. *Hans and Rudolf: The True Story of the German Jew Who Tracked Down and Caught the Commandant of Auschwitz.* New York: Simon and Schuster, 2013.

Hoess, Rudolf. *Commandant of Auschwitz: The Autobiography of Rudolf Hoess.* London: Weidenfeld and Nicolson, 1959.

Holocaust, The

The Holocaust is the term in English most closely identified with the attempt by Germany's National Socialist regime, together with its European allies, to exterminate the Jews of Europe during the period of World War II—particularly during its most destructive phase between 1941 and 1944. While an exact number of those murdered is impossible to determine, the best estimates settle at a figure around 6 million Jews, 1 million of whom were children under the age of 12 and half a million of whom were aged between 12 and 18.

While the term "Holocaust" has entered common parlance to describe the event, two other terms are also employed, particularly within the Jewish world. The Hebrew word *Churban*, or "catastrophe," which historically has been employed to describe the destruction of the two temples in Jerusalem, is one of these; the other, utilized increasingly by Jews, is the Hebrew term *Shoah* ("calamity," or, sometimes, "destruction").

The first step on the road to the Holocaust can be said to have taken place on the night of February 27, 1933, when the Reichstag building in Berlin, the home of the German parliament, was burned in a fire. The day after the fire, on the pretext that it had been set by communists, and that a left wing revolution was imminent, newly appointed chancellor Adolf Hitler persuaded President Paul von Hindenburg to sign a Decree for the Protection of the People and the State, suspending all the basic civil and individual liberties guaranteed under the constitution. It empowered the government to take such steps as were necessary to ensure that the current threat to German society was removed. In a mass crackdown, hundreds were detained in the first few days, and tens of thousands in succeeding weeks.

Then, on March 20, 1933, Reichsführer-SS Heinrich Himmler announced the establishment of the first compound for political prisoners, about 15 kilometers northwest of Munich, on the outskirts of the town of Dachau. Other camps soon followed, among them Oranienburg, Papenburg, Esterwegen, Kemna, Lichtenburg, and Borgermoor. These camps were originally places of political imprisonment. In their most basic sense, they removed political opposition from the midst of the community and intimidated the population into accepting the Nazi regime.

Jews had often previously been arrested for transgressing within the framework of the existing political classifications, but from 1935 onward they were frequently being victimized for their Jewishness alone. This was due largely to the effects of the so-called Nuremberg Laws on Citizenship and Race. According to these laws, the formal status of Jews in the Nazi state was defined and put into practice. Jewish businesses were boycotted, Jewish doctors excluded from public hospitals and only permitted to practice on other Jews, Jewish judicial figures were dismissed and disbarred, and Jewish students were expelled from universities. Jews were increasingly excluded from participation in all forms of German life. The Nuremberg Laws also withdrew from Jews the privilege of German citizenship. It became illegal for a Jew and a non-Jew to marry or engage in sexual relationships. Life was to be made so intolerable for Jews that they would seek to emigrate; those who did not often found themselves arbitrarily arrested and sent to concentration camps. These arrests did not become widespread until 1938, and in most cases the victims were only held for a short time. The emphasis was to terrorize them into leaving the country.

The first large-scale arrests of Jews were made after November 9, 1938, as "reprisals" for the assassination of consular official Ernst vom Rath by Jewish student Herschel Grynszpan in Paris. The event precipitating these arrests has gone down in history as Kristallnacht, the "Night of Broken Glass." The resultant pogrom was thus portrayed as a righteous and spontaneous outpouring of anger by ordinary German people against all Jews, even though for the most part it was Nazis in plain clothes who whipped up most of the action in the streets. The pogrom resulted in greater concentrated destruction than any previous anti-Jewish measure under the Nazis, and spelled out to those Jews who had up to now thought the regime was a passing phenomenon that this was not the case.

Henceforth, Jews were targeted for the sole reason of their Jewishness. Prior to the Kristallnacht, Nazi persecution of Jews was not premised on acts of wanton destruction or murder; the November pogrom, however, had the effect of transforming earlier legislative measures against Jews into physical harassment on a broader and more indiscriminate scale. From now on, physical acts of an anti-Semitic nature became state policy. At the same time that Germany's Jews began frantically seeking havens to which they could emigrate in order to save their lives, however, the Western world began to close its doors to Jewish immigration. And, with Hitler's foreign policy appetite growing and new areas becoming annexed to the Third Reich, the number of Jews coming under Nazi control increased to less manageable proportions.

The outbreak of war on September 1, 1939, saw the establishment of a system of ghettos in occupied Poland from October 1939 onward, in order to confine Poland's Jewish population. Here, they were persecuted and terrorized, starved, and deprived of all medical care. From the summer of 1942 onward, the ghettos began to be liquidated, with the Jews sent to one of six death camps located throughout Poland.

Prior to this, mobile killing squads known as Einsatzgruppen ("Special Action Groups"), accompanying the German military during the Nazi assault on the Soviet Union beginning in June 1941, had been at work murdering all Jews found within their areas of domination and control. The initial means by which they operated was to round up their captive Jewish populations—men, women, and children—take them outside of village and town areas, forcing the victims themselves to dig their own mass graves, and then shooting them to death. When the repetition of that activity proved psychologically troublesome, mobile gas vans using carbon monoxide poisoning were brought in both to remove the intimacy of contact and sanitize the process. While technologically at times quite inefficient, from an economic perspective it was cost-effective regarding the use of both men and material.

It is estimated that between 1941 and 1943, the Einsatzgruppen were responsible for the death of more than 1 million Jews. It is not known precisely when the decision to exterminate the Jews of Europe was made, though best estimates settle on sometime in the early fall of 1941. At a conference held at Wannsee, Berlin, on January 20, 1942, the process was systematized and coordinated among Nazi Germany's relevant government departments, and in the months following a number of camps were established in Poland by the Nazis for the express purpose of killing large numbers of Jews. These six camps—Auschwitz-Birkenau, Bełżec, Chełmno, Majdanek, Sobibór, and Treblinka—were a departure from anything previously visualized, in both their design and character. With the exception only of Auschwitz, these camps were different from all others in that they did not perform any of the functions—political, industrial, agricultural, or penal—attributed to those farther west or north. These were the Vernichtungslager, the death (or extermination) camps.

The death camps were institutions designed to methodically and efficiently murder millions of people, specifically Jews. These mass murders took place in specially designed gas chambers, employing either carbon monoxide from diesel engines (either in fixed installations or from mobile vans), or crystallized hydrogen cyanide (known as Zyklon B), which on contact with air oxidized to become hydrocyanic (or prussic) acid gas.

As the Nazi armies on the Eastern Front began to retreat before the advancing Soviet forces (and later from American and British troops in the west), renewed efforts were made at annihilating Jews while there was still time. Then, in March 1944, a shock of cataclysmic proportions fell upon the Jews of Hungary, the last great center of Jewish population still untouched by the Holocaust. Some 400,000 Jews were murdered in the space of four months, with the killing facilities working nonstop, day and night. This was the fastest killing operation of any of the Nazi campaigns against Jewish populations in occupied Europe.

When viewing this campaign and the means employed to attain it, one reservation must be made: Bełżec, Treblinka, Sobibór, and Chełmno had by this time already been evacuated. Only Auschwitz remained to carry out the massive undertaking during the spring of 1944, as April had already seen the start of the evacuation of Majdanek. With the Soviet armies continuing their advance toward Germany throughout the latter half of 1944, the position of Auschwitz itself seemed uncertain, and the complete evacuation of the complex was ordered for January 17, 1945. The earliest date of free contact with Soviet forces was January 22, 1945; when the site was formally occupied two days later, there were only 2,819 survivors left.

Any prisoners still alive in the eastern camps at the end of the war were evacuated by the Nazis so as not to fall into the hands of the advancing Russians. These evacuations have properly been called death marches, as vast numbers of prisoners died or were killed while en route. Evidence that the Nazis tried to keep their prisoners alive is scant; any prisoners who did not make it to their final destination were treated with the same contempt as they would have been had they remained in the camp. Evacuated in the winter and early spring of 1944–1945, they had to contend with bitter cold, fatigue, hunger, and the SS guards, as well as their own debilitated condition, and for those who had already reached the limit of their endurance the death marches could have only one result. For others, the experience represented yet another challenge which had to be overcome. Often, the Russians were so close while the prisoners were marching away that the sounds of battle could be clearly distinguished, further adding to their distress. When they arrived at their new destination, their trials were hardly eased, as they faced massive overcrowding in the camps to which they had been evacuated.

The prisoners, dropped into places like Bergen-Belsen to await liberation through death or an Allied victory, had little time to wait in real terms, though each day dragged by unendingly. Painfully slowly, as German units both west and east surrendered, the camps were liberated. On April 12, 1945, Westerbork was set free. The day before, Buchenwald's inmates rebelled against their SS guards and took over the camp, handing it to the Americans on April 13. Belsen was liberated by the British Army on April 15, and on April 23 the SS transferred Mauthausen to the International Committee of the Red Cross. The next day, Dachau was overrun by the U.S. Army. Five days later, on April 29, Ravensbrück was liberated. Theresienstadt was handed over to the Red Cross by the Nazis on May 2, and on May 8 American troops occupied Mauthausen—the last major camp to be liberated in the west.

Paul R. Bartrop

See also: Arbeitslager; Auschwitz; Bełżec; Bergen-Belsen; Birkenau; Buchenwald; Bullet Decree (1944); Chełmno; Colditz; Concentration Camps; Dachau; Death Camps; Dora-Mittelbau; Eichmann, Adolf; Extermination Centers; Gas Chambers; Gestapo; Gross-Rosen; Hitler, Adolf; I.G. Farben Case (1947); J.A. Topf & Söhne; Kinderblock 66; Koch Trial (1951); Kramer, Josef; Krupp Case (1948); Lamsdorf; Mauthausen-Gusen; Medical Experimentation during World War II; Monowitz; Natzweiler-Struthof; Neuengamme; Niederhagen; Nuremberg Trials; Ravensbrück; Sachsenhausen; Slave Labor (World War II); Sobibór; Sonderkommando; Stalag; Stutthof; Treblinka; Trostinets; Zyklon B Case (1946).

Further Reading

Arad, Yitzhak, Gutman, Yisrael, and Margaliot, Abraham, eds. *Documents on the Holocaust: Selected Sources on the Destruction of the Jews of Germany and Austria, Poland and the Soviet Union.* Lincoln: University of Nebraska Press, 2004.

Bauer, Yehuda. *A History of the Holocaust.* New York: Franklin Watts, 2001.

Gutman, Israel, ed. *Encyclopedia of the Holocaust.* 4 vols. New York: Macmillan, 1990.

Marrus, Michael R, ed. *The Nazi Holocaust: Historical Articles on the Destruction of European Jews.* 9 vols. Westport, CT: Meckler, 1989.

Holzminden

A German prisoner-of-war camp during World War I. Located near the town of Holzminden (in Lower Saxony), the camp opened in September 1917 to house the British prisoners of war. The German X Army Corps, under whose auspices the camp was established, converted cavalry barracks into two large prisoner compounds that were supervised by General Karl von Hänisch, a disciplinarian who maintained a strict regime at the camp. Overall, conditions at the camp were tolerable, but prisoners did suffer from lack of food due to the Allies economic blockade of Germany. On July 23–July 24, 1918, in what became the largest prisoner of war escape of World War I, 29 British officers escaped through a tunnel that they had been building for almost nine months; although over 80 officers planned to escape, the 30th escapee became stuck in a tunnel and prevented others from crawling through. Of the escaped prisoners, only 10 succeeded in evading German authorities and made their way to Britain via the Netherlands.

Holzminden was also a site of a large German internment camp (*internierungslager*) where some 10,000 civilian internees from Allied nations were held during World War I. The internment camp was far larger than the neighboring POW camp and comprised of some 120 huts surrounded by a perimeter fence and watchtowers. The detainees were mostly Polish, Russian, Serbian, Belgian, and French nationals.

Alexander Mikaberidze

See also: Germany; World War I Prisoners of War.

Further Reading

Cook, Jacqueline. "Holzminden Prisoner of War Camp and the Great Escape of 1918," *Journal of the World War One Historical Association,* 1/3 (2012): 27–34.

Durnford, Hugh. *The Tunnellers of Holzminden.* Cambridge: Cambridge University Press, 1920.

Farcy, Jean-Claude. *Les camps de concentration français de la première guerre mondiale (1914–1920)*. Paris: Anthropos, 1995.

Hanson, Neil. *Escape from Germany: The Greatest POW Break-out of the First World War.* London: Doubleday, 2011.

HOMECOMING, Operation (1973)

Return of U.S. prisoners of war (POWs) who had been held in Southeast Asia, an event that generated a homecoming never before seen during a POW repatriation effort. In August 1972, a final planning conference for Operation HOMECOMING occurred in Honolulu. A month later, the 9th Aeromedical Evacuation Group, heading the recovery operation, had a rehearsal opportunity when the Democratic Republic of Vietnam (DRV) released three POWs early.

On January 27, 1973, the "Agreement on Ending the War and Restoring Peace in Viet-Nam" (the Paris Agreement) called for both the release of U.S. POWs (591 men) and the simultaneous final reduction in active U.S. forces (24,000) within 60 days. The parties agreed to four stages, the first on February 12 and the last, which included nine Americans captured in Laos, ending on March 29 (one day late). The operation consisted of three phases. First, after initial reception at Saigon (for those imprisoned by the Viet Cong, the political arm of which was known as the Provisional Revolutionary Government of South Vietnam, or PRG), Hanoi (for those imprisoned by the DRV), and Hong Kong (for the three to be freed from China), all U.S. POWs would be flown to Clark Air Force Base in the Philippines. Second, at the Joint Homecoming Reception Center at Clark, the former POWs would go through processing, debriefing, and medical examinations. Third, those released could go to any of 31 U.S. military hospitals for recovery.

Of the 591 U.S. POWs returned, 566 were military personnel (497 officers, 69 enlisted) and 25 were civilians. Not only had some of these former POWs survived the longest captivity of any prisoners in U.S. military history, but many had become, from reports of their courage, the focus of widespread affection and respect. This important event gave many Americans, on a personal level, a successful final closure to the POW story, whose increasing publicity they had followed for so long.

On the other hand, Operation HOMECOMING also represented a major public relations event orchestrated by the White House and Pentagon. The POWs were among the few popularly recognized heroes of the war, and their release represented possibly the only positive result of negotiations in Paris. After elaborate receptions at each stop along their journey home, POWs arrived in the United States to a hero's welcome. Although President Richard M. Nixon proudly spoke of the return of "all" POWs, and Walter Cronkite, CBS news anchor, thought the United States was ending one of the most difficult periods in its history, the joy that Operation HOMECOMING generated for some still left the door ajar for questions by others. Had any men been left behind and when would there be an accounting of those missing in action? It would take many more years to answer these questions, and for some, the answers that were eventually provided never did satisfy completely.

Paul S. Daum, with assistance from *Joseph Ratner*

Further Reading

Berger, Carl, ed. *The United States Air Force in Southeast Asia, 1961–1973: An Illustrated Account.* Washington, DC: Office of Air Force History, 1984.

Franklin, H. Bruce. *M.I.A. or Mythmaking in America.* Brooklyn, NY: Lawrence Hill Books, 1992.

Gruner, Elliott. *Prisoners of Culture: Representing the Vietnam POW.* New Brunswick, NJ: Rutgers University Press, 1993.

Isaacs, Arnold R. *Without Honor: Defeat in Vietnam and Cambodia.* Baltimore, MD: Johns Hopkins University Press, 1983.

I

I.G. Farben Case (1947)

In *United States of America v. Carl Krauch, et al.* (May 3, 1947 to July 30, 1948), Military Tribunal VI tried 24 directors and managers of the chemical cartel, Interessengemeinschaft Farbenindustrie Aktiengesellschaft (Community of Interests, Dye Industry, Public Corporation). Accused were Krauch, Hermann Schmitz, Georg von Schnitzler, Fritz Gajewski, Heinrich Hőrlein, August von Knierem, Fritz ter Meer, Christian Schneider, Otto Ambros, Max Brűggemann, Ernst Bűrgin, Heinrich Bűtefisch, Paul Häfliger, Max Ilgner, Friedrich Jähne, Hans Kűhne, Carl Lautenschläger, Wilhelm Mann, Heinrich Oster, Karl Wurster, Walter Dűrrfeld, Heinrich Gattineau, Erich von der Heyde, and Hans Kugler. The indictment listed five counts: I) crimes against peace; II) war crimes and crimes against humanity (plunder and spoliation); III) war crimes and crimes against humanity (complicity in mass murder, illicit medical experiments, and slave labor); IV) membership in a criminal organization; and V) conspiracy. All defendants were charged with counts I, II, III, and V, but count IV applied only to Schneider, Bűtefisch, and von der Heyde. The case against Brűggemann was later suspended for health reasons.

Some I.G. Farben prosecutors, like deputy counsel Josiah E. DuBois, worked in the Treasury and Justice Departments of the Roosevelt Administration, which predisposed them to view I.G. as a trust to be busted or integral to German imperialism. Arguing that directors supplied Hitler the means necessary for war-making, DuBois contended that they harmonized their foreign business in league with Nazi espionage and propaganda. The defendants represented a menace to future peace, as had their predecessors at Fried[rich] Bayer AG and Badische Anilin und Sodafabrik (BASF), two of eight companies that formed I.G. Farbenindustrie in 1925.

Similarly to the Krupp Case, Tribunal VI acquitted all defendants on counts I and V. The court argued that Krauch was too far removed from Adolf Hitler's inner circle to be privy to his aggressive plans. Among all defendants, he had the closest connections to the Nazi leadership, serving from 1937 to 1945 as Plenipotentiary for Special Chemical Questions in Hermann Göring's Four-Year Plan Office, as well as top executive positions in I.G. These facts rendered all the more problematic the peace charges against the other accused.

The prosecution presented a stronger case regarding spoliation. After German conquest, I.G. Farben took over chemical firms in Austria, Czechoslovakia, Poland, Norway, and France, and examined properties in occupied Soviet territory. Attempting to rationalize the French dye industry, it exerted undue pressure upon French manufacturers, by proposing the revision of previous cartel arrangements before the German-dominated Armistice Commission at Wiesbaden. In November 1941, it obtained a 51 percent interest in the new Francolor cartel, transferring in exchange to three French companies (Kuhlmann, Saint-Denis, Saint-Clair) 1 percent of I.G.'s total stock, or about 13 million Reichsmark in 1941 terms, inalienable except among participants. The Tribunal excluded allegations concerning properties in Austria and the Sudetenland, since these takeovers had occurred before the war. Deeming voluntary certain transactions with companies in occupied territories, it agreed with a ruling in the Flick Case, that the Aryanization of Jewish property did not comprise a crime against humanity. On count II, it convicted Schmitz, von Schnitzer, ter Meer, Bürgin, Häfliger, Ilgner, Jähne, Oster, and Kugler.

The prosecution combined several charges under count III. These involved I.G.'s knowledgeable participation in the sale of poison gas for the purpose of mass murder, involuntary pharmaceutical experimentation on concentration camp inmates, and the deployment and maltreatment of forced and slave labor. Unlike the Zyklon B Case, Tribunal VI found little evidence to prove that the directors responsible for overseeing I.G.'s interest in Degesch (German Society for Pest Control), Mann, Wurster, and Hörlein, knew how the Nazi Schutzstaffel (SS) were using Zyklon B, despite receiving Degesch's sales reports. While the prosecution established that the SS physicians had forcibly injected camp detainees with anti-typhus and other I.G. drugs, the court determined that its executives summarily ended the tests upon suspicion of malfeasance.

Against Krauch, Ambros, Bütefisch, ter Meer, and Dürrfeld, the synthetic rubber and oil project called I.G. Auschwitz furnished damning evidence. While the prosecution contended that the nearby concentration camp determined the site's location, the Tribunal lukewarmly endorsed the defense claim that technical criteria (proximity of natural resources and layout) informed the decision, but concluded that availability of slave labor played a secondary role. Scholars still debate I.G.'s degree of culpability in the initiation of slave labor deployment. Founded in 1941 at government urging, I.G. Auschwitz fostered a lethal working environment for slave laborers, especially during the first two years. Conditions were still awful when British prisoners of war arrived in late 1943 (some of these POWs, like Charles Coward, subsequently gave moving testimony at Nuremberg). Determining that I.G. initiated the project, and that approximately 25,000 prisoners lost their lives in consequence, the Tribunal found the defense's claim of necessity unconvincing in this case.

The prosecution alleged that Bütefisch, Schneider, and von der Heyde were active members in the Nazi SS after September 1, 1939. In this connection Tribunal VI deemed insufficient the evidence against the first two, and ruled that von der Heyde ought to have been charged as a member of the illegal Sicherheitsdienst (Security Service), not the SS. The court acquitted ten defendants on all charges (Gajewski, Hörlein, von Knierem, Schneider, Kühne, Lautenschläger, Mann, and Wurster). It imposed terms of confinement ranging from one and a half to eight years upon the remainder, and reserved the lengthiest sentences for those connected with I.G. Auschwitz.

Joseph Robert White

See also: Germany; Hitler, Adolf; Holocaust, The; Nuremberg Trials; Zyklon B Case (1946).

Further Reading

Borkin, Joseph. *The Crime and Punishment of I.G. Farben.* New York: The Free Press, 1978.

Hayes, Peter. *Industry and Ideology: I.G. Farben in the Nazi Era.* Cambridge: Cambridge University Press, 2001.

United Nations War Crimes Commission. Law Reports of Trials of War Criminals. Vol. X. London: HMSO, 1949.

United States. *Nuremberg Military Tribunals. Trials of War Criminals before the Nuernberg Military Tribunals under Control Council Law No. 10.* Vols. VII & VIII. Washington, D.C.: GPO, 1950–1953.

White, Joseph Robert. "'Even in Auschwitz . . . Humanity Could Prevail': British POWs and Jewish Concentration-Camp Inmates at I.G. Auschwitz, 1943–1945." *Holocaust and Genocide Studies* 15:2 (Fall 2001): 266–295.

Indian Removal Act (1830)

Congressional legislation signed into law by President Andrew Jackson on May 26, 1830, that provided legal justification for the wholesale and forcible removal of Native Americans from the east to the west, principally Indian Territory (modern-day Oklahoma and parts of Kansas). The Indian Removal Act of 1830 was the culmination of a decades-long struggle between whites and Native Americans over who would control vast tracts of territory that had traditionally been Native American ancestral lands, for several centuries in some cases. The Act rendered most prior agreements and treaties between the U.S. government and Native American nations null and void, and set the stage for the government to negotiate new treaties with various tribes that would affect their removal to Indian Territory. Jackson believed that prior Indian treaties were an "absurdity" and that Native Americans were "subjects" of the United States who could not claim any rights to sovereignty, as a foreign nation could.

The Indian Removal Act was immediately aimed at the so-called five civilized tribes (Choctaw, Cherokee, Chickasaw, Creek, and Seminole), who had inhabited lands in the Southeast, ranging from parts of Alabama, Mississippi, Tennessee, Georgia, and Florida. Many southerners, principally wealthy planters, coveted the lands these tribes inhabited because they knew that they were prime agricultural lands, which could be planted with crops such as cotton, an extremely lucrative commodity in the early nineteenth century. Of course, the land would be worked with slave labor, making large-scale agricultural enterprises even more lucrative.

The first removal treaty was with the Choctaw (chiefly in Mississippi) and saw the movement of some 14,000 Choctaw to the Red River Valley. About 7,000, however, refused to leave and stayed behind. In the ensuing years, they came under greater and greater pressure from white encroachment. During 1838–1839, the U.S. Army used force to remove thousands of Cherokee to Indian Territory, precipitating the so-called Trail of Tears, during which Cherokees were held for weeks in miserable internment camps, most notably at Fort Cass, where many became ill and died. There were in fact numerous other trails of tears, as most of the affected tribes suffered similar fates. When the Seminole refused forcible removal, the U.S. Army sought to forcibly remove them in what became known as the Seminole Wars; the captured Seminoles were kept in internment camps, including one on Egmont Key island off the coastline of Tampa, before being forcibly relocated to the Indian Territory. The Indian Removal Act also affected tribes further north and west, including the Shawnee, Potawatomi, Sauk, and Fox, who were eventually removed to Indian Territory. The Black Hawk War of 1832 was largely a result of attempts to relocate Sauk and Fox, as well as the Kickapoo.

It is estimated that as many as 100,000 Native Americans were forced to move between 1830 and 1869. By the end, 37 Native American tribes were held in 25 reservations in Indian Territory, which functioned as a vast internment system. This mass relocation caused untold suffering. Perhaps as many as one-third of those forcibly removed died on the marches west, or died shortly after, because of disease, starvation, dehydration, or exposure. The removal permanently altered tribes' cultures, social constructs, and familial institutions. Some, like the Seneca, Navajo, Seminole, and Cherokee, were successful in resisting removal, partly or wholly. Some of these people remain today on part of their ancestral homelands. Other tribes who were removed to the west became the beneficiaries of new lands that had rich natural resources, such as minerals and oil. Those people and tribes who did relocate quickly established their own communities and began farming with considerable success. However, by the end of the nineteenth century, many were once more under pressure to cede land to whites in Indian Territory (Oklahoma), where oil attracted white speculators in droves.

Paul G. Pierpaoli, Jr.

See also: Apache Wars; Fort Cass; Seminole Wars; Trail of Tears (1838).

Further Reading

Cave, Alfred A. "Abuse of Power: Andrew Jackson and the Indian removal Act of 1830." *Historian* 65 (Winter 2003): 1130–1153.

Jahoda, Gloria. *The Trail of Tears.* New York: Holt, Rinehart & Winston, 1975.

Johansen, Bruce E. *Shapers of the Great Debate on Native Americans: Land, Spirit, Power.* Westport, CT: Greenwood Press, 2000.

Satz, Ronald. *American Indian Policy in the Jacksonian Era.* Lincoln: University of Nebraska Press, 1973.

Wallace, Anthony C. *The Long, Bitter Trail: Andrew Jackson and the Indians.* New York: Hill and Wang, 1993.

Internment of Japanese Americans

Following the December 7, 1941, Japanese attack on Pearl Harbor, the U.S. government relocated and detained anyone of Japanese ancestry (Nikkei) living on the West Coast of the United States. During the Japanese American internment, ordered under the pressure of wartime expediency, nearly 120,000 men, women, and children of Japanese descent were uprooted and exiled regardless of their citizenship status.

Despite anti-Asian racism prevalent on the West Coast at the time, by the 1930s, Japanese immigrants (Issei), had established thriving communities in all of the major coastal cities from San Diego to Seattle, as well as in the major agricultural areas of inland California, Oregon, and Washington. However, as tensions mounted in the Pacific between the United States and Japan prior to World War II, some in the U.S. government and military saw West Coast Nikkei as a potential security risk. They feared that the Nikkei might supply sensitive information to the Japanese government or sabotage military or industrial centers on the West Coast. In 1939, the Federal Bureau of Investigation (FBI) began compiling a "threat list" of prominent members of the Nikkei community. Meanwhile, the West Coast media fueled racial hostility with widespread characterizations of Nikkei as the "yellow peril."

Within 24 hours of the attack on Pearl Harbor, the FBI had taken Nikkei thought to pose the highest risk into custody for questioning; they were later transferred to Justice Department holding facilities. For months, their families had no knowledge of their location or even if they were still alive. Additionally, those not in custody were faced with frozen bank accounts, foreclosed loans, seized property, and an 8:00 P.M. curfew enforced by the military.

On February 19, 1942, President Franklin D. Roosevelt was persuaded by his advisers to sign Executive Order 9066, under which—without due process of law—all persons of Japanese descent on the West Coast were to be forcibly removed from their homes and sent to holding facilities located throughout the western United States. Though Nikkei in Hawaii were included under the order, they made up a significant portion of the territory's population, and agriculture in the state was dependent on Nikkei labor. As a result, Hawaii's military governor refused to enforce the internment order on constitutional grounds, though martial law was imposed and civil rights were restricted.

The government agency in charge of removing Nikkei from the West Coast was the War Relocation Authority (WRA). The internment took place in two phases: first, the Nikkei were transported to one of 18 quickly constructed assembly centers to be held until permanent facilities further inland were built; they were then transported to 1 of 10 new, permanent camps to be held for the remainder of the war with Japan. The assembly centers consisted of hastily converted fairgrounds and racetracks, and many families found themselves housed in horse stalls that had been made into living quarters. The permanent internment camps were built further inland under the direction of the U.S. Army. Like the assembly centers, the internment camps were surrounded by barbed wire fences and had armed guards at the gates and in the watchtowers. The barracks in the permanent camps were grouped together in blocks to serve as the physical and social focus for the interned Nikkei. Each block consisted of 14 barracks, lavatories and showers, a laundry room and ironing facility, one mess hall, and a recreation hall.

The WRA tried to develop "self-government" programs as a way to run the camps more efficiently and win the support of the interned Nikkei. In each camp, a council of Nikkei internees were to advise the camp administration and help implement government policies in the camps. However, the self-government programs never really worked; camp administrations were fearful of giving the councils too much authority, and internees felt the councils were another arm of a government that had imprisoned them and stripped them of their rights.

During the internment, many Nikkei fought to join the U.S. military; almost all of them felt that military service would be the best way to prove that they were loyal to America. In early 1942, Congress had designated all persons of Japanese descent, even American citizens, as "4C," or "aliens not subject for military service." After intense lobbying by the Japanese American Citizens League, Nikkei who were U.S. citizens were allowed to register for military service. Many Nisei—literally "second generation," Nikkei who were U.S. citizens by virtue of being born in the United States—promptly volunteered for service or registered for the draft. As the 442 Regimental Combat Team, internees were sent to Italy along with Hawaii's 100th Infantry Battalion, largely made up of Hawaiian-born Nikkei. The 442nd became one of the most decorated units in U.S. military history.

In 1943, the WRA began a series of programs designed to close the camps and relocate the Nikkei to areas in the East and Midwest. However, many of the Nikkei were fearful of leaving the camps, worrying that they would simply be turned out without any means of supporting themselves. Others feared that outside the camps, they would be attacked by anti-Japanese mobs. Also of concern was the fact that, once outside the camps, the Nikkei may not have the traditional support structure of the community available to them.

From 1943 to 1944, the WRA made the process of leaving the camps easier. By the end of May 1944, all that the Nikkei had to do was sign a statement saying that they were loyal to the United States and would register with the WRA field office wherever they resettled. By December 1945, only the Tule Lake camp remained open (it closed in 1946). Upon being released, each Nikkei family was given a government grant of $100 and several booklets of government-issued food coupons.

After leaving the camps, many Nikkei eventually returned to the West Coast. What they found there varied greatly. Some had been able to make arrangements with non-Nikkei friends to care for their houses and property and were able to resume their lives with relatively little difficulty. However, most Nikkei found that their houses and businesses had been looted, and many had their property seized by the various state governments for failure to pay their taxes while they were interned.

The Japanese American internment continues to be black mark on the U.S. government's record. Though there were German and Italian immigrants and German and Italian Americans living on the West Coast during the war, the Japanese were the only ethnic group subjected to internment. In addition, despite the government's concerns, there was not a single documented case of espionage carried out by a member of the Nikkei community during the war. In 1988, based largely on the recommendations of the Commission on the Wartime Relocation and Internment of Civilians, the Civil Liberties Act contained a provision for monetary reparations for Nikkei who had been detained in the camps as well as a formal apology for the internment.

Alexander Mikaberidze

See also: Britain; Canada; U.S. POW Camps, 1941–1948.

Further Reading

Bosworth, Allan R. *America's Concentration Camps*. New York: W. W. Norton & Company 1967.

Daniels, Roger, Sandra C. Taylor, and Harry H. L. Kitano. *Japanese Americans: From Relocation to Redress*. Seattle: University of Washington Press, 1991.

Daniels, Roger. *Asian America: Chinese and Japanese in the United States since 1850*. Seattle: University of Washington Press, 1988.

Hosokawa, Bill. *JACL: In Quest of Justice*. New York: William Morrow, 1982.

Hosokawa, Bill. *Nisei: The Quiet Americans*. New York: William Morrow, 1969.

J

J.A. Topf & Söhne

A German engineering and manufacturing company that supplied crematoria equipment (incineration furnaces) employed at Nazi extermination and concentration camps beginning in 1939. J.A. Topf & Söhne (J.A. Topf and Sons) was established in 1878 in Erfurt, Germany, not far from the future site of the Buchenwald concentration camp. Leadership of the firm passed to Ludwig and Ernst-Wolfgang Topf, the sons of the founder, in 1935. During the 1920s, the company's fortunes rose considerably as more Germans chose cremation for the disposal of their loved ones' remains. J.A. Topf & Söhne also produced brewery and malting equipment, although by the early 1930s their principal product lines were dedicated to cremation and funeral services. Indeed, the company pioneered the design and production of crematoria that were virtually smoke- and odor-free. In 1939, a major outbreak of typhus at the Buchenwald camp necessitated the disposal of large numbers of corpses. Nazi officials contacted J.A. Topf & Söhne, which provided a portable incineration oven for Buchenwald. Officials were so impressed by the equipment that they placed an order for more crematoria and exhaust systems, which were capable of handling far larger quantities of bodies. By 1944, with the mass killing of the Holocaust reaching its zenith, Nazi officials had contracted with Topf for large quantities of crematoria equipment, which was employed at concentration and death camps at Auschwitz, Buchenwald, Mauthausen, Dachau, Bełżec, and Gusen. Company officials certainly knew that their equipment was being used for nefarious purposes, but they perpetuated their contracts nevertheless. Indeed, Kurt Prufer, the company's chief engineer, paid at least five visits to Auschwitz. He later told Soviet officials that he knew about the mass killing as early as the spring of 1943.

When World War II ended in May 1945, Prufer was arrested by Soviet occupation authorities and sent to a gulag, where he died in captivity sometime in 1952. Ludwig Topf was also arrested by the Soviets, but he committed suicide on May 31, 1945, leaving a note that attempted to absolve him from participation in the Holocaust. His brother, Ernst-Wolfgang, was put on trial for war crimes, but was found not guilty. He later took up residence in West Germany and established another incinerator company in 1951; the firm entered bankruptcy in 1963.

Paul G. Pierpaoli, Jr.

See also: Concentration Camps; Death Camps; Gas Chambers; Holocaust, The; I.G. Farben Case (1947).

Further Reading

Bauer, Yehuda. *A History of the Holocaust*. Rev. ed. New York: Franklin Watts, 2001.
Morgan, Patrick. *The Holocaust: Nazi Death Camps*. Los Angeles: Pegasus, 2011.

Jadovno Concentration Camp

A concentration and extermination camp, directed by Juco Rukavina, in the Independent State of Croatia (Nezavisna Država Hrvatska, NDH) during World War II. In April 1941, after the Axis forces invaded the Kingdom of Yugoslavia, the radical Croat nationalist and fascist government (Ustaše), led by Ante Pavelić, came to power and established the Independent State of Croatia. The Ustaše's fascist and racist policies soon led to the establishment of a wide network of concentration camps, where ethnic minorities (Serbs, Jews, Romanis) and political opponents were detained and systematically murdered.

Established about 12 miles from the town of Gospić, the Jadovno concentration camp operated only from May to August 1941. However, in these four months, at least 20,000 prisoners (most of them Croatian Serbs) were methodically executed; groups of prisoners were taken to nearby hill, where they were shot or thrown down into pits. In late August 1941, the camp was closed as the area where it was located was about to be handed over to Italy. The surviving prisoners were moved to the Jasenovac concentration camp.

Alexander Mikaberidze

See also: Jasenovac; Sisak; Ustaše.

Further Reading

Israeli, Raphael. *The Death Camps of Croatia. Visions and Revisions, 1941–1945*. London: Routledge, 2017.

Mojzes, Paul. *Balkan Genocides: Holocaust and Ethnic Cleansing in the Twentieth Century*. New York: Rowman & Littlefield, 2011.

Tomasevich, Jozo. *War and Revolution in Yugoslavia, 1941–1945: Occupation and Collaboration*. Stanford, CA: Stanford University Press, 2001.

Japan

During World War II, Japanese authorities, which had never signed the Second Geneva Convention of 1929, developed a vast network of concentration and prisoner-of-war camps, where over 140,000 Allied POWs, 180,000 Chinese, Filipino, Indian, and other Asian troops and thousands more civilian internees were held during the war. These camps were scattered across much of Asia, including in Indonesia, Malaya, Singapore, Burma, Thailand, China, Korea, Philippines, and Japan itself.

Japanese culture and traditional mores played an important role shaping Japanese perceptions of POWs. The Japanese believed that those who allowed themselves to be taken prisoner had dishonored themselves and therefore did not deserve to be treated with dignity and respect. Thus, prisoners faced unrelentingly lethal conditions at camps, and almost a third of all prisoners perished in captivity. Prisoners were often denied medical care and, with malaria and dysentery almost universal at camps, men were quickly reduced to living skeletons. The Japanese guards routinely abused and tortured prisoners; it was common to receive a *binta* (strong slap on the face) or various kinds of beatings for slight infractions of the rules. On top of these dreadful conditions at camps, most prisoners worked as slave

Table 1   Major Japanese POW and Concentration Camps

Philippines	Cabanatuan
	Davao Prison and Penal Farm
	Camp O'Donnell
	Los Baños
	Santo Tomas Internment Camp
	Bilibid Prison
	Puerto Princesa Prison Camp
	Camp John Hay
	Camp Holmes Internment Camp
	Camp Manganese, Guindulman, Bohol
	Camp Malolos, Bulcan
Malaya and Singapore	Changi Prison
	Salarang Barracks
	River Valley Camp
	Blakang Mati
	Anderson School, Ipoh, Perak State, Malaya
	Outram Road Prison
	Sime Road
Taiwan	Kinkaseki#1 Jinguashi
	Taichu#2 (Taichung)
	Heito#3 (PingTung)
	Shirakawa#4 (Chiayi)
	Taihoku#5 Mosak (Taipei)
	Taihoku#6 (Taipei)
China	Ash Civilian Assembly Center (Shanghai)
	Chapei Civilian Assembly Center (Shanghai)
	Columbia Country Club Civilian Assembly Center (Shanghai)
	Fengtai Prison
	Kiangwang POW Camp
	Lunghua Civilian Assembly Center (Shanghai)
	Lushun (Port Arthur) POW Camp
	Mukden POW Camp
	Woosung POW Camp (Shanghai)
	Weihsien Civil Assembly Center (Weihsien)
	Yu Yuen Road Civilian Assembly Center (Shanghai)
	Yangtzepoo Civilian Assembly Center (Shanghai)
	Zikawei Camp
Manchuria	Hoten Camp

(*continued*)

Table 1   Major Japanese POW and Concentration Camps (continued)

Dutch East Indies (Indonesia)	Ambon (Ambon Island)
	Ambarawa, Central Java
	Bangkong, Java
	Fort van den Bosch, Ngawi Regency, East Java
	Bicycle Camp, Batavia, West Java
	Tandjong Priok POW camp, Tandjong Priok, Java
	Pontianak POW camp, Pontianak (Dutch Borneo) (modern Kalimantan)
	Balikpapan POW camp, Balikpapan (Dutch Borneo)
Hong Kong	Argyle Street Camp
	Stanley Internment Camp

laborers to keep Japan's industry going. They toiled relentlessly in mines, factories, docks, airfields, shipbuilding yards, and construction sites, most famously the Burma-Thailand Railway that claimed thousands of lives. Prisoners captured in Philippines, Singapore, and elsewhere were usually transferred to prison camps in Japan or Manchuria to supplement the shortage of the work force; entombed below decks of what became known as Hell Ships, prisoners had little or no access to fresh air or water, causing hundreds of them to perish; several of these unmarked ships were destroyed by Allied planes and submarines. The Japanese military, notably the infamous Unit 731, conducted biological and chemical warfare research and testing on prisoners.

Alexander Mikaberidze

See also: Bataan Death March (1942); Batu Lintang Camp; Cabanatuan; Changi; Far East, British Military Trials; Sandakan Death Marches; Selarang Barracks Incident; Unit 731.

Further Reading

Daws, Gavan. *Prisoners of the Japanese: POWs of World War II in the Pacific.* Victoria: Scribe Publications, 2004.

Emerson, Geoffrey Charles. *Hong Kong Internment, 1942–1945: Life in the Japanese Civilian Camp at Stanley.* Hong Kong: Hong Kong University Press, 2008.

Roland, Charles G. *Long Night's Journey into Day: Prisoners of War in Hong Kong and Japan, 1941–1945.* Waterloo, ON: Wilfrid Laurier University Press, 2001.

Tanaka, Toshiyuki. *Hidden Horrors: Japanese War Crimes in World War II.* Lanham, MA: Rowman & Littlefield, 2018.

Waterford, Van. *Prisoners of the Japanese in World War II.* Jefferson, NC: McFarland & Company, 1994.

Jasenovac

Site of five concentration camps established by the Croatian ultranationalist and fascist organization Ustaše between August 1941 and February 1942 on the banks of the Sava River, some 60 miles south of Zagreb in central Croatia. The five facilities were Krapje, Brocica, Ciglana, Kozara, and Stara Gradiska; the first two were in existence for only four months. The Jasenovac complex was created and administered entirely by the Ustaše party, although both the Italian and German governments had encouraged its establishment as a way to neutralize dissidents and enemies of the Independent State of Croatia. Most of the prisoners were Serbs, Jews, and Romanis. Political and religious dissidents were also incarcerated at Jasenovac, most of them Muslims or Croats.

Jasenovac was one of numerous concentration camp facilities constructed by the Ustaše during World War II; it was also the largest. Conditions in the camps were absolutely appalling. Barracks were hopelessly overcrowded, food rations meager, and sanitation facilities crude. In the cold winter months, the flimsily constructed buildings offered little in the way of warmth or shelter. Disease and sickness were rampant, and prisoners—men, women, and children—were routinely subjected to savage beatings and even torture by camp guards. Inmates were often murdered over the slightest infraction, or when guards were in a bad mood. Many of the Jews imprisoned at Jasenovac were shot and killed at nearby sites such as Gradina or Granik. In August 1942 and again in May 1943, German authorities transferred most of the surviving Jews from Jasenovac to Auschwitz-Birkenau in southern Poland.

The few Jews at Jasenovac who were spared death or deportation were those individuals with useful backgrounds, including carpenters, tailors, physicians, and electricians. Between 1941 and 1945, it is estimated that as least 100,000 people may have died at Jasenovac, though estimates vary considerably. The range includes 45,000–50,000 Serbs; 12,000–20,000 Jews; 15,000–20,000 Romanis; and 5,000–12,000 political and religious dissidents.

Toward the end of the war, in April 1945, a group of prisoners at Jasenovac sensed an opportunity to rebel and staged a major uprising. Guards, however, brutally suppressed it, and several hundred prisoners died. Most of the remaining survivors were killed before Ustaše guards hastily dismantled the facilities. By early May, Yugoslav partisan troops under Josip Broz Tito had taken control of the area and made known the wartime activities there.

Paul G. Pierpaoli, Jr.

See also: Holocaust, The; Sisak; Ustaše.

Further Reading

Gitman, Esther. *When Courage Prevailed: The Rescue and Survival of Jews in the Independent State of Croatia, 1941–1945.* St. Paul: Paragon House, 2011.

Lituchy, Barry M. (Ed.). *Jasenovac and the Holocaust in Yugoslavia.* Brooklyn, NY: Jasenovac Research Institute. 2006.

Ofer, Dalia, and Lenore Weitzman, eds. *Women in the Holocaust.* New Haven, CT: Yale University Press, 1998.

Roth, John, and Carol Rittner, eds. *Different Voices: Women and the Holocaust.* St. Paul, MN: Paragon House, 1993.

K

Kang Kek Iew (1942–)

A middle-level communist leader of Cambodia during the regime of Pol Pot and the Khmer Rouge between 1975 and 1979. Commonly known by his revolutionary nickname as "Comrade Duch" (sometimes spelled Deuch), Kang Kek Iew (Kaing Guek Eav) was born in the village of Choyaot, in Kampong Thom Province. A brilliant student, he entered the prestigious and elite Lycée Sisowath in Phnom Penh in 1962 and excelled in mathematics. Obtaining his teaching qualification in 1966, Duch was posted to a school in his home province of Kampong Cham. In 1967, he joined the Communist Party of Kampuchea (CPK), after which, on account of a crackdown against the party by Cambodia's Prince Norodom Sihanouk, he fled into the jungle to join the Khmer Rouge. He was arrested by government forces later in 1967, and held without trial for the next two years. He was released in 1970, after Sihanouk was ousted in a coup led by General Lon Nol, and rejoined the Khmer Rouge in the jungle along the Cambodia-Thailand border. He immediately returned to his opposition against Lon Nol's right-wing government, and his immediate superior, Vet, saw the potential for Duch to serve as a committed warden over political prisoners captured by the Khmer Rouge during the ensuing civil war (1970–1975).

Duch set up his first prison, codenamed M-13, as a detention facility in the forest of Kampong Speu Province, in which pits were dug as prisoner "accommodation." These pits were two meters deep, and prisoners were shackled and fed little. Later, Duch acknowledged that the conditions at M-13 were inhumane, saying, "It wasn't a school, it was a Khmer Rouge prison." Here, Duch began perfecting his interrogation techniques and the purging of perceived enemies from within the ranks of the Khmer Rouge. Two years later, Duch established a second prison, M-99, where as many as 20,000 Cambodians may have been sent for torture and execution. Few prisoners left these early camps alive.

After the Khmer Rouge victory in April 1975, the prison system was developed and extended as an arm of the state. In particular, Phnom Penh became home to the infamous Tuol Sleng Prison, codenamed S-21, a prison intended to serve as a political detention center that would periodically purge the Khmer Rouge of suspected enemies of the revolution. Under Duch's direction, Tuol Sleng became a byword for Khmer Rouge brutality. At least 16,000 prisoners were incarcerated there between 1975 and 1979, and all—save seven, who outlived the regime—perished by torture or execution. Duch ordered that all prisoners should be photographed and interrogated prior to their death. His viciousness embraced party members considered to have been disloyal, male and female civilians denounced by party cadres for not being supportive enough of the communist revolution, and even small children, the family members of those already apprehended.

Vet and Sen were particularly impressed with Duch's work, so much so that they appointed him deputy head of the Santebal, the special branch of the security police, under Sen's leadership. Later, Duch became head of the Santebal in his own right. After the fall of the Khmer Rouge government to invading Vietnamese forces in January 1979, Duch (who was the last high-ranking Khmer Rouge leader to leave Phnom Penh in the face of the invasion) made his way to Thailand and then China. In 1998, after several years of alternately fighting for the Khmer Rouge and hiding from the government, he returned to Cambodia and attempted to settle down and put the past behind him. In 1999, he was interviewed by journalists Nic Dunlop and Nate Thayer and admitted participating in the activities at Tuol Sleng. He expressed sorrow for the killings and declared he would be willing to face an international tribunal and provide evidence against others. Soon after this, he surrendered to Cambodian authorities in Phnom Penh.

At this time, there was not yet any formal mechanism for the trial of members of the former Khmer Rouge regime. This had to wait until the establishment of the Extraordinary Chambers in the Courts of Cambodia (ECCC), the tribunal made up of international and Cambodian judges that brought formal charges against Duch on July 31, 2007. He was charged with crimes against humanity. His lawyer argued that Duch had already been denied natural justice on the basis of the eight years he had so far spent without trial in Cambodian military detention, but this was rejected and on August 14, 2008, the tribunal issued its indictment after completing its investigation of Duch. His trial began on February 16, 2009, and on March 31, 2009, Duch accepted responsibility for torturing and executing thousands of inmates at Tuol Sleng. On July 26, 2010, he was found guilty of crimes against humanity, torture, and murder, and was sentenced to 35 years' imprisonment. The judges decreed in sentencing that in their opinion he had already served 11 years in custody before and during the trial, and that an additional controversial five years should automatically be deducted from his sentence as a penalty against the state because his period of pre-trial detention exceeded the maximum allowed under Cambodian law.

Outside the court, victims of the Khmer Rouge regime were furious with the sentence, saying it was too short and should have been one of life imprisonment, the heaviest penalty the court could impose. The prosecution also objected to the verdict, seeking at least the maximum requested, 40 years, while Duch's lawyers lodged an appeal citing the lack of competence of the ECCC to try the case.

On February 3, 2012, the Supreme Court Chamber issued its appeal judgment—Duch's sentence was increased to life in prison. This sentence cannot be appealed.

Paul R. Bartrop

See also: Cambodian Killing Fields.

Further Reading
Chandler, David P. *The Tragedy of Cambodian History: Politics, War, and Revolution since 1945.* New Haven, CT: Yale University Press, 1991.
Deac, Wilfred P. *Road to the Killing Fields: The Cambodian War of 1970–1975.* College Station: Texas A&M University Press, 1997.

Kapos

"Kapo" was a term used to describe prisoners in German concentration camps who worked with the Nazi administration to enforce discipline and perform various other functions. Kapos, derived from the Latin/Italian word for "head" (as in, "head of"), were utilized widely in German camps and prisons to free up men for service in the armed services. They were utilized in regular prisons, forced labor camps, and concentration camps. Oftentimes, Kapos were Jews overseeing other Jews in concentration and death camps. They assumed these roles sometimes by coercion, but sometimes willingly. These prison functionaries were usually granted special privileges by prison administrators, including more and better food, better quarters, and sometimes even parole or early release. The use of Jewish Kapos in German concentration and death camps was particularly troubling, and made postwar prosecution of them highly problematic, as some were forced to undertake such duties under the ever-present threat of death or harm to their families.

Most Kapos were appointed to their positions by SS officers who usually administered the Nazis' extensive prison and internment system. They often enticed these prisoner-functionaries (*Funktionshäftlinge*) with rewards that sometimes included private quarters, access to clean linen and bathing facilities, and little or no manual labor. Most Kapos did not want to see these privileges revoked, so they carried out SS orders to the letter.

Many Kapos were cruel and unforgiving toward their fellow prisoners, and so it is no surprise that they were intensely disliked by other inmates. Indeed, there were ample examples of prisoners murdering Kapos. There were several different levels—or ranks—of Kapos, depending upon their roles and seniority. There was often a single Kapo over the entire camp or prison; under him were block (or barracks leaders), room (or cell) leaders, and block/barracks clerks who did mainly clerical work. Kapos who oversaw forced labor gangs often did no work at all while prisoners under them worked until exhaustion in appalling conditions. These Kapos often met untimely ends at the hands of disgruntled prisoners.

SS chief Heinrich Himmler decreed in February 1944 that Jews would no longer serve as Kapos because Nazi dogma stipulated that no Jew could be put into a superior position over non-Jews. After World War II ended, a number of Kapos, some of them Jews, were tried and convicted under the Israeli Nazi and Nazi Collaborators Punishment Law of 1950; most of the trials took place between 1951 and 1964, and there were at least 15 convictions of Jews during that period. Without the extensive network of Kapos, the Germans could never have administered such a large and far-flung prison camp system.

Paul G. Pierpaoli, Jr.

See also: Germany; Holocaust, The; Sonderkommando; Trawniki Men.

Further Reading

Bartrop, Paul R. *Surviving the Camps: Unity in Adversity during the Holocaust.* Lanham, MD: University Press of America, 2000.

Gutman, Yisrael, and Michael Berenbaum, eds. *Anatomy of the Auschwitz Death Camp.* Bloomington: Indiana University Press, 1994.

Todorov, Tzvetan. *Facing the Extreme: Moral Life in the Concentration Camps.* New York: Henry Holt, 1996.

Katyń Forest Massacre (1943)

A mass murder of Polish prisoners of war by the Soviet Union during World War II. On April 13, 1990, the Soviet news agency Tass announced that a joint commission of Polish and Soviet historians had found documents proving the involvement of personnel from the Narodnyy Kommissariat Vnutrenniakh Del (NKVD, or People's Commissariat for Internal Affairs) in the deaths of some 15,000 Polish officers in the Katyń Forest of eastern Poland in 1940; however, the total number of the executed at Katyń amounted to almost 22,000. The general secretary of the Communist Party of the Soviet Union and president of the USSR, Mikhail Gorbachev, handed over a list of the victims to Polish president Wojciech Jaruzelski. In October 1992, Russian president Boris Yeltsin produced more archival documents, helping to determine the burial sites of missing officers not found near Katyń. Even in the light of Gorbachev's glasnost and perestroika policies, this admission of Soviet responsibility for the massacre was still a bombshell.

The USSR had consistently denied murdering captured Polish army officers after its occupation of eastern Poland ever since Radio Berlin announced, on April 13, 1943, that German troops, tipped off by local inhabitants, had discovered mass graves near Smolensk. That June, the German Field Police reported that 4,143 bodies had been found in the Katyń Forest, all fully dressed in Polish army uniforms. Some 2,815 corpses were later identified by personal documents in their pockets. Without exception, all the officers, ranking from general to noncommissioned officer, had been killed by shots in the back of the head. Medical examination later showed that a few bodies had jaws smashed by blows or bayonet wounds in their backs or stomachs, probably sustained when the individuals tried to resist execution.

The Germans predictably tried to exploit the Katyń Forest murders for propaganda purposes, pointing out to their wartime enemies that any alliance with the "Bolshevik" perpetrators of this atrocity was too dangerous to continue. By then, General Władysław Sikorski's London-based Polish government-in-exile and General Władysław Anders, then commander of the Polish forces in the USSR and the Middle East, had been concerned for a considerable time over the fate of the missing Polish officers. Following the Soviet-Polish agreement in the summer of 1941, a small but steady trickle of Poles arrived at the reopened Polish Embassy in Kuibyshev. These individuals, from prison camps scattered over the western parts of the USSR, agreed that their fellow servicemen had been transferred to unknown destinations when the NKVD liquidated these camps in April 1940. The arrivals at Kuibyshev turned out to be the few survivors of the Katyń Forest Massacre. The massacre was apparently a Soviet effort to deprive the Poles of their natural leaders, who would have undoubtedly protested a Soviet takeover.

After numerous fruitless discussions on the subject with Soviet authorities, including dictator Joseph Stalin himself, the Polish government-in-exile came to believe the German announcement of April 1943 and demanded an independent investigation by the International Committee of the Red Cross (ICRC). This move caused the Kremlin to accuse the Polish government-in-exile of siding with the "fascist aggressors" and to break off diplomatic relations. The ICRC, pursuing its policy of neutrality, could take no action without Soviet consent. London, although embarrassed by this development, made it plain that it was unwilling to risk the breakup of the alliance with the Soviet Union against Nazi Germany over such an investigation. The United States took a similar stance.

When the Red Army finally drove the German armies westward, Moscow determined it needed to present its own investigation results in 1944. A Soviet "special commission," pointing out that the bullets found on the crime scene were manufactured in Germany, concluded that the Germans had killed the Polish officers in 1941. British and American protests notwithstanding, the Soviet prosecution raised the Katyń affair at the International Military Tribunal in Nuremberg, but because the Soviets were unable to prove the Germans guilty, the tribunal simply dropped the case. Throughout the Cold War, the issue of the Katyń Forest Massacre resurfaced time and again, partly because of the efforts of the Polish émigré community. However, it remained unresolved until the demise of the USSR in 1991.

Pascal Trees

See also: NKVD.

Further Reading

Paul, Allen. *Katyń: The Untold Story of Stalin's Massacre.* New York: Scribner's, 1991.

Zawodny, Janusz. *Death in the Forest: The Story of the Katyn Forest Massacre.* 4th ed. Notre Dame, IN: University of Notre Dame Press, 1980.

"Killing Fields." *See* Cambodian Killing Fields

Kim Il Sung (1912–1994)

Founder and president of the Democratic People's Republic of Korea (DPRK, North Korea) during 1948–1994, general secretary of the Korean Workers' Party, and instigator of the Korean War. Born Kim Song Ju on April 15, 1912, to a peasant family in Mangyongdae near Pyongyang, he later assumed the name of Kim Il Sung, a legendary hero of the Korean independence movement, and under this name became a well-known anti-Japanese guerrilla commander in the 1930s. During the Japanese occupation, he led his guerrilla forces on raids against Japanese outposts all across northern Korea. Fleeing the Japanese crackdown on guerrillas in Manchuria, he sought refuge in eastern Siberia in the Soviet Union in 1941.

Kim returned to Korea in September 1945 after the end of World War II and used both his guerrilla record and the support of Soviet occupation authorities to become the undisputed leader of North Korea. When North Korea was formally established on September 9, 1948, he became premier. The pro-Western Republic of Korea (ROK, South Korea) had already been established under the leadership of Syngman Rhee.

Kim possessed a burning ambition to reunite the Korean Peninsula under his rule. With Soviet and Chinese acquiescence and support, he launched a surprise military invasion across the 38th Parallel against South Korea on June 25, 1950. After initial success, however, the assault was repulsed by the forces of South Korea, the United States, and other nations under the flag of the United Nations (UN).

Only the massive November 1950 Chinese intervention saved North Korea from defeat. The war eventually stalemated and ended with an uneasy cease-fire in 1953 that left the peninsula divided at the 38th Parallel. To this day, North and South Korea are still technically in a state of war, as no formal peace treaty has been signed.

In the aftermath of the Korean War, Kim used *juche*, or the ideology of self-reliance, to legitimize his regime and to keep foreign influences out of North Korea. He tightened his control of the country by purging his party and establishing a vast ring of concentration and forced labor camps—the *kwanliso*, the North Korean equivalent of gulag—throughout the country. Kim Il Sung demanded that up to three generations must be punished in order to wipe out the "seed" of a class enemy, meaning those individuals suspected of wrong thinking, wrong knowledge, wrong association, or wrong background. As a result, whole families, including children, were often incarcerated for "guilt by association." The Kim Il Sung's dictatorship painstakingly engineered North Korean society, categorizing all citizens into three classes—the "core" of loyalists at the top, the "wavering" class in the middle," and the bottom "hostile" class which was then subdivided into over 50 groups; a citizen was demoted at the slightest disloyalty and were subject to arbitrary arrests and internments in labor camps. Kim Il Sung supervised detentions of hundreds of thousands of Koreans who were used as a slave labor in huge economic infrastructure projects (road making, dam construction, bridge building, irrigation drainage, and the like), during which scores of thousands died as a result of exposure, starvation, and overwork. He systematically purged his political opponents, creating a highly regimented and centralized system that accorded him unlimited power and generated a formidable cult of personality. It is estimated that Kim's rule claimed between 700,000 and 3.5 million lives, with a mid-estimate of almost 1.6 million (Rummel 1997).

Since the 1960s, the country slid further into despair, owing to a massive reduction in what few economic relationships remained after two decades of war, centralized economic control, and repression. In particular, after Kim's death of a massive heart attack on July 8, 1994, in Pyongyang, North Korea became increasingly unable to stabilize its sinking economy and to feed its own people; by the twenty-first century, this country remains one of the most enigmatic and closed societies in the world.

Jinwung Kim

See also: North Korea.

Further Reading

Bai, Bong. *Kim Il Sung: A Political Biography*. 3 vols. New York: Guardian Books, 1970.

Oberdorfer, Don. *The Two Koreas: A Contemporary History*. Revised and updated ed. New York: Basic Books, 2002.

Rummel, R.J. "Statistics of North Korean Democide: Estimates, Calculations, and Sources," in *Statistics of Democide*. Charlottesille, VA: Center for National Security Law, School of Law, University of Virgina, 1997. Available at: http://www.hawaii.edu/powerkills/SOD.CHAP10.HTM

Suh, Dae-Sook. *Kim Il Sung: The North Korean Leader*. New York: Columbia University Press, 1988.

Kinderblock 66

A special, segregated set of barracks for youths at the Buchenwald concentration camp, located in east-central Germany. Young detainees in Kinderblock 66 were protected by a number of "elders," most of whom were members of the underground resistance movement at Buchenwald. Mainly adult men, by early 1945, the elders were virtually running the day-to-day operations of the camp, and thus were in a prime position to protect the children and youth interned there. Among the youthful detainees was famed Holocaust survivor and writer Elie Wiesel, who was a teenager at the time. He later wrote about his experiences in Kinderblock 66. Under the leadership of Antonin Kalina, a communist Czech detainee, and his deputy, Gustav Schiller, a Polish-Jewish prisoner, as many children and young adults as possible were gathered together in one area of Buchenwald. There they could be better protected from the depredations of German guards, be given larger food rations, and be exempted from hard manual labor. Most, but not all, of the young prisoners were Jewish. Adult prisoners even taught their young charges history, literature, and mathematics lessons to help prevent boredom and give them a sense of encouragement.

In late 1944 and early January 1945, the situation at Buchenwald became dire. As the Germans were being pushed to the west by advancing Soviet troops, they began liquidating concentration camps in the east, relocating them to places like Buchenwald. As many as 1,200 Jewish and non-Jewish boys, ages 12–16, arrived

Internees, many of them children, leave the Buchenwald concentration camp to receive treatment at an American hospital after the camp was liberated by troops of the U.S. Third Army. (Bettmann/Getty Images)

at Buchenwald in January 1945. Kalina and others concentrated these detainees, along with most of the other youths in the camp, in a windowless, separate barracks located beneath the main camp. In early April 1945, as the Germans began to liquidate Buchenwald itself, the camp's elders took extraordinary measures to prevent the camp's youth from being deported. Kalina, Schiller, and other elders ordered the boys not to report for roll-call or assembly. They also falsified their records and changed the religion on their badges to give the appearance that all were Christians. In the end, the ruse worked, and the elders prevented the deportation of Kinderblock 66. On April 10, the Germans planned on deporting the remaining prisoners at Buchenwald, but the operation was foiled by the presence of U.S. warplanes in the vicinity. The following day, the camp was liberated by advanced armor units of the U.S. Third Army, and Kinderblock 66 was saved.

In 2012, a documentary film entitled *Kinderblock 66* chronicled the return to Buchenwald of four adult survivors of Kinderblock 66 on the 65th anniversary of their liberation.

Paul G. Pierpaoli, Jr.

See also: Buchenwald; Concentration Camps; Holocaust, The.

Further Reading

Jones, David H. *Moral Responsibility in the Holocaust: A Study in the Ethics of Character*. Lanham, MD: Rowman & Littlefield, 1999

Koch Trial (1951)

Ilse Koch was the wife of Karl Koch, the former chief of Buchenwald. She was accused of killing inmates who had tattooed skin, in order to collect their skin.

After Allied troops entered Buchenwald in April 1945, many of the 21,000 survivors were interviewed. Some of them talked about a *Kommandeuse*, a fierce, red-haired woman who was perverse and heartless. The prisoners called her the "Witch of Buchenwald," which the press transformed into the "Bitch of Buchenwald." In June 1945, Ilse Koch was denounced by an ex-inmate and arrested. Subsequent inquiries in Buchenwald produced a huge amount of evidence against her. Among the physical evidence was a lampshade made of human tattooed skin, a discovery that inflamed international public opinion.

The trial started two years later in Dachau. As Buchenwald was situated in the Soviet occupation zone, the American military administration had first to secure permission to conduct the trial. The Soviets, who were issuing propaganda claiming the auto-liberation of the camp by internal Communist groups, did not immediately answer American requests. Eventually, April 11, 1947, began one of the most complex events in Nazi crimes judicial history.

The court was made up of nine military judges and the prosecution consisted of three civilian lawyers. The task of defending Ilse Koch fell to a mixed staff of both military and civil lawyers. The trial had no connection with the Nuremberg Tribunal. Ilse Koch was charged with war crimes and violation of the Geneva and The Hague conventions. She was indicted for having concurred at the National Socialist's common design by killing and ill-treating thousands of people. The 16 prosecution and 11 defense witnesses helped to sketch out Ilse Koch's worst nature.

Frau Koch had brutally abused prisoners in the camp, using the power that her husband had arbitrarily granted her to perpetrate sadistic and perverse acts on the Buchenwald's inmates. The heart of the trial in Dachau was the famous articles made of human skin.

During the investigation, several finds of tattooed human skin were discovered at the pathological surgery of the camp. Most of this evidence was handed over to military staff, which had taken them to Nuremberg. The prosecution had only a receipt and the impossibility of producing the finds as evidence; nevertheless, the Allies knew the existence of a trade of human skin intended for SS fetishism.

The trial ended August 12, 1947. The prosecution asked for the death penalty, but Ilse Koch was at that time seven months pregnant, which made it impossible for her to be sentenced to death. On August 14, 1947, she was condemned to life imprisonment. The unanimous verdict declared her guilty of having broken the war laws and of having concurred at the National Socialist's common design. The defense asked for a rehearing, challenging the credibility of the witnesses and attacking the procedural weakness concerning the lack of evidence against Ilse Koch. The trial was actually reheard. A central commission of the U.S. occupation force in Europe accepted the problem of the witnesses' integrity and the deficiency of tangible evidence against Ilse Koch. On June 8, 1948, General Lucius D. Clay, commandant of the American occupation troops in Europe, reduced her sentence to four years imprisonment.

Clay's decision was kept confidential until a journalist discovered and divulged it, causing a negative reaction in the American public opinion. The press coverage of Clay's decision turned it quickly into a political problem, and a commission of the U.S. Congress inquired on the case, drawing it to the attention of President Truman. The Bavarian government gave notice that if Ilse Koch were released, new proceedings would be brought against her. Nevertheless, she was set free in October 1949 and, after a political-bureaucratic discussion between the United States and the Deutsche Demokratische Republik (East Germany), she was handed over to West German authorities, which again arrested her.

Seven pages enumerated the German accusations against Ilse Koch, among them the charge for having selected inmates in Buchenwald to die in order to obtain their tattooed skin. On November 26, 1950, the new trial began; this was the first independent German trial of a Nazi criminal. The 15 members of the jury heard almost 200 witnesses, but the prosecution failed to produce any new evidence against her. Ilse Koch was found guilty of abuse of prisoners and of incitement to homicide, but again, the tattooed skin could not be directly connected to her.

Ilse Koch was condemned to life imprisonment. Her defense attorney put forward several petitions for pardon arguing that, because of the great clamor surrounding her case, Ilse Koch had never received a fair trial. On September 2, 1967, Ilse Koch committed suicide in her cell.

Massimiliano Livi

See also: Buchenwald; Holocaust, The.

Further Reading
"Best Years of Her Life," *Newsweek*, September 18, 1967: 31.

Conduct of Ilse Koch War Crimes Trial. Interim report of the Investigations Subcommittee on the Committee on Exenditures in the Executive Departments, Pursuant to S.

Res. 189 (80th Congress), a Resolution Authorizing the Committee on Expenditures in the Executive Departments to Carry Out Certain Duties. Washington: U.S. Government Printing Office, 1948.

Whitlock, Flint. *The Beasts of Buchenwald: Karl & Ilse Koch, Human-Skin Lampshades, and the War-Crimes Trial of the Century.* Brule, WI: Cable Publishing, 2011.

"The Witch of Buchenwald," *Newsweek,* July 28, 1947: 28–29.

Kogan, Lazar (1889–1939)

Soviet intelligence officer and head of Gulag. Born into an affluent Jewish family in the Eniseiskaya province of the Russian Empire, Kogan in his youth became involved in radical circles, was involved in armed robberies, and sentenced to hard labor in Siberia. Joining the Bolshevik party in 1918, he participated in the Russian Civil War and quickly advanced through the ranks of the newly established secret police, Cheka.

After serving in the North Caucasus, Kogan became second head of Ulag (The Directorate of Camps), a predecessor to the Gulag, in 1930, and supervised the expansion of the labor camp system for two years. After the Gulag system was formally established, he became its deputy head in 1932 and also directed the notorious Belomorstroi forced labor camp that was tasked with constructing a dam project near the White Sea. In 1935–1936 he supervised construction of the Moscow-Volga Canal that involved some 200,000 slave laborers, many of whom perished. Transferred to the Forest Industry Commissariat, Kogan was arrested during Joseph Stalin's purges and executed in 1939. He was legally rehabilitated in 1956.

Alexander Mikaberidze

See also: Gulag; NKVD; Stalin, Joseph.

Further Reading

Applebaum, Anne. *Gulag: A History.* New York: Broadway Books, 2003.

Ivanova, Galina Mikhailovna, with Donald J. Raleigh. *Labor Camp Socialism: The Gulag in the Soviet Totalitarian System.* trans. Carol Fath. Armonk, NY: M. E. Sharpe, 2000.

Khevniuk, Oleg. *History of the Gulag.* New Haven, CT: Yale University Press, 2003.

Solzhenitsyn, Aleksandr. *The Gulag Archipelago, 1918–1956: An Experiment in Literary Investigation.* 3 vols. New York: Harper and Row, 1974–1978.

Koje-Do Incident (1952)

A revolt by North Korean and Chinese prisoners of war at the American prisoner camp at Koje-do in May 1952. As the Korean War entered the second year, the United Nations Command (UNC) was engaged in truce negotiations with North Korean Communist authorities. The North Koreans demanded the return of all prisoners of war (over 130,000 men) but the UNC insisted on the principle of voluntary repatriation. Unbeknownst to the UNC, the North Korean agents had let themselves to be captured as POWs and fomented disturbances within the POW camps. Responding to the rioting in several compounds on February 18 and

March 13, 1952, the UNC opened fire at POWs, killing 89 and wounded over 160. Denouncing the UNC "atrocities," the North Korean side broke off the peace talks and encouraged further riots.

The most serious of these incidents occurred on May 7, 1952, at the Koje-do camp, which was located on a small island near Pusan. U.S. camp commander, Brigadier General Francis T. Dodd, visited Compound 76 to listen to complaints aired by the Communist prisoners. While standing near the gate of the compound, he was forcibly seized as the gate opened to allow a work detail to pass through. U.S. Eighth Army commander, General James A. Van Fleet, dispatched Brigadier General Charles Colson to negotiate with the prisoners, whose chief demand was an admission that UNC forces had been responsible for bloodshed at the POW camps. After Colson conceded to this demand, Dodd was freed. North Korean authorities exploited Colson's statement as confirming UNC atrocities and staining American forces involved. Although U.S. Army investigation found Dodd and Colson blameless, Van Fleet convened another inquiry that reversed this decision and held both generals accountable; they were relieved of command, reduced in rank, and forced out of the army. The new camp commander, Brigadier General Haydon Boatner, received strict instructions to restore order at Koje-do by any means necessary. On June 10, he sent troops, with six tanks, to restore the UNC authority at the camp. In the ensuing battle, more than 150 prisoners were killed and hundreds more injured.

Alexander Mikaberidze

See also: Korean War.

Further Reading

Cummings, Bruce. *The Korean War: A History.* New York: Modern Library, 2011.

Vetter, Hal. *Mutiny on Koje Island.* Rutland, VT: Charles E. Tuttle, 1965.

Korean War

During the twentieth century, ideological wars have produced countless examples of brutality and crimes against humanity. The Korean War was no exception. From 1950 to 1953, the armies and governments of both the Democratic People's Republic of Korea (DPRK, North Korea) and the Republic of Korea (ROK, South Korea) committed or encouraged the killing of civilians and prisoners of war. Ever since, there has been historical debate over the degrees of responsibility on both sides.

U.S. and British troops were appalled by the casual brutality that they observed routinely inflicted on South Koreans by their own government. One British soldier, a Private Duncan, described a typical scene: "Forty emaciated and subdued Koreans were . . . shot while their hands were tied, and also beaten unnecessarily by rifles. The executioners were South Korean military police." Such incidents created great confusion and ill-feeling toward the ROK among Western troops. "We are led to believe that we are fighting against such actions," Duncan wrote, "and I sincerely believe that our troops are wondering which side in Korea is right or wrong."

ROK treatment of Communist prisoners was particularly harsh in the days after the savage and sudden Korean People's Army (KPA, North Korean) occupation of the South. "At least many hundreds [of alleged Communists] have been shot," reported Australian delegate to the United Nations (UN) Commission for Korea John Plimsoll. He related how prisoners had been forced to dig their own graves, then "rather clumsily and inexpertly shot before the eyes of others waiting their own turn." Feelings of bitterness and the desire for revenge after the atrocities committed during the Communist occupation drove South Korean government officials to such retaliatory measures.

But the KPA occupation of much of the South conditioned this. Indeed, the widespread cruelty of the Communist occupation of South Korea during the opening months of the conflict set the moral tone for the rest of the war. It also led South Koreans who were lukewarm or opposed to the government of Syngman Rhee to rally to it as far preferable to that of the Communists.

From June to September 1950, some 26,000 South Korean civilians were murdered by the Communists. At one site near Taejon alone, 5,000 bodies were discovered after the North Korean retreat. Members of the South Korean government, police, and intelligentsia were systematically rounded up and executed. Sometimes this included entire families. During the liberation of Seoul, one group of U.S. Marines came upon a trench filled with hundreds of dead South Korean men, women, and children. "It was a ghastly sight," marine Ed Simmons recalled, "The stench was unbearable. For days civilians were coming out from the center of Seoul in the hope of identifying them." The 5th Cavalry Regiment encountered a similar scene where 200 civilians had been executed. "Many of the murdered," Private First Class Victor Fox remembered, "were professional and business people, educators, artists, politicians, [and] civil servants. The dead appeared to include entire families, from children to the very aged."

Even more shocking to Americans were discoveries of the corpses of American POWs who had been executed by their North Korean captors. Bodies were typically found in roadside ditches or gullies, hands tied behind the backs with barbed wire, and a single bullet wound to the back of the head. One group of 100 executed American prisoners was found in a railway tunnel during the UN advance into North Korea. Such sights enraged U.S. troops and inspired random acts of revenge killing of North Korean prisoners. One such incident occurred when the 21st Infantry Regiment took a hill along the Naktong River after a brief firefight. The retreating North Koreans had left a wounded officer behind. "Our officers asked for volunteers to carry him off the hill," Sergeant Warren Avery recalled. "Of course, no one volunteered; we had all heard about atrocities the North Koreans had participated in. After a little bit of argument about what we should do with this wounded officer, the platoon leader went over to him and shot him between the eyes with his .45."

The Chinese, unlike their North Korean allies, were eager to take prisoners alive for propaganda purposes. For American prisoners fortunate enough to survive capture, a long, terrible march into captivity awaited them. This was particularly true during the winter of 1950–1951, when hundreds of Americans died of disease and hypothermia, or were simply murdered by their guards. The survival rate for wounded soldiers during these marches was particularly dismal, although in fairness to the Chinese, with their primitive medical facilities, their own wounded were not likely to fare much better. "The signal for death was the oxcart following the column," remembered Captain James Majury. "If you had to be placed upon that, you would freeze to death."

Arrival at POW camps rarely provided any solace for American prisoners. North Korean-administered camps were the worst. The guards made little attempt to keep their prisoners alive. Starvation, disease, beatings, and months of solitary confinement were the lot of many captives. Conditions improved slightly when the Chinese assumed control of the prison camps in the spring of 1951. That summer, conditions improved further when the Chinese determined that live prisoners made better bargaining chips. Thereafter, prisoner deaths declined rapidly. But the final figures tell a stark tale: of 7,190 Americans captured by the Communists, 2,730 died in captivity. Nearly 99 percent of these died in the bitter first year of the war.

After the truce ending the Korean War on July 27, 1953, there were no trials to prosecute war criminals, as had been the case at the Nuremberg Trials after World War II. However, there had been discussion, early in the war, over prosecution of war criminals. During the Wake Island conference between U.S. president Harry Truman and his advisers and General Douglas MacArthur in October 1950, MacArthur had outlined a plan whereby those North Koreans who had committed atrocities would be tried by military tribunals. But the Chinese intervention in late November and the resulting stalemate precluded any formal UN attempt to bring war criminals to justice.

Duane L. Wesolick

See also: Koje-Do Incident (1952).

Further Reading

Blair, Clay. *The Forgotten War: America in Korea 1950–1953*. New York: Times Books, 1987.

Halliday, Jon, and Bruce Cumings. *Korea: The Unknown War*. New York: Pantheon, 1988.

Hastings, Max. *The Korean War*. New York: Simon & Schuster, 1987.

Kraków-Plaszow

A Nazi forced labor and concentration camp located in Poland, near the Kraków suburb of Plaszow. Established in 1942, it was initially begun as a forced labor facility, mainly for Polish Jews. It had a separate camp for men and women, and a special section for non-Polish Jews who were detained there because they had violated German occupation policies. As labor needs increased and more manufacturing facilities were built in or near Plaszow, the Germans continued to expand the facility to meet demand. At the height of its operations, in 1944, the camp held about 20,000 prisoners simultaneously.

Run by the SS, Kraków-Plaszow was notorious for its wretched living conditions and the overworking of its detainees. Food was scant and often inedible, medical care was essentially nonexistent, housing quarters overcrowded and squalid, and camp personnel were cruel. Harsh punishments, some of which resulted in deaths, were commonplace. Starvation and disease alone killed several thousand prisoners, while hundreds more died of exhaustion and overwork. Precise casualty figures are almost impossible to determine because the Germans went out of their way to cover up their activities, including the mass cremation of bodies.

German industrialist Oskar Schindler, who operated an enamelware factory in the vicinity of Kraków, exploited labor from the Plaszow camp. He shielded his mostly-Jewish workforce, however, and when he was forced to relocate his factory in 1944, he managed to take some 1,100 Jewish workers with him, saving them from deportation and likely death.

In early 1944, the focus of the camp shifted from forced labor to concentration. During that year, Plaszow became temporary home to Jews in transit to death camps in the east. As well, more and more of the camp's permanent detainees were being deported to camps further east. In the summer of 1944, however, as Soviet troops began approaching from the east, the Germans attempted to completely liquidate the Plaszow facility. They shipped many prisoners to Auschwitz, where most were killed. Soon, the Germans engaged themselves in a major effort to erase any evidence of wrongdoing. Barracks and buildings were demolished, and mass graves were opened. The bodies contained in them were then exhumed and burned. The last prisoners left Plaszow in January 1945; many died during a forced march to Auschwitz, while many more were killed after their arrival. It is not possible to determine exactly how many people died at Plaszow, but deaths most certainly numbered in the several thousands, of all causes.

Paul G. Pierpaoli, Jr.

See also: Arbeitslager; Auschwitz; Belżec; Bergen-Belsen; Birkenau; Buchenwald; Chełmno; Concentration Camps; Dachau; Death Camps; Dora-Mittelbau; Eichmann, Adolf; Extermination Centers; Gas Chambers; Gestapo; Gross-Rosen; Hitler, Adolf; Holocaust, The; I.G. Farben Case (1947); J.A. Topf & Söhne; Mauthausen-Gusen; Monowitz; Natzweiler-Struthof; Neuengamme; Niederhagen; Nuremberg Trials; Ravensbrück; Sachsenhausen; Slave Labor (World War II); Sobibór; Sonderkommando; Stalag; Stutthof; Treblinka; Trostinets

Further Reading

Hilberg, Raul. *The Destruction of the European Jews.* New York: Holmes and Meier, 1962.

Kogon, Eugen. *The Theory and Practice of Hell: The German Concentration Camps and the System behind Them.* New York: Farrar, Straus and Giroux, 2006.

Kramer, Josef (1906–1945)

Known as the "Beast of Belsen," Josef Kramer was born on November 10, 1906, in Munich. Trained as a bookkeeper, he joined the Nazi Party in 1931 and volunteered for the SS in 1932. Originally assigned to the Dachau concentration camp in 1934 as a guard, Kramer's slavish devotion to orders earned him promotions and transfers to camps at Sachsenhausen and Mauthausen.

In 1940, Kramer was assigned to assist Rudolf Hoess, commandant of the Auschwitz concentration camp. Ostensibly tasked with choosing a site for the development of a synthetic fuel plant, their true mission was to select a suitable site for the implementation of the Final Solution, the mass killing of Jews. Kramer's attention to strict discipline and sadistic demeanor earned him the praise of Reichshührer-SS Heinrich Himmler.

From May 1941 to August 1943, Kramer served as commandant of the Natzweiler concentration camp in France. At Natzweiler, one of Kramer's duties was to provide suitable human remains to August Hirt, an anatomist at the Strasburg Medical University. Eighty inmates were transported from Auschwitz to Natzweiler, where Kramer participated in their execution. In November 1943, Kramer was again stationed at Auschwitz, where Hoess assigned him to oversee the gas chambers at Birkenau.

In December 1944, Kramer was promoted to the rank of Hauptsturmführer-SS (captain) and appointed commandant of the Bergen-Belsen camp. Kramer brought to Belsen the strict discipline and sadism he had already demonstrated. Lengthy roll calls, harsh labor, and insufficient food became common at Belsen. As Nazi Germany began to disintegrate in early 1945, more and more transports continued to bring prisoners to the already overcrowded Belsen. With a population of 15,257 inmates at the end of 1944, the number soared to 44,000 by March 1945.

By April 1945, order within the camp had vanished, and Allied bombings had disrupted the camp's water and food supplies. As a typhus epidemic raged, the camp's crematorium could no longer handle the increasing number of dead bodies. Kramer reported that up to 300 inmates per day were dying. Corpses were simply left where they had died. As Allied armies pushed further into Germany, prisoners from threatened camps were transported to Belsen. During the week of April 13, more than 20,000 additional prisoners were transported to Belsen.

On April 15, 1945, British troops liberated Belsen. They found some 40,000 starving survivors along with some 35,000 unburied corpses that littered the camp. To his surprise, Kramer was arrested. On September 17, 1945, Kramer and 44 others stood trial before a British military tribunal. The prosecution detailed the horrific conditions of Bergen-Belsen, and also presented evidence of Kramer's time spent at Auschwitz. His defense argued that he was merely following orders in a time of war and had been following German laws, but this defense was not permitted or accepted by the court. Kramer was found guilty and hanged on December 13, 1945, in Hamelin, Germany.

Robert W. Malick

See also: Bergen-Belsen; Holocaust, The.

Further Reading

Shephard, Ben. *After Daybreak: The Liberation of Bergen-Belsen, 1945.* New York: Schocken Books, 2005.

Snyder, Louis L. *Hitler's Elite.* New York: Brinkley Books, 1990.

Krupp Case (1948)

In *United States of America v. Alfried Krupp, et al.,* Military Tribunal No. III tried 12 executives of the firm Fried(rich) Krupp under the authority of Allied Control Council Law No. 10, between August 16, 1947 to July 31, 1948. The indictment charged the defendants with: I) crimes against peace; II) war crimes and crimes against humanity (plunder and spoliation); III) war crimes and crimes against humanity (forced and slave labor); and IV) conspiracy. The accused were

Alfried Krupp von Bohlen und Halbach, Ewald Lőser, Eduard Houdremont, Erich Műller, Friedrich Janssen, Karl Pfirsch, Max Ihn, Karl Eberhardt, Heinrich Korschan, Friedrich von Bűlow, Werner Lehmann, and Hans Kupke. The prosecution later dropped the first and fourth counts against von Bűlow, Lehmann, and Kupke.

In October 1945, the Allies indicted Alfried Krupp's father, Gustav Krupp, as a major war criminal before the International Military Tribunal (IMT). After serving the indictment, the IMT determined the elder Krupp's unfitness to stand trial, and considered four possibilities for adjudicating his case, as proposed by the prosecution and defense: trial in absentia, dismissal, indefinite postponement, or indictment of Alfried Krupp. In the interest of fairness, the IMT adopted the third course and rejected the proposal of charging the son for allegations against the father. The U.S. Office of the Chief of Counsel for War Crimes thereupon tried the firm's executives as Case IX of the Nuremberg Subsequent Proceedings.

Despite the insistence of prosecutor Telford Taylor that the accused sat in the dock for their misdeeds, the postponed case against Gustav Krupp cast a shadow over the proceedings. According to the prosecution, the firm conspired in 1919 to prepare future German aggression and matched Adolf Hitler's imperialistic ambition. After a unanimous defense motion, the Tribunal dismissed the charges of crimes against peace and conspiracy against all defendants, on grounds that private citizens could not wage war, and that the IMT Charter fixed strict temporal limits to the court's jurisdiction.

After marrying Bertha Krupp, Gustav von Bohlen und Halbach presided over Fried. Krupp AG from 1906 to 1943. His eagerness to please Hitler resulted from a determination to preserve family control over the business, not ideological affinity. His persistent lobbying led to Hitler's issue of Lex Krupp in November 1943: by decree, the public corporation (*Aktiengesellschaft*) was transformed into a perpetual proprietorship, whose owner had to bear the Krupp name. The von Bohlens attached "Krupp" to their name and Alfried took possession of the newly-minted Fried. Krupp Essen.

The prosecution recounted Krupp's participation in the spoliation of steel plants and collieries in Austria, France, Belgium, the Netherlands, Yugoslavia, and the Soviet Union. During the German retreat in 1944, the firm looted machinery and other goods from French and Dutch companies. The defense described such behavior as excusable under emergency conditions, but the Tribunal convicted defendants Krupp, Lőser, Houdremont, Műller, Janssen, and Eberhardt for spoliation. On two occasions, Krupp participated in the Aryanization of Jewish-owned steel plants in Liancourt and Paris. In contrast to the Flick Trial, Tribunal III accepted the argument that offenses against industrial property may constitute crimes against humanity. A majority acquitted the defendants of spoliation in Austria, Yugoslavia, and the Soviet Union.

The most damaging evidence against Krupp concerned the deployment of forced and slave labor. In western and eastern Germany, the firm utilized 100,000 conscripted foreign civilians, prisoners of war, and concentration-camp prisoners. Noted for generous if paternalistic care of Kruppianer (the main German workforce), Krupp brutalized its captives. From fall 1942 to spring 1944, it attempted to establish an automatic gun, then a fuse, factory at Auschwitz concentration camp. Accepting the Reich's proposal of location, it abandoned the project due to economic bottlenecks and its inability to meet contractual obligations, not humanitarian considerations.

Withdrawal from Auschwitz did not spell the end of Krupp's involvement with slave labor, however. Gross-Rosen inmates erected the Bertha-Werke at Markstädt, in Upper Silesia. Five hundred female Jewish internees from Buchenwald also toiled at the main Krupp Essen plant in late 1944 and early 1945. According to the defense, the regime caught Krupp between the Scylla of inflexible production quotas and the Charybdis of labor allocation imposed from above. The defendants thus had no choice but to accept whatever labor the State supplied. While the judges in the Flick and I.G. Farben cases endorsed a similar defense of necessity, Tribunal III found that such pleadings ought to apply strictly to life-and-death circumstances, not cases concerning the potential loss of property. The court also determined that Krupp had aggressively procured and exploited coercive labor, and thereby demonstrated initiative, an exception to the Flick ruling. Eleven defendants were convicted on the slave labor count.

The court sentenced all but one defendant to terms of imprisonment that ranged from 2 years and 10 months to 12 years. It also ordered the confiscation of Alfried Krupp's industrial property, as provided by Allied Control Council directives. Pfirsch was acquitted. Two of three judges, President H.C. Anderson and William Wilkins (the third was Edward Daly), issued concurring and dissenting opinions. Anderson found the sentences against all defendants except Krupp too severe, and expressed reservations about the seizure of the latter's property. By contrast, Wilkins opined that the Tribunal had erred in acquitting the defendants on certain spoliation charges. In January 1951, U.S. high commissioner for Germany John J. McCloy restored the firm to Krupp's ownership and commuted his twelve-year sentence.

Joseph Robert White

See also: I.G. Farben Case (1947); J.A. Topf & Söhne; Koch Trial (1951); Nuremberg Trials; Zyklon B Case (1946).

Further Reading

International Military Tribunal. *Trial of the Major War Criminals: Nuremberg, 14 October 1945–1 October 1946.* Vols. I & II. Nuremberg: Secretariat of the IMT, 1949.

United Nations War Crimes Commission. *Law Reports of Trials of War Criminals.* Vol. X. London: HMSO, 1949.

United States Nuremberg Military Tribunals. *Trials of War Criminals Before the Nuremberg Military Tribunals under Control Council Law No. 10.* Vol. IX. Washington: GPO, 1950–1953.

Young, Gordon. *The Fall and Rise of Alfried Krupp.* London: Cassell, 1960.

L

Lamsdorf

Site of the Stalag VIII-B Lamsdorf prisoner-of-war camp during World War II. Established in 1939, the camp initially comprised of barracks built to house British and French prisoners during World War I. The camp size quickly grew as Nazi Germany gained military victories in Europe, and eventually held some 100,000 prisoners; in 1941, following the German invasion of the Soviet Union, a separate camp, Stalag VIII-F, was established for the Soviet prisoners of war. In 1943, the main camp was reorganized; some prisoners were moved to two new facilities—Stalag VIII-C Sagan (modern Żagań) and Stalag VIII-D Teschen (modern Český Těšín)—while the base camp itself was renamed to Stalag 344. In January 1945, as the Soviet armies approached the camp, the German authorities moved the surviving prisoners on what became known as the Long March or Death March; many prisoners perished from cold and exhaustion.

Alexander Mikaberidze

See also: Colditz; Stalag.

Further Reading
Vourkoutiotis, Vasilis. *The Prisoners of War and German High Command: The British and American Experience.* New York: Palgrave Macmillan, 2003.

Libby Prison

A prison facility maintained by the Confederacy to hold Union officers captured during the Civil War. Libby Prison was located in Richmond, Virginia, in an urban area bordered by Canal Street, 20th Street, Carey Street, and a vacant lot. Although practically in the middle of the city, the three-story, 150-by-100-foot building was self-contained, and thus easily guarded. Libby, along with Andersonville in Georgia, which housed enlisted Union prisoners of war (POWs), was the most famous—or infamous—of the Southern prison facilities.

Libby had originally been the Libby & Son Chandlers and Grocers before being converted into a prison. While conditions and death rates did not rise to the levels associated with Andersonville, conditions were nevertheless grim. Prisoners slept together in squads, lined along the cold, hard floor on their sides for warmth. Several times during the night, an elected squad leader would order his squad to turn over in unison as the hardness of the floor became unendurable. The food was execrable, and the amounts usually inadequate to sustain a grown man. Many officer prisoners bartered with each other, and sometimes with the guards to augment their meager rations.

Libby Prison was also the scene of one of the most daring escapes of the entire war. Under the direction of Colonel Thomas Rose of the 77th Pennsylvania, prisoners painstakingly dug a 50-foot-long tunnel underground through a kitchen fireplace to a warehouse shed located in the vacant lot across the street from the prison. On February 9, 1864, 109 men made their escape through the tunnel. Two of them drowned while trying to swim across the nearby James River, 48 (including Rose) were recaptured by local authorities, but 59 managed to avoid capture. The escapees provided an exciting account of their adventure and lurid stories of conditions inside Libby Prison.

During the final months of the war, Confederate officials began moving prisoners from Libby Prison to more secure locations throughout the South. When Richmond fell and the war ended in April 1865, Libby Prison was used by federal authorities to house a number of Confederate officials awaiting trial in Washington.

The life of Libby Prison did not end with the war. In 1888, W. H. Gray, A. G. Spalding, Charles Gunther, and three other Chicago businessmen formed the Libby Prison War Museum Corporation, dedicated to generating a profit from the infamous facility. In April 1889, the entire building was disassembled and transported via railroad from Richmond to Chicago. The prison was then reassembled brick by brick in the city's central business district. Libby was converted into a museum that housed an array of Civil War artifacts and that drew more than 100,000 visitors during the first three months of operation; thousands more were attracted to it during the 1893 World's Columbian Exposition. Interest in the museum soon faded, however, and it was razed in 1899.

Jeffery B. Cook

See also: Andersonville Prison; Confederate States of America; U.S. POW Camps, 1861–1865.

Further Reading

Hesseltine, William. *Civil War Prisons: A Study in War Psychology.* Columbus: The Ohio State University Press, 1998.

McPherson, James. *Battle Cry of Freedom: The Civil War Era.* New York: Oxford University Press, 1988.

Morgan, Michael. "Breakout of Rat Hell," *Civil War Times* (October 2001): 29–37.

Lieber Code

Military manual developed by the U.S. Army during the American Civil War. Published on April 24, 1863, as "General Orders No. 100—Instructions for the Government of Armies of the United States in the Fields," the Lieber Code consisted of 10 sections and 157 articles laying out rules of warfare.

The Code was named after the German American Dr. Francis Lieber, who drafted the military manual. U.S. president Abraham Lincoln had asked him to prepare a codification of the rules of land warfare to be used in the Civil War. At that time, it was the first codification of the rules and customs of war by a State, and included more than rules concerning the methods and means of warfare. The Lieber Code had great impact on other codifications of international humanitarian law, including

The Hague Conventions of 1899 and 1907, the St. Petersburg Declaration of 1874, and the Geneva Conventions of 1864, 1906, 1929, and 1949. The Lieber Code also became the model for similar military manuals distributed by Germany, France, England, and many other countries to their soldiers in the field.

Section I of the code dealt with certain general principles of the laws of war, including martial law, military jurisdiction, military necessity, and retaliation. Sections II, III, and IV dealt with public and private property of the enemy, protection of persons, punishment of crimes, prisoners of war, and partisans. Sections V, VI and VII included rules concerning spies, war traitors, abuse of the flag of truce, exchange of prisoners, and parole. Sections VIII, XI and X dealt with armistice, assassination, and civil war.

The Lieber Code contained important provisions on the treatment of prisoners of war. Article 49 defined what category of persons should be treated as prisoners of war:

> Prisoner of war is a public enemy armed or attached to the hostile army for active aid, who has fallen into the hands of the captor, either fighting or wounded, on the field or in the hospital, by individual surrender or by capitulation.
>
> All soldiers, of whatever species of arms; all men who belong to the rising en masse of the hostile country; all those who are attached to the Army for its efficiency and promote directly the object of the war, except such as are hereinafter provided for; all disabled men or officers on the field or elsewhere, if captured; all enemies who have thrown away their arms and ask for quarter, are prisoners of war, and as such exposed to the inconveniences as well as entitled to the privileges of a prisoner of war.

The Lieber Code also specified that "citizens who accompany an army for whatever purpose, such as sutlers, editors, or reporters of journals, or contractors, if captured, may be made prisoners of war and be detained as such. . . . The monarch and members of the hostile reigning family . . . the chief, and chief officers of the hostile government, its diplomatic agents, and all persons who are of particular and singular use and benefit to the hostile army or its government, are, if captured on belligerent ground, and if unprovided with a safe-conduct granted by the captor's government, prisoners of war." Under Article 56, a prisoner of war should face "no punishment for being a public enemy, nor is any revenge wreaked upon him by the intentional infliction of any suffering, or disgrace, by cruel imprisonment, want of food, by mutilation, death, or any other barbarity." At the same time, prisoners of war could be held answerable for any crimes they had committed before he was captured and for which they had not been punished yet. The code protected POWs' personal possessions and considered "the appropriation of [POW] valuables or money [as] dishonorable and prohibited" (Article 72). Article 120 set up a mechanism for the prisoner release, stating that "the pledge of individual good faith and honor to do, or omit doing certain acts" was a sufficient condition for being released. It is noteworthy that Article 105 specified that any prisoner exchange should be done "number for number—rank for rank—wounded for wounded—with added condition for added condition."

The Lieber Code had a major impact on the development of the laws and rules of war. The Prussian Army used it as a model for the military manual which was distributed to its troops in the Franco-Prussian War of 1870. It also provided the basis for the adoption of the Brussels Declaration of 1874 and the Oxford Manual of 1880. Some of the code's provisions were later codified in the Hague Conventions of 1899 and 1907.

Alexander Mikaberidze

See also: Brussels, Declaration of (1874); Confederate States of America; U.S. POW Camps, 1861–1865.

Further Reading

Baxter, R.R. "The First Modern Codification of the Law of War," *International Review of the Red Cross* 3 (1963): 171–187.

Carnahan, Burrus M. "Lincoln, Lieber and the Laws of War: The Origins and Limits of Military Necessity," *American Journal of International Law* 92 (1998): 213–231.

"General Orders No. 100: The Lieber Code," The Avalon project, http://avalon.law.yale.edu /19th_century/lieber.asp

Hartigan, Richard S. *Lieber's Code and the Law of War*. Chicago: Precedent, 1983.

Los Baños

Japanese POW and civilian internment camp at Los Baños, Laguna, Philippines. After the occupation of the Philippines in 1942, the Japanese established a prisoner of war and civilian internment camp amidst the foothills of Mount Makiling

Internees of Los Baños, Laguna, Philippines. Wedged between the foothills of Mount Makiling and the northern shore of Los Baños, the Los Baños internment camp was established in 1943. In February 1945, a joint raid by U.S. Army Airborne and Filipino guerrilla task forces freed over 2,000 Allied civilian and military internees. (Carl Mydans/The LIFE Picture Collection/Getty Images)

and the northern shore of Los Baños facing Laguna de Bay. Throughout 1943 the camp received several groups of prisoners that included American, British, Australian, Polish, Dutch, Norwegian, Italian, and Canadian soldiers. At first conditions at the camp were tolerable, but they progressively worsened and, by late 1944, prisoners suffered from dwindling rations, poor housing, abysmal sanitation, and inhumane treatment by the camp guards. On February 23, 1945, a combined U.S. Army Airborne and Filipino guerrilla task force successfully raided the camp, killing over 200 Japanese troops and rescuing 2,147 civilian and military internees. One of the most successful rescue operations in modern military history, it came on the heels of another successful rescue mission launched by combined U.S.-Filipino forces at Cabanatuan at Luzon on January 30.

Alexander Mikaberidze

See also: Bataan Death March (1942); Batu Lintang Camp; Cabanatuan; Changi; Far East, British Military Trials; Sandakan Death Marches; Selarang Barracks Incident; Unit 731.

Further Reading

Henderson, Bruce. *Rescue At Los Baños: The Most Daring Prison Camp Raid of World War II.* New York: HarperCollins Publishing, 2016.

Rottman, Gordon L. *The Los Baños Prison Camp Raid: The Philippines 1945.* Oxford: Osprey, 2010.

Lublin. See Majdanek

M

Majdanek

A Nazi forced labor and death camp established by the Nazis in Poland on October 1, 1941, which remained operational until July 22, 1944, when it was liberated by Soviet troops. Majdanek was located just outside the Polish city of Lublin; unlike other Nazi camps in Poland, it was the only one not to be situated in a rural, isolated locale. Throughout its existence, the capacity of the camp continued to be expanded as more and more prisoners were transported there. Majdanek also served as a transit camp, where prisoners were temporarily housed while en route to other camps. Initially, SS leader Heinrich Himmler ordered the construction of Lublin-Majdanek as a forced labor camp that was to house Soviet war prisoners. The camp was to have a prisoner population of 50,000. By the end of 1941, that capacity had been raised to 250,000. Much of the early construction was done by Soviet prisoners of war and Jews deported from nearby Lublin.

Like most of the Nazi death camps, Lublin-Majdanek was staffed with SS officials along with locally recruited police forces. Prisoners also helped run the camp. Kapos helped maintain order and discipline in the barracks, while slave labor working in the crematoria (Sonderkommandos) readied prisoners for the gas chambers and later moved their bodies to crematoria or mass graves.

During 1942 and 1943, the camp's population continued to expand as Jews from other parts of Poland were deported there. By 1943, Lublin-Majdanek had 145 barracks; that same year, the sub-camps of Budzyn, Trawniki, Krasnik, Pulawy, Luopwa, and Poniatowa were subsumed by Majdanek's administration. Perhaps the largest single influx of Jews to arrive at Majdanek occurred in 1942, when some 25,000 were transferred from Bełżec, another death camp. The following year, 18,000–22,000 more Jews were sent to the camp; most had been residents of the Warsaw Ghetto, which had been liquidated as a result of the April 13, 1943, uprising there.

Beginning on a massive scale in the fall of 1943, camp officials began exterminating prisoners using carbon monoxide and Zyklon B gas. Most of the bodies were incinerated in the facility's crematoria. Beginning on November 3, Nazi officials forced prisoners and Jews detained in nearby sub-camps to begin digging mass graves. SS officials then shot and killed 18,000 Jews outside Lublin-Majdanek (8,000 from the camp alone) and buried them in the graves that the victims themselves had dug.

On July 22, 1944, Soviet troops rushed toward the camp. Because of their hasty arrival, camp officials were unable to disguise or hide their activities, as they did at other mass murder sites. What the Soviets found was deeply disturbing— detainees who were near starvation and rail-thin; gas chambers with bodies still in them; and crematoria with human remains and mounds of ashes. In August, the Soviets cordoned off the entire camp and convened a Soviet-Polish commission designed to investigate the Nazis' activities at Lublin-Majdanek. This was one of the first efforts to document German war crimes in eastern Europe, and it occurred almost a year before the end of World War II. Because the Soviets secured the camp before the Nazis could properly dismantle it, it is considered the best-preserved death camp site from the Holocaust era.

Estimates as to the death toll at Lublin-Majdanek vary considerably, from as low as 78,000 to as high as 1.5 million. Holocaust scholars have since determined that the death toll may have been around 360,000, although an exact number is impossible to determine. Some 75,000–90,000 Jews (60,000 of them Polish Jews) were deported to the camp between 1941 and 1944. While many were gassed to death, many also died from the brutal conditions in the camp as well as from forced labor.

Numerous camp personnel were prosecuted for war crimes and crimes against humanity. The first trial occurred in late 1944, when four SS soldiers and two Kapos were tried; five of the men were executed on December 4, 1944, while the sixth man committed suicide. Of the approximately 1,037 SS personnel who worked at Lublin-Majdanek, only 170 were prosecuted for war crimes; the last trial occurred in West Germany in 1981. After World War II ended in 1945, three of the camp's commandants were also tried, convicted, and executed.

Paul G. Pierpaoli, Jr.

See also: Arbeitslager; Auschwitz; Bełżec; Bergen-Belsen; Birkenau; Buchenwald; Bullet Decree (1944); Chełmno; Colditz; Concentration Camps; Dachau; Death Camps; Dora-Mittelbau; Eichmann, Adolf; Extermination Centers; Gas Chambers; Gestapo; Gross-Rosen; Ninzert; Hitler, Adolf; Holocaust, The; I.G. Farben Case (1947); J.A. Topf & Söhne; Kinderblock 66; Koch Trial (1951); Kramer, Josef; Krupp Case (1948); Lamsdorf; Mauthausen; Medical Experimentation during World War II; Monowitz; Natzweiler-Struthof; Neuengamme; Niederhagen; Nuremberg Trials; Ravensbrück; Sachsenhausen; Slave Labor (World War II); Sobibór; Sonderkommando; Stalag; Stutthof; Treblinka; Trostinets; Zyklon B Case (1946).

Further Reading

Mailänder, Elissa. *Female SS Guards and Workaday Violence: The Majdanek Concentration Camp, 1942–1944.* East Lansing: Michigan State University Press, 2015.

Wachsmann, Nikolaus. *KL: A History of the Nazi Concentration Camps.* New York: Farrar, Straus and Giroux, 2015.

Maly Trostinets. *See Trostinets*

Manjača

An internment camp near the city of Banja Luka in northern Bosnia and Herzegovina during the Croatian War of Independence (1991) and the Bosnian War (1992–1995). Manjača was a Yugoslav National Army base before the war. In 1991, the Republika Srpska (RS) turned it into an internment camp where Croat prisoners were held in facilities on top of the mount Manjača. The prisoners were subjected to regular mistreatment and abuse, including beatings and killings; one of the prisoners described, "we were kept in stables, just like cattle, with nothing to sleep on but concrete floor and mown grass . . . in the morning we would get a thin slice of bread and plain tea. Lunch [consisted of] another slice of bread and a small amount of cooked food, usually soup or gruel . . ."

International outcry over prisoner abuse led to the camp being closed in 1993, but it reopened during the Bosnian War in October 1995. As many as 6,000 Bosnian prisoners passed through the camp before it was captured by Bosnian forces; dozens of prisoners were murdered at the camps. In 2007, the International Court of Justice's judgment in the Bosnian Genocide case described atrocities committed in detention camps, including Manjača.

Alexander Mikaberidze

See also: Bosnian War; Yugoslavia.

Further Reading

Nizich, Ivana. *War Crimes in Bosnia-Hercegovina* (Helsinki Watch, 1992), II, 132–137. New York: Human Rights Watch, 1992.

Sells, Michael A. *The Bridge Betrayed: Religion and Genocide in Bosnia.* Berkeley: University of California Press, 1998.

Mao Zedong (1893–1976)

Leader of the People's Republic of China (1949–1976) and one of history's deadliest dictators. Born into a prosperous peasant family in Hunan Province, in central China, Mao Zedong graduated from a Teacher's Training School, but soon became involved in radical political circles and supported the Chinese Communist Party (CCP). In the 1920s he opposed the Guomindang (GMD, Nationalist) government of China and established a Communist base in Jiangxi (Kiangsi) Province, where he helped found the Jiangxi Soviet Republic (JSR) in 1931. When the GMD forces encircled the JSR in 1934, Mao broke out and led more than 100,000 followers on the epic Long March of 6,000 miles to Yenan in northern China. He was elected chairman of the CCP in 1935.

During World War I, Mao agreed to cooperate with the Nationalist authorities against the Japanese, and Mao's Red Army played an important role in the eventual victory. The Communist-GMD union broke down as soon as the war ended and the two sides engaged in a brutal civil war that GMD lost. In 1949, Mao proclaimed the new People's Republic of China (PRC), and served as its supreme leader until his death. He was responsible for several controversial and costly policies, including the Great Leap Forward (1958–1962), a disastrous attempt to industrialize China, and the Cultural Revolution (1966) that sought to induce a state of permanent revolution in China.

To combat internal opposition, Mao transplanted elements of the Soviet model and developed a vast machinery of state repression that included hundreds of internment and forced labor camps. A highly controversial figure, Mao Zedong is one of the most important individuals in modern history, but also a person who oversaw mass repressions, purges, executions, and forced labor that claimed an estimated 40 to 70 million lives.

Alexander Mikaberidze

See also: China.

Further Reading

Feigon, Lee. *Mao: A Reinterpretation.* Chicago: Ivan R. Dee, 2002.

Short, Philip. *Mao: A Life.* New York: Henry Holt, 2000.

Spence, Jonathan D. *Mao Zedong.* New York: Viking, 1999.

Terrill, Ross. *Mao: A Biography.* Stanford, CA: Stanford University Press, 1999.

Maschke Commission

Between 1962 and 1974, Erich Maschke, a respected German historian from University of Heidelberg and former German prisoner of war in the Soviet Union, led the Scientific Commission for the History of the German Prisoners of War that produced a vast study on the German prisoners of war. The 22-volume series, *Zur Geschichte der deutschen Kriegsgefangenen des Zweiten Weltkrieges* (The History of German Prisoners of War of the Second World War) examined documentary evidence and conducted interviews with German POWs to describe conditions in the Allied POW camps and demonstrate mistreatment and abuse of the captured German soldiers, especially those held by the Soviets.

Of the 22 volumes, 13 dealt with Eastern Europe (Poland, Czechoslovakia, Yugoslavia and Soviet Union), where the German POWs were treated the worst. The commission reported that by the end of the war, some 940,000 German soldiers were held by the French, 3.64 million by the British and 3.1 million by the Americans. It also showed many cases of maltreatment and referred to some 25,000 German prisoners who died in French custody, some of them perishing when forced to clear wartime minefields.

The Maschke Commission also found that about 5,000 German POWs died in in American custody and 1,300 in British custody. The commission concluded that the Western powers demonstrated cruel indifference to the captured German soldiers, who were treated with certain vindictiveness and subjected to harsh conditions, including lack of adequate food and shelter; this treatment was partly explained by the Allied awareness of the horrors of the German concentration camps. Despite some criticisms, the latest scholarship has largely corroborated the story told by the Maschke Commission.

Alexander Mikaberidze

See also: Rheinwiesenlager; World War II Prisoners of War.

Further Reading

Kochavi, Arieh J. *Britain and the United States and Their POWs in Nazi Germany.* Chapel Hill: The University of North Carolina Press, 2005.

Steininger, Rolf. "Some Reflections on the Maschke Commission," in Gunther Bischof and Stephen E. Ambrose, eds. *Eisenhower and the German POWs: Facts against Falsehood.* 170–80. Baton Rouge: Louisiana State University Press, 1992.

Mauthausen-Gusen

Located approximately 12 miles east of the city of Linz in Upper Austria, this concentration camp was actually two sites—Mauthausen and Gusen (Gusen I, II, and III)—and further establishments numbering more than 100 sub-camps throughout Austria. Its specific locale was between the small villages of Mauthausen and Sankt Georgen an der Gusen (or, simply, Gusen). This was, after construction, located in what was formerly a heavily forested area away from the larger population centers, and close to the stone quarry of Wienergraben. In terms of its horrific conditions and brutality, as well as the numbers of murdered victims (Jews, interestingly enough, being a decided minority), it rivalled Auschwitz-Birkenau in southeastern Poland. In fact, it was the only camp(s) given Category III status, and thus identified by the twin understandings *Rückkehr unerwüunscht* ("return not desired") and *Vernichtung durch arbeit* ("extermination by work"). In the offices of the Reich Security Main Office (Reichssicherheitshauptamt) in Berlin, it was also known, somewhat colloquially, as the Knochenmühle ("bone mill").

Its primary victims were political and social dissidents and intellectuals, initially from Austria, but later from Spain (more than 7,000 anti-Franco Republicans and communists, members of the so-called International Brigade who also fought against the fascist takeover), Czechoslovakia, Soviet Russia, and Poland. Prior to liberation, in 1944 these groups began organizing serious resistance efforts which culminated in an unsuccessful insurrection on February 1, 1945. It was organized primarily by Soviet prisoners, almost all of whom were either killed or captured. This "action" was labelled Mühlviertler Hasenjagd ("rabbit chase") by the SS and those who assisted them. Jews, however, played a relatively minor role in both the organizing of such efforts and their implementation, due primarily to their smaller numbers and late arrival.

Mauthausen-Gusen was established under the direct imprimatur of Reichsführer-SS Heinrich Himmler on August 8, 1938, after an initial visit to select the location, almost five months to the day after the German Anschluss with Austria on March 12, 1938. It would ultimately become one of the largest—if not the largest—slave labor complex in the whole of Nazi-occupied Europe. Although under the direct control of the Nazi state, Mauthausen-Gusen was initially founded by a private company as an economic enterprise. Its first commandant was SS captain Albert Sauer (August 1, 1938–April 1 1939), until he was replaced by SS colonel Franz Ziereis. He remained at the helm until the camp's liberation on May 5, 1945. From March 1940 onward, SS captain Georg Bachmayer was tasked with internal control of all prisoners inside the camps. Though estimates of victims vary, due largely to the destruction of vital records, overall numbers approached 200,000 between August 1, 1938 and May 5, 1945, with almost 100,000 murdered, included approximately 14,000 Jews. Of the more than 300,000 imprisoned in the various sub-camps, no more than 80,000, representing 26 percent, survived. The liberation of Mauthausen-Gusen was achieved by members of the 41st Reconnaissance Squad, 11th Armored Division, 3rd US Army, and it was the last such camp to be liberated by Allied forces.

Among the more famous of those liberated was Simon Wiesenthal, acclaimed Austrian Nazi hunter and writer, and Hungarian Tibor Rubin, who would later go on to win the U.S. Congressional Medal of Honor for his military service in the Korean War.

As a slave-labor enterprise, Mauthausen-Gusen was the most successful operation under Nazi control in terms of both production outputs and profits, generating more than 11 million Reichsmark by 1944. Among the major German corporations which benefitted from these slave laborers were: Accumulatoren-Fabrik AFa (military batteries); Bayer Pharmaceuticals (medicines and medications); DEST cartel (bricks and quarry stone); Flugmotorenwerke Ostmark (airplane engines); Heinkel und Messerschmitt (airplane and rocket production); and Otto Eberhard Patronenfabrik (munitions).

As regards the prisoners themselves, gas chambers for their deaths were originally in operation by 1940 and permanently by 1941, and, by war's end, 10 functioning gas chambers were constructed and in use. The standard litany of abuse—beatings, torture, starvation, random shootings, and disease—was equally fully in evidence. Perhaps the most notoriously brutal method was that of requiring the stone quarry prisoners to race up the 186 "Stairs of Death" carrying their stones, often close to their own body-weights and averaging 110 pounds, falling to their deaths, being trampled by other prisoners, and then, finally, making it to the top only to stand in line and being shot from behind—to the amusement and delight of their captors. Then, too, on many occasions prisoners were assembled in the various collection sites, sprayed with water and left to freeze to death in sub-zero temperatures, or forced to take cold showers at the end of their work-day with the same effect. Camp diseases, such as dysentery, also took an enormous toll.

In the spring of 1946, 61 defendants were tried by the U.S. Military Tribunal stationed at Dachau. Fifty-eight were sentenced to death (49 executions were carried out), and three to life imprisonment. Later, nine of the initial death sentences were commuted to life sentences; and, between 1950 and 1951, the remaining 12 prisoners were released. However, more than 90 percent of the additional 224 Mauthausen-Gusen perpetrators (202) were found guilty and sentenced to varied prison terms.

The Mauthausen-Gusen site was declared an important historical site by Austria in 1949; its museum officially opened in 1974. Mauthausen has remained largely intact, but Gusen I, II, and III have been transposed into residential dwellings.

Steven Leonard Jacobs

See also: Arbeitslager; Auschwitz; Bełżec; Bergen-Belsen; Birkenau; Buchenwald; Bullet Decree (1944); Chełmno; Colditz; Concentration Camps; Dachau; Death Camps; Dora-Mittelbau; Eichmann, Adolf; Extermination Centers; Gas Chambers; Gestapo; Gross-Rosen; Ninzert; Hitler, Adolf; Holocaust, The; I.G. Farben Case (1947); J.A. Topf & Söhne; Kinderblock 66; Koch Trial (1951); Kramer, Josef; Krupp Case (1948); Monowitz; Natzweiler-Struthof; Neuengamme; Niederhagen; Nuremberg Trials; Ravensbrück; Sachsenhausen; Slave Labor (World War II); Sobibór; Sonderkommando; Stalag; Stutthof; Treblinka; Trostinets; Zyklon B Case (1946).

Further Reading
Haunschmeid, Rudolf A., Jan-Ruth Mills, and Siegl Witzany-Durda. *St. Georgen-Gusen-Mauthausen: Concentration Camp Mauthausen Reconsidered.* Books on Demand www.gusen.org, 2008.

Horwitz, Gordon J. *In the Shadow of Death: Living Outside the Gates of Mauthausen.* New York: Free Press, 1990.

Jardim, Tomaz. *The Mauthausen Trial: American Military Justice in Germany.* Cambridge, MA: Harvard University Press, 2012.

Kulish, Nicholas, and Souad Mekhennet. *The Eternal Nazi: From Mauthausen to Cairo, the Relentless Pursuit of SS Doctor Aribert Heim.* New York: Doubleday, 2014.

Le Chêne, Evelyn. *Mauthausen: The History of a Death Camp.* London: Methuen Publishers, 1971.

Medical Experimentation during World War II

During World War II, German doctors and scientists performed a wide variety of medical experiments on individuals imprisoned in concentration camps. These experiments were usually based on faulty or pseudo-scientific premises and were conducted with virtually no regard for the victims' well-being or survival. Indeed, many experiments ended in the permanent disfigurement or death of the people involved. The Nazi experiments may be divided into three broad categories: exercises that involved the testing of new drugs and the treatment of various illnesses or injuries; tests designed to ascertain certain physical effects on soldiers and pilots; and experiments that sought to "prove" Nazi racial theories or purge the German bloodline of so-called inferior peoples.

The development of new drugs and the treatment of injuries—especially those sustained in battle—were of particular importance to doctors at the Buchenwald, Dachau, Natzweiler, Sachsenhausen, and Neuegamme concentration camps. There doctors administered untested pharmaceutical compounds, inoculations, and serums to various individuals to gauge their effectiveness against such maladies as typhoid fever, malaria, tuberculosis, infectious hepatitis, and yellow fever. While it may have been commendable to seek treatments or cures for such illnesses, the experiments were forced upon internees, and many died during or after the experiments. At Ravensbrück, prisoners' legs and arms were broken to test bone-grafting and amputation techniques. Many of these tests were done using little or no anesthetic. At other camps, internees were exposed to mustard and phosgene gas as doctors experimented with various antidotes; many of the victims died. There were even attempts to transplant limbs, although the results were disappointing and many of the victims died of massive infections.

At Dachau particularly, prisoners were employed to test various conditions that pilots and soldiers might have to endure. These included placing people into low-pressure chambers to gauge the effects of high altitude on air force personnel. Physicians here were joined by German civilian physicians from the Institute of Aviation. Other prisoners were studied to gauge the effects of hypothermia on the human body. Victims were either forced to lie in the snow in winter with no clothes on or were immersed into tanks of ice-cold water for an hour or more at a time. Many of the victims died or suffered greatly. Still others were compelled to drink seawater until they passed out or died.

The last category of experiments, which aimed to prove or sustain Nazi racial and social policies, was perhaps the most cruel and bizarre of all. Many tests involved young children. At Auschwitz and Ravensbrück, mass sterilization experiments were conducted on men and women, who had their sex organs irradiated. Many were badly burned in the process. Doctors also engaged in wide-scale surgical castration to ensure that prisoners did not engage in sexual intercourse. At Auschwitz and Sachsenhausen, doctors conducted serological tests on Romanis, which included children, to study how different "races" contracted or responded to communicable diseases.

No other German physician became as widely known for his bizarre and cruel experimentation as did Josef Mengele, who became chief medical officer at Auschwitz in 1943. Mengele took a special interest in child twins and those who exhibited some sort of physical abnormality. He would often ingratiate himself to children by offering them sweets and then perform inhumane experiments on them. One experiment witnessed the injection of different chemicals into children's eyes to see if their eye color could be altered. Other children underwent bizarre amputations and other experimental surgeries, oftentimes without proper anesthesia. One particularly grotesque experiment involved sewing together two Romani twins to create conjoined twins. They eventually died of gangrene and massive infections. Young girls were routinely sterilized and given shock treatments to gauge their reactions to such stimuli. One night saw the rounding up of 14 pairs of Romani twins; they were taken to a lab, killed by the injection of chloroform into their hearts, and meticulously dissected by Mengele himself.

It is estimated that the Germans conducted at least 70 different "medical research" programs, supervised by nearly 200 physicians and scientists. At least 7,000 prisoners were involved, many of whom were killed or permanently injured. A number of these programs were connected to civilian laboratories, hospitals, and universities, which was an indictment of the entire German medical establishment. After the war, more than 20 Nazi physicians were tried for crimes against humanity at Nuremberg, beginning in October 1946. Seven were given the death penalty, nine were handed long prison terms, and seven were found not guilty. Unfortunately, Mengele fled Germany, finally taking up residence incognito in South America. He was never brought to justice for his many crimes. There was but one silver lining in the darkness of the Nazi experiments: after 1946, the international medical community put in place specific guidelines for medical experimentation so that the grotesque excesses of World War II would not be repeated.

The Japanese also engaged in extensive biological warfare research on humans during World War II in China. Unit 731 of the Japanese Army, under the leadership of microbiologist Lieutenant General Shiro Ishii, was the primary research group located out of Harbin, China. The Japanese experimented on prisoners at a disguised "water purification" plant. After the experiments, there were no survivors. The Japanese also conducted field trials across the Chinese countryside to test various disease (e.g., anthrax, smallpox, cholera) delivery systems.

See also: Germany; Holocaust, The; Mengele, Josef; Unit 731.

Further Reading
Lifton, Robert Jay. *The Nazi Doctors: Medical Killing and the Psychology of Genocide.* New York: Basic Books, 2000.

Posner, Gerald L., and John Ware. *Mengele: The Complete Story.* New York: Cooper Square, 2000.

Proctor, Robert. *Racial Hygiene: Medicine under the Nazis.* Cambridge, MA: Harvard University Press, 1988.

Mengele, Josef (1911–1979)

German medical doctor who performed quasi-scientific experiments on prisoners in Nazi concentration camps. He was born on March 16, 1911, in Gunzburg, Bavaria, and began studying medicine in 1930, showing a special interest in anthropology and genetics. From 1935, he worked at a medical clinic. Having joined Germany's National Socialist Party, Mengele became a research assistant at an institute for heredity and "racial purity" at Frankfurt University; by 1938 he was a member of the SS. He volunteered for the German Army in 1940, and took part in the invasion of the Soviet Union in 1941 before an injury rendered him unfit for further military service.

In May 1943, Mengele volunteered to become the senior physician in the women's section of the Auschwitz concentration camp. One of his duties was to examine arriving prisoners and decide whether they were to be sent to the gas chambers or to forced labor. A number of the prisoners also became the subjects of Mengele's medical experiments. Auschwitz provided him an unending supply of research subjects, especially Romanis, people with physical deformities, and twins. Mengele's particular interest was twin research, because he believed that if the Nazis could duplicate multizygotic births, the population could attain Aryan perfection. He observed each twin couple under the same life conditions and killed them in the best of health—an ideal assumption for postmortem research. Mengele's crude surgery included amputations and deliberate infections with diseases

Josef Mengele in Paraguay in 1960. At the Auschwitz extermination camp, he performed deadly human experiments on prisoners and was a member of the team of doctors who selected victims to be killed in the gas chambers. When the war ended, the doctor escaped prosecution and died in Brazil in 1979. (Bettmann/Getty Images)

in order to observe reactions. He also used methods involving electricity and radiation. Observers noted that he never expressed regret over the suffering of his human subjects. Over time, he became known to the prisoners as the Angel of Death.

Mengele continued his experiments until the advance of the Red Army forced him to leave Auschwitz on January 17, 1945. U.S. forces captured him, but he managed to escape despite being listed as a war criminal. He returned to Gunzburg and, in 1948, with financial assistance provided by his family, was able to travel to and settle in Argentina under an assumed name. In 1956 Mengele returned to Germany and married for a second time, and in 1961 fled once more, this time to Paraguay. Fearing capture, he moved on to Brazil in 1978. On February 7, 1979, Mengele went for a swim, suffered a stroke, and drowned. After investigations ordered by the U.S. Justice Department, his gravesite at Bertioga was revealed and experts were able to prove that the skeleton was that of Mengele. The discovery of his death ended a worldwide manhunt.

Martin Moll

See also: Auschwitz; Heim, Aribert; Holocaust, The; Oberheuser, Herta; Unit 731.

Further Reading

Astor, Gerald. *The Last Nazi: The Life and Times of Dr. Josef Mengele*. New York: Donald I. Fine, 1985.

Cefrey, Holly. *Doctor Josef Mengele—The Angel of Death*. New York: Rosen, 2001.

Posner, Gerald L., and John Ware. *Mengele: The Complete Story*. New York: Cooper Square, 2000.

Weinberg, David J. *Mengele's Legacy*. Danbury, CT: Rutledge Books, 2001.

Monowitz

One of the three primary camps which, along with numerous sub-camps, made up the Auschwitz complex. It was distinguished from the other camps by its focus on the provision of slave labor to a new chemical plant built by I.G. Farben in the same area as the other two primary Auschwitz camps. It was in operation from October 1942 to January 1945, when it was liberated by the Soviet army.

The initiative for the camp came from I.G. Farben, Germany's largest corporation—actually, a cartel—and chemical manufacturer. It had decided to build a chemical plant not far from Auschwitz. More specifically, the plant was to be located on the site of the village of Monowice, in the southern part of the section of Poland that was annexed by Germany. This site offered all of the basics required for a major plant, including flat ground and access to water and rail lines.

I.G. Farben saw another reason—this one compelling—to build its plant where it did. It was located so that it could avail itself of the seemingly unlimited source of slave labor that could be provided by the nearby Auschwitz main camp. Building a concentration camp on site to house the slave labor that would be made available to construct and work in the chemical facility represented a significant financial incentive to I.G. Farben. The SS "leased" these prisoners to I.G. Farben for an extraordinarily low daily rate. As a result, a concentration camp was built by slave labor so that a corporate entity could profit from the ongoing Final Solution of the Jews. This explains why Monowitz has been referred to as I.G. Farben's "corporate concentration camp."

The camp was given several names over its years of operation. The primary product to be manufactured at the camp was Buna, a type of synthetic rubber named for two of its components: butadiene and sodium, which has the chemical symbol of NA. Thus, the camp was called Buna/Monowitz (and the plant built there, Buna Werke). Its name was later changed to reflect an administrative restructuring of the Auschwitz complex, made in late 1943 to provide for three autonomous primary camps. Monowitz became Auschwitz III, with the main camp called Auschwitz I, and Birkenau, the extermination center, called Auschwitz II.

Although its initial group of prisoners came from other concentration camps, the main source of manpower for Monowitz came from Jews who had been sent to Auschwitz. The vast majority of Jews deported to Auschwitz went immediately to their death in the extermination center, Birkenau, but others were assigned to the main camp for slave labor, and still others were sent to Monowitz.

The proposal for a camp for the housing of "employees" and the building of industrial facilities was submitted by I.G. Farben to Rudolf Hoess, the Auschwitz commandant, in October 1941. The proposal was also submitted to the management and board of directors of I.G. Farben in early 1942, resulting in an agreement in June of that year to go forward with the construction of a concentration camp—more accurately, a labor camp—that would be the Monowitz concentration camp (Konzentrationslager Monowitz).

With the help of a major German engineering company—the Organisation Todt, named for the Nazi leader, Fritz Todt—Monowitz was ready to receive its first group of prisoners at the end of October 1942. In December 1942, some 3,500 prisoners were housed in the Monowitz concentration camp, but that number grew to more than 11,000 by July 1944.

Monowitz was not headed by a commandant until the administrative restructuring in November 1943 that resulted in it being an autonomous camp. At that time, SS-Hauptsturmführer Heinrich Schwarz was named commandant, and served as such until January 1945. Prior to then, the camp was led by a Lagerführer (Camp Leader), SS-Obersturmführer Vinzens Schöttl.

Conditions in the Monowitz camp were in some ways better than in the Auschwitz main camp, with the possibility of working indoors, out of the elements, and even windows and heat in some of the barracks, but the overcrowded conditions, with poor sanitation, the constant risk of disease, and inadequate food took a heavy toll on the population. Prisoners were also subject to grueling production demands from factory supervisors, with failure to meet them resulting in beatings, and sometimes death, either on the spot in Monowitz or by transfer to Birkenau.

With the Soviet army closing in, the entire Auschwitz complex, including Monowitz, was evacuated. This resulted in a death march that began on January 18, 1945, with thousands of Monowitz prisoners walking away from I.G. Farben's corporate concentration camp. Few would survive.

Michael Dickerman

See also: Arbeitslager; Auschwitz; Bełżec; Bergen-Belsen; Birkenau; Buchenwald; Bullet Decree (1944); Chełmno; Colditz; Concentration Camps; Dachau; Death Camps; Dora-Mittelbau; Eichmann, Adolf; Extermination Centers; Gas Chambers; Gestapo; Gross-Rosen; Ninzert; Hitler, Adolf; Holocaust, The; I.G. Farben Case (1947); J.A. Topf & Söhne; Kinderblock 66; Koch Trial (1951); Kramer, Josef; Krupp Case (1948); Mauthausen-Gusen; Natzweiler-Struthof; Neuengamme; Niederhagen; Nuremberg Trials; Ravensbrück; Sachsenhausen; Slave Labor (World War II); Sobibór; Sonderkommando; Stalag; Stutthof; Treblinka; Trostinets; Zyklon B Case (1946).

Further Reading

Dwork, Deborah, and Robert Jan van Pelt. *Auschwitz: 1270 to the Present*. New York: Norton, 1997.

Jeffreys, Diarmuid. *Hell's Cartel: I.G. Farben and the Making of Hitler's War Machine*. London: Bloomsbury, 2008.

Levi, Primo. *Survival in Auschwitz*. New York: Simon & Schuster, 1996.

N

Natzweiler-Struthof

A Nazi concentration camp located some 30 miles southwest of Strasbourg (Alsace) in northeastern France. It opened in May 1941 and was initially designed as a forced labor facility. It was not a site of systematic mass murder, as were other German camps, although several thousand people did die there between 1941 and 1944, when it was largely liquidated. The camp was designed to hold about 1,500 prisoners, but as many as 52,000 were interned there in the three years of its operation. Internees included Polish, Russian, French, Dutch, German, and Norwegian prisoners.

Prisoners worked in nearby quarries, on various construction projects and, beginning in early 1944, in German munitions factories. To curb accelerated activities on the part of the anti-German resistance movement in western Europe, in the summer of 1943 the Germans began imprisoning many resistance fighters at Natzweiler-Struthof; the largest percentage of these prisoners was from the French Resistance.

In August 1943, the Germans erected a makeshift gas chamber at Natzweiler-Struthof, where medical experimentation was carried out against a number of prisoners, especially the Romani in captivity there. Shortly thereafter, 80 Jewish internees were killed in the gas chamber; their bodies were transferred to Strasbourg University, where German scientists hoped to prove their bogus theories of racial hierarchy by studying the skeletons of the murdered prisoners.

Although the prison was not an extermination camp, there were at least 4,431 documented deaths at Naztweiler-Struthof. Some prisoners died from overwork, while others died from disease, malnutrition, and beatings. In total, as many as 10,000–12,000 people probably died at the main camp and its numerous subsidiary camps. In September 1944, after Allied troops had landed in France, the Germans liquidated most of the camp, sending prisoners to Dachau, where many more perished. On November 23, 1944, Allied troops entered Natzweiler; it was the first such camp discovered in western Europe. It was later determined that this was the only permanent concentration camp established within France, even though there were many others, such as Drancy, that were not permanent and had different functions.

After the war, several members of the camp's administration were tried and convicted of war crimes, including the commandant. Two were sentenced to death, and one was given a 10-year prison term.

Paul G. Pierpaoli, Jr.

See also: Arbeitslager; Auschwitz; Bełżec; Bergen-Belsen; Birkenau; Buchenwald; Bullet Decree (1944); Chełmno; Colditz; Concentration Camps; Dachau; Death Camps; Dora-Mittelbau; Eichmann, Adolf; Extermination Centers; Gas Chambers; Gestapo; Gross-Rosen; Hitler, Adolf; Holocaust, The; I.G. Farben Case (1947); J.A. Topf &

Söhne; Kinderblock 66; Koch Trial (1951); Kramer, Josef; Krupp Case (1948); Mauthausen-Gusen; Monowitz; Neuengamme; Niederhagen; Ninzert; Nuremberg Trials; Ravens-brück; Sachsenhausen; Slave Labor (World War II); Sobibór; Sonderkommando; Stalag; Stutthof; Treblinka; Trostinets; Zyklon B Case (1946).

Further Reading

Natzweiler-Struthof Official Site: http://www.struthof.fr/en/home/

Webb, A.M., ed. *Natzweiler Trial: Trial of Wolfgang Zeuss and Others*. London: W. Hodge, 1949.

Zuccotti, Susan. *The Holocaust, the French, and the Jews*. Lincoln: University of Nebraska Press, 1999.

Neuengamme

A concentration camp established by Nazi Germany in December, 1938, originally intended to be a sub-camp of the older and larger camp at Sachsenhausen. It was located on the banks of the Dove Elbe River, a tributary of the Elbe, and close to the city of Hamburg. It was chosen because of an abandoned brickworks factory, which the SS hoped to renovate and restore to full production to assist in constructing new public buildings in the city under contract with its own Deutsche Erd- und Steinwerke (German Earth and Stoneworks Corporation). In so doing, it could turn a significant profit. Its first 100 prisoners were transferees from Sachsenhausen, who were sent to begin the construction of the camp itself. In the meantime, they were housed in the abandoned factory.

Six months later, in June 1940, Neuengamme became an independent camp, with 96 sub-camps under its jurisdiction. It has been estimated that between 1940 and its liberation by British forces on May 4, 1945, between 95,000 and 106,000 prisoners were incarcerated at Neuengamme, both men and women (13,500 in the main camp, and the rest at the various sub-camps). It has been estimated that the following groups, arranged by nationality, constituted its prisoner population: Soviets, 34,500; Poles, 16,900; French, 11,500; Germans, 9,200; Dutch, 4,800; Belgians, 4,800; and Jews, 13,000 (Polish and Hungarian Jews transferred from Auschwitz in 1944).

Neuengamme's first commandant, appointed by Reichsführer-SS Heinrich Himmler, was SS major Walter Eisele, who was replaced in April 1940 by SS captain Martin Weiss, and, finally, SS lieutenant colonel Max Pauly, who would later be hanged for his crimes.

As was the case through the entire camp system, conditions for the prisoners were atrocious, to say the least, made all the more so by their intensive labor activities and lack of caloric intake. Inadequate and poor quality food supplies, even poorer shelters, lack of medicines and sanitary facilities, beatings, tortures, starvation, random killings; all of these, and more, resulted in the spread of various diseases such as dysentery, pneumonia, typhus, and tuberculosis. In December, 1941, for example, more than 1,000 prisoners died from a typhus outbreak.

In 1942, as the prison population increased and the number of workers unable to continue working also increased, Neuengamme became one of the sites for the implementation of Aktion 14f13 (which remained in effect until 1944), whereby those who were sick, elderly, or unfit were murdered after having been "examined" by SS and other physicians. That same year, the SS increased its energies at

Neuengamme by become the primary slave labor provider for the German armaments industry.

Neuengamme was also the site of medical experiments upon the prisoners, the most horrific of which took place at the Dullenhuser Damm School on April 20, 1945. Twenty Jewish children, 10 boys and 10 girls, selected by SS physician Josef Mengele at Auschwitz, accompanied by 4 Jewish caretakers and Soviet POWs, were transported to Neuengamme and injected with active tuberculosis bacilli under the watchful eye of Dr. Kurt Heissmayer, enabling their bodies to produce their own antibodies and vaccines. All the children became infected but did not produce the required antigens, and were subsequently murdered along with the adults who accompanied them. SS-Obersturmführer Arnold Strippel oversaw the murders; he would later be convicted and given a life sentence; later freed, he died in Frankfurt in a condominium he would purchase with restitution funds from the German government. Heissmeyer, too, would later be given a life sentence, but would die in prison.

In the early spring of 1945, prior to liberation and the end of the war, the Swedish Red Cross and the Danish government successfully attempted a rescue mission to free, initially, Scandinavian prisoners in the camps, but, ultimately, others as well, including Jews, and bring them to Sweden in their "White Buses" (painted all white with red crosses on their sides so as to avoid Allied bombs). The mission was led by Swedish diplomat Count Folke Bernadotte, who, ironically, would later be murdered by Jewish radicals in Jerusalem on September 17, 1948, four months after Israel was officially recognized as a sovereign nation-state. On March 29, 1945, the buses arrived at Neuengamme and remained there until April 2, as other Scandinavians were brought there. Though estimates vary, upwards of 15,000 prisoners were rescued from various locations; half Scandinavian, half not, including more than 400 Jews rescued from Theresienstadt in Czechoslovakia.

Of the maximum of 106,000 prisoners who passed through Neuengamme, it is now estimated that between 55,000 and 56,000 perished at the hands of the Nazis between 1940 and 1945 by hangings, gassings, shootings, lethal injections, and/or being transported to their deaths in Auschwitz.

Steven Leonard Jacobs

See also: Arbeitslager; Auschwitz; Bełżec; Bergen-Belsen; Birkenau; Buchenwald; Bullet Decree (1944); Chełmno; Colditz; Concentration Camps; Dachau; Death Camps; Dora-Mittelbau; Eichmann, Adolf; Extermination Centers; Gas Chambers; Gestapo; Gross-Rosen; Ninzert; Hitler, Adolf; Holocaust, The; I.G. Farben Case (1947); J.A. Topf & Söhne; Kinderblock 66; Koch Trial (1951); Kramer, Josef; Krupp Case (1948); Mauthausen-Gusen; Monowitz; Natzweiler-Struthof; Niederhagen; Nuremberg Trials; Ravensbrück; Sachsenhausen; Slave Labor (World War II); Sobibór; Sonderkommando; Stalag; Stutthof; Treblinka; Trostinets; Zyklon B Case (1946).

Further Reading

Buggein, Marc. *Slave Labor in Nazi Concentration Camps.* Oxford: Oxford University Press, 2014.

Feig, Konnilyn. *Hitler's Death Camps.* New York: Holmes and Meier, 1979.

Persson, Sune. *Escape from the Third Reich: Folke Bernadotte and the White Buses.* South Yorkshire, UK: Frontline Books, 2009.

Schwarberg, Gunther. *The Murders at Bullenhuser Damm: The SS Doctor and the Children.* Bloomington: Indiana University Press, 1984.

Wachsmann, Nikolaus. *KL: A History of the Nazi Concentration Camps*. New York: Farrar, Straus and Giroux, 2015.

Wachsmann, Nikolaus, and Jane Caplan, eds. *Concentration Camps in Nazi Germany: The New Histories*. London: Routledge, 2010.

Niederhagen

A German concentration camp on the outskirts of Büren-Wewelsburg (in North Rhine-Westphalia region of Germany) during World War II. The Niederhagen concentration camp was established as the result of Heinrich Himmler's private folly. He acquired a castle at Wewelsburg which he renovated and expanded. Due to labor shortages, Himmler decided to use prisoner labor and established a satellite camp of the Sachsenhausen concentration camp at Wewelsburg. Two years later the subcamp Wewelsburg became a camp in its own right, where hundreds of prisoners, including political prisoners, religious groups (Jehovah's Witnesses) and minorities (Sinti and Romani people, Jews), and prisoners of war were forced to work in mines and quarries and the castle construction. Exposed to poor conditions, mistreatment, and diseases, hundreds of prisoners did not survive their imprisonment. In April 1943, with Germany's war effort requiring more labor, Himmler could no longer justify existence of the Niederhagen camp. It was closed, and prisoners were transferred to other concentration camps.

Alexander Mikaberidze

See also: Arbeitslager; Auschwitz; Bełżec; Bergen-Belsen; Birkenau; Buchenwald; Bullet Decree (1944); Chełmno; Colditz; Concentration Camps; Dachau; Death Camps; Dora-Mittelbau; Eichmann, Adolf; Extermination Centers; Gas Chambers; Gestapo; Gross-Rosen; Ninzert; Hitler, Adolf; Holocaust, The; I.G. Farben Case (1947); J.A. Topf & Söhne; Kinderblock 66; Koch Trial (1951); Kramer, Josef; Krupp Case (1948); Mauthausen-Gusen; Monowitz; Natzweiler-Struthof; Neuengamme; Nuremberg Trials; Ravensbrück; Sachsenhausen; Slave Labor (World War II); Sobibór; Sonderkommando; Stalag; Stutthof; Treblinka; Trostinets; Zyklon B Case (1946).

Further Reading

Rammerstorfer, Bernhard. *Taking the Stand. We Have More To Say. Interviews with Holocaust Survivors and Victims of Nazi Tyranny*. Herzogsdorf, AT: [n.p.] 2013.

Wachsmann, Nikolaus. *KL: A History of the Nazi Concentration Camps*. London: Little, Brown Book Group, 2015.

NKVD

Soviet secret police that was responsible for the maintenance and operation of internment and labor camps in Soviet Union. NKVD is an abbreviation of Narodnyy Komissariat Vnutrennikh Del (The People's Commissariat for Internal Affairs) and represents the fourth reincarnation of the Soviet secret police.

Shortly after the October Revolution of 1917, the Bolshevik government set up the All-Russian Extraordinary Commission for Combating Counterrevolution and Sabotage under the Council of People's Commissars of the RSFSR (VCheka under

CPC RSFSR). Better known under its abbreviated name, the CHEKA played a crucial role in the consolidation of the Soviet power in Russia and its leader Felix Dzerzhinsky (The Iron Felix) came to symbolize the ruthless efficiency of Soviet regime. CHEKA was tasked with liquidating any suspected counterrevolutionary and sabotage activities. It became the scourge of the counterrevolution through its extensive authority to conduct summary trials and executions, and used its vast powers to arrest and execute tens of thousands of peoples whose loyalties came to be suspect.

In 1922, CHEKA was reorganized into Gosudarstvennoe politichseskoe upravlenie (GPU, State Political Directorate) that developed a vast network of branches and agents across Russia. Its Secret Section comprised of eight divisions, each of them focusing on a particular political or social group; thus, the first division dealt with anarchists; the second, third, and fourth, various ideological and political opponents (Mensheviks, the SRs, Whites, etc.); while the sixth division targeted the Orthodox Church. In addition, there were sections for counter-intelligence and propaganda dissemination. With the formation of the Soviet Union in December 1922, a more centralized organization was required to exercise control over state security. In November 1923, the Soviet State Political Directorate was therefore transformed the all-union Joint State Political Directorate (OGPU, Obyedinyonnoye gosudarstvennoye politicheskoye upravleniye), with Felix Dzerzhinsky becoming its first chief. As with CHEKA and GPU, the OGPU's primary task was suppressing "political and economic counterrevolution, espionage, and banditry."

OGPU survived for 11 years before it was reorganized into NKVD, which played a decisive role in organizing and perpetrating Soviet repressions and purges of the late 1930s. Established in 1934, NKVD enjoyed a monopoly over all law enforcement activities until the end of World War II. In this capacity, it both upheld public order through policing and performed functions of secret police, earning notoriety for its involvement in the Great Purges of 1936–1937. Under leadership of Genrikh Yagoda and Nikolai Yezhov, the NKVD was responsible for arrests and mass extrajudicial executions of hundreds of thousands of Soviet citizens, and was entrusted with setting up and administering the notorious Gulag system of forced labor camps, where millions of Soviet citizens had been interned. During World War II, the NKVD's functions and power vastly expanded as a way to shore up the Soviet war effort. In addition to running Gulag, NKVD provided general policing and ruthlessly dealt with any cases of insubordination and desertion. It was responsible for the massive deportations of Volga Germans, Crimean Tatars, and other ethnic groups suspected of possible collaboration with the enemy. NKVD was also responsible for prisoners of wars and, in what was the most infamous NKVD operation of the war, supervised massacre and burial of over 20,000 Polish prisoners of war; the Soviet Union blamed the murders on Nazi Germany until admitting its culpability in 1990.

During World War II, NKVD was responsible for suppression of internal dissent and maintenance of order within the Soviet society and military. During the summer of 1941, as the German army launched its invasion of Soviet Union, the NKVD was involved in mass executions of political prisoners in Poland, Ukraine, and the Baltic States. In Tartu (Estonia) and Vilnius (Lithuania), hundreds of

Table 1   Soviet Military Administration Camps in Germany, 1945–1949

Camp No.	Location
NKVD special camp No. 1	The former Stalag IV-B near Mühlberg
NKVD special camp No. 2	Buchenwald Concentration Camp
NKVD special camp No. 3	Hohenschönhausen
NKVD special camp No. 4	Bautzen
NKVD special camp No. 5	Ketschendorf
NKVD special camp No. 6	Jamlitz near Lieberose
NKVD special camp No. 7	Sachsenhausen Concentration Camp
NKVD special camp No. 8	Torgau (Fort Zinna)
NKVD special camp No. 9	Fünfeichen, Neubrandenburg
NKVD special camp No. 10	Torgau (Seydlitz-Kaserne)

detainees were summarily shot at local prisons, while in Poland the NKVD executed almost 10,000 Polish citizens before Soviet forces withdrew. Some of the worst NKVD massacres took place in Lviv (Ukraine), where the Soviet secret police shot several thousand inmates, many of them killed with explosives thrown into crowded cells. At Kharkiv (Ukraine), the NKVD set fire to a local prison, burning over 1,000 prisoners alive.

After World War II, the NKVD took over the German concentration camps and set up a network of ten special camps (also known as silence camps, or *Schweigelager*) where over 150,000 Germans, suspected of the Nazi membership or collaboration, were detained; over a third of them died due to mistreatment, diseases, and starvation. Furthermore, as the Iron Curtain descended over the Eastern Europe, NKVD established numerous internment camps, filtration camps, and prisons in Poland, Czechoslovakia, Hungary, Romania, and Bulgaria, where thousands of individuals were detained; in Poland alone, over 200,000 people were interned, with over 145,000 of them eventually sent to Gulag camps in Soviet Union. The explicit goal of these camps was to quarantine people who might oppose the Communist regime, and sustained an atmosphere of fear in the wider society.

Following the end of World War II in 1945, the Soviet security apparatus underwent further reorganization. In March 1946, the NKVD was turned into the new Ministry of State Security (Ministerstvo Gosudarstvennoe Bezopasnosti, or MGB), led by Lavrenty Beria. Following Stalin's death in March 1953 and Beria's subsequent arrest and execution, the MGB underwent a new round of reforms that led to the creation of the notorious the Committee for State Security (Komitet Gosudarstvennoi Bezopasnosti, or KGB), which remained the primary state security organ of the Soviet Union until 1991.

Alexander Mikaberidze

See also: Beria, Lavrenty; Gulag; Stalin, Joseph.

Further Reading
Applebaum, Anne. *GULAG: A History.* New York: Doubleday, 2003.
Applebaum, Anne. *Iron Curtain: The Crushing of Eastern Europe, 1944–1956.* New York: Doubleday, 2012.

Butler, Rupert. *Stalin's Secret Police: A history of the CHEKA, OGPU, NKVD, SMERSH & KGB, 1917–1991.* London: Amber Books, 2015.

Getty, J. Arch, and Oleg Naumov. *The Road to Terror: Stalin and the Self- Destruction of the Bolsheviks, 1932–1939.* New Haven, CT: Yale University Press, 2010.

Knight, Amy. *Beria: Stalin's First Lieutenant.* Princeton, NJ: Princeton University Press, 1993.

Shearer, David R. *Policing Stalin's Socialism: Repression and Social Order in the Soviet Union, 1924–1953.* New Haven, CT: Yale University Press, 2009.

Norman Cross

The site of the world's first purpose-built prisoner of war camp at Norman Cross, Cambridgeshire. During the French Revolutionary and Napoleonic Wars, over 100,000 prisoners were brought to Britain, causing British prisons and prison hulks to fill up rapidly. To deal with the growing POW population, British government decided to construct a prisoner-of-war camp at Norman Cross in late 1796. The camp layout was based on that of an artillery fort and formed a vast rectangle, which was surrounded by a ditch, a wooden stockade fence (later brick wall) and guard towers.

Opened in 1797, the camp became far more than just an internment facility—it evolved into a small town, with houses, offices, craft shops, a hospital, a school, a market, and a banking system. The camp was divided into four compounds, each of them featuring several barracks and a large exercise yard. The average prisoner population was about 7,000 men, who had access to basic education and were at full liberty to entertain themselves and make and sell artefacts. Conditions at the camps were, overall, tolerable, but an outbreak of typhus epidemic in 1800–1801 did claim over 1,000 prisoners' lives.

Prisoners were freed and repatriated upon the end of the Napoleonic Wars in 1814. The POW camp was then slowly dismantled and sold.

Alexander Mikaberidze

See also: Dartmoor Massacre (1815); French Revolutionary and Napoleonic Era.

Further Reading

Chamberlain, Paul. *The Napoleonic Prison of Norman Cross.* Stroud, UK: The History Press, 2018.

Chamberlain, Paul. *Hell Upon Water: Prisoners of War in Britain, 1793–1815.* Stroud, UK: The History Press, 2016.

North Korea

The first internment camps appeared in North Korea following its liberation from Japanese colonial rule at the end of World War II. The Communist government, led by Kim Il Sung and his successor Kim Jong-il, quickly moved to consolidate its power by arresting individuals whose loyalties became suspect. An extensive system of spies and informers was (and still is) used to monitor citizens' political, social, and other infractions without reference to formal civil rights. After World War II, the government shut down all religious institutions and launched a harsh crackdown on religious groups. The vast majority of Buddhist temples were closed and priests imprisoned; at the same time, thousands of Korean Christians have been detained and some killed, as in the case of Ri Hyon-ok was executed in 2009 for distributing Bibles.

North Korean government still relies on a vast system of internment camps that hold about quarter of a million prisoners. At least six camps—at Kaechon, Yodok, Hwasong, Bukchang, Hoeryong, and Chongjin—have been identified as internment sites for prisoners accused of political offences or denounced as politically unreliable. The camps usually comprise of forced labor colonies located in secluded mountain valleys, where prisoners are engaged in mining and agriculture. North Korea also maintains the so-called reeducation camps, most notably at Kaechon and Chongori, where prisoners undergo ideological brainwashing.

During the Korean War (1950–1953), the North Korean regime captured some 90,000 United Nations Command (UNC) troops, most of them South Koreans, who were sent to the newly established prisoner-of-war camps. The Korean POW camps evolved throughout the war, from three temporary camps established in 1950–1951 to permanent facilities constructed by 1953. Prisoners captured early in the war endured extreme abuse, and were forced to march on foot over rugged terrain in cold weather and deprived of food; many of them perished during these forced marches; the wounded and stragglers were oftentimes shot by the side of the road. Conditions had significantly improved by the end of the war, primarily because of the intervention of Chinese forces that took charge of the POW camps. The POW network of at least 17 camps was centered at Pyoktong (North Pyongan province) where the North Korean POW administration was located. Each POW camp was divided into companies that averaged about 200–300 men. Prisoners were subjected to indoctrination programs and required to undertake various tasks at camps. After the signing of the 1953 Armistice Agreement, North Korea failed to release thousands of prisoners of war, and South Korea currently estimates that at least 500 of them might be still alive; over the past six decades, over 70 prisoners of wars have managed to escape from North Korea, including the 70-year-old Young-Bok Yoo, who escaped in 2000 and published his memoirs.

Alexander Mikaberidze

See also: Kim Il Sung; Korean War.

Further Reading

Carlson, Lewis. *Remembered Prisoners of a Forgotten War: An Oral History of Korean War POWs*. New York: St. Martin's, 2002.

French, Paul. *North Korea: State of Paranoia*. London: Zed Books, 2015.

Han, Tong-ho. *Prison Camps in North Korea*. Seoul: Korea Institute for National Unification, 2016.

Kim, Ŭn-ju, and Sébastien Falletti. *A Thousand Miles to Freedom: My Escape from North Korea*. New York: St. Martin's Press, 2015.

White, William. *The Captives of Korea: An Unofficial White Paper on the Treatment of War Prisoners. Our Treatment of Theirs; Their Treatment of Ours*. New York: Scribner, 1955.

Yoo, Young-Bok. *Tears of Blood: A Korean POW's Fight for Freedom, Family, and Justice*. Los Angeles: Korean War POW Affairs, 2012.

Nuremberg Trials (1945–1946)

The Allies were determined to hold German leaders, both civilian and military, accountable for the war and the mass killings that had taken place in German-occupied Europe. British prime minister Winston L. S. Churchill and Soviet leader Joseph Stalin agreed in 1941 to try those guilty of war crimes. The logistics and framework needed to carry out this policy were discussed throughout the war. At Moscow in October 1943, a declaration signed by British, Soviet, and U.S. representatives stated that war criminals would be brought to trial. Such a procedure was further discussed at important meetings at Tehran (November–December 1943), at Yalta (February 1945), and at Potsdam (July 1945). Finally, the London Agreement of August 8, 1945, set forth the method—a court trial—and identified jurisdiction. Although the Soviets proposed that the trials be held within their zone of occupation, in Berlin, the Western Allies insisted on Nuremberg.

The city of Nuremberg was selected because the palace of justice there had received only minimal damage during the war. The large stone structure had 80 courtrooms and over 500 offices, and thus offered sufficient space for a major international legal proceeding. Furthermore, an undestroyed prison was part of the justice building complex, so all prospective defendants could be housed on site. Moreover, the proclamation of the Third Reich's racial laws against the Jews had been made at Nuremberg. U.S. Army personnel prepared the palace of justice for the trial, repairing damage and laying thousands of feet of electrical wire.

The defendants' dock during the Nuremberg war crimes trials, ca. 1945–46. Organized shortly after the end of World War II in 1945, and continuing through 1946, the Nuremberg Trials convicted nearly two dozen high-level Nazi officials of war crimes. (National Archives)

Broadly speaking, the Nuremberg proceedings fell into two categories. The first set—and the subject of this essay—took place between November 1945 and October 1946, and involved the trial of 22 defendants before an international military tribunal (IMT) established by Britain, France, the Soviet Union, and the United States. Subsequently, a series of other trials were held at Nuremberg until the spring of 1949, before U.S. tribunals in the American zone of occupation, involving nearly 200 other defendants.

The Nuremberg IMT opened on October 8, 1945. Judges from France, Great Britain, the Soviet Union, and the United States presided. The Western judges dressed in traditional robes, whereas the Soviet judge wore a military uniform. Judge Iola T. Nikitschenko, a Soviet, presided during the first session.

The prosecution presented indictments against 24 major criminals and six organizations. The individuals were Martin Bormann, deputy Führer after 1941 (tried in absentia); Karl Dönitz, admiral and commander of the navy from 1943 to 1945; Hans Frank, governor-general of Poland; Wilhelm Frick, minister for internal affairs; Hans Fritzsche, head of the Radio Division of the Ministry of Propaganda; Walther Funk, minister of Economic Affairs; Hermann Göring, Reichsmarschall (Reich Marshal) and commander of the Luftwaffe; Rudolf Hess, deputy Führer until May 1941; Alfred Jodl, army general and head of Operations, Oberkommando der Wehrmacht (OKW); Ernst Kaltenbrunner, head of the Sicherheitsdienst (SD, Security Service); Wilhelm Keitel, army field marshal and chief of OKW; Gustav Krupp von Bohlen und Halbach, industrialist and head of Krupp armaments; Robert Ley, head of the Labor Front (he committed suicide on October 16, 1945); Konstantin Neurath, protector of Bohemia and Moravia from 1939 to 1943; Franz von Papen, former vice chancellor and ambassador to Turkey; Erich Raeder, grand admiral and commander of the navy until 1943; Joachim von Ribbentrop, foreign minister; Alfred Rosenberg, minister for the Occupied Territories in the East until 1941; Fritz Saukel, plenipotentiary for the mobilization of labor; Hjalmar Schacht, president of the Reichsbank, from 1933 to 1939 and minister of economics from 1934 to 1937; Baldur von Shirach, leader of the Hitler Youth and Gauleiter (area commander) of Vienna; Arthur Seyss-Inquart, commissioner for the Netherlands from 1940 to 1945; Albert Speer, minister of armaments from 1942 to 1945; and Julius Streicher, publisher of the newspaper Der Sturmer. The indicted organizations were the Nazi Party (NSDAP), the Schutzstaffel (SS), the SD, the Gestapo, the General Staff, and Hitler Cabinet.

The charter governing the proceedings declared that the IMT's decisions would be made by majority vote. British lord justice Geoffrey Lawrence, president of the court, would cast the deciding vote in the event of a tie among the four sitting judges. The charter identified four categories of crimes: (1) crimes against peace: planning and/or preparing a war of aggression and violating international agreements; (2) crimes against peace: participating in a conspiracy to plan a war of aggression; (3) war crimes: a violation of custom and laws of war, use of slave labor, killing of hostages; and (4) crimes against humanity.

The trial itself lasted 218 days, and some 360 witnesses gave either written or verbal testimony. A new simultaneous translation system allowed the trial to proceed efficiently and swiftly in four languages. Although the defense was given the right to call its own witnesses, it was not allowed to bring forth any evidence against the Allies.

The proceedings at Nuremberg laid bare before the world the horrific crimes committed by the Third Reich. Most revealing were testimonies regarding the brutalities of the death camps. When shown German films of concentration camps, some of the defendants wept or became noticeably upset.

One aspect of the trial that caused debate at the time was the legality of trying military officers. Some suggested it was the role of military officers to carry out orders, but this defense was disallowed at Nuremberg. The prevailing view held that German military leaders had knowingly approved and planned aggressive war and had sanctioned war crimes.

On October 1, 1946, U.S. Army colonel Burton Andrus led 21 defendants into the somber courtroom. (Martin Bormann was tried in absentia, Robert Ley had committed suicide, and Gustav Krupp von Bohlen und Halbach was too weak to be present). Sir Geoffrey Lawrence announced that the verdicts would be delivered first, followed by the sentencing. Twelve defendants were sentenced to death by hanging (the counts on which they were found guilty are in parentheses): Hans Frank (three and four), Wilhelm Frick (two, three, and four), Hermann Göring (all four), Alfred Jodl (all four), Ernst Kaltenbrunner (three and four), Wilhelm Keitel (all four), Robert Ley (all four), Joachim von Ribbentrop (all four), Alfred Rosenberg (all four), Fritz Saukel (three and four), Arthur Seyss-Inquart (two, three, and four), and Julius Streicher (one and four).

Göring escaped the hangman's noose by committing suicide with poison smuggled into the prison. Franz von Papen, Hans Fritzsche, and Hjalmar Schacht were the only defendants to be acquitted. Charges against Gustav Krupp von Bohlen und Halbach were dropped on the grounds that he was physically unable to stand trial. The remaining defendants received various terms, ranging up to life in prison: Karl Dönitz, 10 years (two and three); Walter Funk, life imprisonment (two, three, and four); Rudolf Hess, life imprisonment (one and two); Konstantin Neurath, 15 years (all four); Erich Raeder, life imprisonment (one, two, and three); Baldur von Schirach, 4 to 20 years (one and four); and Albert Speer, 4 to 20 years (three and four). Of those imprisoned, Rudolf Hess lived the longest. He died in Spandau Prison in 1987 at age 93.

Even before the trial ended in 1946, debate began on the validity of the tribunal. Although some have argued that the IMT was merely a case of the victor trying the vanquished, it nonetheless exposed the horrors of the Third Reich, most especially the Holocaust, the use of slave labor, and the heinous war crimes.

Gene Mueller

See also: Concentration Camps; Death Camps; Extermination Centers; Gas Chambers; Gestapo; Hitler, Adolf; Holocaust, The; I.G. Farben Case (1947); Koch Trial (1951); Kramer, Josef; Krupp Case (1948); Slave Labor (World War II); Zyklon B Case (1946).

Further Reading
Andrus, Burton C. *I Was the Nuremberg Jailer.* New York: Coward-McCann, 1969.

Conot, Robert W. *Justice at Nuremberg.* New York: Harper and Row, 1983.

Davidson, Eugene. *The Trial of the Germans.* London: Macmillan, 1966.

International Military Tribunal. *Trial of the Major War Criminals.* 41 vols. Washington, DC: U.S. Government Printing Office, 1949.

Persico, Joseph. *Nuremberg: Infamy on Trial.* New York: Penguin, 1994.

Smith, Bradley F. *Reaching Judgment at Nuremberg.* New York: Basic Books, 1977.

Smith, Bradley F. *The Road to Nuremberg.* New York: Basic Books, 1981.

Sprecher, David A. *Inside the Nuremberg Trials: A Prosecutor's Comprehensive Account.* 2 vols. Lanham, MD: University Press of America, 1999.

Taylor, Telford. *Final Report of the Secretary of the Army on the Nuremberg War Crime Trials under Control Council Law No. 10.* Washington, DC: U.S. Government Printing Office, 1949.

Taylor, Telford. *The Anatomy of the Nuremberg Trials: A Personal Memoir.* New York: Alfred A. Knopf, 1992.

Oberheuser, Herta (1911–1978)

A German medical doctor who conducted cruel and sadistic medical experimentation on concentration camp inmates, Herta Oberheuser was born on May 11, 1911, in Cologne and received her medical degree in Bonn in 1937, with specialty training in dermatology. Following the completion of her medical training, the 26-year-old Oberheuser joined the Nazi Party as an intern and later as a physician for the League of German Girls. By 1940, she had been assigned as assistant physician to Dr. Karl Gebhardt, chief surgeon of the SS and personal physician to Reichsführer SS Heinrich Himmler.

The May 27, 1942, assassination of German security Police Chief Reinhardt Heydrich, who died primarily due to infection, led to the establishment of a branch of the Hohenlychen Sanatorium within the Ravensbrück concentration camp. Hoping to expand their knowledge of infections and how to fight them, Gebhardt and Oberheuser arrived at the facility intent on using the camp's inmates as subjects for their medical experiments.

On July 27, 1942, 75 women at Ravensbrück were ordered to the commandant's headquarters. Once there, Oberheuser physically examined the women and evaluated their suitability for the experiments. Those chosen had their legs cut and bacteria strains placed in the wounds. The subsequent infections were then treated with new sulfanilamide drugs. All of the experiments were conducted without the subjects' consent.

The results of the initial experiments were disappointing because they failed to replicate actual combat injuries. Later experiments sought to correct this. Inmates were subjected to gunshot wounds infected with dirt and foreign material; they also endured severed muscles and broken bones. Wounds were then injected with streptococcus, gas gangrene, and tetanus. Prisoners who survived these experiments were often crippled for life.

Experiments involving bone and muscle transplantation were also conducted by Oberheuser. Oberheuser also oversaw the transfer of inmates to the Hohenlychen Sanatorium, where unnecessary amputations and transplants were conducted. The goal of these experiments was to provide "spare parts" for wounded German soldiers. Once a subject's usefulness had passed, Oberheuser hastened death with injections of gasoline.

Following the end of the war, Oberheuser was the only woman to stand trial at the Nuremberg Doctors' Trial. On August 20, 1947, she was found guilty for her part in conducting human experimentation at Ravensbrück and at Hohenlychen. Originally sentenced to 20 years' imprisonment, her sentence was later reduced to 10 years, and she was released in 1952 after serving only 5 years. She returned to practice as a doctor, establishing a family medical practice in Stocksee, Germany. In 1958, her medical license was revoked after she was recognized by a former Ravensbrück inmate. Oberheuser died on January 24, 1978, in Linz am Rhein, West Germany.

Robert W. Malick

See also: Heim, Aribert; Holocaust, The; Nuremberg Trials; Ravensbrück; Unit 731.

Further Reading

Annas, George J., and Michael A. Grodin. *The Nazi Doctors and the Nuremberg Code: Human Rights in Human Experimentation.* New York: Oxford University Press, 1992.

Lifton, Robert Jay. *The Nazi Doctors: Medical Killing and the Psychology of Genocide.* New York: Basic Books, 2000.

O'Donnell, Camp. *See* Camp O'Donnell

Okahandja

Perhaps the least well known and least documented of the many concentration camps in German South West Africa was the Osona camp in Okahandja, some 70 kilometers north of Windhoek. It is likely that this camp was less well-documented due to the strategic military importance of Okahandja during the Herero Revolt, which limited access for non-military personnel.

The Osona camp was first set up by General Lothar von Trotha, who, before the battle at Ohamakari on August 11, 1904, asked for the building of an enclosure large enough to contain any potential prisoners of war brought back from the Waterberg campaign. Osona remained a major camp throughout the war.

As was the case in other major towns, Osona was actually comprised of a number of separate camps. According to Missionary Inspector Spiecker, who visited the camp in July 1905, there were four camps in total. Spiecker did not use the term Konzentrationslager to describe the camps—which was the normal term—but rather described them as Kraals, a word usually relating to enclosures for cattle.

The first camp was run by the Rhenish Mission and was built to house those who were not deemed fit for labor, meaning the very young and the very old.

The second camp was the main POW camp and, as such, was heavily guarded by the military. At any given time the camp housed between 800 and 900 prisoners, the majority of whom were women and children.

The third camps housed sick and dying prisoners. In the early parts of the war, little to no medical attention was afforded the infirm prisoners. The construction of a separate camp was likely done to avoid contamination of healthy, workable prisoners, as well as the German garrison.

The last camp was the so-called Police Camp, falling outside the purview of the military. It housed a couple of hundred free "natives," mostly Damara-speakers.

At the time of Spiecker's visit there were an estimated 2,000 Herero prisoners in these camps. Similar to Windhoek and Karibib camps, the Osona camp complex in Okahandja gradually became a transit center for prisoners who were ushered on to the railway and general infrastructure projects introduced by Frederick von Lindequist in early 1906.

A number of notable prisoners were interned at Osona, including the wife and daughter of Samuel Maharero, the paramount chief and military leader of the Herero campaign as well as Chief Zeraua of Omaruru.

Casper W. Erichsen

See also: Herero Genocide, Concentration Camps and; Shark Island; Windhoek.

Further Reading

Drechsler, Horst. *"Let Us Die Fighting:" The Struggle of the Herero and Nama against German Imperialism (1844–1915).* Berlin: Academie-Verlag, 1996.

Erichsen, Casper W. *"The Angel of Death Has Descended Violently among Them" Concentration Camps and Prisoners-of-War in Namibia, 1904–1908.* Leiden, NL: ASC University of Leiden, 2005.

Olusoga, David, and Casper W. Erichsen. *The Kaiser's Holocaust: Germany's Forgotten Genocide and the Colonial Roots of Nazism.* London: Faber and Faber, 2010.

Omarska

Notorious detention camp established by the Serbs in May 1992 to house Croats and Bosnian Muslims (Bosniaks) in the aftermath of ethnic cleansing in the municipality of Prijedor. The concentration camp was located in northwestern Bosnia's Prijedor Province at the site of an abandoned iron ore mine. Prisoners there were subjected to starvation, terrible overcrowding, rape, torture, beatings, and murder. Although it is not known exactly how many may have perished in the facility, which was only in operation until August 1992, estimates range from hundreds to a thousand or more. A number of individuals responsible for the establishment and operation of Omarska were later successfully prosecuted for crimes against humanity.

Serb records pertaining to Omarska indicate that a total of 3,335 people—the vast majority of them Bosniak men—were detained at the camp from about May 25, 1992, until August 20, 1995. Outside officials, however, have estimated that the number of detainees may have been closer to 5,000–7,000. Serbs imprisoned most of the detainees after they had fled their homes during Serbian assaults against the town. The Serbs claimed to be holding them because they had been involved in "paramilitary activities" against Serb forces, a charge that had virtually no basis in truth.

The conditions at Omarska were appalling. Prisoners had no access to medical care or adequate potable water supplies. Many became ill or died from drinking contaminated water. There were virtually no sanitation facilities, which meant that much of the camp quickly became an open sewer. Overcrowding was so bad that some internees suffocated during the night; their bodies would be pulled out of their cells in the morning and thrown into mass graves. At best, prisoners were fed one meal per day, usually a small piece of bread and perhaps some rancid jelly. Many were beaten for real or imagined infractions, tortured when they would not provide Serb authorities with the information they sought, and women were routinely raped and abused. Foreign visitors likened the facility to a Nazi concentration camp during World War II.

Survivors have testified that on some nights, between 30 and 150 men were taken out of their cells and tortured or killed. Inmates were normally killed by way of beating, shooting, or throat-slashing. Prisoners were often forced to bury the victims of these crimes; many never returned, and it is presumed that they too had been murdered. On one evening in late July 1992, a group of prisoners were burned atop a pile of old tires; survivors claim that some were still alive and struggled as the flames consumed them. In early August, a group of foreign journalists visited Omarska and immediately publicized the horrors there. The Serbs shut down the facility by month's end, but there were still more than 675 other camps in other parts of Bosnia and Herzegovina that were still operational.

Paul G. Pierpaoli, Jr.

See also: Bosnian War.

Further Reading

May, Larry. *War Crimes and Just War*. Cambridge: Cambridge University Press, 2007.

Wesselingh, Isabel, and Arnaud Vaulerin. *Raw Memory*. London: Saqi Books, 2005.

P

Palawan Massacre (1944)

During World War II, the Japanese set up a prisoner-of-war camp, formally known as Camp 10-A, near the bay of Puerto Princesa on the Palawan Island of the Philippines. Its garrison comprised the 131st Airfield Battalion under the command of Captain Nagayoshi Kojima (whom the American prisoners called the Weasel). As in most Japanese camps, the prisoners suffered from dilapidated housing, poor sanitation, malnutrition, lack of medical care, and abuse. By 1944, the camp held some 150 American prisoners. On December 14, 1944, with American forces rapidly advancing in the wake of the successful landings at Leyte, the Japanese troops made decision to kill prisoners. During a camp lunchtime, an air raid warning was sounded, forcing POWs to seek cover in trenches. The Japanese then set the trenches on fire using barrels of gasoline; as prisoners, engulfed in flames, tried to escape burning trenches, the Japanese guards machine gunned, bayoneted, and clubbed them to death; some American POWs managed to get to the shoreline and tried swimming across the Puerto Princesa bay, only to be shot in the water. Ultimately, only 11 men survived the massacre. After Palawan was liberated, the U.S. Army's 601st Quartermaster Company, under Major Charles Simms, excavated the burned and destroyed trenches and properly interred the remains of American prisoners of war. In 1952, the remains of 123 of the Palawan victims were transferred to the Jefferson Barracks National Cemetery near St. Louis, MO, where they lie in a mass grave.

In 1948, the Military Tribunal for the Far East prosecuted Japanese military officials for the Palawan Massacre. Six defendants were acquitted of the charges, while 10 others were given prison sentences. The death sentence for kempeitai (military police) sergeant Taichi Deguchi was eventually commuted to confinement and hard labor for 30 years; Toru Ogawa, a company commander in the 131st Airfield Battalion who presided over the massacre, was also sentenced to 2 years of hard labor.

The Palawan Massacre is particularly important because it demonstrated Japanese readiness to murder prisoners, and caused the American high command to consider taking measures to rescue them; thus, in January–February 1945, a series of POW rescue missions were launched to liberate prisoners at Cabanatuan Camp, Santo Tomas Internment Camp, Bilibid Prison, and Los Baños Camp.

Alexander Mikaberidze

See also: Far East, British Military Trials; Japan; World War II Prisoners of War.

Further Reading

Nielsen, Eugene. *Oral History Interview with Eugene Nielsen*, December 11, 1989, World War II Prisoners of War Oral History Project, University of North Texas https://oralhistory.unt.edu/oh-0802

Wilbanks, Bob. *Last Man Out: Glenn McDole, USMC, Survivor of the Palawan Massacre in World War II*. Jefferson, N.C.: McFarland & Co., 2009.

Persian Gulf War (1991)

During their August 1990 invasion of Kuwait, Iraqi forces captured some 22,000 Kuwaitis, and during the 1991 Persian Gulf War (Operation DESERT STORM), they captured 46 coalition military personnel. In the Persian Gulf War, coalition forces captured 86,743 Iraqis. Of the estimated 22,000 Kuwaiti military personnel and civilians captured or taken hostage during Iraq's invasion and occupation of Kuwait, more than 1,000 were killed during the occupation. Most of the remaining were released or escaped during the Iraqi withdrawal from Kuwait in February 1991. At the end of the conflict, Iraq released 5,722 Kuwaiti prisoners of war and freed 500 Kuwaitis held by rebels in southern Iraq. Kuwait subsequently claimed that 605 Kuwaitis and foreigners were missing after being taken to Iraq. Some of their bodies were later found in a mass grave near Samawah, Iraq. Most remain unaccounted for, however.

Of the 46 coalition military personnel taken prisoner by the Iraqis during DESERT STORM, 22 were Americans. All of the captured coalition personnel were subsequently repatriated, except for U.S. Navy pilot captain Michael Scott Speicher, who remains missing. Captured coalition personnel also included 12 British, 2 Italians, 9 Saudis, and 1 Kuwaiti. Most of these POWs were airmen, although four survivors of a controversial British Army reconnaissance patrol with radio call sign Bravo Two Zero were also captured.

American POWs were driven to Baghdad and interrogated at an intelligence facility known as the Bunker. They were then taken to an intelligence headquarters

American soldiers escorting captured Iraqi soldiers. During the war, the coalition forces captured some 80,000 Iraqi troops. (Peter Turnley/Corbis/VCG via Getty Images)

nicknamed the Biltmore. The prisoners were later transferred to either Abu Ghraib prison or Al-Rashid Military Prison, where they were held until repatriation. All coalition prisoners were subjected to physical abuse and most were tortured, deprived of food, and subjected to cold temperatures. Both American women POWs were sexually abused. Some POWs were forced to make propaganda statements.

Prior to the commencement of DESERT STORM, coalition forces established a three-stage system of POW camps in Saudi Arabia through which war prisoners would be processed. Most prisoners would be sent to forward holding camps administered by the United States, Britain, and France. They were then transferred to U.S.-administered theater level camps and lastly transferred to Saudi camps. POWs captured by coalition Arab states were taken directly to the Saudi camps.

Temporary POW camps included one constructed by U.S. Navy Seabees at Kibrit, which could hold 40,000 prisoners. Similar facilities were established by XVII Airborne Corps and VII Corps, as well as by the British and French. The British camp near Qaysumah, known as Maryhill, could hold 5,000 prisoners, and the French Clemence camp near Rafha could hold 500 POWs. The four theater-level camps were designed to hold a total of 100,000 prisoners. Two of the camps, collectively known as Bronx, were constructed to the southwest of Mishab. The other two camps, known as Brooklyn, were constructed north of King Khalid Military City. The Saudi Arabia National Guard also maintained four camps: Number one at Hafr al-Batin, Number two near Nuariyah, Number three near Artawiyah, and Number four near Tabuk. These camps could hold a combined total of 41,000 Iraqis.

POW camps constructed by U.S. forces each covered nearly 1.5 square miles. Materials used to construct and maintain the camps included 35,000 rolls of concertina wire, 450 miles of chain-link fence, 296 guard towers, 10,000 tents, 1,500 latrines, 5,000 wash basins, as well as 100,000 towels, 300,000 meals, and 1.5 million gallons of water per day. A field medical hospital and an interrogation facility were located at each major camp.

During interrogations, American forces determined that 1,492 prisoners appeared to be displaced civilians, some of whom had surrendered seeking food and shelter. To determine their status, 1,196 tribunal hearings were held. Subsequently, 310 people were classed as enemy POWs, while the rest were classified as displaced civilians—none was found to have been an unlawful combatant. Among the Iraqi POWs were an American citizen and an Iraqi whose mother was an American. Both had been impressed into the Iraqi Army. They were released and allowed to join their families in the United States.

By war's end, coalition forces had captured 86,743 Iraqis: 63,948 were captured by the United States; 5,005 by the British; 869 by the French; and 16,921 by Arab forces. Over 13,000 Iraqis refused repatriation to Iraq and were reclassified as refugees.

Glenn E. Helm

See also: Abu Ghraib; Korean War; Vietnam War; World War II Prisoners of War.

Further Reading

Department of Defense. *Conduct of the Persian Gulf War: Final Report to Congress.* Washington, DC: U.S. Government Printing Office, 1992.

Marolda, Edward, and Robert Schneller. *Shield and Sword: The United States Navy and the Persian Gulf War.* Annapolis, MD: U.S. Naval Institute Press, 2001.

Yarsinske, Amy Waters. *No One Left Behind: The Lieutenant Commander Michael Scott Speicher Story.* New York: Dutton, 2002.

Pliner, Izrail

Soviet intelligence officer and head of the Gulag. Born into a Jewish family in the Vilna province of the Russian Empire, Pliner joined the Red Army in 1919 and became a member of the Communist Party in 1922. After serving at various positions in the Red Army, Pliner joined the reorganized Soviet secret police, Joint State Political Directorate (OGPU) in 1926 and quickly advanced through its ranks. In 1933 he became Deputy Head of the Gulag system and, in 1935–1937, he was the head of the Gulag.

During the Great Purges of 1937–1938, Pliner was a close aide and collaborator to Nikolai Yezhov, the infamous head of the Soviet secret police, NKVD, and participated in mass arrests, imprisonments, and deportations. He was a key participant in the mass deportation of the Koreans residing in the USSR's Far East regions. Originally conceived in 1926, the deportation was carried out to prevent the alleged "penetration of the Japanese espionage into the Far East." It constituted the first mass forced relocation of an entire nationality in the Soviet Union as over 170,000 Koreans were forcibly moved from the Russian Far East to unpopulated areas of the Central Asia; conservative estimates show that almost a third of them had died from starvation, exposure, and mistreatment.

In 1938, Pliner became a victim of the very purges that he had orchestrated. He was expelled from NKVD, charged with involvement in "counter-revolutionary terrorist organization" and executed in early 1939. He was legally rehabilitated in 1956.

Alexander Mikaberidze

See also: Gulag; NKVD.

Further Reading

Applebaum, Anne. *Gulag: A History.* New York: Broadway Books, 2003.

Petrov, N., and K. Skorkin. *Kto rukovodil NKVD, 1934–1941.* Spravochnik. Moscow: Memorial, 1999.

Solzhenitsyn, Aleksandr. *The Gulag Archipelago, 1918–1956: An Experiment in Literary Investigation.* 3 vols. New York: Harper and Row, 1974–1978.

Pohl, Oswald (1892–1951)

Born in Duisburg-Ruhrort, Germany, on June 30, 1892, Oswald Pohl became one of the most powerful men in the Nazi SS and supervised its economic component, as well as the administration of the Nazi concentration camp system. In 1912, Pohl enlisted in the German Imperial Navy and served throughout World War I, rising to the position of paymaster. Following the end of the war, he became active with the Friekorps movement, drawing on his naval training as paymaster. In 1925, he joined the SA, and a year later, the Nazi Party.

By 1934, Pohl had come to the attention of Reichsführer-SS Heinrich Himmler. Himmler tasked Pohl with overseeing the administration of the Allgemeine-SS, the largest branch of the SS overall. Pohl quickly expanded his influence to include the administrative and financial control of the Totenkopfverbände (SS Death Head's units), the Verfuegungstruppe (later renamed the Waffen-SS), and the Budget and Building Department of the Reichsführer-SS, which oversaw the construction of concentration camps. By 1939, Pohl's authority had expanded to the administration of the concentration camp system. In 1942 his power was consolidated into the Wirtschafts-und Verwaltungshauptamt (SS Economic and Administrative Department, or WVHA).

As leader of the WVHA, Pohl had emerged as the third most powerful man in the SS, superseded only by Heinrich Himmler and Reinhard Heydrich. The WVHA oversaw the administration and supplying of the entire Waffen-SS, exercised control over 20 concentration and labor camps, controlled all SS and police building projects, and managed all SS business concerns.

Overseeing the concentration and labor camps provided Pohl with some 600,000 slave laborers. Originally organized to punish and exterminate the enemies of the Nazi regime, he now reorganized the camps to exploit their victims' labor. Not exclusive to the SS, Pohl rented out his slave workforce to meet the labor needs of private industries. By 1944, 250,000 laborers were working in the private armament industries, and many industries were allowed to open factories within or adjacent to the camps. As labor needs grew, Pohl and the WVHA also appropriated the labor of surviving Jews in the ghettos and eastern camps.

Pohl and the WVHA also controlled all SS-owned industries, such as the German Excavating and Quarrying Company, the German Equipment Company, the German Experimental Establishment for Foodstuff and Nutrition, and the Society for Exploitation of Textiles and Leatherworks. Industries not owned by the SS were indirectly controlled by the WVHA, including mineral water production and the furniture industry. Jewish-owned and foreign industries were also seized by the WVHA.

Captured by the British at the end of the war, Oswald Pohl was sentenced to death by an American military court on May 27, 1946. Imprisoned rather then immediately executed, he rejoined the Catholic Church and in 1950 published *Credo: My Way to God.* Pohl was hanged on June 7, 1951, at Landsberg Prison.

Robert W. Malick

See also: Germany; Holocaust, The; Slave Labor (World War II).

Further Reading

Buggeln, Mark. *Slave Labor in Nazi Concentration Camps.* Oxford: Oxford University Press, 2014.

Höhne, Heinz. *The Order of the Death's Head: The Story of Hitler's SS.* New York: Penguin, 2001.

Tooze, Adam. *The Wages of Destruction: The Making and Breaking of the Nazi Economy.* New York: Viking Penguin, 2007.

Pul-i Charkhi (Pul-E-Charkhi)

An Afghan village on the Kabul River east of Kabul, and the site of a notorious prison camp. Built from a West German design, the camp had a capacity of 5,000 prisoners, but during the 1970s it was said to have housed more than twice that number. The prison has separate sections for political prisoners, foreigners, and women.

After the Saur Revolution of 1978, the government of Nur Muhammad Taraki executed thousands of prisoners at Pul-i Charkhi; the Hafizullah Amin government later produced a list of approximately 12,000 Afghans who had been killed there, although current estimates point to a much higher number of killed. The prison complex was partially destroyed during the Afghan Civil War, but the surviving parts served as a detention center for the Burhanuddin Rabbani regime until it was captured by the Taliban in September 1996.

After the U.S. invasion of Afghanistan in 2001, the prison was renovated by the United States Army Corps of Engineers, and it remains the only modern prison complex in Afghanistan, although its reputation remains stained by past crimes.

Alexander Mikaberidze

See also: Afghanistan.

Further Reading

Kaplan, Robert D. *Soldiers of God: With Islamic Warriors in Afghanistan and Pakistan.* New York: Vintage Books, 2001.

Qala-i-Jangi Revolt (2001)

Qala-i-Jangi is a nineteenth-century fortress that had been converted into a make-shift prisoner detention facility during the U.S. Invasion of Afghanistan in 2001. During the fighting at the Afghan city of Kunduz, the United States and its allies (the Northern Alliance) captured hundreds of Taliban fighters who were transported to the Qala-i-Jangi fortress for detention, interrogation, and processing; many prisoners were the Al Ansar or foreign fighters, who had come from Pakistan and countries of the Middle East. During their transportation, the prisoners had not been properly searched, and some of them had managed to conceal and smuggle their weapons. In another blunder, the Northern Alliance forces did not reinforce security at the prison.

On November 25, just as the CIA agents arrived to conduct interrogations, the prisoners revolted, killing one U.S. agent—Johny Micheal Spann, the first American known to have died in the conflict—and dozens of Afghan troops, and seizing control of the prison facility and its armory. The ensuing fighting quickly escalated into one of the bloodiest engagements of the entire war. Facing a determined and well-armed enemy, the Northern Alliance fighters, supported by British and American special forces and air support, battled for six days to crush the prisoner revolt. The U.S. forces called in missile and air strikes on the prison and launched a systematic assault supported by tanks and other armored vehicles. With the above-ground prison facilities destroyed, the Taliban fighters retreated into underground vaults, where they continued to resist for several days until the Afghan forces flooded the basement with water and forced their surrender.

Of the estimated 500 prisoners held at Qala-i-Jangi, only 86 survived the fighting, although a few later died of their wounds. Among the surviving prisoners were two American citizens who had served with the Taliban, Yaser Esam Hamdi and John Walker Lindh. Hamdi was transferred to Guantanamo Bay where he was held until 2004 before striking a deal with the U.S. government—after renouncing his U.S. citizenship and committing to travel restrictions, he was deported to Saudi Arabia. Lindh was prosecuted, found guilty of aiding and supporting the enemy, and sentenced to 20 years in prison without parole.

Alexander Mikaberidze

See also: Afghanistan; Guantanamo Bay Detention Camp.

Further Reading

Perry, Alex. "Inside the Battle at Qala-I-Jangi," *Time*, 1 December 2001.

Sennott, Charles M. "The First Battle of the 21st Century: Returning to the Site of America's Earliest Casualty in Afghanistan," *The Atlantic*, May 5, 2016, https://www.theatlantic.com/international/archive/2015/05/war-afghanistan-spann-qala-i-jangi/392402/

R

Rab

One of the several Italian concentration camps established during World War II. Established in July 1942 on the Italian-occupied island of Rab (now in Croatia), the camp played a crucial role in mass killing and ethnic cleansing that Italian forces, under General Mario Roatta, unleashed against the Slovene civilian population. The "Camp for the Concentration and Internment of War civilians—Rab" (Campo di concentramento per internati civili di Guerra—Arbe) interned Slovenian and Croatian prisoners, as well as Jews transported from the neighboring Croatia; by summer of 1943, over 10,000 prisoners were held at the camp. Conditions were horrifying, and about 20 percent of prisoners died in 1942–1943; Metod Milač, an inmate at the camp, described in his memoirs how prisoners slowly starved to death on a daily diet of thin soup and a few grains of rice. In September 1943, after the fall of the fascist government of Italy, the camp was closed.

Alexander Mikaberidze

See also: Chieti; Fossoli di Carpi; World War II Prisoners of War.

Further Reading

Milač, Metod. *Resistance, Imprisonment and Forced Labour: A Slovene Student in World War II.* New York: Peter Lang, 2002.

Pedaliu, Effie. "Britain and the 'Hand-over' of Italian War Criminals to Yugoslavia, 1945–48," *Journal of Contemporary History* 39/4 (2004): 503–529.

Rape Camps, Former Yugoslavia

During the 1992–1995 Bosnian War, Serb forces routinely subjected Croat and Bosniak (Bosnian Muslim) women and girls to mass rapes, many of which occurred in dedicated areas, mostly concentration camps, which also became known as rape camps. Although mass rapes certainly occurred during the 1998–1999 Kosovo War, and despite the fact that rumors of rape camps during that conflict circulated widely, their existence has never been substantially proven. During the Bosnian War, the estimated number of rapes committed by the Serbs was estimated to be between 20,000 and 50,000. Some victims were as young as 12. The shocking level of sexual violence, which was extensively covered by the international media, prompted numerous human rights groups to classify mass rape as an international war crime. After the war, a number of Serbs charged with sexual violence were convicted; this marked the first time in history such a crime was recognized and prosecuted by an international tribunal.

The Serbs promptly systematized their program of mass rape, which took two principal forms. First, when Serb forces moved into a given area that was to be ethnically cleansed, they quickly separated the men and boys from women and girls. Most of the males were either deported to prisons or murdered, leaving the women and girls entirely defenseless. Sometimes, the mass rapes occurred within the villages or towns that were being liquidated. More often, however, the Bosniak women and girls were sent to concentration camps, which functioned as de facto rape camps. There, Serbian troops subjected them to sexual enslavement and mass rapes. Sometimes these rape centers were located in private homes, schools, or other public buildings, which served as de facto brothels for Serbian forces.

The Serbs employed mass rape as a weapon to humiliate Bosnian Muslims, whose cultural conditioning made such crimes particularly degrading, even sacrilegious. Rape was frequently used as part of a larger plan to punish and torture Bosniak women. It was also employed to diminish the Muslim bloodline by forcing Muslims to give birth to children of mixed parentage.

There were a number of rape camps throughout Bosnia and Herzegovina. The most infamous of these were: the Keraterm Camp (near Prijedor); Omarska (also near Prijedor); Vilina Vlast (near Visegrad), and the Foca Rape Camp, which was perhaps the most notorious of all. In the summer of 1992, Roy Gutman, an American journalist, and British journalist Ed Vulliamy first reported on the existence of the Serbian rape camps. Gutman and Vulliamy's reporting on the sexual atrocities in eastern Bosnia quickly garnered international attention. The Serbians and Montenegrins in turn worked feverishly to cover up or destroy all evidence of the camps, fearing that they could be accused of war crimes and crimes against humanity.

Eventually, some 14 Serbian leaders were tried and convicted for their participation in the Foca atrocities, including Dragan Gagovic, Gojko Jankovic, Janko Janjic, Radomir Kovac, Zoran Vukovic, Dragan Zelenovic, Dragoljub Kunarac, Radovan Stankovic, Savo Todovic, Milorad Krnojelac, and Mitar Rasevic. Some of the defendants were tried by the International Criminal Tribunal for the Former Yugoslavia, and others by the Court of Bosnia and Herzegovina. Radovan Karadzic, former president of the Republika Srpska, was also arrested and tried for his part in the Foca calamity, but his trial is ongoing, and other charges are also pending.

Paul G. Pierpaoli, Jr.

See also: Srebrenica Massacre.

Further Reading

Allen, Beverly. *Rape Warfare: The Hidden Genocide in Bosnia-Hercegovina and Croatia.* Minneapolis: University of Minnesota Press, 1996.

Zinsstag, Estelle. "Sexual Violence against Women in Armed Conflicts: Standard Responses and New Ideas," *Social Policy & Society* 5:1 (2005), 137–148.

Ravensbrück

A Nazi concentration camp for women, located 56 miles north of Berlin on swampy land near the Havel River. On May 15, 1939, the first prisoners arrived when 867 women were transferred from Lichtenburg. The camp was staffed by 150 female SS supervisors (*Aufseherinnen*), male guards, and male administrators. In 1942 and

1943, Ravensbrück served as a training base for female guards, and 3,500 women were trained there for work in Ravensbrück and other camps.

In late 1939, the camp held 2,000 prisoners. By late 1942, there were 10,800. In 1944, the main camp contained 26,700 female prisoners and several thousand female minors grouped in a detention camp for children. Most of the camp was evacuated in March 1945 as the Russians approached, and 24,500 prisoners were marched into Mecklenburg. When the camp was liberated by Soviet troops during April 29–30, they found only 3,500 ill and famished women left.

During its existence, at least 107,753 (123,000 according to Germaine Tillion) women were interned in Ravensbrück and its satellite camps, most of which were industrial slave labor sites. There was a concentration camp for men near Ravensbrück, but it was connected with the Sachsenhausen camp rather than being allocated to the Ravensbrück administration. It has been estimated that approximately 50,000 inmates died at Ravensbrück across the camp's duration. In addition to general overwork, exposure, malnutrition, disease, and abuse, individual women were subjected to excruciating medical experimentation while in the camp, including bone transplants, induced gas gangrene, and deliberately infected incisions. Early in 1945, a gas chamber was constructed at the camp, where, it is asserted, between 2,200 and 2,400 women were gassed. Max Koegel, who had been commandant from the opening of the camp until the summer of 1942, committed suicide in 1946. His successor, Fritz Suhren, was tried and executed in 1950.

Bernard A. Cook

See also: Arbeitslager; Auschwitz; Bełżec; Bergen-Belsen; Birkenau; Buchenwald; Bullet Decree (1944); Chełmno; Colditz; Concentration Camps; Dachau; Death Camps; Dora-Mittelbau; Eichmann, Adolf; Extermination Centers; Gas Chambers; Gestapo; Gross-Rosen; Ninzert; Hitler, Adolf; Holocaust, The; I.G. Farben Case (1947); J.A. Topf & Söhne; Kinderblock 66; Koch Trial (1951); Kramer, Josef; Krupp Case (1948); Mauthausen-Gusen; Monowitz; Natzweiler-Struthof; Neuengamme; Niederhagen; Nuremberg Trials; Sachsenhausen; Slave Labor (World War II); Sobibór; Sonderkommando; Stalag; Stutthof; Treblinka; Trostinets; Zyklon B Case (1946).

Further Reading

Helm. Sarah. *Ravensbrück: Life and Death in Hitler's Concentration Camp for Women.* New York: Nan E. Talese/Doubleday, 2015.

Tillion, Germaine. *Ravensbrück: An Eyewitness Account of a Woman's Concentration Camp.* Garden City, NY: Anchor, 1975.

Wachsmann, Nikolaus. *KL: A History of the Nazi Concentration Camps.* New York: Farrar, Straus and Giroux, 2015.

Rheinwiesenlager (1945)

The Rheinwiesenlager or Rhine Meadow Camps refer to some 17 to 19 "Prisoner of War Temporary Enclosures" (PWTE) set up by American forces from late March to June 1945, shortly before and after the end of World War II. Although most of these camps were on the west side of the Rhine River, the locations spanned from the northernmost camp at Büderich to as far south as Heilbronn on the Neckar. These temporary installations, which eventually accommodated over a million Axis fighting forces and auxiliaries, became known as starvation camps, where prisoners were crowded in large fields surrounded by barbed wire and forced to burrow holes for shelter in earth deluged by spring rains. Although death tolls continue to be debated, estimates range from 10,000 to 40,000 fatalities. Consequently, the Rheinwiesenlager are notoriously the worst detention centers set up by the Western Allies during and immediately after World War II.

Although the American Army had already drawn up a provisional plan, code-named Operation ECLIPSE, for the detention of surrendered Axis forces, it became clear by February 1945 that this was unworkable in view of the huge numbers of captured and surrendering troops. Prisoners of War were initially to have been transported to France and Belgium, but transport problems arose when the front line crossed the Rhine. With the occupation of the Rhineland early in 1945, 250,000 prisoners had fallen into U.S. hands with at least 325,000 more captured in the Ruhr pocket in the first two weeks of April. During the two months of April and May 1945, approximately 1.8 million soldiers had surrendered.

The sheer volume of prisoners caught the Allied forces relatively unprepared, a problem exacerbated by millions of refugees and displaced persons from former Axis-occupied territory also flooding into western-controlled zones of Germany. The country had been devastated and food supplies were minimal. Therefore, in conjunction with Supreme Headquarters, Allied Expeditionary Forces (SHAEF), the U.S. command decided to reclassify prisoners as Disarmed Enemy Forces (DEF; the British used the term Surrendered Enemy Personnel, SEP). This move allowed SHAEF to bypass the terms of the Geneva Convention and to feed prisoners at a lower level than Allied troops. While outrage at the discovery of the full extent of Axis war crimes against the Jewish population of Europe may well have influenced the treatment of prisoners in the Rheinwiesenlager, current scholarship indicates that logistics played the primary role.

Therefore, it was decided to set up the PWTEs, most located on the west bank of the Rhine. By May 1945, 13 enclosures had already been built and 2 more were in preparation. The total number of camps varies, largely because of mistakes or omissions in the American records of the Prisoner of War Division (POWD). Among the camps, Remagen, established at the end of March 1945, was one of the earliest. Like most other Rheinwiesen camps, the location was chosen because of its open spaces and its proximity to a rail line. Each barbed-wire enclosure was designed to accommodate about 1,000 inmates. Nevertheless, the five-kilometer-long and two-kilometer-wide stretch between Remagen and Sinzig to the south ended up accommodating as many as 400,000 prisoners. In these camps, as in the neighboring one at Bad Kreuznach, various eyewitnesses reported that corpses were removed daily. The Rheinberg camp to the north, initially established on April 18, 1945, to hold about 1,000 occupants, held some 20,000 by May and 140,000 when the camp was turned over to the British by the beginning of summer.

Although it is cannot be determined exactly how many inmates of the Rheinwiesenlager were classified as DEFs, it is nevertheless certain that a total of approximately 1 million inmates were held in execrable conditions. Herded into immense fields without tents, toilet facilities, canteens, or medical care, and erratically provided with minimal rations, it is little wonder that death tolls were inordinately high in comparison with those in other western Allied detention centers. One survivor recounts that he received his first rations almost 40 hours after imprisonment; the whole time until his transfer to a French camp, he lay on bare ground that a wet spring rapidly transformed into mud. Most inmates had been deprived, not only of weapons, but of all other supplies they still retained, including German-issue tarpaulins that could be fastened together to form tents. In the haste of construction, many pens were at first fenced by only a single strand of barbed wire. According to the eyewitness account of one American at the Sinzig camp, guards were thus forced to fire at the slightest movement at night; nevertheless, few prisoners attempted to escape. However, when the guard service consisted of non-American personnel, particularly Polish, guards became more trigger-happy, sometimes firing at random into the interior of camps.

Inclement weather, unsanitary conditions, food deprivation, and occasionally hostile guards were not, however, the only problems that German inmates faced. In the Rheinberg camp, for instance, American forces had handed over the responsibility for preparation and distribution of supplies to German personnel. Prisoners complained that German camp police or translators were relatively well fed, but deprived their own countrymen of their rightful share of provisions. In addition, although civilian populations in adjacent communities were generous in sharing their limited provisions through the barbed wire with inmates, in some centers, such as Bad Kreuznach, inhabitants were threatened with death if they provided prisoners with food or water.

Fortunately, however, the American Rheinwiesenlager existed only for a short time. By the summer of 1945, most prisoners had been transferred to British or French custody. On June 12, 1945, the camps of Rheinberg, Büderich, and Wickrathberg were surrendered to the British, who shortly thereafter transferred prisoners to the U.K.; on July 10, a further eight camps were transferred to the French. Many prisoners from the latter camp were, however, engaged in mining and dangerous tasks such as clearing landmines (officially forbidden by the Geneva Conventions). Additionally, conditions in most French post-war internment camps fell far short of Geneva agreements. Meanwhile, American forces had released a large number of internees, particularly those with essential skills or those connected with the Hitler Youth (Hitlerjugend, HJ).

As a result of the huge number of Rheinwiesenlager internees and their transfer to French or British custody in a short matter of time, great difficulty emerged in assessing an accurate number of death tolls in these notorious camps. In 1989, with the publication of *Other Losses*, Canadian journalist/historian James Bacque created a furor with his claim that 1 million unacknowledged deaths among former German military personnel stemmed, in large part, from "other losses;" i.e., the deliberate starvation of German soldiers in U.S. detention camps, particularly those in the Rheinwiesenlager. The true number of deaths, he contended, were disguised in U.S. statistics as "other losses." Recent historiography has largely refuted Bacque's sources and methodology, even though his works remain popular, particularly among revisionist circles. More convincingly, studies such as those of Bischof and Ambrose (see Further Reading), and particularly that of Arthur Smith, deal far more objectively with the Rheinwiesenlager. Agreeing largely with the

German government-backed study of Erich Maschke et al., Smith concludes that the statistician can come to conclusions only on the basis of inaccurate and contradictory evidence: first, the highly inaccurate records of the U.S. Army, which was overwhelmed by an influx of prisoners; second, the somewhat larger estimates of German government researchers, who have delved into records from localities, burial sites, and former inmates; and third, the records of the locality of the given camp. The last group, Smith contends, raises the death total, for it also takes into consideration the eyewitness reports of former prisoners. Nevertheless, although Smith's maximum figure of 40,000 fatalities is somewhat higher than that of the Maschke commission (32,000). Still, each of these studies refutes Bacque's exaggerated claims.

Despite the inaccuracy of death figures for the Rheinwiesenlager, it is undeniable that the conditions under which prisoners were held constituted a contravention of Geneva Conventions.

Anna M. Wittmann

See also: Maschke Commission; World War II Prisoners of War.

Further Reading

Bacque, James. *Other Losses*. Toronto: Stoddart, 1989.

Bischof, Günter, and Stephen E. Ambrose. *Eisenhower and the German POWs: Facts Against Falsehood*. Baton Rouge: Louisiana State University Press, 1992.

Boehme, Kurt W. *Zur Geschichte der deutschen Kriegsgefangenen des 2. Weltkrieges: Die deutschen Kriegsgefangenen in amerikanischer Hand In: Zur Geschichte der deutschen Kriegsgefangenen des zweiten weltkrieges*. Ed. Erich Maschke et al. Vol. X/2. München 1971.

Overmans, Rüdiger. *"Die Rheinwiesenlager 1945."* In: *Ende des Dritten Reiches—Ende des Zweiten Weltkrieges. Eine perspektivische Rückschau*. Ed. Hans-Erich Volkmann. Munich: Militärgeschichtlichen Forschungsamt, 1995.

Smith, Arthur L. *Die "vermisste Million": Zum Schicksal deutscher Kriegsgefangener nach dem Zweiten Weltkrieg. Schriftenreihe der Vierteljahrshefte für Zeitgeschichte 65*. Munich: Oldenbourg, 1992.

Ruhleben

A civilian internment camp in Germany during World War I. Located at Ruhleben, near Berlin, the camp was originally a racing track that was converted into an internment camp after the start of World War I in August 1914. The camp detainees comprised of nationals of the Allied Powers who happened to be in Germany at the outbreak of the war; the camp's size varied between 4,000 and 5,000 prisoners, most of them British.

Ruhleben was, by no means a typical internment camp. Conditions at the camp were rather satisfactory, and detainees were allowed to manage their own internal affairs. In fact, Ruhleben developed a vibrant cultural life. The detainees formed various clubs and groups, including Debating Society and Dramatic Society, and published journals, including a fortnightly magazine, *In Ruhleben Camp*. The camp school taught detainees a variety of subjects, including foreign languages, literature, music, bookbinding, and sciences. Furthermore, the detainees staged theatrical performances and sporting events (including boxing matches), and even organized a mock election into the British Parliament in the summer of 1915. The detainees even developed their own postal system, though it was later suppressed by the German authorities since private postal systems were illegal in Germany.

As World War I entered its third year, Germany began to release detainees and, by late 1917, the only prisoners left in Ruhleben were military men, who had to await the end of the war in 1918 before being repatriated.

Alexander Mikaberidze

See also: Holzminden.

Further Reading

Ketchum, Davidson J. *Ruhleben: A Prison Camp.* Toronto: University of Toronto Press, 1965.

"Prisoners of War in World War I: British and Allied Civilian Internees at Ruhleben Camp, Germany," in Dowling, Timothy C., ed. *Personal Perspectives: World War I,* 259–272. Santa Barbara: ABC-CLIO.

S

Sachsenhausen

Nazi concentration camp established north of Berlin, near Oranienburg, in July 1936. Administered by the SS, Sachsenhausen initially housed political prisoners and others deemed "dangerous" to the German government. Beginning in 1937, and continuing into 1945, the camp expanded dramatically, and soon became home to a wide array of detainees, including Jews, Jehovah's Witnesses, male homosexuals, individuals deemed "asocial," and Romanis. Between 1936 and 1945, some 200,000 detainees were either incarcerated at Sachsenhausen or transited through it. A few Soviet civilians were held there, and the camp became a major staging area for Soviet prisoners of war. By 1945, the number of Jewish prisoners at Sachsenhausen totaled about 11,000. In the period immediate following Kristallnacht in 1938, at least 6,000 German Jews were rounded up and imprisoned at Sachesenhausen. Most Jews were released, however, and by early 1939, only 1,345 remained.

After World War II began in September 1939, however, Sachsenhausen once again became home to many Jews, mainly resident aliens who had been residing in Germany, or Polish Jews. Many of those people were transferred to death camps in the east, where most perished. In 1944, Hungarian and Polish Jews who had been residing in various ghettos began arriving in large numbers, while Soviet POWs began arriving in the late summer of 1941; as many as 18,000 of these men were shot and killed there between 1941 and 1945. Their bodies were cremated in an on-site crematorium. In the autumn of 1944 German officials arrested thousands of Polish civilians, of whom approximately 6,000 were sent to Sachsenhausen. Most were non-Jews.

As in all concentration camps, conditions at Sachsenhausen were appalling. Food was scant and of poor quality, living quarters were overcrowded, sanitation facilities were crude at best, and medical care was essentially nonexistent. Many prisoners were ordered to perform forced labor in area factories, where some were worked to the point of exhaustion and death. Malnutrition and disease were perhaps the biggest killers. Including the Russian POWs who died at Sachsenhausen, a total of some 30,000 people died at the camp between 1936 and 1945. Others were beaten to death or executed, and some became the victims of Nazi medical experimentation.

In early April 1945, as Allied troops closed in on Berlin, the SS decided to liquidate the facility. Prisoners were force marched toward the north and east, a brutal process that resulted in many more deaths. When the Soviet Army liberated Sachsenhausen on April 22, 1945, there were still some 3,000 prisoners there, including 1,400 women.

Paul G. Pierpaoli, Jr.

See also: Arbeitslager; Auschwitz; Bełżec; Bergen-Belsen; Birkenau; Buchenwald; Bullet Decree (1944); Chełmno; Colditz; Concentration Camps; Dachau; Death Camps; Dora-Mittelbau; Eichmann, Adolf; Extermination Centers; Gas Chambers; Gestapo; Gross-Rosen; Ninzert; Hitler, Adolf; Holocaust, The; I.G. Farben Case (1947); J.A. Topf & Söhne; Kinderblock 66; Koch Trial (1951); Kramer, Josef; Krupp Case (1948); Mauthausen-Gusen; Monowitz; Natzweiler-Struthof; Neuengamme; Niederhagen; Nuremberg Trials; Ravensbrück; Slave Labor (World War II); Sobibór; Sonderkommando; Stalag; Stutthof; Treblinka; Trostinets; Zyklon B Case (1946).

Further Reading

Bartrop, Paul R. *Surviving the Camps: Unity in Adversity during the Holocaust.* Lanham, MD: University Press of America, 2000.

Kogon, Eugen. *The Theory and Practice of Hell: The German Concentration Camps and the System behind Them.* New York: Farrar, Straus and Giroux, 2006.

Wachsmann, Nikolaus. *KL: A History of the Nazi Concentration Camps.* New York: Farrar, Straus and Giroux, 2015.

Sajmište

A Nazi concentration and extermination camp during World War II. Located near the town of Zemun (present-day Serbia), the camp was established by the German SS Einsatzgruppen units, which were part of the German invasion of Yugoslavia in early 1941. Yugoslavia was dismembered, with the Ustaše (extreme Croat nationalist and fascist) government of Ante Pavelić leading the Independent State of Croatia while Milan Nedić became head of the collaborationist Government of National Salvation in Serbia.

In the fall of 1941, the German military authorities ordered that all Jewish women and children in Serbia be moved to a concentration camp set up at Zemun. The camp, formally designated as the "Jewish Camp in Zemun" (German: Judenlager Semlin) opened in October 1941 when thousands of Jewish and hundreds of Romani women, children, and old men were brought to the camp. Kept in squalid conditions, the prisoners suffered from malnutrition, abuse, and exposure to elements, with hundreds of them dying during the winter of 1941–42. In the spring of 1942, the Germans set up a gas facility at the camp and began methodical killing of the Jewish inmates.

With the extermination of the Jewish inmates completed, the camp was renamed to Zemun Concentration Camp (German: Anhaltelager Semlin) and served to hold captured Yugoslav Partisans, Chetniks, members of Greek and Albanian resistance movements, etc. Conditions in the camps remained horrific and greatly contributed to prisoners' high mortality. In late 1943, as the tide of war turned against Germany, SS-Standartenführer Paul Blobel led an effort to erase evidence of atrocities committed in the camp—thousands of corpses were exhumed from mass graves and incinerated. In early 1944, the Germans transferred control of the camp over to the Ustaše, which closed the facility in late summer.

Alexander Mikaberidze

See also: Concentration Camps; Jasenovac; Ustaše.

Further Reading

Browning, Christopher. *The Origins of the Final Solution: The Evolution of Nazi Jewish Policy, September 1939–March 1942*. Lincoln: University of Nebraska Press, 2007.

Israeli, Raphael. *The Death Camps of Croatia. Visions and Revisions, 1941–1945*. London: Routledge, 2017.

Salaspils

The site of a concentration camp near small city of Salaspils in Latvia, situated on the Daugava River, about 11 miles (18 kilometers) to the southeast of Latvia's capital, Riga. In late 1941, a concentration camp, a little over one mile out of town, was established at Salaspils. Originally it was intended for former Soviet prisoners of war and political prisoners, but by the time it was at its peak, the camp became the largest civilian concentration camp in any of the Baltic republics. Officially, Salaspils (known in German as Kurtenhof) was designated as a Police Prison and Work Education Camp (Polizeigegfängnis und Arbeitserziehungslager), spread over an area measuring about 650 by 450 yards.

In October 1941, a senior Einsatzgruppen officer, SS-Sturmbannführer Rudolf Lange, began planning a detention camp to be built at Salaspils. He then oversaw the planning and implementation of the Rumbula massacre, a program that saw the murder of 24,000 Latvian Jews from the Riga ghetto, which occurred between November 30 and December 8, 1941. Later in December he began working as commander of both the security police (*Sicherheitspolizei*) in Latvia and also of the Security Service (*Sicherheitsdient*). His idea for the Salaspils camp was to create a place in which to not only confine those arrested in Latvia for political reasons or as resisters, but also as an end point for Jews deported from Germany. Eventually, this would also extend to other occupied countries.

There was a precedent for this, dating to before the establishment of Salaspils. On November 29, 1941, a trainload of approximately 1,000 Jews from Germany arrived in Riga, where they were murdered. This served as a precedent for others, starting on December 3, 1941. Salaspils now became a convenient location for the Nazis' grisly task, situated on the main rail line between Riga and the next largest city in Latvia, Daugavpils.

Development of the camp took place during January 1942, when around 1,000 Jews from the Riga ghetto were conscripted to work on the site. By the fall of 1942, Salaspils was comprised of 15 barracks. In addition, there were two camps for Soviet prisoners of war nearby, which also fell under the overall jurisdiction of the camp administration. The death rate here, as in other compounds holding Soviet POWs, was high; while the exact number is unclear and subject to varying estimates; perhaps up to 1,000 Soviet prisoners died, the victims of inferior accommodation and sanitary conditions and poor nutrition.

There was a juvenile barrack block at Salaspils, where children aged from 7 to 10 years old, upon being separated from their parents, were held. It has been recorded that these children were often victims of medical experimentation, which, together with typhoid fever, measles, and other diseases, saw a death rate that numbered at least half of the children incarcerated. Indeed, in one of the burial places discovered after the war, 632 corpses of children of ages five to nine were found. While imprisoned, moreover, children were given special badges with their names and family information on them, but should the badges be lost—which happened, particularly with younger children, who would often play with their badges or swap them around—their identities would be lost.

On January 20, 1942, in recognition of his anti-Jewish measures in Riga, Lange was invited to attend the Wannsee Conference in Berlin. This only served to encourage him (as well as those around him) to push for higher results in the mass killing of Jews. Plans for the camp at Salaspils camp were then revised, with a projected population of 15,000 Jews deported from Germany anticipated. While this did not eventuate, nonetheless between 12,000 and 15,000 people did transit through the camp in one way or another during its existence.

Figures concerning the overall mortality rate at Salaspils have fluctuated considerably over time. A reasonable estimate for the total number of deaths has landed at anywhere between 2,000 and 3,000. Not all were Jews, though it is certain that hundreds of German Jews were deliberately murdered or died as a result of sickness, overwork as slave labor, or callous treatment on the part of the guards. During the Cold War, Soviet estimates placed the number of deaths at anywhere between 50,000 and 100,000, but these figures are clearly way too high, on account of the camp never taking in that many prisoners to begin with.

On October 13, 1944, the Soviet army liberated Riga—now completely emptied of all of its Jewish population—and on the same day the camp at Salaspils was also overrun. On October 31, 1967, a memorial complex was opened at the site of the Salaspils concentration camp, embracing a small museum and various forms of commemorative artwork.

Michael Dickerman

See also: Holocaust, The.

Further Reading

Buttar, Prit. *Between Giants: The Battle for the Baltics in World War II*. Oxford: Osprey Publishing, 2013.

Ezergailis, Andrew. *The Holocaust in Latvia, 1941–1944: The Missing Center*. Riga, LV: The Historical Institute of Latvia, 1996.

Salisbury Prison (North Carolina)

Confederate prison facility. On November 2, 1861, the Confederate government bought an 11-acre parcel of land, which included an old cotton mill to be converted into a prison. The prison was designed to hold Confederate soldiers convicted of crimes, suspected spies, disloyal citizens, and prisoners of war, and was commanded by commandant major John H. Gee. The complex included a four-story, brick mill and six smaller brick outbuildings. Initially, the smaller buildings were used to house detainees; some were later converted into hospital wards. Salisbury Prison was supposed to house a maximum of 2,500 prisoners.

Drawing of the prisoner-of-war camp in Salisbury, North Carolina. Three regiments of North Carolina Senior Reserves were stationed here as prison guards. (Buyenlarge/ Getty Images)

The first detainees arrived on December 2, 1861. Until the autumn of 1864, the prison population remained below the 2,500-inmate threshold, and conditions were generally quite good. Food was abundant, cells were spacious, medical care was generally good, and the death rate was quite low. That all changed, however, in October 1864, when the prison population exploded, nearing 10,000 by year's end. The change was due chiefly to the end of the May 5–September 2, 1864, Atlanta Campaign and the unraveling of the prisoner exchange system.

Salisbury was one of the South's most notorious prisoner of war camps. Water supplies became scarce and unreliable, illness and disease spread like wild fire, housing was in such short supply that many prisoners had to dig holes in the ground for shelter, and the on-site hospital lacked basic medicines and personnel. Food became scarce, and many inmates augmented their meager rations by eating acorns from nearby oak trees. Between December 1861 and October 1864, only 255 detainees died at the facility, but between November 1864 and February 1865 alone, an astounding 3,419 more died. The death rate was so high that the deceased were buried without coffins, in mass graves. On November 25, 1864, a massive riot resulted in the deaths of 250 inmates.

In late 1864, Brigadier General Bradley Johnson replaced Gee as prison superintendent. Johnson directed the emptying of the facility, which was accomplished by the end of February 1865. When Union forces reached the site in April 1865, they burned the buildings to the ground. Gee was later accused of mass murder and cruelty, but was acquitted of all charges in July 1866. The court reasoned that the conditions at Salisbury had not deteriorated until late 1864, when Gee was burdened with an impossibly large influx of prisoners.

Paul G. Pierpaoli, Jr.

See also: American Civil War; Confederate States of America; U.S. POW Camps, 1861–1865.

Further Reading

Brown, Louis A. *The Salisbury Prison: A Case Study of Confederate Military Prisons.* Wendell, NC: Broadfoot Publishing, 1992.

Speer, Lonnie. *Portals to Hell: Military Prisons of the Civil War.* Mechanicsburg, PA: Stackpole Books, 1997.

Sandakan Death Marches

A series of forced marches by Allied prisoners of war in Borneo from Sandakan to Ranau, which resulted in the deaths of about 1,000 men. With the start of World War II, Japan captured thousands of Australian and British soldiers who were transported to North Borneo to construct an airstrip and prisoner of war camps at Sandakan. Conditions deteriorated rapidly, and prisoners suffered from lack of supplies, diseases, and maltreatment. In January 1945, as the advancing Allied powers bombed the airfield, the Sandakan camp commandant captain Hoshijima Susumi received orders to move the remaining prisoners to the town of Ranau, located about 160 miles to the west. In a series of marches, the prisoners had to pass through marshland and dense jungle while deprived of food and water; many died en route while the survivors were herded into unsanitary and overcrowded huts where they suffered from lack of bare necessities; many perished from dysentery. By August 1945, of 2,434 prisoners held at Sandakan at the start of the year, only 6 Australians survived, and only because they managed to escape. The Sandakan death marches constitute the single worst atrocity suffered by Australian servicemen during World War II. After the war Captain Hoshijima and several other Japanese officers were found guilty of war crimes and executed.

Alexander Mikaberidze

See also: Bataan Death March (1942); World War II Prisoners of War.

Further Reading

Braithwaite, Richard W. *Fighting Monsters: An Intimate History of the Sandakan Tragedy.* Melbourne: Australian Scholarly Publishing, 2016.

Daws, Gavan. *Prisoners of the Japanese: POWs of World War II in the Pacific.* New York: Simon & Schuster, 2008.

Silver, Lynette Ramsay. *Sandakan: A Conspiracy of Silence.* Bowral, AU: Sally Milner Publishing, 2011.

Sandarmokh

One of the largest Soviet killing sites, located in the remote Karelia region in the Soviet Union, where victims of Joseph Stalin's Great Purge were shot and buried there in 236 communal pits. The 20-acre site witnessed over 9,000 executions by NKVD in 1937–1938, including 1111 prisoners from Solovki Special Camp who were executed between October 27 and November 4, 1937. The killing site remained secret through the Soviet era and was only revealed to the public in late 1990s. Today Sandarmokh serves as a memorial to the crimes of the Soviet regime.

Alexander Mikaberidze

See also: Gulag; NKVD; Solovki Special Camp; Stalin, Joseph.

Further Reading

Haynes, John E., and Harvey Klehr. *In Denial: Historians, Communism and Espionage.* San Francisco: Encounter Books, 2003.

Sandarmokh Memorial Cemetery, https://sand.mapofmemory.org/

Sarposa

Prisoner detention facility near Kandahar, Afghanistan. After the U.S. invasion of Afghanistan in 2001, Sarposa emerged as one of the largest prisoner detention facilities and housed some of the country's most dangerous Taliban militants. On June 13, 2008, the Taliban insurgents orchestrated a well-planned attack on the prison complex, detonating an explosive-laden truck at the front gates of the prison before launching an assault. They freed over 1,200 prisoners, who were evacuated by minibuses waiting for them outside the prison during the attack; almost 400 of prisoners were Taliban fighters.

The U.S.-led coalition launched a major operation to apprehend escaped prisoners, which resulted in several major clashes with the Taliban insurgents. The Sarposa prison, which suffered major damage in the attack, was thoroughly rebuilt and received new batch of prisoners. Yet, in 2011, it became the site of a major prisoner escape. After several months of clandestine planning and work, the Taliban insurgents managed to dig almost 1,200-foot-long tunnel and rescued over 500 Taliban commanders and fighters.

Alexander Mikaberidze

See also: Abu Ghraib; Bagram Air Base; Guantanamo Bay Detention Camp; Qala-i-Jangi.

Further Reading

"Afghanistan's Great Escape: How 480 Taliban Prisoners Broke Out of Jail," *The Guardian*, April 25, 2011.

"Afghan Officials Try to Limit Damage from Prison Break," *New York Times*, April 25, 2011.

"Taliban Free 1,200 Inmates in Attack on Afghan Prison," *New York Times*, June 14, 2008.

"Taliban Reveal Details of Daring Kandahar Prison Escape," *BBC News*, April 25, 2011.

Selarang Barracks Incident (1942)

A revolt of British and Australian prisoners of war at the Japanese camp in Changi, Singapore. After the occupation of Singapore in 1942, the Japanese authorities transformed the Changi military barracks (part of a heavily fortified coastal defense that the British had built) into a POW camp, where some 20,000 Allied soldiers (majority of them British and Australian) were kept. The Selarang Barracks housed the 2nd Battalion Gordon Highlanders, while the Royal Engineers and the 9th Coastal Artillery Regiment of the Royal Artillery were at the Kitchener Barracks and Roberts Barracks respectively.

On August 30, 1942, after the Japanese guards recaptured several Allied POWs who had escaped from the Selarang Barracks camps, Japanese commander general Shimpei Fukuye required all British and Australian POWs interned at Selarang Barracks to sign a "No Escape Pledge," which they all refused. As a punishment, the prisoners were forced to remain in the areas around the barracks square for nearly five days with little food or water and no sanitation. Furthermore, to break POW's spirit, Fukuye ordered executions of the recaptured POWs—Australian corporal Rodney Breavington and Private Victor Gale, and British privates Harold Waters and Eric Fletcher—but this drastic measure failed to produce the desired results, and prisoners remained firm in their defiance. However, by September 5, as prisoners began to fall sick and die from dysentery, Commander of the British and Australian troops in Changi, Lieutenant General E. B. Holmes and his deputy, Lieutenant Colonel Frederick Galleghan felt compelled to concede to the Japanese demands. Upon signing the pledge (though many signed under false names, with "Ned Kelly" being a popular choice), the POWs were allowed to return to the barracks buildings.

After the war, General Fukuye was tried at the Singapore War Crimes Trial in 1946 and was sentenced to death; he was shot by a firing squad on April 27, at the same spot where the four prisoners were executed four years earlier.

Alexander Mikaberidze

See also: Changi; Japan.

Further Reading

Havers, R.P.W. *Reassessing the Japanese Prisoner of War Experience: The Changi POW Camp, Singapore, 1942–1945*. London: Routledge, 2012.

Seminole Wars

A series of wars, in 1817–1819, 1835–1842, and 1855–1858, between the Seminoles and the United States over control of Florida. The First Seminole War (1817–1819) began as the Seminoles—an amalgam of Upper Creek, Yamasees, Guales, Hitchitis, and Oconees tribes—resisted the U.S. efforts to acquire Florida from Spain. American general Andrew Jackson led an invasion of the Florida peninsula in late 1817, defeated the Seminoles living west of the Suwannee River, and captured Pensacola and St. Marks. The American invasion convinced Spain to part with Florida in 1819.

As the United States took possession of the peninsula, hundreds of American settlers moved into the region to claim the land. Throughout the 1820s, there were ongoing tensions and skirmishes between white planters and the Seminoles, who sought to preserve their territory and sovereignty. Upon his election as the U.S.

president, Andrew Jackson was determined to implement a forceful resolution to the "Seminole Question" and insisted on relocation of the Seminoles west of the Mississippi. The Seminoles rejected the Treaty of Fort Gibson (1833) that would have resettled them into Indian Territory, and subsequent American efforts to enforce it resulted in a new war.

Led by chiefs Osceola, Jumper, Alligator, and others, the Seminoles resorted to guerrilla warfare tactics and resisted American forces for seven years before the war ended in 1842. The war resulted in hundreds of Seminoles getting killed in battle, or through starvation and disease, while hundreds of Seminoles were moved to an internment camp that the U.S. Army had built on Egmont Key, an island just off the coast of Tampa. At Ford Dade, as this internment facility became known, the U.S. troops detained Seminoles before their removal to the Indian Territory (in modern Oklahoma), and kept a close watch for any Seminoles who tried to wade into the swift currents around Egmont Key to escape to freedom.

Most of the Seminoles were ultimately relocated to Indian Territory, which in itself served as a vast internment facility. A few hundred Seminoles managed to remain in an unofficial reservation in southwest Florida, where they became involved in the Third Seminole War in 1855, when American settlers encroached upon their lands. Led by chief Billy Bowlegs, the Seminoles fought for three years before they were defeated and forced to surrender. The captured Seminoles were detained at the Egmont Key internment camp before being relocated to Oklahoma. About 100 Seminoles who survived the war retreated deep into the Everglades, where they lived on land that was unwanted by white settlers.

Alexander Mikaberidze

See also: Apache Wars; Indian Removal Act (1830); Trail of Tears.

Further Reading

Covington, James W. *The Billy Bowlegs War, 1855–1858: The Final Stand of the Seminoles against the Whites.* Chuluota, FL: Mickler House, 1982.

Josephy, Alvin M. *Now That the Buffalo's Gone.* Norman: University of Oklahoma Press, 1989.

Mahon, John K. *History of the Second Seminole War, 1835–1842.* Gainesville: University of Florida Press, 1967.

Serpantinka

A sub-camp of the Sevvostlag (a directorate of the Gulag), Serpantinka served as a special death camp where prisoners were worked to death or summarily executed. Located in the midst of the forest in the Far Eastern part of the Soviet Union, Serpantinka was part of a vast network of internment camps that the Soviet government set up in the Kolyma region in order to mine natural resources. By late 1930s, as the political repression increased, the primary purpose of the Sevvostlag (North-Eastern Corrective Labor Camps) directorate shifted from industrial output to punishment of presumed traitors and other undesirables. A special death camp was created in Serpantinka for the purpose of prisoner extermination and about 30,000 individuals were killed here in 1937–1938, either through overwork or executions; to put it a wider context, more prisoners were killed at Serpantinka than were executed in the last century of the Russian imperial rule. Eyewitness testimonies reveal that horrifying conditions at the camp, where "the barracks were so overcrowded that prisoners took turns sitting on the floor while everyone else remained standing" (Vilensky 1999). The camp became so notorious that its very name frightened people since being sent here meant a certain death.

Alexander Mikaberidze

See also: Gulag; NKVD.

Further Reading

Bollinger, Martin. *Stalin's Slave Ships: Kolyma, the Gulag Fleet, and the Role of the West.* Westport, CT: Praeger, 2003.

Conquest, Robert. *Kolyma. The Arctic Death Camps.* Oxford: Oxford University Press, 1979.

Vilensky, Simeon, ed. *Till My Tale Is Told: Women's Memoirs of the Gulag.* Blomington: Indiana University Press, 1999.

Sevvostlag

A Soviet directorate of forced labor camps; the name is an abbreviation of the official title, Severo-vostochnye ispravitelno-trudovye lagera (North-Eastern Corrective Labor Camps). The directorate was established in 1931 to satisfy the workforce demands of the Dalstroy, an organization set up by the Soviet secret police (NKVD) in order to manage industrial development in the Soviet Far East. In late 1930s, the directorate was transferred to NKVD's Main Administration of Camps (GULAG) but was returned back to Dalstroy after World War II. Sevvostlag represented a vast network of labor camps, with over 350 camps and over 190,000 prisoners in 1940. The inmates were employed in mining (especially gold) and road construction, including the infamous Kolyma Highway. Tens of thousands of prisoners perished due to overwork, starvation, cold weather, and abuse. From 1945 to 1949, the directorate included a camp for Japanese prisoners of war in Magadan.

In 1953, after the death of Joseph Stalin, the Soviet government announced amnesty for many prisoners held in labor camps; some 76,000 inmates were released from the Sevvostlag. The directorate was then reorganized and was partly transferred under control of the Soviet Ministry of Metallurgy while some camps formed the Directorate of North Eastern Corrective Labor Camps (USVITL, Upravlenie Severo-Vostochnykh ispravitelno-trudovykh lagerei) within the Soviet Ministry of Justice.

Alexander Mikaberidze

See also: Gulag; NKVD; Serpantinka.

Further Reading

Batsaev, I., and A. Kozlov. *Dalstroy and Sevvostlag NKVD SSSR v tsifrakh i dokumentakh.* Magadan: DVO RAN, 2002, 2 volumes.

Conquest, Robert. *Kolyma. The Arctic Death Camps.* Oxford: Oxford University Press, 1979.

Shark Island

Concentration camp located at Luderitz Bay in German South West Africa. Luderitz Bay, also known as Angra Pequena, was the southernmost seaport in the German colony of South West Africa. It lies in a barren natural harbor wedged between the southern Namib Desert and the Atlantic Ocean. The town was named after Adolf Luderitz, the Bremen-based businessman who first created a beachhead for German annexation of the territory.

The Nama uprising in the south of the colony in October 1904 increased the strategic importance and size of Luderitz town almost overnight. From being a dormant outpost it rapidly became the main supply line for the colonial army, the Schutztruppe, in the campaign against the Nama. There were several military installations in the town, chief among which was the supply command of the Rear, the Etappenkommando. The responsibility for the containment, care, and utilization of the several thousand prisoners of war sent to the town fell to the supply command.

At the edge of the harbor, sheltering the town from the gale-force winds blowing in from the South Atlantic, is a rocky outcrop known as Shark Island. The Luderitz concentration camp was placed at the western-most tip of the island, which is fully exposed to the elements and surrounded by icy waters on three sides.

There were several reasons why prisoners were sent to Luderitz. It was a remote town surrounded by desert, which prevented attempts of escape. More importantly though, the prisoners, who were mainly women and children, were forced to build up the local infrastructure of the town, which until recently had been an insignificant outpost. The need for labor increased manifold by early 1906 when the German Reichstag in Berlin approved the construction of a railway between Luderitz and Keetmanshoop in the interior. This railway was built on the backs of prisoners of war, of whom some 2,000 people died in the process.

From missionary accounts, it is known that mortality on the island was extraordinarily high from the outset. In the annual report for Luderitz district during 1906, compiled by local government officials, the concentration camp was given the nickname "Death Island."

In September 1906, some 2,000 Nama, mainly from the Witbooi, Bethanie, and Veldshoendrager communities arrived in the southern town. They had been banished to Shark Island by the colonial governor, Friedrich von Lindequist, who deemed them too weak to perform meaningful labor. Instead, he hoped that their numbers might be reduced somewhat in order to bring down the costs of a potential future deportation to another German colony. In other words, he expected a number of them to die.

The Nama, who were separated from the Herero prisoners by a barbed wire fence, very quickly started to break down as a result of the climate, the violence of overseers, bad and sparse food rations, the forced labor, and the spread of viral diseases and bacterial infections. By the end of the year, missionary Herman Nyhof could report to his headquarters in Wuppertal that "the nation is doomed," counting upwards of 18 deaths per night. By March, 1,200 of the Nama had died with a further 120 so sick that they were expected to die soon. The majority were women and children.

The camp was closed in April 1907 by the recently appointed head of the colonial army, Major Ludwig von Estorff, who overruled the civil authorities in Windhoek by refusing to perform this "hangman's duty" as he phrased it. One of the more notable casualties of the Island was Bethanie leader and famed guerrilla fighter Cornelius Fredericks.

Casper W. Erichsen

See also: Herero Genocide, Concentration Camps and; Swakopmund; Windhoek.

Further Reading

Drechsler, Horst. *"Let Us Die Fighting:" The Struggle of the Herero and Nama Against German Imperialism (1844–1915).* Berlin: Academie-Verlag, 1996.

Olusoga, David, and Casper W. Erichsen. *The Kaiser's Holocaust: Germany's Forgotten Genocide and the Colonial Roots of Nazism.* London: Faber and Faber, 2010.

Sisak

A concentration camp set up by the Ustaše government of the Independent State of Croatia during World War II. Led by Ante Pavelić, the Ustaše adopted many of the Nazi German policies, including forming concentration camps and persecuting ethnic minorities and political opponents.

With the start of World War II, the Ustaše developed a network of concentration camps where the government detained and exterminated its opponents. In the summer of 1942 one such camp was established at Sisak (near the town of Jasenovac, Croatia) and was formally designated as "Shelter for Children Refugees." The first group of almost 1,000 children arrived in August 1942. At its height, the camp held almost 7,000 children (most of them of Serbian, Romani, and Jewish origins), who were kept in unsanitary conditions, deprived of basic essentials and medical care.

The camp's commander, physician Antun Najžer, performed tests on the children held in the camp, starving them death or torturing them in various ways; some 1,600 children perished as the result. One German eyewitness described "frightful conditions" at the camp: "Few men, many women and children, without sufficient clothing, sleeping on stone at night, pining away, wailing and crying . . . and then worst of all: a room along whose walls, lying on straw which had just been laid down . . . something like fifty naked children, half of them dead, the other dying" (West 2012).

The camp was shut down after the end of World War II; Najžer was arrested and sentenced to death in 1946.

Alexander Mikaberidze

See also: Jadovno Concentration Camp; Jasenovac; Ustaše.

Further Reading

Israeli, Raphael. *The Death Camps of Croatia. Visions and Revisions, 1941–1945.* London: Routledge, 2017.

"Sisak Camp," Jasenovac Memorial Site, http://www.jusp-jasenovac.hr/Default.aspx?sid=7375

West, Richard. *Tito and the Rise and Fall of Yugoslavia.* London: Faber & Faber, 2012.

Slave Labor (World War II)

During World War II, prisoners in most of the Nazi concentration camps were exploited mercilessly as slave labor. Political prisoners included communists, political dissidents, and other opponents of Germany (broadly defined), as well as captured partisans and even citizens of countries occupied by the Germans, randomly picked up for conscripted work details. In addition, people who had volunteered for well-paid positions in German war factories ended up as slave prisoners of the Germans once Germany began losing the war. Most abundantly, however, were Jews in every country occupied by the Nazis.

The foreign workers came from Germany's satellite states or occupied territories to work for the German Reich. As early as March 1938, when Germany invaded Austria, some 100,000 Austrian civilians were taken to work in Germany, and by August 31, 1939, 70,000 workers from Bohemia and Moravia had been conscripted for work in the Reich. After Germany's invasion of Poland in September 1939, and its invasion of the Soviet Union in June 1941, harsh methods were used to press workers into laboring on behalf of the German war effort, as replacements for the millions of Germans who were fighting in the army.

In opposition to international law, Germany also used prisoners of war to help support the German economy. As early as fall 1939, 340,000 Polish POWs were being compelled to work the land, and in August 1942, Germany enacted a decree that made forced labor possible in all occupied countries and POW camps. In western Europe, local authorities cooperated with the Germans in recruitment in an effort to have their own POWs released, or to have the status of their POWs changed to that of foreign workers in Germany.

Although Germany recruited millions of workers between 1942 and 1944, there were never enough for the country's needs, partly because word had spread about the terrible working conditions and the treatment of foreign workers, and partly because of Germany's impending military defeat. Nevertheless, by late 1944 there were 9 million foreign workers (including POWs) in Germany. One out of every five workers was a foreigner, and one out of every four tanks and every four aircraft manufactured in Germany was made by foreign workers.

In most instances, foreign workers were supervised by the Sicherheitspolizei (Security Police, or SiPO) and the Auslandische Arbeiter (Foreign Worker) section of the Gestapo, and members of those groups were guided by racism, xenophobia, and arbitrary decisions. They regarded Poles and Russians as inferior and subhuman beings. Thus, the east European workers were subjected to hard physical labor, humiliated, and severely penalized for misdeeds. They received very low pay, they had to wear special signs on their clothes—"P" for Poles and "Ost" (East) for Russians—and they could not socialize or mix with German society in any way. Germans who had sexual intercourse with foreign workers could be sentenced to death. Even though western European workers were treated better, they also complained that they were treated like slaves. Jews who became foreign workers or were taken as POWs tried to avoid being identified as Jewish.

The majority of the millions of Jews caught in the Nazi net and earmarked for death were gassed upon arriving by train at one of the six Nazi death camps in

Poland. In these camps, only a relatively small minority were selected for labor (with the exception of Auschwitz and Majdanek), but hundreds of thousands were sent to work as slave labor in other camps, as well as in the Nazi-imposed ghettos throughout eastern Europe. When Germany invaded Poland in September 1939, army units recruited Jews at random for forced labor, including removing roadblocks and paving roads. Not only were the Jews mistreated, but their work was specifically chosen to degrade them. At the same time, Jews were subject to constant beatings and harassment.

From October to December 1939 in Poland, the Nazis issued decrees drafting into compulsory labor Jewish men and women aged 14 to 60 and children aged 12 to 14. Jews had to register with the local Judenrat, the Nazi-enforced Jewish council, and they had to carry out temporary work assignments like removing snow, loading goods the Nazis had confiscated from other Jews, and building ghetto walls. Eventually, special labor camps were set up for the Jews; in the Lublin district in Poland alone, there were 29 such camps by July 1940. In August 1940, 20,000 Jews from the ages of 19 to 35 were ordered to report to the labor camps. Many defied the recruitment despite the danger involved in doing so.

Conditions in the labor camps were horrific. Often, the men had no sleeping quarters and had to sleep outside. Sometimes they were not fed even their meager rations, and were humiliated and persecuted by dogs, Nazi threats, and beatings. Those working on land amelioration projects sometimes had to stand in water to work. Out of 6,000 men sent from the Warsaw Ghetto to labor camps, 1,000 were no longer fit for labor after only two weeks. In Poland's Łodz ghetto, the entire Jewish population had to partake in forced labor as the ghettos themselves became labor camps.

Large numbers of Jews worked in German factories in Poland and in workshops during the last years of the ghettos. At the end of 1940, more than 700,000 Jews were engaged in forced labor in Poland. The figure dropped to 500,000 in 1942 and to little more than 100,000 in mid-1943, owing to the high ghetto death rate and to deportations of the Jews from the ghettos to the death camps. Factories using Jewish labor had to pay sizable sums to the German secret police, and Jews had to pay bribes in order to obtain such employment, which they naïvely believed would exempt them from being deported to the concentration camps.

In mid-1942 and April–May 1943, some of the Jews in the ghettos were taken to the Trawniki and Poniatowa labor camps in Poland, and in November 1943, the Germans murdered 40,000 Jews in those camps. In most work camps, the Jews had to work at least 10 to 12 hours a day. In those rare circumstances where they were paid, they were paid less than the meager wage that people of other nationalities received. Jewish wages did not enable them to purchase food on the black market, so most of the workers starved.

Jews arriving in Auschwitz who were selected for work and not death faced the horrors of forced labor. Eating only a small piece of bread and watery soup either before or after a long, tough workday, most Jewish prisoners succumbed to diseases like typhus. Health conditions in the camps were primitive and the water undrinkable, and epidemics spread quickly. The Germans kept the Jews in a constant state of terror. People could be shot anytime and for any reason.

Jews had to do the dirty work in the Nazi-instigated death camps against their fellow Jews, often relatives or fellow Jewish community members. Unlucky men and women were selected for the most hideous medical experiments. Jewish prisoners had to clear rocks, fill trains full of dirt, dig trenches and tunnels, sort the possessions of new arrivals (which were confiscated by the Germans), and work in ammunition factories. Mostly, Jews were slave laborers in factories for the German military effort. Whether Jews were making or putting together airplane parts or ammunition, working in coal mines, or working in machine shops, they were thoroughly and completely abused and exploited. Jews were compelled to steal in order to survive, and some Jewish women were forced into prostitution.

Toward the end of World War II, Jewish prisoners were often shot in forests or on long marches by foot, or journeys by train, after camps were evacuated because of Allied bombings. Many Jewish prisoners ended up in Bergen-Belsen, where they were neglected and left to die of typhus. In the last days before liberation, the Germans poisoned potato storehouses so that many Jews died when eating that food, the only food to be found. After liberation by the Allies, many prisoners died from overeating. Most Jews selected for labor in the death camps did not survive until liberation.

Junius P. Rodriguez

See also: Germany; Holocaust, The.

Further Reading

Browning, Christopher R. *Remembering Survival: Inside a Nazi Slave-Labor Camp.* New York: Norton, 2010.

Buggeln, Mark. *Slave Labor in Nazi Concentration Camps.* Oxford: Oxford University Press, 2014.

Von Plato, Alexander, Almut Leh, and Christoph Thonfeld, eds. *Hitler's Slaves: Life Stories of Forced Labourers in Nazi-Occupied Europe.* New York: Berghahn, 2010.

Sobibór

Death camp established by the Nazis in Poland in April 1942. It was located in modern-day eastern Poland, five miles south of Włodawa, and like most death camps, it was situated in a sparsely-populated, remote area. Measuring 1,969 feet long and 1,312 feet wide, Sobibór was erected along the Chełm-Włodawa rail line, which facilitated the shipment of condemned Jews into the camp. Surrounded by a high, wire fence, it was masked by trees planted along its perimeter, so outsiders would not be aware of its true purpose. Beyond the fence and trees was a 50-foot-wide minefield to thwart escape attempts.

Sobibor was administered by 20–30 SS and security officials; the guard force numbered between 90 and 120 men, some of whom were Polish or Ukrainian civilians or Soviet prisoners of war. SS first lieutenant Franz Stangl ran the facility from April until August 1942; he was replaced by SS captain Franz Reichleitner, who headed the camp until it was decommissioned in November 1943. Most of the Jews sent to Sobibór were from the eastern and northern parts of Poland's Lublin District, although Jews from Austria, Germany, Bohemia, Slovakia, Moravia, France, and the Netherlands were also sent there.

In May 1942, Sobibór officials began systematically gassing arriving detainees. As trainloads of Jews pulled into the reception area, they were herded onto platforms, had their valuables taken, and then were forced to disrobe. They were then

Sobibór death camp sign taken in 2004. Situated at the Polish village of Sobibór (near Włodawa, Poland), this German extermination camp was part of the secretive Operation REINHARD, which sought to exterminate Jews in the German-occupied territories. As many as 250,000 people perished here before the war ended. (Benoit Gysembergh/Paris Match via Getty Images)

led into the "tube," a leafy and wooded tunnel that connected the reception area to the gas chambers. The system could accommodate up to 20 freight cars as a time. Once the victims were in the gas chambers, which the Germans cruelly told them were showers, the doors were sealed and they were gassed to death with carbon monoxide. Sonderkommandos, prisoners forced to work in the camps, then emptied the chambers and buried the dead in mass graves; before doing so, they extracted any jewelry or gold fillings from the corpses.

Sobibór was the site of a major prisoner uprising in October 1943, led by Alexander Pechersky and Leon Feldhendler. On October 14, after learning that they would likely be deported to other camps where they would meet certain death, about 600 prisoners killed some 12 German prison administrators and guards. Amid the chaos, at least 300 prisoners managed to exit the camp. About 100 were caught in the days immediately after the uprising, and up to 60 managed to survive the war.

The following month, SS officials decided to close Sobibór. The remaining prison guards shot any surviving internees still in camp, and were ordered to dismantle the gas chambers and bulldoze the facility to the ground. By March 1944, when the last of the guard contingent had left the area, trees had been planted over the site of Sobibór to mask its existence. No prisoners were taken to the facility after November 1943. Sobibór was one of six dedicated death camps operated by the Nazis and situated in Poland during the Holocaust.

Paul G. Pierpaoli, Jr.

See also: Arbeitslager; Auschwitz; Bełżec; Bergen-Belsen; Birkenau; Buchenwald; Bullet Decree (1944); Chełmno; Colditz; Concentration Camps; Dachau; Death Camps; Dora-Mittelbau; Eichmann, Adolf; Extermination Centers; Gas Chambers; Gestapo; Gross-Rosen; Ninzert; Hitler, Adolf; Holocaust, The; I.G. Farben Case (1947); J.A. Topf & Söhne; Kinderblock 66; Koch Trial (1951); Kramer, Josef; Krupp Case (1948); Mauthausen-Gusen; Monowitz; Natzweiler-Struthof; Neuengamme; Niederhagen; Nuremberg Trials; Ravensbrück; Sachsenhausen; Slave Labor (World War II); Sonderkommando; Stalag; Stutthof; Treblinka; Trostinets; Zyklon B Case (1946).

Further Reading

Arad, Yitzhak. *Belzec, Sobibor, Treblinka: The Operation Reinhard Death Camps.* Bloomington: Indiana University Press, 1987.

Blatt, Thomas Toivi. *From the Ashes of Sobibor: A Story of Survival.* Evanston, IL: Northwestern University Press, 1997.

Schelvis, Jules. *Sobibor: A History of a Nazi Death Camp.* London: Bloomsbury Academic, 2007.

Rashke, Richard. *Escape from Sobibor.* London: Michael Joseph, 2013.

Solovki Special Camp

Soviet prison and forced labor camp on the remote Solovetskii Islands in the White Sea. Established in 1923, the Solovki Special Designation Concentration Camp (Solovetsky Lager Osobogo Naznachenia or SLON) was housed within the famous Solovetskii Orthodox Monastery, and was designed to incarcerate opponents to Soviet Russia's new Bolshevik regime. In its structure, administration, and purpose, the Solovki served as a prototype for the Gulag camps and its very name soon became the euphemism for a "corrective labor camp."

Between 1923 and 1933, the Solovki camp processed tens of thousands of prisoners, with the height of prisoner population reaching 65,000–70,000 in 1929–1930. In 1933 the "special designation camp" was formally transferred to the new and much larger Belbaltlag camp that was tasked with the construction of a canal connecting White Sea and Baltic Sea. The construction of this 140-mile-long canal involved a labor force of over 120,000 prisoners, thousands of whom died from mistreatment, exposure, and overwork. In 1937 the Solovki became the site of a "special prison" where hundreds of prisoners were abused, tortured, and executed during Joseph Stalin's Great Purges; thus, in late October 1937 alone, over 1100 prisoners were moved from Solovki to Sandarmokh where they were summarily executed. The prison was closed in 1939.

Alexander Mikaberidze

See also: Belomorkanal; Gulag; NKVD; Vorkuta Camps.

Further Reading

Applebaum, Anne. *Gulag: A History.* New York: Broadway Books, 2003.

Ivanova, Galina, Carol Apollonio Flath, and Donald J. Raleigh. *Labor Camp Socialism: The Gulag in the Soviet Totalitarian System.* New York: M.E. Sharpe, 2000.

Robson, Roy P. *Solovki: The Story of Russia Told Through its Most Remarkable Islands.* New Haven, CT: Yale University Press, 2004.

Solzhenitsyn, Aleksandr (1918–2008)

Soviet-Russian dissident and writer. Born in Kislovodsk, he was the son of an artillery officer. After graduating from the University of Rostov-on-Don in 1941, he was drafted into the army during the German invasion of the Soviet Union and served as an artillery captain. In February 1945, Solzhenitsyn was arrested in East Prussia for his criticism of the policies of Soviet dictator Joseph Stalin and sentenced to eight years of hard labor in a gulag. In March 1953, after his sentence ended, Solzhenitsyn was sent to internal exile at a remote village in Kazakhstan. After Stalin's death, Solzhenitsyn was released and worked as a high school math teacher.

In 1962, the leading Soviet literary journal Novyi Mir (with the approval of then Soviet leader Nikita Khrushchev) published Solzhenitsyn's novella *One Day in the Life of Ivan Denisovich* that became an instant hit and initiated public discussion of Stalin's repressions; never before had the conditions in a Soviet Gulag system been described in such gritty detail and poignancy. After Khrushchev's downfall from power in 1964, the political and cultural climate in the Soviet Union again became more repressive and Solzhenitsyn found it impossible to publish his works. The Soviet secret service (KGB) seized his papers and regularly harassed him. Nevertheless, Solzhenitsyn persevered and undertook his most ambitious project—the three-volume *The Gulag Archipelago* (published in 1973–1975) that offered an in-depth look into Soviet system of repression, detailing conditions in prison and internment camps, prisoner transports, prison camp culture, etc. The work was based upon Solzhenitsyn's own experience as well as the testimony of hundreds of former prisoners. *The Gulag Archipelago* was not published in the Soviet Union, but was smuggled out of the country and released in the West, where it sold over 30 million copies in 35 languages. It caused a cultural and political uproar in the Soviet Union and resulted in Solzhenitsyn expulsion from the country in 1974.

After living briefly in Zurich, Solzhenitsyn moved to the United States, where he spent most of his remaining life. In 1990, as the Soviet Union was about to collapse, Solzhenitsyn's Soviet citizenship was restored and he was allowed to return. He passed away in Moscow in 2008.

Alexander Mikaberidze

See also: Gulag; NKVD.

Further Reading

Scammel, Michael. *Solzhenitsyn: A Biography*. London: Palatin, 1986.
Thomas, D.M. *Alexander Solzhenitsyn: A Century in his Life*. New York: St. Martin's Press, 1998.

Sonderaktion 1005

The 'special action', launched by Nazi Germany, of systematically removing all trace of atrocities and mass murders perpetrated during World War II. Sonderaktion 1005 was launched in the spring of 1942 on the orders of the Chief of the Reich Main Security Office (including the Gestapo, Kripo, and SD) Reinhard Heydrich. The operation was directed by SS-Standartenführer Paul Blobel who initially experimented on disposing of corpses at the German concentration camp at Chełmno. It was discovered that the most effective way was giant pyres on iron grills. Under Blobel's direction, prisoners were forced to form special work groups (*Leichenkommandos* or "corpse units") to construct large pyres, burn corpses, and crush the remaining bone fragments in grinding machines before re-burying them in pits.

The Sonderaktion 1005 officially began at the Sobibór extermination camp and gradually involved other extermination camps, including Bełżec and Treblinka. In 1943, the German authorities returned to the sites of earlier mass killings, including at Babi Yar and Ponary, where they began "cleaning" mass graves. Upon finishing their grim work, the prisoners who had carried it out were oftentimes executed. The German efforts were only partly successful before the advancing Soviet troops reclaimed the site of mass murder. After the war, the Allied powers prosecuted individuals involved in the Sonderaktion; Blobel was sentenced to death by the U.S. Nuremberg Military Tribunal and was hanged at Landsberg Prison on June 8, 1951.

Alexander Mikaberidze

See also: Extermination Centers; Gas Chambers; Holocaust, The; Nuremberg Trials; Sobibór.

Further Reading

Levene, Mark. *The Crisis of Genocide: Volume 2: Annihilation: The European Rimlands, 1939–1953*. Oxford: Oxford University Press, 2013.

Marrus, Michael R. *The Nazi Holocaust. Volume 6: The Victims of the Holocaust.* London: Meckler, 1989.

Sonderkommando

Sonderkommando is a term that refers to prisoners in Nazi death camps who helped herd newly-arriving prisoners into the gas chambers and then deposited their corpses into crematoria. The term, meaning "special commandos," was also used on other occasions to describe special killing units of the SS, which targeted Jews and other "undesirables," as German armies advanced into newly-conquered territory. However, its most common usage refers to death camp workers.

Sonderkommandos were invariably young, able-bodied Jewish males who were selected for slave labor soon after their arrival in the death camps. They helped process newly-arrived prisoners and readied them for the gas chambers. This included the removal of their clothing and the shaving of women's heads. After the victims were gassed to death, they also gathered the personal possessions of those who had been murdered, removed any gold that victims might have had in their teeth, and moved the corpses from the gas chambers into the crematoria. The work was grim and gruesome, and shifts lasted for 12 hours, seven days a week.

Because the Sonderkommando were intimately familiar with the Nazis' factory-like extermination procedures, they were housed in separate barracks, so they could not interact with other internees or tip them off as to their fate. And because the Nazis wished to keep the particulars of their death camps a secret,

Sonderkommandos were routinely killed and replaced by newly-arriving recruits. The average life span of a Sonderkommando was three to four months. To entice the workers to do such horrific labor, and to prevent them from influencing other inmates, the camp's administrators usually gave the Sonderkommando special privileges, including better and more abundant food and better housing.

Only a very few Sonderkommando workers survived their ordeal, and some rebelled against their captors. On August 2, 1943, a number of Sonderkommando men participated in an uprising at the Treblinka death camp, and nearly 100 prisoners managed to escape. At Auschwitz-Birkenau on October 7, 1944, a carefully planned revolt took place involving a number of men from the XII Sonderkommando, who managed to destroy one of the camp's crematoria. For several months prior to the rebellion, prisoners had been hiding gunpowder, which was used to blow up one of the ovens. Almost all those who participated in this revolt were caught and executed.

Paul G. Pierpaoli, Jr.

See also: Auschwitz; Concentration Camps; Extermination Centers; Germany; Holocaust, The; Kapos; Trawniki Men.

Further Reading
Müller, Filip. *Eyewitness Auschwitz: Three Years in the Gas Chambers.* Chicago: Ivan R. Dee, 1979.

Rees, Laurence. *Auschwitz: The Nazis and the Final Solution.* New York: Random House, 2005.

Venezia, Shlomo. *Inside the Gas Chambers: Eight Months in Sonderkommando at Auschwitz.* Cambridge: Polity, 2011.

Soviet Union. *See* Gulag

Soviet Union, Deportations in

The German invasion of the Soviet Union began in June 1941, and proceeded rapidly through the Ukraine and beyond. By the following June, Hitler's forces had advanced as far as the Crimea. The initial military setbacks for the Soviet Union occasioned the adoption by Stalin's government of repressive measures aimed at certain nationality groups. Those communities singled out by the new policy were subjected to forcible resettlement, a procedure carried out with the utmost brutality and disregard for human life.

The first ethnic community to feel the effect of the resettlement policy was the long-established Volga German Autonomous Region and its ethnic German population. Already in August 1941, the Presidium of the Supreme Soviet decreed the deportation of the Volga Germans on the pretext that thousands of "diversionists and spies" were awaiting a signal from the German invader to commit acts of sabotage. Ethnic Germans residing in the Crimea and north Caucasus were subjected to similar measures, all concerned being removed to Central Asia and Siberia, where they remained in highly restrictive circumstances for over 14 years.

Whereas the deportation of ethnic Germans was a preventive move, no actual treason or disloyal conduct having been charged, the ensuing deportations were justified by the imputation of treasonous activity by members of the affected groups. Seven additional nationality groups were deported in their entirety: Balkars, Chechens, Crimean Tatars, Ingushi, Karachai, Kalmyks, and Meskhetians. The removals, which began in 1943 and extended through 1944, were accomplished in a singularly inhumane manner. The targeted groups were given minimal notice of their impending departure and had minimal opportunity to retain their belongings. Like the Ethnic Germans, these groups were dispersed to remote regions to work in mines, labor camps, factories, and farms. Conditions under which they were transported were similar to the conditions of the trains bound to Auschwitz, and the conditions awaiting them at their destination resembled those of a Gulag, the Soviet penal system. Estimates of loss of life are not very exact, but in the worst case, that of Crimean Tatars, mortality reportedly approached 50 percent. And in the vacated areas, homes and belongings were seized by neighbors or newcomers, the latter including many Russians encouraged to move into the vacuum left by the removals.

The justification for this draconian program was quite specious. Although there were instances of disloyalty and even sabotage by members of the groups to be deported, that was equally true for other nationalities, and for the Russian population itself. Yet, despite the arbitrariness of Stalin's choices for deportation, corrective measures were slow in coming.

The Supreme Soviet issued an amnesty decree in 1955 that accomplished little more than easing some of the restrictions still in force for the deported people. The 20th Party Congress, held in February of the next year, featured Khrushchev's famous speech denouncing Stalin's cult of personality and including the deportations among Stalin's crimes. This paved the way for corrective action by the Party Central Committee in the form of a decree, "On the Restoration of the National Autonomy of the Kalmyk, Karachai, Balkar, Chechen, and Ingush peoples." While failing to provide restitution or atonement for losses and suffering, the new policy allowed for gradual depatriation for the peoples named. Strangely missing from the list, however, were the Volga Germans, the Crimean Tatars, and the Meskhetians. Of these, the Crimean Tatars case is the most dramatic, for it became a major element in the dissident movement of the 1970s and the 1980s, giving rise to serious discussions of the genocidal implications of the deportation program. Finally, late in 1989, an official declaration acknowledged that the deportations had been unlawful and criminal, cold comfort for peoples whose suffering had begun more than four decades earlier.

Lyman H. Legters

See also: Gulag.

Further Reading

Conquest, Robert. *The Nation Killers: The Soviet Deportation of Nationalities.* New York: Macmillan, 1970.

Legters, Lyman H. "Soviet deportation of whole nations: A genocidal process," in Samuel Totten, William S. Parsons, and Israel W. Charny, eds. *Century of Genocide:*

Eyewitness Accounts and Critical Views. 113–135, New York: Garland Publishing, 1997.

Naimark, Norman M. *Stalin's Genocides.* Princeton, N.J.: Princeton University Press, 2010.

Nekrich, Aleksander M. *The Punished People: The Deportation and Fate of Soviet Minorities at the End of the Second World War.* New York: W. W. Norton, 1978.

Soviet Union, POW Camps (1941–1956)

During World War II, the Soviet Union captured some 3 million Axis prisoners of war, with the vast majority of them falling into captivity in the last two years of the war; after the battle of Stalingrad alone, the Soviets captured over 90,000 Germans soldiers. The vast majority of prisoners of wars were Germans (over 2.3 million), followed by Hungarians (over 500,000), Austrians (over 150,000), Romanians (almost 200,000), and Italians (close to 50,000). These prisoners were held in a vast system of POW camps that included over 200 permanent base camps and over 2,400 branch camps scattered across the 15 economic regions (ERs) that the Soviet Union had been divided into. The highest number of camps was in the Central (50 base camps and 655 branch camps), Southern (34 and 515) and Western (30 and 515) ERs. Due to desperate economic situation and labor shortages in the Soviet Union, POWs served as an important source of labor, especially after the war when they were employed in clearing devastated Soviet cities and towns, rebuilding infrastructure, as well as mining coal, iron, and other natural resources. Overwork, maltreatment, cold weather, malnutrition, and disease resulted in high mortality rates among the prisoners of war, and as many as 1 million men

German soldiers taken prisoner by the Red Army in World War II stand in queue for water on the Khodynka Field, Moscow, 1945. (TASS via Getty Images)

perished during their captivity. The last surviving German POWs were repatriated in late 1950s.

In 1945, as the Soviet Union declared war on Japan and invaded Manchuria and Korea, the Red Army captured over 650,000 Japanese who were also sent to prisoner-of-war camps and employed in postwar reconstruction. The Japanese POWs were largely held in camps in the Far East where they were treated more benevolently than the German prisoners; thus, they were allowed to leave camps, interacted with local civilian population, and published a Japanese-language newspaper in Khabarovsk. The repatriation of Japanese prisoners began in 1946 and completed four years later.

Alexander Mikaberidze

See also: Gulag.

Further Reading

Gavrilov, V.A., and E.L. Katasonovva, eds. *Yaponskie voennoplennye v SSSR: 1945–1956. Sbornik Dokumentov.* Moscow: MFD, 2013.

Hilger, Andreas. *Deutsche Kriegsgefangene in der Sowjetunion 1941–1956: Kriegsgefangenenpolitik, Lageralltag und Erinnerung.* Essen, DE: Klartext Verlag, 2000

Kim, S. P. "Repatriatsia yaponskikh voennoplennykh iz SSSR v 1946–1950 gg," in *Voenno-Istoricheskii zhurnal* 3(2015): 69–75.

Overmans, Rüdiger. *Deutsche militärische Verluste im Zweiten Weltkrieg.* Berlin: Oldenbourg Wissenschaftsverlag, 2009.

Vsevolodov V. A. *'Srok khraneniya—postoyanno!' Kratkaja istoriya lagerya voennoplennyh i internirovannyh UPVI NKVD-MVD SSSR #27 (1942–1950).* Moscow: Moskovskij izdatel'skij dom, 2003.

Vsevolodov V. A. *Stupajte s mirom: k istorii repatriatsii nemetskikh voennoplennykh iz SSSR (1945–1958 gg.)* Moscow: Moskovskij izdatel'skij dom, 2010.

Spanish-American War (1898)

During Cuban efforts to throw off Spanish colonial rule during the Cuban War of Independence (1895–1898), both sides engaged in atrocities. Although perceived Spanish brutality in Cuba was a key factor in the U.S. decision to declare war on Spain, the perception that the Spanish deliberately and routinely committed atrocities was primarily the creation of the yellow press, which ran stories reported by Cuban revolutionaries without scrutiny or investigation. Spanish governor-general Valeriano Weyler y Nicolau attempted through his reconcentrado (reconcentration) policy of 1896 to weaken the insurgency in the countryside. Weyler initially ordered civilians in one province to detention camps near garrisoned military headquarters. He also gave military commanders broad powers to execute people who evaded the requirement to register with the government, and he subjected those who aided the rebels to military rather than civilian law. Later, the reconcentration camps were greatly expanded. The camps were overcrowded, and shelter consisted mostly of dilapidated warehouses without plumbing. The government also failed to provide adequate food or arable land for the internees. As a result, between 200,000 and 400,000 civilians in the camps died from diseases, such as yellow fever and smallpox, or starvation during the two years that the policy remained in effect.

The Cuban rebels also committed atrocities as part of their military strategy, but few of these are well documented. One major exception is José Maceo Grajales's march of some 6,000 men through Havana Province in the spring of 1897. In an effort to put economic pressure on Spain to end its rule of the island, the rebels raided fellow Cubans' shops and killed civilians working on railways and in sugarcane fields.

Atrocities were relatively few during the brief Spanish-American War of 1898. One grisly incident occurred when Americans in the Cuban village of El Caney placed some prisoners of war captured during the Battle of San Juan Hill under the control of Cuban rebels, who murdered 40 of the prisoners by decapitation. Some historians have argued that the U.S. Navy's bombardment of the city of Santiago de Cuba for two days prior to the August 12, 1898, truce may also be considered an atrocity.

While atrocities have been a part of warfare since the beginning of history, the modern press's reporting of such acts and increased government scrutiny of them before, during, and after the Spanish-American War led to a general heightened awareness of such acts. Indeed, a number of atrocities and massacres occurred during the American pacification of the Philippines, which began in 1899 and lasted until 1902. As a result of the Spanish-American War, the United States had annexed the Philippines, a former Spanish colony where an independence movement had also been underway before that conflict began.

Matthew J. Krogman

See also: Boer War (1899–1902); Concentration Camps.

Further Reading

Perez, Louis A. *Cuba Between Empires, 1878–1902.* Pittsburgh, PA: University of Pittsburgh Press, 1983.

Tone, John Lawrence. *War and Genocide in Cuba, 1895–1898.* Chapel Hill: University of North Carolina Press, 2008.

Trask, David F. *The War with Spain in 1898.* Lincoln: University of Nebraska Press, 1996.

Srebrenica Massacre

The worst bloodbath on European soil since the Holocaust, the Srebrenica Massacre involved a systematic killing of more than 8,000 Muslim Bosniaks during the Bosnian War. Srebrenica is a town located near the Dvina River in eastern Bosnia. After the collapse of Yugoslavia and outbreak of war, this predominantly Bosniak town defended itself successfully against the advance of the Bosnian Serb army in the spring of 1992. The Serbs conducted a wide-scale ethnic cleansing of the region, expelling Bosniaks and increasing the share of Serbian population. Besieged by the Bosnian Serbs, Srebrenica was isolated from Bosniak-controlled territories to the west and was dependent on humanitarian aid provided by the United Nations Protection Force (UNPROFOR). Nevertheless, the Bosnians, under command of Naser Oric, successfully repelled the Serbs throughout 1992 and early 1993. In the spring of 1993, the United Nations declared Srebrenica a "safe area," along with five other Bosnian Muslim cities, then under siege at the hands of the Bosnian Serbs.

Despite its new status, Srebrenica was never properly defended by UNPROFOR; of over 30,000 UN troops requested for Bosnian Muslim "safe areas", only 7,600 arrived, of which 750 Dutch troops were deployed at Srebrenica; the UN troops were lightly armed and operated under a stringent mandate that made them powerless to successfully engage either of the conflicting sides. The Bosniak population continued to suffer from extreme privation as the Serbs tested the UN's resolve by blocking aid convoys.

By 1995, after almost three years of resistance, Srebrenica became a symbol of Bosniak resistance, which further increased the town's importance. In July 1995, encouraged by UN vacillation over whether or not to maintain safe areas, the Bosnian Serb forces, under command of General Ratko Mladic, launched a major campaign to capture Srebrenica. The UNPROFOR troops failed to stop the Serbs because of a lack of support further up the UN chain of command. As the Serbian forces overran the enclave, over 15,000 Bosniaks fled into the woods, while many sought shelter at the UNPROFOR base at Potocari, where the members of the Dutch peacekeepers sheltered over 8,000 Bosnian Muslims. The Serb forces overwhelmed the Dutch forces, seized the base, and turned it into an internment camp, where the Bosnian prisoners were methodically massacred between July 11 and 22, 1995.

The Srebrenica Massacre became the worst single war crime of the entire Bosnian conflict, and the worst case of mass murder in Europe since the end of World War II. It also stands as a symbol of the failure by the international community, especially the UN, to prevent mass killings. The massacre led to the indictment of several Serbian commanders, including Mladic, as war criminals by the International Criminal Tribunal for the former Yugoslavia (ICTY) at The Hague. In 2004, in a unanimous ruling, the ICTY ruled that the massacre constituted a genocide. Mladic was convicted of various crimes, including his role at Srebrenica, in 2017.

Alexander Mikaberidze

See also: Bosnian War.

Further Reading

Cigar, Norman. *Genocide in Bosnia: The Policy of "Ethnic Cleansing."* College Station: Texas A&M University Press, 1995.

Rohde, David. *A Safe Area, Srebrenica: Europe's Worst Massacre since the Second World War.* London: Pocket Book, 1997.

Sremska Mitrovica

Location of one of the largest Serbian concentration camps during the Yugoslavian Civil Wars in 1991–1992. Situated in Sremska Mitrovica (Vojvodina province, Serbia), the facility served as a prison dating back to the late nineteenth century. During the Yugoslavian Civil Wars, it was turned into the main internment facility where some 4,000 Croatian and Bosnian prisoners were held by the Serbian authorities. The camp acquired notoriety for widespread prisoner abuse, torture, and rape.

Alexander Mikaberidze

See also: Bosnian War.

Further Reading

Mojzes, Paul. *Balkan Genocides: Holocaust and Ethnic Cleansing in the Twentieth Century.* New York: Rowman & Littlefield, 2011.

Sri Lanka

Starting in 1983, the Liberation Tigers of Tamil Eelam (Tamil Tigers) had been waging a full-scale war to establish an independent state of Tamil Eelam in the north and east of Sri Lanka. The fighting between the two sides raged for 25 years, causing widespread hardship and devastation and claiming an initial estimated 80,000–100,000 people.

In 2007, after the failure of the fourth peace process, the Sri Lankan military launched a major military offensive aimed at crushing the insurgency. By 2008, the military seized control over the entire Eastern Province of the island and shifted its focus to the north. In January 2009, the Sri Lankan authorities announced the establishment of 12-square-mile-wide Safe Zone and began evacuating local population to newly set up camps. Ultimately, some 372,000 civilians were moved to the so called "welfare centers," where they were detained and prevented from leaving. Conditions inside these internment camps worsened rapidly, especially after heavy rains caused considerable flooding. Despite international criticism, Sri Lankan government kept the detainees in the camps and denied access to international observers. After the Tamil Tigers were defeated and sued for peace, Sri Lanka began the process of repatriation and the vast majority of detainees was able to return home.

Alexander Mikaberidze

See also: Concentration Camps.

Further Reading

Goodhand, Jonathan, Jonathan Spencer, and Benedikt Korf, eds. *Conflict and Peacebuilding in Sri Lanka: Caught in the Peace Trap?* New York: Routledge, 2011.

Thiranagama, Sharika. *In My Mother's House: Civil War in Sri Lanka.* Philadelphia: University of Pennsylvania Press, 2011.

SS-Totenkopfverbände

Specially trained SS personnel whose primary job was to provide administrative and guard duties for Nazi German concentration camps. The term SS-Totenkopfverbände (SS-TV) can be translated as "Death's Head Squad." By early 1934, the head of the SS, Heinrich Himmler, had gained control over Germany's nascent system of concentration camps and created an Inspectorate of Concentration Camps under Theodor Eicke as Chief Inspector. Eicke already had charge over the camp at Dachau, which would serve as a model for all subsequent camps. In April 1934 he established the SS-TV. All SS-TV personnel were highly trained, and were thus well-placed to maintain day-to-day operations in the camps, including discipline, which, as time progressed, became more and more brutal for those incarcerated. In 1937, there were just four concentration camps in Germany; that number increased dramatically as Germany established many other camps within its borders, as well as in those areas occupied by German troops after the war began in 1939. In 1939, the SS-TV had some 24,000 personnel, a number that had nearly doubled to 40,000 by early 1945.

After 1938, concentration camps became important not only in terms of the Holocaust, but also as a centerpiece of Germany's forced labor system, particularly in occupied areas outside Germany. The SS-TV created a string of forced labor camps, which farmed out prisoners as slave labor to civilian contractors for a profit. In some instances, the SS-TV actually owned companies, using concentration camp prisoners as forced labor. Meanwhile, in 1939 a combat division of the SS-TV was formed, which later became part of the Nazi Party army, the Waffen-SS. The uniforms of the SS-TV, designed by Hugo Boss, were adorned with a menacing skull-and-crossbones patch, a grim reminder of its major role in the Holocaust.

Between 1939 and 1945 alone, it is estimated that the SS-TV was directly responsible for the murders of at least 2 million people. They included Jews, political dissidents, Romanis, Jehovah's Witnesses, homosexuals, alleged career criminals, and others. After the war ended in 1945, a number of SS-TV officers were tried for various war crimes and crimes against humanity.

Paul G. Pierpaoli, Jr.

See also: Concentration Camps; Gestapo; Sonderkommando.

Further Reading

Höhne, Heinz. *The Order of the Death's Head: The Story of Hitler's SS.* New York: Penguin, 2001.

Wachsmann, Nikolaus. *KL: A History of the Nazi Concentration Camps.* New York: Farrar, Straus and Giroux, 2015.

Weale, Adrian. *Army of Evil: A History of the SS.* New York: NAL Caliber, 2012.

Stajićevo

A former agricultural farm in Stajićevo (near Zrenjanin, Serbia) where Serbian authorities set up a concentration camp and held between 1,500 and 6,500 Croatian prisoners of war and civilians during the Yugoslavian Civil Wars (1991–1995). The Serbian abuse of prisoners at Stajićevo was cited in the International Criminal Tribunal for the former Yugoslavia's case against former Serbian president Slobodan Milošević and former president of the Republic of Serbian Krajina Goran Hadžić. According to the eyewitness testimonies, prisoners at Stajićevo were denied medical treatment, sanitary facilities, adequate bedding, and food. They were subjected to psychological and physical abuse, and some were executed. Detainees were released in a prisoner exchange in January 1992, after spending over three months in the camp. After the war the camp buildings at Stajicevo were razed to the ground.

Alexander Mikaberidze

See also: Bosnian War.

Further Reading

Prosecutor v. Hadžić (IT-04-75), International Criminal Tribunal for the former Yugoslavia.

Stalag

A contraction of "Stammlager" (itself short for Kriegsgefangenen-Mannschafts-Stammlager), stalag was a camp for official prisoners of war captured by Germany. These camps were established and operated under the aegis of the Hague and Geneva conventions on prisoners of war; consequently, German officials differentiated between stalags, where capture enemy noncommissioned personnel was kept, and oflags, where capture enemy officers were confined; partisans and other prisoners of the Nazi regime were sent to concentration camps. Furthermore, German prisoner-of-war camps were also categorized by branches of service: the Luftwaffe (German air force) operated Stalag Luft where flying personnel was held while the Kriegsmarine (German navy) operated Marlag for Navy personnel and Milag for Merchant Navy personnel.

Stalags were identified by roman numerals that corresponded to one of military districts where they were located in (Germany was divided into seventeen such districts, or *wehrkreise,* see table); camps within a military district then received a letter designation and the name of the nearest town. Thus, Stalag II-A Neubrandenburg referred to the first POW camp in the second (II) *wehrkreise* of Stettin and located near the town of Neubrandenburg.

Stalags were usually established near specific industrial centers or work locations (i.e. factories, coal-mines, etc.). Individual camp layouts varied, but they were all enclosed with barbed wire and contained guard towers manned by armed

Table 1

District Number	Center
I	Königsberg
II	Stettin
III	Berlin
IV	Dresden
V	Stuttgart
VI	Munster
VII	Munich
VIII	Breslau
IX	Kassel
X	Hamburg
XI	Hannover
XII	Wiesbaden
XIII	Nurnberg
XVII	Vienna
XVIII	Salzburg
XX	Danzig
XXI	Posen

German soldiers. Camps comprised of labor compounds (*Arbeitskommando*) where prisoners could be put to work; the Third Geneva Convention (Section III, Article 49) allows use of POWs for work in agriculture and industry (but not in a war-effort related industry), but requires prisoners to be housed and paid. German stalags frequently violated these requirements, especially when dealing with Soviet and east European prisoners. Prisoners of various nationalities were usually separated from each other by barbed-wire fences, although prisoners speaking the same language were permitted to intermingle.

Upon being captured and before getting to a stalag, a captured prisoner of war went through a Dulag (short for the German *Durchgangslager*) or a transit camp where he was interrogated and processed. Under the terms of the Geneva Convention, prisoners only had to divulge their name, rank, and serial number, but interrogating officers often sought to extract more information from captured servicemen. Once processed, POWs were then assigned and transported (generally, by train) to a stalag, where they typically housed in wooden barracks that contained bunk beds and a charcoal burning stove in the middle of the room. Food allowance was rather meager, and malnutrition and hunger was a feature of most prisoners' lives; while British and American POWs did occasionally receive deliveries of Red Cross food parcels, Soviet POWs experienced far harsher treatment at stalags and were frequently deprived of food and medical care; up to 2 million Soviet POWs, out of 5.1 million captured, perished in German camps.

Alexander Mikaberidze

See also: Dulag Luft; Germany; World War II Prisoners of War.

Further Reading

Durand, Arthur A. *Stalag Luft III: The Secret Story.* Baton Rouge: Louisiana State University Press, 1999.

Vercoe, Tony. *Survival at Stalag IVB: Soldiers and Airmen Remember Germany's Largest POW Camp of World War II.* Jefferson, NC: McFarland, 2006.

Wylie, Neville. *Barbed Wire Diplomacy: Britain, Germany, and the Politics of Prisoners of War, 1939–1945.* Oxford: Oxford University Press, 2010.

Stalin, Joseph (1879–1953)

As the general secretary of Soviet Communist Party, Stalin led the Soviet Union for almost three decades, and presided over a brutal regime that claimed millions of lives. Born Iosif Vissarionovich Dzhugashvili in the Georgian town of Gori, Stalin had a difficult childhood that shaped his character. Admitted to a theological seminary in Tbilisi, he was soon introduced to Russian socialism and Marxism, and was expelled for revolutionary activity. Joining the Bolshevik faction of the Russian Social Democratic Labor Party (RSDLP), he earned notoriety for "expropriations" (robbery) and counterfeiting. By 1912, he was included in the Bolshevik-controlled RSDLP Central Committee and adopted the nom de guerre "Stalin" (the man of steel). After the Bolshevik seizure of power in October 1917, Stalin emerged as commissar for nationalities in the new Bolshevik government. He played an active role in the Russian Civil War and his day-to-day management of the party gradually earned him considerable power. In 1922, he was appointed general secretary of the Central Committee of the Communist Party.

In 1924, upon the death of the Bolshevik leader Vladimir Lenin, Stalin skillfully exploited his power to secure control of the key institutions of Soviet governance and to methodically destroy all the old leaders of the Communist Party. By 1929, his accumulation of power was complete and unchallengeable. In the 1930s, Stalin presided over a series of purges, or "repressions" as they are known in Russia, that targeted not only the Party elite but also wider society. Carefully orchestrated show trials initially "unmasked" prominent Soviet political leaders as "enemies of the people" and sentenced them to death. The purge then evolved into a mass campaign of political repression, targeting the Red Army leadership and anyone suspected of being "enemy of the state," "saboteur," or "counterrevolutionary" for imprisonment and arbitrary executions. The Soviet military saw 3 of 5 marshals, 13 of 15 army commanders, 8 of 9 admirals, 50 of 57 army corps commanders, and 154 out of 186 division commanders arrested, with many sent to the newly established labor camps or summarily executed; Stalin also sanctioned execution of over 22,000 Polish prisoners of war at the Katyń Forest in April–May 1940.

Stalin's call for rapid modernization and industrialization of the Soviet Union resulted in one of the greatest humanitarian calamities of the twentieth century. Millions of Soviet peasants resisted Stalin's policy of collectivizations, and were therefore branded as "kulaks" and "enemies of the working class," which led to their executions or internment in labor camps. Ukraine witnessed the man-made famine in 1932–1933 that killed at least 3 million people, while tens of thousands were interned.

During the 1930s, Stalin supervised the expansion of the Main Administration of Corrective Labor Camps and Settlements (Glavnoye upravleniye ispravityelno-trudovykh lagerey i koloniy, GULAG), a vast system of Soviet forced labor camps that interned hundreds of thousands of individuals, from petty criminals to political dissidents. Managed by the Soviet secret police (NKVD), the Gulag system served as a key pillar of Stalin's regime and claimed the millions of lives. Stalin used prisoners as slave labor to pursue vast infrastructure projects and promoted rapid exploitation of Soviet natural resources and development of heavy industry. Although considerable progress was indeed made, much of it came at the expense of human lives.

In 1941, after ignoring numerous warnings, Stalin found himself at war with Nazi Germany. Soviet forces, still recovering from the purges, were largely unprepared for the German onslaught and suffered catastrophic defeats in the summer and fall of 1941. By appealing to patriotism and resorting to utmost repression, Stalin sought to rally Soviet citizens and the Red Army to the defense of the "motherland." He ordered a scorched earth policy of laying waste to entire regions as the Red Army retreated and instructed the NKVD to kill tens of thousands of political prisoners in areas the German army approached. Stalin's Order No. 270 ordered Soviet soldiers facing capture to commit suicide or fight to the death; those who allowed themselves to be captured were considered as traitors. A separate, Order

No. 227, declared that those soldiers who retreated without order had to be placed in "penal battalions" that served as cannon fodder on the front lines.

By late 1943, the Red Army was able to turn the tide of war, scoring important victories at Stalingrad and Kursk that shattered the German army. As supreme commander, Stalin played a major role in the Soviet success, and gave personal approval to all important strategic and operational decisions. By the time the Soviet army stormed Berlin in April 1945, Stalin had secured major concessions from the Western powers at Tehran, Yalta, and Potsdam, and established Soviet control over eastern and parts of central Europe. In the newly occupied Poland, Czechoslovakia, Hungary, Romania, and Bulgaria, Stalin facilitated campaigns of political terror that destroyed fledgling democracies and set up Communist dictatorships. Stalin's NKVD used former German concentration camps to set up a network of concentration camps across much of eastern Europe and Germany to isolate "dubious" individuals and consolidate Communist power. On Stalin's instructions, over 2 million Soviet prisoners of war, who were freed from German camps, were interned at filtration camps to determine if they were traitors; about half of them were then sent into the Gulag system.

Stalin continued to rule the Soviet Union with an iron fist until his death on March 5, 1953, at Kuntsevo near Moscow.

Alexander Mikaberidze

See also: Beria, Lavrenty; Gulag; NKVD; Soviet Union, Deportations in; Soviet Union, POW Camps (1941–1956).

Further Reading

Applebaum, Anne. *Gulag: A History.* New York: Anchor Books, 2004.

Applebaum, Anne. *Iron Curtain: The Crushing of Eastern Europe, 1944–1956.* New York: Doubleday, 2012.

Applebaum, Anne. *Red Famine: Stalin's War on Ukraine.* New York: Doubleday, 2017.

Conquest, Robert. *Stalin: Breaker of Nations.* New York: Penguin, 1991.

Kotkin, Stephen. *Stalin.* New York: Penguin, 2014–2017, 2 volumes.

Stangl, Franz (1908–1971)

Nazi extermination camp commandant. Born in Austria on March 26, 1908, his original profession was as a weaver. In 1931, he became a police officer, and soon thereafter joined the then-illegal Austrian Nazi Party, but the German Anschluss with Austria provided him with opportunities denied him under domestic Austrian rule. By 1940 he had become the superintendent at Hartheim Castle, where he oversaw the mass murder of people with physical and psychological disabilities, under the auspices of Aktion T-4, or the "euthanasia" program.

In 1942, Stangl was transferred to the new death camp at Sobibór as commandant. During his term there, between March and September 1942, Stangl's approach to the mass annihilation of Jewish prisoners won him admiration in Berlin. As a consequence, he was moved on to another death camp, this time at Treblinka, where he served as its commandant from September 1942 through the camp's closure in

August 1943. While at Treblinka, Stangl was responsible for the system that would see the murder of most of Treblinka's 870,000 Jewish victims.

After Germany's defeat in 1945, Stangl went into hiding, was identified and interned in Austria, then escaped to Syria with the assistance of Nazi sympathizers in the Vatican, such as Bishop Alois Hudal. In 1951 he was spirited into Brazil, where he lived until he was tracked down by Nazi-hunter Simon Wiesenthal and extradited to Germany in 1967. In 1970, following a trial, Stangl was sentenced to life imprisonment. In prison, British journalist Gitta Sereny conducted some 70 hours of interviews with him, attempting to penetrate to the core of his consciousness vis-à-vis his role as a mass murderer. Her study of Stangl based on these (and other) interviews was published in 1974 as *Into that Darkness: An Examination of Conscience.* On June 28, 1971, the day after Sereny completed the last of her interviews with him, Stangl suffered a heart attack and died.

Throughout his trial, Stangl claimed that his conscience was clear; this he reaffirmed in his last interview with Sereny, adding that he "never intentionally hurt anyone . . . But I was there [and] in reality I share the guilt."

Paul R. Bartrop

See also: Concentration Camps; Hoess, Rudolf; Holocaust, The; Kramer, Josef.

Further Reading

Fest, Joachim C. *The Face of the Third Reich: Portraits of the Nazi Leadership.* New York: Pantheon Books, 1970.

Sereny, Gitta. *Into That Darkness: An Examination of Conscience.* New York: Vintage, 1983.

Stutthof

Nazi forced labor and concentration camp located in a sparsely-populated area west of the town of Stutthof, some 22 miles east of Danzig (Gdansk), Poland. The camp was established in September 1939, in the immediate aftermath of the German invasion of Poland on September 1. Initially, it served as a civilian prison camp and was administered by the Danzig police; in November 1941, it became a "labor education" camp, which was supervised by the Sicherheitzpolizei (German Security Police, or SiPO). In January 1942 it became a fully-fledged concentration camp. At that time, the SS provided guards for the facility, and these were joined by Ukrainian auxiliary personnel beginning in early 1943. The camp expanded exponentially between 1939 and 1944, eventually encompassing 105 sub-camps throughout central and northern Poland. The two principal sub-camps were Elbing and Thorn.

Nearly all the prisoners at Stutthof were compelled to work as forced laborers. Some worked in workshops on premises, while others worked in local agriculture, various privately-owned industries, brickyards, or the German Equipment Works (Deutsche Ausrüstungswerke, DAW). Overwork and exhaustion were commonplace, and a sizable number of prisoners became sick or died as a result. The camp was greatly enlarged in 1943, as a new camp was built adjacent to the original facility. In 1944, a large aircraft manufacturing facility was built in nearby Stutthof, which caused the prisoner population to increase markedly.

Prisoners at the Stutthof concentration camp in Poland line up for their food rations, late 1939. Food for prisoners in Nazi concentration camps was meager at best, and consisted of things like watery soup made from spoiled vegetables, and bread made from flour and sawdust. (United States Holocaust Memorial Museum, courtesy of Panstwowe Muzeum Stutthof)

At first, most of Stutthof's prisoners were non-Jewish civilian Poles. Later, as the Jewish population increased, many Jews from Białystok and Warsaw were housed there. Beginning in 1944, as Soviet troops pushed east, the Germans transferred a large number of Jews to Stutthof from concentration camps located in the Baltic States. It is estimated that Stutthof and its sub-camps housed more than 100,000 prisoners in its six-year lifespan.

Conditions at Stutthof were grim. Food and adequate clothing were always in short supply, living conditions were squalid, and medical care was nonexistent. Typhus epidemics took a dreadful toll during the winters of 1942 and 1944. Guards routinely brutalized prisoners, and those who fell ill from disease or overwork were gassed in the on-site gas chamber. Others were given lethal injections.

As Allied forces began to press into the region, in January 1945 the Germans decided to evacuate Stutthof's prisoners. At least 50,000 prisoners, most of them Jews, were force-marched out of the camp. Some 5,000 people were marched to the Baltic Sea, forced into the water, and mown down by machine-gun fire. Most of the others were marched into eastern Germany amid brutal cold and snow. Many died of exposure or were killed by guards. In April 1945, the rest of the prisoners were forced toward the sea, where hundreds were murdered. About 4,000 were sent to Germany by boat, and a sizable number drowned during the perilous voyage. At least 25,000 prisoners died during the evacuations alone, or one out of every two detainees. A total of 60,000 prisoners died between 1939 and 1945. When Soviet troops liberated the camp in May 1945, they found only about 100 prisoners, who had survived the camp's final liquidation by hiding in order to escape the brutal evacuations.

In the aftermath of the war, four Stutthof trials were held in Gdańsk against former guards and Kapos, who were charged by the Polish government with crimes of war and crimes against humanity. The first trial was held against 30 former camp personnel between April 25, 1946 and May 31, 1946. All were found guilty, and 11 were sentenced to death, while the others were sentenced to a range of terms of imprisonment. The second trial, held between October 8 and 31, 1947, saw charges brought against 24 former Stutthof officials and guards. Found guilty, 10 received the death penalty. The third trial was held across the period of November 5–10, 1947. Twenty were brought before a Polish Special Criminal Court; 19 were found guilty, and 1 was acquitted. The final trial, a short time later, was held from November 19 to November 29, 1947. Twenty-seven were tried, of whom all but one were found guilty.

Paul G. Pierpaoli, Jr.

See also: Arbeitslager; Auschwitz; Bełżec; Bergen-Belsen; Birkenau; Buchenwald; Bullet Decree (1944); Chełmno; Colditz; Concentration Camps; Dachau; Death Camps; Dora-Mittelbau; Eichmann, Adolf; Extermination Centers; Gas Chambers; Gestapo; Gross-Rosen; Ninzert; Hitler, Adolf; Holocaust, The; I.G. Farben Case (1947); J.A. Topf & Söhne; Kinderblock 66; Koch Trial (1951); Kramer, Josef; Krupp Case (1948); Mauthausen-Gusen; Monowitz; Natzweiler-Struthof; Neuengamme; Niederhagen; Nuremberg Trials; Ravensbrück; Sachsenhausen; Slave Labor (World War II); Sobibór; Sonderkommando; Treblinka; Trostinets; Zyklon B Case (1946).

Further Reading

Clark, Peter B. *The Death of East Prussia: War and Revenge in Germany's Easternmost Province.* Chevy Chase, MD: CreateSpace, 2013.

Ferencz, Benjamin B. *Less than Slaves: Jewish Forced Labor and the Quest for Compensation.* Cambridge, MA: Harvard University Press, 1979.

Kogon, Eugen. *The Theory and Practice of Hell: The German Concentration Camps and the System behind Them.* New York: Farrar, Straus and Giroux, 2006.

Wachsmann, Nikolaus. *KL: A History of the Nazi Concentration Camps.* New York: Farrar, Straus and Giroux, 2015.

Swakopmund

Founded in 1892, Swakopmund lies at the mouth of the ephemeral Swakop River that runs seasonally from the central plateau to the Atlantic Ocean. The river is mainly dry and in colonial times was the main transport route to the colonial capital Windhoek. Unlike the British-owned enclave of Walvis Bay, some 30 kilometers to the south, Swakopmund did not have a natural harbor. Instead the large Woermann ocean liners connecting the colony with Germany were offloaded via flat-bottom boats pushed through the often-rough surf.

The official policy to introduce concentration camps was implemented from January 1905 onward, but in Swakopmund there had been Herero prisoners since the start of the Herero Revolt. The majority of these were workers who had been employed at the coast, many doing railway work. In August 1904, as a measure of control, Lieutenant-General Lothar von Trotha issued orders that the Hereros should bear numbered brass tags with the inscription G.H. (Gefangener Herero). Some of the early prisoners of war were also interred in the cargo hull of two anchored Woermann ocean liners.

From January 1905 onward, large numbers of prisoners were transported to Swakopmund by rail. The first rudimentary concentration camp was placed at the northern entrance of the town, but due to soil pollution it was soon moved to the beach where more permanent structures were constructed out of corrugated iron sheets and blankets.

As in the other major towns, the main purpose of the camp was to provide labor to build up the local infrastructure and buildings. Sexual and physical abuse was not uncommon, as noted by countless eyewitnesses. Mortality statistics kept by the Swakopmund Rhenish missionary Heinrich Vedder indicate how bad conditions were. At the end of 1905, as many as 800 prisoners out of the estimated 1,000 had died. The dying was so commonplace that the military issued pre-printed death certificates with the words "death through exhaustion," "bronchitis," or "scurvy" written on them.

Apart from the maltreatment and forced labor, the food was a contributing factor in the high mortality. Rations consisted mostly of rice and flour. Rice was a food-stuff that was not familiar to the prisoners, and without proper cooking utensils both rice and flour were near impossible to prepare—as noted by the missionaries.

The missionaries, who were allowed to work among the prisoners, were very vocal about the treatment and the high mortality. Due to pressure from the missionary headquarters in Wuppertal, the colonial authorities commissioned a report into the matter. The author of the report, which appeared in June 1905, Dr. Fuchs, blamed the military for its neglect and noted that the deaths were entirely preventable. The report was widely ignored, and the modus operandi of the military was essentially sanctioned by German authorities in Windhoek and Berlin. As a result, the dying in the Swakopmund concentration camp and the other camps around the colony continued unabated for a further three years.

Casper W. Erichsen

See also: Herero Genocide, Concentration Camps; Okahandja; Shark Island; Windhoek.

Further Reading
Olusoga, David, and Casper W. Erichsen. *The Kaiser's Holocaust: Germany's Forgotten Genocide and the Colonial Roots of Nazism.* London: Faber and Faber, 2010.

Sweden

During World War II, Sweden created a network of internment camps where communists, pacifists, and others were detained. These camps included Naartijärvi (east of Luleå), Öxnered (at Vänersborg), Grytan (near Östersund), Vindeln and Stensele (in Västerbotten), and Lövnäsvallen (near Sveg). Probably the most infamous of these camps was Storsien (in Norrbotten) where about 400 detainees were held in

1939–1940. In addition, Sweden's State Board of Social Affairs established 12 internment camps (i.e. Långmora in Dalarna, heartland Sweden, and Tjörnarp in Skåne) to detain foreigners with suspicious political affiliations. Most of these camps comprised of modest country manors, but some had a perimeter of barbed wire. Overall, Sweden had interned about 3,000 foreigners and had over 190,000 registered with state officials. Among the internees were also American pilots, who had landed in Sweden and were formally detained by Swedish authorities.

Alexander Mikaberidze

See also: Denmark; Finland.

Further Reading

Barker, Vanessa. *Nordic Nationalism and Penal Order: Walling the Welfare State.* London: Routledge, 2018.

Switzerland

During World War II, Switzerland, a neutral power, interned thousands of Allied soldiers who had either fled combat to Switzerland or were shot down over the Swiss territory. By late 1944, Swiss internment camps held almost 40,000 internees, including over 20,00 from Italy, 10,000 from Poland, 2,643 from the United States and 1,121 from the United Kingdom. The most notorious of the Swiss internment camps was located at Wauwilermoos, near the towns of Wauwil and Egolzwil in the Canton of Luzern. The camp was set up and maintained by the Swiss army and served as the punishment camp for prisoners who had tried to escape from other camps. The camps comprised a vast complex of 25 barracks surrounded by a barbed wire fence and watchtowers. Led by a Nazi sympathizer André-Henri Béguin, it earned notoriety for its harsh discipline and mistreatment of Allied prisoners.

Alexander Mikaberidze

See also: Germany; France; World War II Prisoners of War.

Further Reading

Mears, Dwight S. *Interned or Imprisoned? The Successes and Failures of International Law in the Treatment of American Internees in Switzerland, 1943–45.* MA Thesis, University of North Carolina, 2010.

Prince, Cathryn J. *Shot from the Sky: American POWs in Switzerland.* Annapolis, MD: Naval Institute Press, 2016.

T

Theresienstadt

Located in the town of Terezín, some 35 miles from Prague in northwestern Czechoslovakia, Theresienstadt was a Nazi-established Jewish ghetto, as well as a concentration and transit camp. The camp was contained within an old fortress constructed in the seventeenth century. It became operational on November 24, 1941, and was liberated by Soviet troops on May 8, 1945.

Theresienstadt was designed to fulfill two primary functions. First, it was a transit point for Czech Jews who were being deported to concentration camps, death camps, and forced labor camps located in eastern Europe and the Balkans. Second, it was a labor camp where elderly, disabled, or prominent Jews were housed. The Nazis perpetrated an elaborate hoax by implying that detainees who remained at Theresienstadt were being treated well as "retirees"; they even called the camp a "spa town."

In 1942, the Nazis began deporting large numbers of Jews at Theresienstadt to the east, where many perished. Nevertheless, the Germans continued to allude to the camp in quite glowing terms, in an effort to disguise their activities and keep the outside world from learning about the true scale of the Holocaust. In 1944, the Germans permitted representatives of the International Committee of the Red Cross (ICRC) to visit the facility, after receiving negative press about the Nazis' deportation of Dutch Jews to Theresienstadt. The visit occurred in June 1944. When ICRC officials arrived, they were impressed with what they saw. Gardens had been cultivated, barracks were clean and renovated, and buildings were freshly painted. Camp officials even staged social and cultural events for their visitors, many of which included detainees. When the ICRC personnel left, however, deportations from Theresienstadt were resumed, and they continued until October 1944. Camp authorities had, of course, forced internees to perform renovations and other projects prior to the visit of the Red Cross.

At least 140,000 Jews were either interned or passed through Theresienstadt between 1941 and 1945. Of that number, some 90,000 were ultimately deported to death or concentration camps in the east; the vast majority of them perished. Some 5,000 children were transported to the east via Theresienstadt, and it is estimated that about 90 percent died in death camps. The death toll within the camp is estimated at 33,000. Many of those individuals died from disease, illness, malnutrition, exposure, or abuse by camp personnel. By mid-1942, the death toll became so high that camp authorities had to build a crematorium just outside the walls that processed as many as 200 bodies per day.

Unlike most concentration camps, Theresienstadt boasted a vibrant cultural scene; in this case, it resembled many Jewish ghettos. Because the camp housed a number of artists, writers, teachers, actors, and musicians from Czechoslovakia, Germany, and Austria, prisoners benefited from concerts, plays, lectures, art exhibits, and other cultural happenings. The library at Theresienstadt held an impressive 60,000 volumes and, although they were officially forbidden from instructing children, older prisoners held daily classes for hundreds of students.

On May 2, 1945, with Adolf Hitler dead and Soviet forces pressing in from the east, camp personnel turned over control of Theresienstadt to the ICRC. Soviet troops officially liberated the camp on May 8.

Paul G. Pierpaoli, Jr.

See also: Holocaust, The.

Further Reading

Green, Gerald. *The Artists of Terezin.* New York: Hawthorn Books, 1959.

Kogon, Eugen. *The Theory and Practice of Hell: The German Concentration Camps and the System behind Them.* New York: Farrar, Straus and Giroux, 2006.

Troller, Norbert. *Theresienstadt: Hitler's Gift to the Jews.* Chapel Hill: University of North Carolina Press, 2002.

Torrens Island

A concentration camp in the estuary of the Port River near Adelaide, Australia. When World War I broke out in August 1914, almost 10 percent of South Australia's population claimed German descent. Concerned about possible threat this large German-speaking community could pose, Australian government initially ordered all of its residents of German heritage to register at local police stations and be subject to weekly paroles. At the same time, it began construction of several concentration camps, including one at the Torren Island, which opened on October 9, 1914. Within several months, the camp housed hundreds of individuals of German and Austrian descent, who were subjected to abuse and mistreatment. Frank Bungardy, who had been interned at the camp, noted in his diary that prisoners suffered from lack of provisions and medical services, and were routinely prodded, and occasionally even stabbed, with bayonets. The camp continued to operate until August 1915, when most of internees were released, while few others transferred to other camps in New South Wales.

Alexander Mikaberidze

See also: Australia.

Further Reading

Fischer, Gerhard. *Enemy Aliens: Internment and the Homefront Experience in Australia, 1914–1920.* St. Lucia: University of Queensland Press, 1989.

Monteath, Peter, Mandy Paul, and Rebecca Martin. *Interned: Torrens Island, 1914–1915.* Adelaide, SA: Wakefield Press, 2014.

Trail of Tears (1838)

Name given to the forced movement of the Cherokee tribe from Georgia to the western United States by the U.S. Army. This movement, which consisted of a series of brutal forced marches, began on May 26, 1838, and was part of the U.S. government's Indian Removal Policy. Some 17,000 Cherokees were gathered together, mostly in Georgia and Tennessee, and were then forced to travel nearly 1,200 miles to Arkansas and Oklahoma. In the Cherokee language, the removal was referred to as "the trail where we cried," a name that has described the grim event ever since.

Tensions between the Cherokee nation and white settlers had reached new heights in 1829, when gold was discovered in Dahlonega in northwestern Georgia. The Cherokees considered this area their tribal land and insisted on exercising sole sovereignty over it. In 1830, the state of Georgia sought legal clarification of the land dispute in a case that went ultimately to the U.S. Supreme Court, which refused to hear it because it did not consider the Cherokee nation a sovereign state. However, in another U.S. Supreme Court case in 1832, the Court ruled that state governments could not invoke sovereignty over the Cherokees, arguing that this was the prerogative of the federal government. After his landslide 1832 reelection to the presidency, Andrew Jackson was more determined than ever to pursue with vigor the removal of the Cherokees, which had been made easier by the 1830 Indian Removal Act.

Soon thereafter, a splinter faction of the Cherokees formed called the "Ridge" or "Treaty" Party, led by Cherokees Major Ridge and Stand Watie. They began negotiations with the Jackson administration to secure equitable treatment, believing that removal was inevitable. However, Ridge and others acted without the support of the Cherokee elected council, headed by Chief John Ross, who was firmly opposed to any kind of removal, and thus unwilling to negotiate such terms. This created a split among the Cherokees, with the Ridge contingent forming its own ruling council and becoming known as the Western Cherokees. Those loyal to Chief John Ross were then known as the Eastern Cherokees.

In 1835, President Jackson appointed Reverend John Schermerhorn as a treaty commissioner to enter into detailed negotiation with the Cherokees. That same year, the U.S. government proposed to pay $4.5 million to the Cherokees as compensation for their land. In return, they were to vacate the area voluntarily. Schermerhorn then organized a meeting with a small number of Cherokee council members who were prepared to accept removal. Not more than 500 Cherokees (out of many thousands) parlayed with the commissioner, but nevertheless, 20 Cherokees—including Ridge—signed the Treaty of New Echota on December 30, 1835. It was also signed later by Ridge's son John and Stand Watie. No members of the main Cherokee Council signed the document, however.

This treaty ceded all Cherokee lands east of the Mississippi River. Naturally, Chief Ross rejected the treaty out of hand. The U.S. Senate nevertheless ratified it—just barely—on May 23, 1836, and set the date of May 23, 1838, as the deadline for the removal of the Cherokees. Although Chief Ross presented a 15,000-signature petition to Congress in support of the Cherokees and against the treaty, this appeal fell on deaf ears. Meanwhile, Cherokees who had supported the removal policy began to migrate from Georgia to Oklahoma and Arkansas. By the end of 1836, it is estimated that at least 6,000 Cherokees had voluntarily left their ancestral lands, but some 17,000 Cherokees remained.

In May 1838, with the removal deadline looming, President Martin Van Buren appointed Brigadier General Winfield Scott to oversee the forcible removal of the recalcitrant Cherokees. By May 17, Scott had reached New Echota, Georgia, the heart of Cherokee country, with 7,000 troops. They began to round up the Cherokees in Georgia beginning on May 26. Operations in Tennessee, North Carolina, and Alabama began on June 5. Systematically, the Cherokees were forced from their homes at gunpoint and marched to a series of camps. They were allowed to take no belongings with them, and they offered little resistance.

Thirty one forts—basically makeshift detention camps—had been built to aid in the removal. Thirteen of them were in Georgia. The Cherokees were then moved from these temporary encampments to 11 fortified camps, of which all but one was in Tennessee. By late July 1838, some 17,000 Cherokees and an additional 2,000 black slaves owned by wealthy Natives were in the camps.

Conditions in the camps were appalling, and diseases, including dysentery, were rife. As a result, there was a very high mortality rate in the camps. The Cherokees were then gradually removed to three transfer points: Ross's Landing (Chattanooga, Tennessee); Gunter's Landing (Guntersville, Alabama); and the Cherokee Agency (at Calhoun, Tennessee).

Three groups of Cherokees, totaling 2,800 people, were moved from Ross's Landing by steamboat along the Tennessee, Ohio, Mississippi and Arkansas Rivers to Sallisaw Creek in Indian Territory by June 19. However, the majority of the Cherokees were moved in groups of between 700 to 1,500 people, along with guides appointed by Chief Ross, on overland routes. Chief Ross had received the contract to oversee the relocation under Cherokee supervision, despite resistance from within his own nation and members of Congress who resented the extra cost. In the end, the army was to be used only to oversee the removal and to prevent outbreaks of violence. There was one exception to this mass removal, which was the small group of Cherokees who had signed the New Echota Treaty. They were escorted by Lieutenant Edward Deas of the army, mainly for their own protection.

The movement of detachments began on August 28, 1838. For most, the journey was about 1,200 miles. Although there were three distinct overland routes, the majority took the northern one through central Tennessee, southwest Kentucky, and southern Illinois. These groups crossed the Mississippi at Cape Girardeau, Missouri and trekked across Missouri to northern Arkansas. They then entered Oklahoma near Westville, having met troops from Fort Gibson.

The conditions on the march varied. The first groups to undertake the journey experienced high temperatures and many suffered from heat exhaustion. In the winter, many Cherokees suffered from frostbite and hypothermia while waiting to cross frozen rivers. Most Cherokees marched on foot, but some were loaded into over-crowded wagons. It was customary for the detachments to be accompanied by a physician and a clergyman. Many died on the way. The official government total was 424, but the most widely cited number is 4,000, half of them in the camps and half on the march. A recent scholarly study, however, has come up with a much higher figure of 8,000 dead.

Many of the Cherokees settled around Tahlequah, Oklahoma, which became the center for the tribal government. Local districts were established, which in turn elected officials to serve on the new National Council. Bilingual schools were created and missionaries from the American Board of Commissioners for Foreign Missions built churches on the reservations. There was great resentment on the part of many Cherokees against Major Ridge, Stand Watie, and the signatories of the New Echota Treaty. Major Ridge and his son John were killed on June 22, 1839, in separate incidents. The Trail of Tears is generally considered to be one of the most deplorable eras in American history.

Ralph Baker and Paul G. Pierpaoli, Jr.

See also: Apache Wars; Indian removal Act (1830); Seminole Wars.

Further Reading

Carter, Samuel. *Cherokee Sunset: A Nation Betrayed.* New York: Doubleday, 1976.

Ehle, John. *Trail of Tears: The Rise and Fall of the Cherokee Nation.* New York: Doubleday, 1988.

Foreman, Grant. *Indian Removal: The Emigration of the Five Civilized Tribes of Indians.* Norman: University of Oklahoma Press, 1989.

Remini Robert V. *Andrew Jackson and his Indian Wars.* New York: Viking Publishers, 2001.

Trawniki Men

Named for the concentration camp in which they were trained, "Trawniki men" (Trawnikimänner) or "Trawnikis" were auxiliary police guards who played a deadly role in the day-to-day process of mass murder that was the Final Solution.

In order to implement Operation REINHARD—the Nazi plan to exterminate the Jews of the Generalgouvernement (the German-controlled section of Poland that was not annexed to Germany)—trained men were needed to guard extermination camps, enforce and escort deportations, liquidate ghettos, and shoot—up close—Jewish men, women, and children into mass graves. Most of the men who trained under this program were Soviet prisoners of war who "volunteered" for this in exchange for release from the horrid, starvation-level conditions in which they were held. As such, they were part of a larger group called Hilfswilliger (volunteers), also called Hiwis.

The facility in which they trained was part of the Trawniki concentration camp, built where there once was a sugar refinery outside the village of Trawniki, some 20 miles southeast of Lublin. The camp was established shortly after the beginning of Operation BARBAROSSA, Germany's invasion of Russia in July 1941, on the orders of SS-Gruppenführer Odilo Globocnik, SS and Police Leader (SS-und Polizeiführer) of the Lublin District. He placed SS-Hauptsturmführer Hermann Höfle in command of the camp, and SS-Hauptsturmführer Karl Streibel in command of the training program and facility for the Trawniki men.

The Trawniki camp served several functions over its three years of operation. For its first three months (July through September 1941) it was used to hold Soviet civilians. Beginning in September 1941 and continuing through to July 1944, it was the training center for Trawniki men who were to be Guard Forces (Wachmannschaften) as part of Aktion Reinhard. It served as a forced labor camp from July 1942 to September 1943, at which point it functioned as a sub-camp for the Majdanek concentration and extermination camp, also located in the Generalgouvernement, near Lublin.

From the inception of the training program through late 1944, more than 5,000 men were screened for sufficient levels of anti-communist and anti-Semitic sentiments, recruited, and trained for their role in the murder of the Jews. Not all were Soviet POWs. Others were conscripted Volksdeutsche, that is, men who were "Germans in terms of people or race," but were not living in, nor citizens of, Germany. Most were from eastern Europe so that the Trawniki men—the Soviets and the civilian conscripts—could communicate (in reality, order) prisoners in a language they could understand, such as Polish, Russian, Ukrainian, Belarusian, Estonian, Latvian, and so forth.

Trawniki men were trained for and participated in some of the most violent aspects of an already monstrous campaign of mass murder. They served as guards at almost all of the Nazi extermination camps, such as Bełżec, Sobibór, and Treblinka (more specifically, Treblinka II, the killing site within the Treblinka camp). They were brutal participants in the deportations of Jews from ghettos to the assigned extermination camp, and in the liquidation of those ghettos. Thus, in the ghettos of Warsaw, Czestochowa, Lublin, Białystok, and others, they killed all Jews who had not yet been deported.

Perhaps their most notorious task was to kill hundreds or thousands of Jews at a time, shooting them individually in the soft spot immediately below the back of the skull, or forcing them to lie down on their stomachs on the rows of bodies that were killed before them, and then shooting them, even as the next row of victims was brought to the edge of the open pit to await their turn. Some of the members of the German army or the Reserve Police Battalions found this task—killing innocent men, women, and children in a close up and personal way—to be psychologically difficult, so it was not unusual that the Trawniki men—who seemed to have no such qualms—would take over the killing operation.

The Trawniki training camp, which remained operational to the very end, was overrun in July 1944. After the war, Globocnik and Höfle committed suicide. Streibel, along with other leaders of the program, was charged and brought to trial, only to be acquitted in 1976.

Michael Dickerman

See also: Concentration Camps; Extermination Centers; Kapos; Sonderkommando.

Further Reading

Browning, Christopher. *Ordinary Men: Reserve Police Battalion 101 and the Final Solution in Poland.* New York: Harper Perennial, 1998.

Douglas, Lawrence. *The Right Wrong Man: John Demjanjuk and the Last Great Nazi War Crimes Trial.* Princeton, NJ: Princeton University Press, 2016.

Stoltzfus, Nathan, and Henry Friedlander (Ed.). *Nazi Crimes and the Law.* Cambridge: Cambridge University Press, 2016.

Treblinka

Consisting of a labor camp and an extermination camp, Treblinka contributed mightily to the death toll of the Holocaust with approximately 870,000 victims—almost all Jews—killed there during its operation.

Aerial view of the Treblinka memorial site. (Mondadori Portfolio via Getty Images)

Treblinka was located near the villages of Treblinka and Malkinia, about 50 miles northeast of Warsaw, in the Generalgouvernement. Two conditions made this an ideal location in which to carry out the tasks of the camps: it was in a lightly populated but heavily wooded area, and it was near a rail line, with a station stop at Malkinia, which allowed for a spur to be built to the camp.

Treblinka was one of three extermination camps established as part of Operation REINHARD (Aktion Reinhard), named after SS Obergruppenführer Reinhard Heydrich, head of the Reich Security Main Office (RSHA), who was assassinated in June 1942. Bełżec and Sobibór were the other two Operation Reinhard extermination camps.

Treblinka consisted of two camps. Treblinka I was a forced labor camp (Arbeitslager), opened in November 1941. Its prisoner population was composed of Jews, and non-Jewish Poles for whom the camp was a means of political detention. Though held in two different areas of the camp, both cohorts did hard labor, primarily in a gravel pit. Deportees who appeared capable of work when they arrived at Treblinka were housed here. The commandant of Treblinka I was SS-Sturmbannführer Theodor van Eupen. He served in that capacity from the camp's inception until its closing in July 1944.

Treblinka II was the extermination camp (Vernichtungslager). It was completed and operational in July 1942. This was where virtually all Jews from each deportation train were sent after being adjudged as incapable of performing the tasks required in Treblinka I. It was here that they were gassed within hours of their arrival.

There were three commandants of Treblinka II. They were: SS-Untersturmführer Dr. Irmfried Eberl, from July to August 1942; SS-Obersturmführer Franz Stangl (who had served as commandant of Sobibór), from August 1942 to August 1943; and SS-Oberscharführer Kurt Franz, from August to November 1943.

Treblinka II was composed of three areas. The first was the reception area where the Jews who made up the human cargo packed into railroad cattle cars detrained. The second area was divided into two sub-sections. One included housing for the German and Ukrainian staff, administrative offices, storerooms, a clinic, and workshops. The staff consisted of 20 to 30 SS men in command and administrative posts, all of whom had received their training through their participation in the Aktion T-4 operation, under which Germans who, due to physical or mental disabilities, were deemed to be living "lives not worthy of living" were killed by carbon monoxide gas. Ninety to 120 Soviet prisoners of war, as well as Ukrainian and Polish civilians, served as guards, and some participated in tasks associated with the gas chambers. They were schooled at the Trawniki labor camp, which was the training center for Operation Reinhard police and guards.

The second sub-section of Treblinka II was composed of the barracks for the Jews who temporarily worked in the camp at the camp's workshops, while the third area was the extermination center. The entire camp was surrounded by two fences of barbed wire and numerous watch towers.

Sometimes referred to as the "upper camp" (and identified to its incoming victims as a transit camp), the extermination site of Treblinka II was maintained in its own fully fenced area, with a large earthen mound and branches intertwined in the fence to make it difficult for anyone outside of the area to see what was happening. It contained three gas chambers (which would be expanded by another 10 as more trainloads of victims kept coming). The process that led to the gas chambers began in the reception area.

Deportation trains were often 50 or 60 cars long. As each train approached the "station" where the victims would detrain, the train would stop and be broken into segments of 20 cars each. Each 20-car train pulled into the reception area and was handled before the next segment of the deportation train pulled in. There, the doors of the train cars were thrown open and the Jews who managed to survive the trip— often lasting for days with no food, water, sanitation, or light—would be berated and beaten in order to bring them all out into the bizarre scene that awaited them. Once they were out of the cars and on their way to the next step in this process, a special work unit (Sonderkommando) of Jewish prisoners jumped into each car, removing the bodies of those who did not survive, collecting whatever food, clothing, and valuables that were left behind, and cleaning the car so it could be put into use for the same purpose again.

Jews who were unable to walk were taken to an "infirmary" (Lazaret) with a Red Cross flag on it. They passed through the building and exited on the other side, where they were shot and thrown into huge pits that were already dug for just this purpose. Those who were able to walk were immediately divided by gender (children with the women). A very few of the men and women—the strongest among them—were selected to go to the forced labor camp—Treblinka I—while all the rest would be just minutes away from their death. The condemned group entered two barracks—men in one, women and children in the other—where they were ordered to remove all their clothing to prepare for a shower before they would be allowed into the camp. During this time, all valuables—money, jewelry, and so forth—were collected from them, to be sorted and stored in large storerooms until shipped back to Germany. Beginning in the fall of 1942, women and children were shorn of their hair.

Then these people—naked and no doubt terrified—were forced by fists and whips to run down a path—itself fenced in and covered with branches to hide what was happening—from the barracks to the building with gas chambers. This path was called the tube. As soon as they left the undressing barracks, another special work unit would gather up all the clothing (which would be examined for valuables and taken to storerooms for sorting) and clean the room so the next group of victims could be brought and the process repeated.

The gas chambers at Treblinka used carbon monoxide as its killing agent. It was generated from a large diesel engine in a shed (although some reports refer to other sources for the carbon monoxide) and then piped through to the "shower heads" in the gas chamber. There unsuspecting victims took up to 30 minutes to die.

Disposal of the bodies began after a second set of doors was opened and the remaining gas dissipated. Not far from the gas chambers' doors were huge trenches where the bodies were buried. This was the case until Reichsführer-SS Heinrich Himmler issued an order in early 1943 to exhume all the buried bodies and burn them in an effort to destroy all evidence of the killing that took place there. This began the horrible process of opening the graves and moving the bodies to large pits with burning pyres, some built using train track railings. The burning continued for several months.

There was a Jewish resistance group at Treblinka that began its planning for an uprising in April 1943, which took place on August 2, 1943. The first step was to break into the armory in the camp and take weapons. Before this could be completed, however, the Germans became aware of the prisoners' actions, meaning that the prisoners were unable to arm themselves sufficiently to take control of the camp as they had planned. Instead, the resistance group set fire to buildings (but the gas chambers remained unscathed), and hundreds of prisoners stormed the fence surrounding the camp. Fewer than 100 were able to escape and survive until liberation.

The killing operation continued through August 1943. The camp was dismantled throughout that fall and winter, with the gas chambers destroyed and a farmhouse built in its place. Soviet forces entered the camp on August 16, 1944.

The number of Jews killed at Treblinka—there were other groups killed there, such as 2,000 Romanis, but the victims were almost all Jews, and almost all from Poland—is staggering. In the 15 months from July 1942, when killing operations first began, until the fall of 1943, when operations ceased, it is estimated that more than 870,000 Jews were killed, including: 254,000 from Warsaw, and another 112,000 from the Warsaw district; some 337,000 Jews from the Radom district; 35,000 from the Lublin district; more than 107,000 from Białystok; and approximately 29,000 Jews from other countries, including Greece, Macedonia, Slovakia, and Salonika.

Two postwar trials were held in Düsseldorf related to the perpetrators of these mass killings. The first—from October 12, 1964 until August 24, 1965—tried and convicted 10 defendants, including Commandant Kurt Franz. At the second trial—from May 13 to December 22, 1970—the only defendant was Commandant Franz Stangl. He was sentenced to life in prison.

Michael Dickerman

See also: Arbeitslager; Auschwitz; Bełżec; Bergen-Belsen; Birkenau; Buchenwald; Bullet Decree (1944); Chełmno; Colditz; Concentration Camps; Dachau; Death Camps; Dora-Mittelbau; Eichmann, Adolf; Extermination Centers; Gas Chambers; Gestapo; Gross-Rosen; Ninzert; Hitler, Adolf; Holocaust, The; I.G. Farben Case (1947); J.A. Topf & Söhne; Kinderblock 66; Koch Trial (1951); Kramer, Josef; Krupp Case (1948); Mauthausen-Gusen; Monowitz; Natzweiler-Struthof; Neuengamme; Niederhagen; Nuremberg Trials; Ravensbrück; Sachsenhausen; Slave Labor (World War II); Sobibór; Sonderkommando; Stalag; Stutthof; Trostinets; Zyklon B Case (1946).

Further Reading

Arad, Yitzhak. *Belzec, Sobibor, Treblinka: The Operation Reinhard Death Camps.* Bloomington: Indiana University Press, 1987.

Rajchman, Chil. *The Last Jew of Treblinka: A Survivor's Memory, 1942–1943.* New York: Pegasus Books, 2009.

Steiner, Jean-Francois. *Treblinka.* New York: Simon and Schuster, 1967.

Trostinets

A German extermination camp, also known as Maly Trostinets, during World War II. Located at the village of Maly Trostinets, near Minsk, the camp was constructed in late 1941 when the German forces occupied Minsk. Starting in 1942, thousands of Jews, who had been rounded up in Europe (especially in Austria and Czechoslovakia) and the German-controlled territory of the Soviet Union, were brought by train to the camps and methodically killed in mobile gas chambers under supervision of the camp administrator SS-Scharführer Heinrich Eiche. At least 60,000 Jews (but probably as many as 200,000) died at the camp before the Red Army liberated it in June 1944. Despite German efforts to destroy evidence of the atrocities, the Soviets discovered dozens of large pits where the corpses of the killed were disposed.

Alexander Mikaberidze

See also: Holocaust, The; Sonderaktion 1005.

Further Reading

Adamushko, V. ed. *Lager sperti "Trostenets": Dokumenty i materialy [The Trostinets Death Camp: Documents and Materials].* Minsk: National Archives of the Republic of Belarus, 2003.

Tuchola Camp

A prisoner-of-war camp that was used by Germany during World War I and by Poland in 1918–1921. After crushing Russian armies at Tannenberg and the First

Battle of the Masurian Lakes, the Germans found themselves with well over 120,000 captured Russian soldiers. To intern them, the Germans hastily constructed a camp near the town of Tuchola. Conditions at the camp were hardly adequate for the high number of prisoners, and the situation was further complicated by the outbreak of diseases that claimed thousands of lives. The prisoners were released after the collapse of the German Empire in November 1918.

The newly independent Republic of Poland took control of the Tuchola Camp and used it to intern prisoners captured during the Polish-Ukrainian War (1918–1919) and the Polish-Soviet War of 1919–1921. By 1920, the camp facilities were in dilapidated condition and suffered from overcrowding and lack of basic necessities; food rations were smaller than required, hospitals were poorly furnished, and medicine lacking. Hunger, abuse, and epidemics (cholera, dysentery, flu, tuberculosis, and typhus) claimed hundreds of lives. After the end of the Polish-Soviet war, Tuchola briefly served as an internment center for those prisoners who decided to remain in Poland. It was formally disbanded in 1922 when the last of internees were released.

Alexander Mikaberidze

See also: World War I Prisoners of War.

Further Reading

Borzecki, Jerzy. *The Soviet-Polish Peace of 1921 and the Creation of Interwar Europe.* New Haven, CT: Yale University Press, 2008.

Karpus, Zbigniew. *Tuchola: obóz jeńców i internowanych: 1914–1923.* Toruń, PL: Uniw. Miko·laja Kopernika, 1998.

Kobialka D., and M. Kostyrka. "The Great War and Its Landscapes between Memory and Oblivion: The Case of Prisoners of War Camps in Tuchola and Czersk, Poland," *International Journal of Historical Archeology,* 21/(2017): 134–151.

Tuol Sleng Prison

A prison and torture/killing center established by the radical Khmer Rouge regime in Phnom Penh, the capital of Cambodia, in 1975. Between 1975, when the Khmer Rouge ascended to power, and 1979, when it was ousted by the Vietnamese, Tuol Sleng incarcerated between 17,000 and 20,000 Cambodians (including many children), and all but a handful died. The prison became a de facto torture and killing factory, and was later referred to as part of the killing field, a mass graveyard nearby that held the remains of thousands of murdered Tuol Sleng detainees. Tuol Sleng is now the site of a memorial and museum complex that bears witness to the atrocities of the Cambodian Genocide and serves as a document center for archives pertaining to the genocide.

Tuol Sleng was a high school before its conversion to a prison. It came to serve as the main "interrogation" center for the dreaded Santebal, which served as the secret police of the Khmer Rouge regime. The facility was code-named S-21 (for Security Complex #21) and was actually one of at least 150 execution centers located throughout Cambodia. Of those, Tuol Sleng was the largest. Tuol Sleng housed perceived enemies of the Khmer Rouge regime and its attendant revolution.

Most were completely innocent individuals who, for one reason or another, were suspected of being subversives. The Santebal also intended the facility to be a potent propaganda tool in an effort to maintain power over the rest of the population. Most Cambodians knew what was occurring at Tuol Sleng, and were petrified of doing anything that might land them in the horrific facility.

When detainees were first brought to the prison, which was run by the sadistic Khang Khek Iev ("Comrade Duch"), they were placed in small, solitary jail cells. They were usually chained to a wall or bed frame. They had no direct access to toilet or bathing facilities and were routinely beaten and tortured. Food was meager and largely inedible.

Soon after being incarcerated, prisoners were "interrogated" using torture, including water boarding, and forced to "confess" their alleged crimes. In most cases, prisoners confessed to crimes they never committed to avoid more torture. They were then promptly executed and their bodies dumped into mass graves. Thus, most of Tuol Sleng's detainees did not spend much time alive at the prison—they were usually executed within weeks of arrival. In the early months of Tuol Sleng's existence, most of the prisoners were members or supporters of the Lon Nol regime, but as time progressed, Tuol Sleng became a death camp for Khmer Rouge leadership, as the paranoid and homicidal Pol Pot began to turn against his own followers, whom he accused of undermining his revolution. Many of the Khmer Rouge detainees who died at the prison were accused of spying and other "traitorous" activity.

Of all the thousands of detainees who cycled through Tuol Sleng, perhaps as few as 12 managed to survive. After Vietnamese forces invaded Cambodia and overthrew the Pol Pot regime, the full horror of Tuol Sleng was discovered when people searching for lost loved ones uncovered vast piles of human skulls, various documents, and many photographs of Tuol Sleng prisoners. Tuol Sleng has since proven to be the "face" of the Pol Pot regime and the calamitous genocide that it unleashed. Indeed, it was a powerful symbol that reflected the regime's maniacal obsession with obedience and irrational paranoia.

Paul G. Pierpaoli, Jr.

See also: Cambodian Killing Fields.

Further Reading

Chandler, David P. *Voices from S-21-Terror and History in Pol Pot's Secret Prison.* Berkeley: University of California Press, 1999.

Cook, Susan E., ed. *Genocide in Cambodia and Rwanda: New Perspectives.* New Brunswick, NJ: Transaction Publishers, 2006.

Deac, Wilfred P. *Road to the Killing Fields: The Cambodian War of 1970–1975.* College Station: Texas A&M University Press, 1997.

U

Unit 731

Japanese army's secret biological warfare unit. Established under the command of Lieutenant Colonel Ishii Shiro in Harbin, Manchuria, in August 1936, Unit 731 was officially known as the Epidemic Prevention and Water Purification Bureau. Some 3,000 personnel worked to produce bacteria for anthrax, bubonic plague, cholera, dysentery, tetanus, typhoid, typhus, and other infectious diseases.

To develop methods to disperse biological agents and enhance their effectiveness, Unit 731 infected prisoners of war. At least 3,000 of them died in the experiments. Unit personnel referred to the prisoners—mostly Chinese, Koreans, and Soviets—as *maruta* (logs) because the Japanese informed the local Chinese that the Unit 731 facility was a lumber mill. U.S., British, and Australian prisoners were also used as human guinea pigs.

Unit 731's activities were outrageous crimes against humanity. After infecting a prisoner with the virus, researchers might then cut open his body, sometimes while he was still alive, to determine the effects of the disease. No anesthetics were employed, as these might affect the results. Medical researchers also confined infected prisoners with healthy ones to determine how rapidly diseases spread. In addition, Unit 731's doctors conducted experiments on compression and decompression and the effects of extreme cold on the body, subjecting limbs to ice water and then amputating them to determine the effects. The Japanese army also repeatedly conducted field tests using biological warfare against Chinese villages.

In a more widespread use, Japanese aircraft spread plague-infected fleas over Ningbo (Ningpo) in Zhejiang (Chekiang) Province in eastern China in October 1940, causing 99 deaths. The Chinese government correctly concluded that an epidemic of plague in these areas was caused by Japanese biological weapons, and it publicized its findings. Japanese troops also dropped cholera and typhoid cultures into wells and ponds. In 1942, germ-warfare units deployed dysentery, cholera, and typhoid in Zhejiang Province.

At the end of the Pacific war, Ishii and other researchers escaped to Japan. They left behind their laboratory equipment, as well as plague-infected mice that produced outbreaks of the disease in the Haerbin (Harbin) area between 1946 and 1948. The U.S. government feared that the Japanese might employ biological warfare against North America via balloon bombs from Japan, but such a plan was never carried out.

After the Japanese surrender, the United States did not bring Ishii and his colleagues before the International Military Tribunal for the Far East (the Tokyo War Crimes Trials) for their crimes. Instead, they were granted immunity in exchange for providing information on the experiments to U.S. authorities, which Washington considered invaluable in its own biological warfare program. The Soviet government did prosecute 12 members of the unit at Khabarovsk in December 1949, all of whom admitted their crimes. They were convicted and received sentences of from 2 to 25 years in a labor camp.

Kotani Ken

See also: Japan; Medical Experimentation during World War II.

Further Reading

Harris, Sheldon. *Factories of Death*. London: Routledge, 1994.

Tsuneishi Keiichi. *Kieta saikin butai* [Vanished biological warfare unit]. Tokyo: Kaimei-sya, 1981.

Williams, Peter, and David Wallace. *Unit 731*. New York: Free Press, 1989.

U.S. POW Camps (1861–1865)

During the Civil War, Union forces captured more than 460,000 Confederate military prisoners. More than half were paroled on the battlefield, but approximately 215,000 were sent into captivity in various Union compounds. Nearly 26,000 Confederate soldiers died in captivity, an overall mortality rate of approximately 12 percent.

Union officials initially expected the war to be a relatively short conflict. Therefore, they made inadequate preparations for the confinement and maintenance of enemy captives. Those who had expected large numbers of detainees believed that an exchange or parole system would be devised, obviating the need for an extensive prison system. Thus, the early Union prisons were primarily in the Eastern Theater, and many were converted state civil prison facilities ill-suited for holding military captives.

Colonel William C. Hoffman served as the Union commissary general of prisoners. His relatively low rank belied the enormity of his task, and greatly hampered his efforts to obtain assistance from higher ranking field and department commanders. Even when he conveyed the urgent need for space, shelter, and sustenance of his charges, his pleas went largely unheeded. His problems were greatly compounded in 1863, when the crude but functional prisoner exchange system collapsed. That same year, major offensives by Union forces increased the number of enemy prisoners by thousands per month.

Hoffman resorted to improvisation, converting recruitment and training camps into prison compounds, which soon became massively overcrowded. The dense prisoner populations soon triggered disease outbreaks, a situation exacerbated by poorly functioning supply systems and a lack of proper hygiene among the captives. By 1864, reports of even worse conditions in Confederate prisons eroded what little compassion remained toward enemy prisoners. Hoffman ordered retaliatory reductions in the rations and medical supplies sent to each camp, allowing the mortality rate to quickly climb.

Both contemporary observers and historians have accused Union officials of deliberately mistreating their captives. Occasional recruitment of Confederate prisoners, offering them the opportunity to escape the camps in exchange for frontier service in the West, provides one possible explanation for the poor treatment of

Confederate detainees. Approximately 6,000 Confederates ("Galvanized Yankees") chose to take the oath of allegiance and don a Union uniform, and most remained on frontier duty for the remainder of the war.

In reality, it is unlikely that Union political and military leaders sought to mistreat the prisoners. They were simply overwhelmed by the demands of coordinating the largest war in the nation's history, and spared little time or effort worrying about the welfare of an enemy who many considered treasonous American citizens. While the mortality rate in the Union camps was high, it was not considered scandalous at the time, and only became so in the decades after the war ended. In short, there is little evidence of intentional mistreatment of Confederate prisoners; rather, they were largely victims of bureaucratic inefficiency, strained logistics, and an inability to predict the future course of the conflict.

Paul J. Springer

See also: American Civil War; Confederate States of America.

Further Reading

Hesseltine, William B. *Civil War Prisons: A Study in War Psychology.* New York: F. Ungar, 1964.

Sanders, Charles W. *While in the Hands of the Enemy: Military Prisons of the Civil War.* Baton Rouge: Louisiana State University Press, 2005.

Speer, Lonnie R. *Portals to Hell: Military Prisons of the Civil War.* Mechanicsburg, PA: Stackpole Books, 1997.

U.S. POW Camps (1941–1948)

During World War II, the United States established a network of camps to house tens of thousands of prisoners of wars captured in the European and the Pacific theaters of war. At first, the U.S. government resisted the idea of POW camps on its soil, but later decided to act, in part because of British requests to alleviate the POW housing problems in Great Britain. Ultimately, over 400,000 POWs had been kept at over 140 permanent base camps and over 300 branch camps scattered across almost every state of the United States, with the exceptions of Alaska, Nevada, North Dakota, and Vermont; the highest number of POW camps was in remote areas of southern states (Arkansas, Louisiana, Texas, Alabama, Georgia, etc.) due to climate conditions that reduced costs of maintaining facilities, but also to alleviate security concerns in metropolitan areas. At its height (in the spring of 1945), these camps held 425,871 prisoners, of whom the vast majority were Germans (371,683), followed by Italians (50,273) and Japanese (3,915). The camps tended to be segregated by the POW's nationality—for example, Camp Belle Mead in New Jersey and Camp Hereford in Texas housed primarily Italian prisoners, while Camp McCoy in Wisconsin held Japanese and Germans. Nearly 23,000 captured troops, mostly Germans and Italians from Erwin Rommel's famed Afrika Korps, were sent to Arkansas, where they were held in several major camps—Camp Robinson in North Little Rock (Pulaski County), Camp Chaffee in Fort Smith (Sebastian County), Camp Dermott in Dermott (Chicot County) Camp Monticello, east of Monticello (Drew County).

Conditions at American POW camps were, in general, excellent. The prisoners had access to good barrack housing, diverse recreational activities, and creative and educational opportunities. They were given ample food and, in case of officers, even alcohol; in the words of one German POW, "when I was captured I weighed 128 pounds; after two years as an American POW weighed 185. I had gotten so fat you could no longer see my eyes." The camps offered a formal reeducation program for German prisoners, which was run by the Special Projects Division and involved American university professors. Prisoners were also allowed to leave camps without guards on the honor system, and many of them socialized with local civilian population. Escape attempts were rather rare. The most famous attempt was that of 25 German prisoners escaping from Camp Papago Park in Arizona in late December 1944 by digging an almost 200 foot tunnel; they were recaptured days later. The camp authorities, however, had to keep die-hard Nazi prisoners of war segregated in separate camps because they harassed or, in some cases, killed fellow POWs; on November 4, 1943, at Camp Tonkawa (Oklahoma), five German POWs beat to death a fellow prisoner, Wilhelm Johannes Kunze, who they accused of being a traitor and collaborator with the Americans; they were all subsequently tried, found guilty, and hanged.

The POWs suffered little mistreatment from the camp authorities, although there was one instance of a massacre. On July 8, 1945, American soldier, Private Clarence V. Bertucci, opened fire on prisoners of war, killing 9 and wounding 20 others at a camp in Salina, Utah. The victims were buried with full military honors at Fort Douglas Cemetery; Bertucci, who explained that "he had hated Germans so he had killed Germans," was prosecuted but was found to be insane and hospitalized.

Due to labor shortages in the United States, many POWS were used for work, both in and around the camp, and outside the facility; in total, nearly 200,000 POWs were thus employed, mostly in farming and timber industry. The prisoners were paid for their labor based on their rank and the minimum pay for enlisted soldiers was $0.80 a day, which was about the same as for an American private. Part of their wages were used to defray costs of running the POW camps—in 1944 the U.S. government received $22 million from prisoner wages—while the prisoners were free to use the rest as pocket money at camp canteens or elsewhere; some were, in fact, able to set aside money and returned home with a few savings.

After the end of World War II, the United States turned over some POWs to France and Britain to help clear and rebuild devastated infrastructure. Most POWs were repatriated to Germany in 1947–1948; some of them later emigrated to the United States and returned in some official capacity, such as Rüdiger von Wechmar, who, after being imprisoned in the United States, served as the Permanent Representative of West Germany to the United Nations.

Alexander Mikaberidze

See also: Internment of Japanese Americans; World War II Prisoners of War.

Further Reading

Carlson, Lewis H. *We Were Each Other's Prisoners: An Oral History of World War II American and German Prisoners of War.* New York: Basic Books, 1997.

Krammer, Arnold. *Nazi Prisoners of War in America.* Chelsea, MI: Scarborough House, 1996.

"Midnight Massacre," *Time,* July 23, 1945 http://content.time.com/time/magazine/article
/0,9171,803557,00.html

Moore, John Hammond. *The Faustball Tunnel: German POWs in America and Their Great
Escape.* Annapolis, MD: Naval Institute Press 2006.

Pritchett, Merrill R., and William L. Shea. "The Afrika Korps in Arkansas, 1943–1946,"
Arkansas Historical Quarterly 37 (Spring 1978): 3–22.

Rabin, Ron. *The Barbed-Wire College: Reeducating German POWs in the United States
during World War II.* Princeton, NJ: Princeton University Press, 1995.

Ustaše

The Ustaše (literally, "rebels") was an extreme right-wing Croat nationalist movement that fought for the secession of Croatia from Yugoslavia. Following the collapse of the Austro-Hungarian Empire in 1918, the Croat nationalists were
disappointed to see their dreams of an independent Croatia crushed with the establishment of a new multi-ethnic state, the Kingdom of Yugoslavia. The Croat radical nationalism eventually expressed itself in the creation of the Ustaše, which
employed terrorist means in order to achieve its nationalist ambitions of an independent state.

The start of World War II provided the Ustaše with an opportunity to try to establish an independent Croatia. In 1941, the Ustaše came to power with the support of
Nazi Germany and Fascist Italy and formed a fascist puppet state in Croatia. Governed by Ante Pavelić (1889–1959), Croatia incorporated Bosnia and Herzegovina
and had a significant Serb population. The Ustaše pursued a policy of ethnic cleansing of Jews, Romanis, Muslims, and Serbs from territories under its control. It
established a network of concentration camps, the largest of which was Jasenovac
(about 60 miles south of the Croatian capital of Zagreb) that became as notorious
in the Balkans as Auschwitz was in the Nazi-occupied territories. Major concentration camps were also at Stara Gradiška (oftentimes referred to as Jasenovac V),
Sisak, Gospić, and Jadovno, while smaller camps existed at Lepoglava, Danica,
Lobor, Kerestinec, Jastrebarsko, Slana, Metajna, and Kruščica. Managed with
merciless brutality, the Ustaše camps were responsible for the deaths of hundreds of
thousands of Serbs, Romanis, Jews, and others. Well over 150,000 Serbs fled or
were deported from Croatia, while thousands Orthodox Christian Serbs were
forced, often at gunpoint, to convert to Roman Catholicism.

Yugoslavian resistance to the Germans and their supporters, the Croatian Ustaše
and the Serbian general Milan Nedić's government, centered on two factions. Colonel Dragoljub "Draza" Mihajlović, who strongly supported restoration of the mon-
archy, set up the Četniks (named for Serb guerrillas who had fought the Turks)
while Josip Broz Tito, leader of the Yugoslav Communist Party since 1937, headed
the second resistance group, the Partisans, which were particularly active in
Montenegro, Serbia, and Bosnia. After failing to develop a cooperative approach
against the Germans and Ustaše, Tito and Mihajlović turned against each other.
Ultimately, the Partisans gained an upper hand, and by the end of the war, their
numbers swelled to over half a million men.

After the war, Tito's Partisans exacted vengeance on their opponents, including the Ustaše and Četniks. Within weeks of the war's end, the Partisans executed, without trial, up to a quarter of a million people who had sided with the Germans, most of them Croats. However, many of the Ustaše leaders were able to flee to safety in South America. Pavelić himself fled to Argentina, where he reorganized the Ustaše in exile. He was, however, wounded in an assassination attempt in Madrid in 1957, and he died two years later from his injuries.

Alexander Mikaberidze

See also: Jasenovac; Sisak; Gospić; Jadovno Concentration Camp.

Further Reading

Goldstein, Ivo. *Croatia: A History.* Kingston, ON: McGill-Queen's University Press, 2000.

Muñoz, Antonio J. For *Croatia and Christ: The Croatian Army in World War II, 1941–1945.* Bayside, NY: Europa Books Inc., 2004.

Tanner, Marcus. *Croatia: A Nation Forged in War.* New Haven, CT: Yale University Press, 2001.

V

Vaivara

A Nazi transit and concentration camp, established in northeastern Estonia in August 1943, near the Vaivara train station. It served as the main concentration camp in Estonia, created originally as a camp for Soviet prisoners of war. Over time, it became the largest concentration camp in Estonia, with about 20 other smaller labor camps. Approximately 20,000 Jews passed through Vaivara, most of them from Latvia and the Lithuanian ghettos of Vilna and Kovno. In addition to serving as a concentration camp, it had the function of a transit camp, housing up to 1,300 prisoners at a time prior to them being sent off to labor and death camps. Most of Vaivara's prisoners were Jews, but also included Russian, Dutch, and Estonian inmates.

Vaivara's commandant was SS-Hauptsturmführer (captain) Hans Aumeier, who also assisted in Dachau, Buchenwald, Auschwitz, and other concentration camps during the Nazi period. Directors of Vaivara included Max Dahlmann, Kurt Panike, and Helmut Schnabel. Franz von Bothmann served Vaivara as the camp's chief physician, while the camp was guarded by an Estonian SS unit.

While in Vaivara, prisoners worked at various forms of hard labor from sun up to sun down. Some of the work in which they engaged included assembling railways, crushing stones into gravel, digging ditches, and felling trees. Daily food rations consisted of seven ounces of bread with ersatz jam or margarine, vegetable soup, and coffee.

At night the prisoners were forced to sleep in wooden huts, divided into five sections. Each section housed anywhere from 70 to 80 prisoners. Prisoners had barely any access to water, and were allowed to wash themselves only rarely and, as a result, sicknesses and lice were prevalent throughout the camp.

The camp administration at Vaivara conducted regular "selections," when they would choose which inmates were fit for work and which ones were not. Those who were deemed too old, too young, or too sick to perform work were killed. The first of these selections took place in 1943, soon after the camp had opened; 150 Jewish men and women were killed after being found unfit to work. Soon after, the same selection and execution process took place again, and 300 Jews were killed. After these first two selections, similar processes leading to the murder of prisoners at Vaivara took place approximately every two weeks; eventually, this was repeated roughly 20 times following the camp's inception. Five hundred more Jews were murdered in these actions. During one of these, Jewish children, who until then had been kept separate from the rest of the camp in their own hut, were taken and killed. Those who survived the selections were nonetheless still subjected to severe beatings and possibly death at the hands of the SS officers who supervised Vaivara.

When the Soviet Army closed in on Estonia and Vaivara in 1945, hundreds of the remaining inmates were taken west on death marches. Some of the prisoners were transported to Saki, another camp in western Estonia. Lagerführer Helmut Schnabel, one of Vaivara's directors, was tried and sentenced for war crimes in 1968, and sentenced to 16 years in prison; his sentence was reduced to 6 years the following year. Hans Aumeier, Vaivara's commandant, was sentenced to death in Kraków, Poland, and executed on December 22, 1947.

Danielle Jean Drew

See also: Concentration Camps; Germany.

Further Reading

Mojzes, Paul. *Balkan Genocides: Holocaust and Ethnic Cleansing in the Twentieth Century.* Lanham, MD: Rowman and Littlefield, 2011.

Press, Bernhard. *The Murder of the Jews in Latvia: 1941–1945.* Evanston, IL: Northwestern University Press, 2000.

Voren, Robert van. *Undigested Past: The Holocaust in Lithuania.* Amsterdam: Rodopi, 2011.

Vietnam War (1964–1973)

In accordance with the 1973 Paris Peace Accords, a total of 565 American military and 26 civilian prisoners of war (POWs) were released by the Democratic Republic of Vietnam (DRV, North Vietnam) in February and March 1973, and two military persons and two civilians held in the People's Republic of China were freed at the same time. The civilians included contract pilots; Central Intelligence Agency (CIA), State Department, and Voice of America personnel; and agricultural specialists, missionaries, and other nonmilitary personnel. Six foreign nationals—two Canadians, two South Koreans, and two Filipinos—also departed.

At various points during the war, Hanoi had turned over a total of 12 POWs to visiting "peace delegations," and early in the war the Viet Cong (VC) released a few prisoners. A small number of Americans escaped from the VC control or from Communist forces in Laos. Although many pilots shot down over hostile territory evaded capture until being rescued, no one actually brought into the prison system successfully escaped from North Vietnam. Only a few civilians captured after the 1973 ceasefire agreement and convicted Marine defector Robert Garwood came home after the 1973 release.

Estimates of POWs who died in captivity vary. The North Vietnamese listed 55 deaths. One American source cited 54 military and at least 13 American and foreign civilians; another source gives the number as 72 Americans. For prisoners so injured and mistreated, the casualty rate was amazingly low in the North Vietnamese camps. The returned POWs cited eight known deaths of military personnel in the Hanoi system—two considered outright murder, three from a combination of brutality and neglect, and three from appallingly substandard medical care. The largest number of deaths of military personnel and civilians occurred in the jungle camps in the South.

Justifiably proud of their communication network, command structure, and memory bank, which attempted to register every individual in the system, the POWs recorded at least 766 verified captives at one point or another. But accountability for those outside the North Vietnamese prison system was less certain. Of the hundreds who disappeared in Laos, only ten came home in 1973, and no one knows the fate of the many captives of local VC units. At the time of release, more than 2,500 men were still listed as missing in action (MIA). Many of those most likely died when shot down, but their deaths were not confirmed. Others known to be alive on the ground and even in the prison system mysteriously disappeared.

All but 71 of the military personnel who returned in early 1973 were officers, primarily Air Force or Navy aviators shot down during combat missions. With the exception of a handful of Air Force personnel, the enlisted men consisted of army and marine personnel captured in the South. The fliers had received survival and captivity training; for the most part those captured in the South had not. The first pilot captured by the North Vietnamese was Navy lieutenant, junior grade Everett Alvarez, shot down on August 5, 1964, in the first bombing raid on the DRV, following the Gulf of Tonkin incidents. But the longest-held POW was Army Special Forces captain Floyd James Thompson, whose light reconnaissance plane was shot down by small-arms fire on March 26, 1964. He spent five years in solitary confinement, three with the Viet Cong in the South and two more after being moved to North Vietnam. Thompson suffered a broken back in the crash, numerous illnesses, and a heart attack during his almost nine years of captivity, becoming the longest-held American POW in history.

Most of the POWs were aviators shot down during the ROLLING THUNDER bombing campaign of North Vietnam during February 1965 through November 1968; 1967 produced the most captives. The Tet Offensive in the first half of 1968 generated the most captives on the ground; almost half the army and marine POWs came in that year. Eighteen of the 26 civilian POWs released in 1973 were captured during a one-week period, the first week of February 1968. With the end of ROLLING THUNDER, the number of captives dropped off dramatically from late 1968 through early 1972, virtually all of them taken in the South or in Laos. The LINEBACKER I bombings lead to an upsurge of captives in the spring of 1972, and during LINEBACKER II, 44 aviators were shot down in December 1972 alone. Only one pilot was added in 1973, captured on January 27, the day that the peace accords were signed. The 131 POWs captured in 1972 and 1973 experienced a short and very different captivity from those held in the earlier years.

Among the military POWs, one commentator surveying the 356 aviators held in 1970 recorded that the average flier was approximately 32 years old, an Air Force captain or Navy lieutenant, and married with two children. They were for the most part career officers, skilled pilots of high-performance aircraft, highly disciplined, intensely competitive, and college graduates.

American POWs were held in 11 different prisons in North Vietnam, 4 in Hanoi, 6 others within 50 miles of the city (more or less up and down the Red River), and 1 on the Chinese border. The most famous of these was North Vietnam's main penitentiary, Hoa Lo Prison in downtown Hanoi, which the POWs dubbed the "Hanoi

Hilton." They gave the other prisons names as well—Briar Patch, Faith, Hope (Son Tay), Skidrow, D-1, Rockpile, Plantation, the Zoo, Alcatraz, and Dogpatch.

From the first captive on, a test of wills existed between the Hanoi camp authority and the American military personnel over the U.S. Code of Conduct, which had been adopted in 1955 in response to the allegedly disgraceful performance of some American POWs during the Korean conflict. The Vietnam POWs were determined to maintain a record of honor that would reflect well upon themselves personally, the U.S. military, and the nation. The camp authority employed every means at its disposal, including isolation, torture, and psychological abuse, to break POW discipline. Senior commanders such as Air Force lieutenant colonel Robinson Risner, Navy commander James Stockdale, Navy lieutenant commander Jeremiah Denton, and many others emerged as the leaders in the POW resistance campaign. And tough resisters such as George Day, George Coker, John Dramesi, George McKnight, and Lance Sijan, to name but a few, played significant roles in the effort. Stockdale, Day, and Sijan (posthumously) received the Medal of Honor for their heroism and leadership as POWs. Army captain Rocque Versace, who was executed in captivity as a prisoner of the VC in the south, also received the Medal of Honor.

The POW experience broke down roughly into several periods. From 1965 through 1969 prisoners were isolated, kept in stocks, bounced from one camp to another, malnourished, and brutally tortured to break their morale, discipline, and commitment to the U.S. Code of Conduct. Following the death of Ho Chi Minh in September 1969, the torture ended, and conditions improved in the camps. After the Son Tay Raid in November 1970, the North Vietnamese closed the outlying camps and consolidated all the POWs in Hanoi. Compound living began in what the prisoners called Camp Unity. In February 1971, Air Force colonel John Flynn, the highest-ranking POW, who had spent most of his captivity isolated from the others, assumed command and organized the military community into the 4th Allied POW Wing. A few Thais and South Vietnamese POWs, who had distinguished themselves in working with the Americans, were included in the Wing.

From this point on, the greatest attention was given to how the POWs would return home. Amnesty was tendered to those who had cooperated with the enemy if they would now adhere to the Code of Conduct. All but a few accepted the offer. During the final two years, the collective POW story was collected, shaped, and honed.

With the end of the war, the POWs returned home in Operation HOMECOMING to great fanfare as the only heroes of a frustrating war. Much to the dismay of senior POW officers, the Defense Department decided that POWs who had collaborated would not be prosecuted. Only Robert Garwood, when he returned to the United States in 1979, faced court-martial. Although many divorces resulted from their captivity, the Vietnam POWs adjusted relatively well. Ten years later, only about 30 had been treated for psychological or mental problems, although 2 had committed suicide and 3 died of other causes. Almost half were still in the military. The POW story is recorded in the more than 50 individual and collective participant narratives.

Joe P. Dunn

See also: Hoa Lo Prison (Hanoi Hilton); HOMECOMING, Operation.

Further Reading

Doyle, Robert C. *Voices from Captivity: Interpreting the American POW Narrative.* Lawrence: University Press of Kansas, 1994.

Dunn, Joe P. "The Vietnam War and the POWs/MIAs," In *Teaching the Vietnam War: Resources and Assessments,* Los Angeles: Center for the Study of Armament and Disarmament, California State University–LA, 1990.

Howes, Craig. *Voices of the Vietnam POWs: Witnesses to Their Fight.* Oxford: Oxford University Press, 1993.

Hubbell, John G., et al. *P.O.W.: A Definitive History of the American Prisoner of War Experience in Vietnam, 1964–1973.* New York: Reader's Digest Press, 1976.

Philpott, Tom. *Glory Denied: The Saga of Jim Thompson, America's Longest-Held Prisoner of War.* New York: W. W. Norton, 2001.

Rowan, Stephan A. *They Wouldn't Let Us Die: The Prisoners of War Tell Their Story.* Middle Village, NY: Jonathan David, 1973.

Vorkuta Camps

One of the major Gulag labor camps. Located 100 miles above the Arctic Circle in the Pechora River Basin in the Komi Republic, the camp complex was established in 1932 to mine natural resources of the Pechora Coal Basin. It comprised of the Vorkutlag forced labor camp complex (which included over 130 branch camps) that housed tens of thousands of prisoners, and of the Rechlag (Special Camp Number 6) that held thousands of political dissidents. The prison population at the Vorkutlag averaged 15,000–20,000 in 1938–1941, and rose to over 50,000 by the end of the World War II; the neighboring Rechlag housed 25,000–35,000 prisoners. In

Vorkuta Gulag (Vorkutlag) in 1945. One of the major Gulag labor camps, Vorkutlag was located in the Pechora River Basin in the Komi Republic (Russian Federation). Tens of thousands of prisoners, kept at over 100 sub-camps, lived in abysmal conditions and labored in coal mines. (Laski Diffusion/Getty Images)

addition to common criminals and political dissidents, these camps held many prisoners of wars, including thousands of Polish POWs captured by the Soviet forces in 1939, and German POWs captured on the Eastern Front during the World War II. American Homer Harold Cox, who had served in the U.S. Army's 759th Military Police Service Battalion in West Berlin and was detained by the Soviet military police in East Berlin in 1949, has spent almost four years in the Vorkuta camps before his release in 1953.

In 1953, the Vorkuta camps were affected by a large prisoner unrest. After the death of Joseph Stalin in March 1953, prisoners hoped for amnesty and release, which was granted only to some prisoners, excluding political dissidents. In the summer of 1953, a major unrest, better known as the Vorkuta Prisoner Uprising, broke out at the Rechlag; according to Aleksandr Solzhenitsyn, it was provoked by two events in June 1953: the arrest of the head of the Soviet secret police, Lavrenty Beria, in Moscow and the arrival of new batch of prisoners who were willing to act. In July, the prisoners refused to follow orders, staged protests, and tried to send appeals to the Soviet government; by August, some 18,000 prisoners were protesting. In early August, prison authorities opened fire at the prisoners, killing and wounding dozens. A similar prisoner uprising at the Gorlag (in Norilsk) was also harshly suppressed, with hundreds of prisoners killed and wounded. Although prisoner uprisings had failed, authorities were forced to react and conditions at camps were marginally improved, especially for political prisoners.

Alexander Mikaberidze

See also: Beria, Lavrenty; Gulag; Solovki Special Camp; Soviet Union, POW Camps (1941–1956).

Further Reading

Kozlov, V. *Istoriya stalinskogo Gulaga. Volume 6. Vosstaniya, bunty i zabastovki zaklyuchennykh.* Moscow: ROSSPEN, 2004.

Vught

A concentration camp established for Dutch political prisoners, located in southern Holland near the city of Hertogenbosch. Called by its Dutch name of Kamp Vught, and to the Germans as Konzentrationslager Herzogenbusch, Vught was, together with Natzweiler-Struthof in France, the only Nazi concentration camp in Western Europe outside of Germany.

Construction on the camp began in May 1942, and it became operational toward the end of the year. The first political prisoners arrived before construction was complete, coming from another Dutch camp at Amersfoort. The initial group of Jewish prisoners arrived at Vught during January 1943, and by May of that year their numbers had increased to 8,684.

In its first design, Vught was divided into two sections, a Jewish camp and one for political prisoners. The Jewish camp was intended to serve as a transit camp, calculated to hold Jews prior to them being deported, first to Westerbork, and from there to death camps situated in Poland. The so-called "security camp" took in Dutch and Belgian political prisoners. In May and August of 1943, two additional areas of Vught were created: a camp exclusively for women, and what was essentially a penitentiary within the camp, where prisoners in detention were kept.

The camp measured 500 by 200 meters and consisted of 36 living and 23 working barracks. Surrounding this complex was a double barbed-wire fence, with watchtowers placed every 50 meters around the perimeter. Just outside the camp were the SS barracks. Some prisoners were permitted to work outside the camp, in a factory owned by the Dutch electrical company Philips. Here, up to 1,200 prisoners were employed, in conditions which the company claimed were decent; these included a cooked meal every day and exemption from deportation. Such conditions were valued, the more so as elsewhere in Vught circumstances were, quite simply, appalling. Particularly at the start, the food was poor, and the SS guards were exceptionally brutal (even by SS standards). Hundreds of prisoners died during the first few months of the camp's existence.

With one of the functions of the camp being the transit of Jews to death camps, a number of convoys left Vught during the course of its existence, bound for Germany and Poland. In June 1943, for instance, hundreds of Jewish children were sent to Sobibór, while there were additional transports of Jews sent in November 1943 and June 1944. Most convoys, however, went first to Westerbork, which was the major transit camp for the Netherlands.

By May 1943, Vught held nearly 31,000 prisoners, of all backgrounds: Jews, political prisoners, resistance fighters, Romanis, Jehovah's Witnesses, homosexuals, and criminals, among others. This period saw the high point of Vught in terms of prisoner numbers, though it took more than another full year before the camp began to be liquidated in the summer of 1944. On June 3, 1944, one final group of prisoners was transported out. It was comprised of 517 workers from the Philips factory. When sent to Auschwitz, they were used as slave labor by another electronics company, Telefunken, though only 160 of these survived. Most of the men had been killed; two-thirds of those who stayed alive until liberation were women, and nine were children.

As Allied forces were approaching Vught during the fall of 1944, the SS began to work on dismantling operation at the camp, and most of the prisoners were transferred to concentration camps further east. Across the period September 4–5, 1944, many of the women were transferred to Ravensbrück; the men were sent to Sachsenhausen. By September 5–6, 1944, Vught was practically empty. On October 26, 1944, the camp was liberated by Canadian troops. They found a total of no more than around 500 prisoners still there, all of whom had been slated for execution by the Nazis that day. Were it not for the arrival of the Canadians, there was every likelihood that they would have been murdered. Another 500 or so inmates were discovered dead in piles near the gates; they had been murdered earlier that same morning.

Altogether, owing to hunger, sickness, murder, and general abuse, some 749 men, women, and children lost their lives during the camp's existence. A large number—329 of them—were killed at an execution site known as the Fusilladeplaats. They were for the most part members of the Dutch resistance, brought to Vught from various prisons and murdered between late July and early September 1944. The perpetrators were members of the Dutch SS, who were routinely used by the Germans to guard the watch towers.

After the war, the camp was used as a prison for Dutch collaborators and up to 6,000 Germans, evacuated from various parts of the Netherlands until their repatriation later in 1945. The camp remained open as an internment facility until 1949. On December 20, 1947, the then-princess Juliana of the Netherlands (who would be crowned the following year) unveiled a memorial at the site with names of all those who had lost their lives at Vught. Then, in April 1990, the National Monument Camp Vught was opened by Queen Beatrix of the Netherlands. It is accompanied by a visitor center and museum, containing exhibitions from the time of the camp's existence. There is also a national monument commemorating the victims of the camp, and all those who passed through it.

Paul R. Bartrop

See also: Concentration Camps; Holocaust, The; SS-Totenkopfverbände; Westerbork.

Further Reading

Boom, Bart van der, and Peter Romijn. *The Persecution of the Jews in the Netherlands, 1940–1945.* Amsterdam: Vossiuspers, 2012.

Camp Vught National Memorial, http://www.nmkampvught.nl/english/

Presser, Jacob. *The Destruction of the Dutch Jews.* London: Dutton, 1969.

Westerbork

A transit camp located about 12 kilometers from the village of Westerbork in the northeast of the Netherlands, had originally been set up in October 1939 by the Dutch government as a place to hold German Jewish refugees who had entered the Netherlands illegally, following the closure of the border on December 15, 1938. Financed partly by Dutch Jews, the first refugees arrived at Westerbork on October 9, 1939.

On May 10, 1940, the German army invaded the Netherlands, and had forced the country to surrender by May 14. At the time of the invasion, there were about 750 Jewish refugees at Westerbork. The occupying authorities imposed their anti-Semitic policies soon after taking over the country, dismissing Jews from the civil service and requiring that they register the assets of their business enterprises. They also took over Westerbork, turning it into a place to detain resisters and then, in late 1941, into a deportation camp. As the year unfolded, the number of Jews increased, to the point where the Nazis had assembled a population of 1,100 Jewish refugees, mostly from Germany, while at the same time the Nazis enlarged the camp for future use.

On July 1, 1942, the Nazis took direct control, and Westerbork became transformed, officially, into a transit camp (Durchgangslager Westerbork). Two weeks later, on July 14, 1942, a "selection" took place to see who was fit enough to work; the rest, numbering 1,135, were deported to Auschwitz two days later. By the end of July, nearly 6,000 Dutch Jews had been similarly deported. An SS officer, Erich Deppner, was appointed as commandant, overseeing initial deportation operations across July and August 1942, and taking responsibility for the first transport of Jews to Auschwitz. Upon being relieved, Reichsführer-SS Heinrich Himmler complimented Deppner for his "good work."

New rail lines were then added, and by November 1942, deportation trains came straight into the camp in order to enable the more rapid loading of Jews for Auschwitz; over time, other trains were sent to in other death camps in German-occupied Poland, as well as places such as Bergen-Belsen, Theresienstadt, and Vittel, France.

From this point onward, deportation trains consisting of around 20 cattle wagons or freight cars would arrive each Monday evening. A list of 1,000 people would be compiled by the Jewish Council (Joodse Raad), and on Tuesday the trains would then leave Westerbork. From that first train on July 16, 1942, until the procedure came to an end on September 3, 1944, a total of 97,776 Jews were deported from Westerbork: 54,930 to Auschwitz in 68 transports; 34,313 to Sobibór (19); 4,771 to Theresienstadt (7); and 3,762 to Bergen-Belsen (9). Taken overall, 101,000 Dutch

Jews and about 5,000 German Jews were deported to their deaths in Poland, together with about 400 Romanis. The camp also served as the location of imprisonment for Dutch resisters, and toward the end of the war some 400 female resisters were also deported to their deaths.

Of all those deported, only 5,200 survived. Some, numbering 876, 569 of whom were Dutch citizens, managed to avoid deportation and outlasted the Nazis at Westerbork. Others who had been deported and survived did so at Theresienstadt or Bergen-Belsen. Almost all those who had been sent to Auschwitz and Sobibór were murdered immediately upon arrival.

Regardless of the camp's core function as a deportation facility, Westerbork also served as a regular concentration camp, with a permanent prisoner population of some 2,000 prisoners. Many of these Jews, possessing British or American citizenship, were exempted from deportation. The Nazis considered that they could be used as "currency" for "exchange"; for each Jew, the idea was that several German prisoners of war could be traded. Moreover, it served the Germans to maintain this presence, as the SS could point to the fixed structures—which included a school, a hair-dresser, an orchestra, and even a restaurant—as evidence to newcomers that this was the type of environment to which they were being sent in Poland. Certainly, this reduced problems during the deportation process, and even encouraged people to board the trains to Auschwitz and Sobibór. The added tragedy of Westerbork was that over time most of the "permanent" residents of the camp were themselves deported to their deaths.

On April 12, 1945, with the Allied approached, the Nazis abandoned Westerbork and the Canadian 2nd Infantry Division liberated the camp. Westerbork was then given over to house Dutch collaborators with the Nazis, with other uses brought into play in later years. The camp was demolished in 1971, and a monument was erected on the site. In 1983, a museum and memorial site was opened at the location of what had been part of the former camp area.

Paul R. Bartrop

See also: Holocaust, The; Vught.

Further Reading

Boas, Jacob. *Boulevard des Misères: The Story of the Transit Camp Westerbork*. Hamden, CT: Archon Books, 1985.

Hillesum, Etty. *Letters from Westerbork*. New York: Pantheon, 1986.

Law, Cecil. *Kamp Westerbork Transit Kamp to Eternity: The Liberation Story*. Ottawa: Canadian Peacekeeping Press, 2000.

Mechanicus, Philip. *Year of Fear: A Jewish Prisoner Waits for Auschwitz*. New York: Hawthorn Books, 1968.

Windhoek

The largest single population of Herero and Nama prisoners were held in Windhoek, the colonial capital. Windhoek had two military run concentration camps, and a number of smaller private camps. The main camp, which started operating around February 1905, was located on a hill overlooking the town next to the main military installation, known today as the Alte Feste (the old fort). The other camp, which was likely started as an overflow facility in 1906, was placed on a flat plain in the hills northwest of the main railway station.

The key catchment areas of the camps were eastern and northeastern parts of the colony, especially along the ephemeral Black and White Nossob rivers. The prisoners were largely captured Herero communities who had fled the Waterberg attack, or were people still living in eastern Hereroland who may or may not have taken part in the war. Between December 1905 and April of 1907, the missionary collection point of Otjihaenena was responsible for a large influx of Herero prisoners of war to the camp. Notably, as was the case in all camps, only one in three prisoners were adult males.

In 1906, the two camps held an average of 5,000 people with more than 7,000 being counted in April of that year. In contrast, the European population of the town of Windhoek was approximately 3,000. The containment was therefore as much a security measure as it was a military strategy. The large fluctuation in the number of prisoners was caused by the onward transport of able-bodied prisoners to the railways and other infrastructure projects, as well as a high mortality rate.

Both archival and oral sources point to commonplace sexual abuse of female prisoners, both by the nearby garrison and the settlers, who routinely rented prisoners from the camp for domestic chores. According to a comprehensive medical report covering the period 1904 to 1907 (the Sanitaets-Bericht), the transmission of sexual diseases from and to the camps was a major cause of morbidity in Windhoek during 1906.

The camps themselves were rudimentary at best. The accommodation consisted of crude round-huts, or Pontoks, made up of blankets, animal skins, and branches, which offered only little protection from the extreme climate. A lack of sanitary facilities, bad food, and poor rations compounded the situation, leading to outbreaks of dysentery, pneumonia, influenza, and syphilis.

As had been the case in the South African concentration camps during the Boer War, the concentration of people in a confined area resulted in a rapid spread of communicable diseases. Rather than improve camp facilities, however, the colonial government increased tighter controls on traffic to and from the camp in order to minimize the risk of infection to the German population. Whereas we do not have complete mortality figures for the two concentration camps, it is known that in peak months like September 1906 more than eight people died per day.

Casper W. Erichsen

See also: Herero Genocide, Concentration Camps and; Okahandja; Shark Island.

Further Reading
Olusoga, David, and Erichsen, Casper W. *The Kaiser's Holocaust: Germany's Forgotten Genocide and the Colonial Roots of Nazism.* London: Faber and Faber, 2010.

Wirth, Christian (1885–1944)

Known for his brutality both to Jewish victims and his own SS staff at Nazi extermination camps, Christian Wirth was involved in—if not directly responsible for—the mass killings of Jews in three of the six Nazi extermination camps situated in Poland.

Wirth was born on November 24, 1885, in Oberbalzheim in Baden-Württemberg, in southern Germany. His years before World War I, and prior to his association with the Nazi party in 1931, were spent first in the construction trade, and then with the police department in Stuttgart. He served valiantly in World War I, where he was wounded and highly decorated. After the war he returned to Stuttgart, where he became a leading police detective, and later was responsible for other detectives working homicide.

His early roles in the Nazi party were in the SA (Sturmabteilung) in 1933; in the SD (Sicherheitsdienst) in 1937; and the SS (Schutzstaffel) in 1939, where he was promoted to Obersturmführer (first lieutenant) in October of that year. His brutality was already well known; his success rate for getting confessions from suspects that no one else could was impressive.

His education in the workings of the Nazi regime continued when he was assigned at the end of 1939 to the German "euthanasia" program, Aktion T-4. That was the Nazis' first large-scale, organized killing operation, addressed this time not at Jews, but at German citizens with physical and mental disabilities that, under Nazi ideology, rendered them as leading "lives not worthy of living." It was while working as the administrative director at a euthanasia station in Brandenburg that Wirth was first involved in killing by gas. He also learned there and at another euthanasia center in Hartheim Castle that carbon monoxide gas was very effective for killing a large group of people relatively quickly, and that for such a program to be efficient, the victims must be deceived into believing that they were not going to their death until it was too late for them to do anything to stop it. Wirth was so good at this work that he was appointed head of the program in mid-1940.

With this as background, Wirth soon found himself involved from the very beginning with the Operation REINHARD (Aktion Reinhard) program. This program focused on the extermination of the Jews of Poland, and to that end it created three so-called Operation REINHARD extermination camps: Bełżec, Sobibór, and Treblinka (all built in the Generalgouvernement). In December 1941, Wirth was ordered to set up the first of these camps, Bełżec, and was appointed its first commandant. By mid-March 1942, Bełżec's killing capacity was operational.

As Bełżec's commandant—in which capacity he was referred to as "Christian the Savage"—Wirth was in a position that allowed him to experiment to determine what steps needed to be taken to make the killing center run as efficiently as possible; "efficiently" meaning, in this case, the ability to kill and dispose of the bodies of as many Jews in as short a time as possible. To that end, Wirth, drawing on his Aktion T-4 experience, recognized the importance of deceiving the victims for as long as possible as to the real purpose of the camp. He often personally made a welcoming speech to new arrivals, assuring them that they had come to a transit camp and that they had nothing to fear.

He also recognized the importance of speed in this operation. It was critical that the victims be moved as quickly as possible from arrival to execution. In a manner that seemed to contradict his principle of keeping victims calm, he ordered that they be forced to run from one place to the next, always being beaten or whipped if they did not do so fast enough. The goal was to disorient them so that any thoughts or feelings other than terror would be impossible. Another decision he made was for Jews themselves to do as much of the work in the extermination process as feasible.

Less than six months into Bełżec's killing operations, Wirth was promoted again, this time to be the supervisor of all three of the Operation REINHARD camps, meaning that his command was extended from Bełżec to include Sobibór and Treblinka. In that capacity, Wirth set out to increase killing efficiency in those camps as well. In the summer of 1943, Himmler promoted him to Sturmbannführer.

A massacre with a particularly cruel name—"Operation HARVEST FESTI-VAL," committed in November 1943—was also Wirth's doing. As the Operation REINHARD camps began to be closed, Wirth saw to it that the Jewish laborers in Nazi camps, including Trawniki and Madjanek, be killed. Some 42,000 Jews were murdered as a result.

Wirth was then assigned to Trieste, where his job was to establish a death camp in San Sabba, and to fight partisans. On May 26, 1944, he was killed by Yugoslav partisans. He was buried with full honors.

Michael Dickerman

See also: Bełżec; Germany; Hitler, Adolf; Hoess, Rudolf; Kramer, Josef; Sobibór; Treblinka.

Further Reading
Arad, Yitzhak. *Belzec, Sobibor, Treblinka: The Operation Reinhard Death Camps.* Bloom-ington: Indiana University Press, 1987.
Bryant, Michael. *Eyewitness to Genocide: The Operation Reinhard Death Camp Trials, 1955–1966.* Knoxville: University of Tennessee Press, 2016.

World War I Prisoners of War

At the beginning of the Great War in 1914, all participating governments antici-pated a short conflict. In consequence, none of the warring states had given ade-quate attention to the incarceration of large numbers of prisoners of war for a prolonged period of time. The result was considerable chaos and suffering for those taken prisoner early in the war.

Most of the warring powers adhered to The Hague Conventions of 1899 and 1907, which codified humane treatment for prisoners of war and required the cap-turing state to accord them the same conditions as its own soldiers. The Hague Con-vention also required governments to compile records on each prisoner and stipulated that prisoners were not to be used for war work; this regulation was ignored as the need for laborers sharply increased.

Within six months, the warring powers had taken almost 1.5 million prisoners. Despite the pressures of total war, most captor states endeavored to treat their pris-oners humanely. There were some incidents of mistreatment, but most came from incompetence and lack of foresight rather than intentional cruelty. The original tem-porary arrangements proved inadequate, and the result was considerable suffering in regard to shelter, food, and clothing. Crowded conditions produced outbreaks of disease, and typhus, typhoid fever, and dysentery were common in the early camps on all sides, especially in the east.

Conditions gradually improved as permanent camps were constructed, and tents gave way to permanent shelters. The widespread use of prisoner-of-war labor also led to improved conditions for many prisoners, as it gave them access to better food and some income.

The various Red Cross societies began distribution of aid to the prisoners in the fall of 1915. The International Committee of the Red Cross compiled information on prisoners and relayed this to family members. It also distributed letters, parcels, and money, and it supervised prison camp conditions on both sides. Red Cross packages included basic foodstuff, as well as luxuries such as tobacco, clothing, chocolate, coffee, and soap. The Red Cross also accounted for those who died in the camps and forwarded their belongings to relatives. The French Bureau de Secours aux Prisonniers de Guerre and the British Prisoners of War Help Committee oversaw volunteer efforts.

Generally speaking, prisoners of war held by the Western Entente powers were the better cared for, while those in the east suffered the most. Living conditions for prisoners in the camps in the east, especially in Russia, were difficult.

Many prisoners held by the Russians were sent to Siberia, where life was especially harsh. Military enlisted prisoners were required to work. Prisoners worked in quarries, factories, and coal and salt mines. They also built roads, cut timber, and worked in agriculture.

As demands for labor increased during the war, many prisoners were forced to labor in war-related work. Private employers often hired prisoner-of-war labor, and prisoners often struck up friendships with local civilians who provided them extra food and clothing. While the income was welcome, many prisoners resented the extra work.

Officers were generally accorded better treatment. They had the best quarters, monthly financial allowances, and release from any type of manual labor. The rampant inflation of the war, however, eroded the purchasing power of their financial stipends.

Infectious diseases were a constant problem. Dysentery, gangrenous wounds, and lice were omnipresent. Nutritional deficiencies caused beriberi and dental problems. Many prisoners also suffered from chronic depression, and suicide was not uncommon.

Prisoners could send and receive mail, although their correspondence was censored. To relieve boredom, prisoners organized libraries and formed dramatic groups, orchestras, and choirs. Sports activities proliferated, and the prisoners also established school systems with workshops to teach new skills and lectures on such subjects as history and foreign language. Prisoners were also permitted to attend church services.

Many World War I prisoners of war made attempts to escape, which was both far easier and less likely to result in severe punishment than in World War II. Future French army general and president Charles de Gaulle, for example, attempted escape a half dozen times; each time he was foiled, in large part due to his conspicuous height.

Prisoners could escape from the poorly guarded camps, from work parties, or from transport trains; many did so, and attempted to reach neutral states such as Switzerland, the Netherlands, and the Scandinavian states. Prisoners escaping in Britain might be able to secure refuge on Dutch ships in British ports. Those caught attempting to escape were usually sent to a more secure facility, or they might be placed in solitary confinement. Prisoners who managed to reach their home countries often provided valuable intelligence about the enemy.

World War I ushered in a new class of war prisoners: alien civilians. These included students, resident workers, travelers, and merchant seamen. After a brief period in which they could depart, such individuals were often placed in camps but not required to work. Not until the 1949 Geneva Conventions was there international agreement on the treatment of alien non-combatants.

WESTERN FRONT

The largest number of prisoners taken by both sides in the war on the Western Front came during the war of maneuver at the beginning of the conflict. Thereafter, some prisoners were taken in trench raids, and more fell in general offensives. By early 1915, for example, the Germans held 245,000 French prisoners. The largest batch of British prisoners, some 100,000, was taken in the Ludendorff Offensives in the spring of 1918. At the end of the war, the Germans held nearly 172,000 British prisoners and another 10,000 from the British dominions and colonies. The Germans also held 350,000 French and 43,000 U.S. prisoners of war.

During the war, the British captured about 328,000 Germans, while the French took another 400,000. The French also held a number of Turkish and Bulgarian prisoners, whom they interned on Corsica.

Generally speaking, conditions were best for German prisoners held in camps in Britain and in U.S.-run camps. The British kept some Germans prisoners on prison ships. Conditions there, while cramped, were nonetheless satisfactory. Conditions were slightly worse for Germans in the French-run camps, especially at the beginning of the war, when the French were unprepared for the huge influx of German prisoners. Conditions improved rapidly as the French built permanent camps.

The French were especially concerned about the German treatment of their many French prisoners, so they were anxious that the German prisoners of war be well cared for under the Hague Convention. They also did not force their prisoners to work in war-related industries until they learned that the Germans were doing so. The French did not release their last prisoners of war until 1920, keeping many of them at work repairing war-related damage.

At first U.S. forces transferred Germans they captured to French control, but this practice ended when Americans began to fall into German hands. U.S. authorities decided that they needed to maintain the German prisoners to ensure that American prisoners held by the Germans were well cared for. Despite considerable time to prepare for this, the United States had given little thought to the care of its prisoners of war, and many were sheltered in tents for some time. The U.S. military also put German prisoners to dangerous work, such as disposing of munitions; in one case, 25 German prisoners of war died in an explosion from such activity, leading to a temporary work stoppage. Later, such work for prisoners would be banned by international law.

The worst conditions for Allied prisoners taken on the Western Front were in Germany. Those sent to agricultural areas to do farm work were fortunate in that most could supplement their diets. Many others ended up working in German factories where they were relatively well cared for. Prisoners sent to work in the lumber industry or coal mines were forced to labor for 10 to 12 hours a day in dangerous conditions with poor rations, little pay, and next to no medical treatment in case of injury.

EASTERN FRONT

Both sides took large numbers of prisoners in the more fluid warfare that characterized fighting on the Eastern Front. In the great Battle of Tannenberg (August 26–31, 1914), the Germans captured more than 90,000 Russian soldiers. Both at Przemysl in March 1915 and in the first three days of the Brusilov Offensive (June 4–September 1, 1916), the Russians took 70,000 Austro-Hungarian soldiers prisoner. During the three and a half years of fighting on the Eastern Front, some 5 million prisoners were taken by both sides. The largest number came from the Russians: 1.43 million taken by the Germans, and 1.27 million captured by Austro-Hungarian forces. The Russians in turn took 2.11 million Austro-Hungarian soldiers and 167,000 Germans.

Conditions in the camps were at first harsh, especially in Russia, due to lack of foresight and inadequate resources. Disease was rampant in some camps on both sides of the Eastern Front. Perhaps the worst example was in Russia where, at the Totskoye camp near Samarrah, a typhus epidemic in the winter of 1915–1916 claimed more than 9,000 of 17,000 prisoners housed there. Conditions for prisoners slowly improved with the construction of permanent shelters and the distribution of aid through the Red Cross. The revolutions in Russia in 1917 produced more freedom for the prisoners, but also brought chaos, as prisoners were often dependent on local authorities for their support.

All three of the major powers fighting on the Eastern Front endeavored to turn prisoners to fight against their own state. They segregated prisoners according to nationality and encouraged them to volunteer for national military formations. Both sides during the war, for example, formed Polish military units and promised that if their side won the war Poland would achieve independence.

At the beginning of the war, the Russians formed a brigade of Czechs living in Russia who desired to fight against Austria-Hungary for Czech independence. This brigade swelled into the Czech Legion as the Russians added to it Czechs who had either deserted or been captured from the Austro-Hungarian Army. Later, the Bolshevik government of Russia had some success in recruiting Hungarian prisoners of war, many of whom were radicalized while incarcerated. The leadership of the short-lived Hungarian Soviet Republic after the war included a number of former Russian prisoners, among them Béla Kun.

Unfortunately for the prisoners of war held on the Eastern Front, the end of the war did not bring their speedy repatriation. Revolution, the collapse of public services, and the Russian Civil War (1918–1922) all imposed additional problems. Perhaps a half million Central Powers prisoners were trapped in Siberia and Central Asia until the end of the Russian Civil War in 1920. The last prisoners were not repatriated until 1922. Norwegian Fridtjof Nansen, appointed by the Council of the League of Nations to coordinate the release of those remaining, was awarded the Nobel Peace Prize in 1922 for his work.

AFRICA

During the initial invasion by South African forces of German South West Africa (today's Namibia), the Germans took a number of prisoners. Held in camps at Tsumeb and Namutoni in the north of the colony, they were generally treated well. When South African forces finally triumphed in South West Africa in mid-1915, they reciprocated the favor regarding prisoner treatment.

In the prolonged fighting on the other side of the continent in German East Africa, the Germans also took a number of Allied prisoners and held them for much of the war. The principal complaint of Allied soldiers held by the Germans in Africa seems to have been that they were guarded by native African troops.

MIDDLE EAST

Prisoners held by the Ottoman Empire during the war suffered difficult conditions indeed. The majority of the British prisoners taken by the Ottomans, most of them in the siege of Kut-al-Amara (December 7, 1915–April 29, 1916), suffered terribly, despite promises that they would be held under humane conditions. Of more than 8,000 British and Indian troops taken at Kut in April 1916, nearly 5,000 died before the end of the war. In part this was because conditions were so difficult for the Turks themselves. According British prisoners, the same standards as Ottoman soldiers condemned a large number to death. In all, 70 percent of British prisoners of war held in Ottoman camps died.

Ottoman prisoners held by the British were significantly better cared for, although there were problems at first, largely due to lack of shelter; trachoma led to blindness in at least one eye in about 10 percent (15,000) of Ottoman prisoners held by the British.

Some 18,000 Ottoman prisoners were also held in India and Burma, but little is known about conditions there. The British also extensively recruited Arab prisoners to fight on the side of the Arab Revolt against Ottoman rule. As was the case with prisoners from other nations held there, Ottoman prisoners in Russia suffered greatly in the course of the war. Perhaps 25 percent of Ottoman prisoners held in Russia died there during the war.

FAR EAST

During the war, the Japanese, Australian, and New Zealand forces captured the German Pacific islands and the German cession at Qingdao (Tsingtao) in China after the siege there during August 23–November 2, 1917. There was little fighting, save at Qingdao, and the number of prisoners taken was small. There was no general internment of German civilians taken, save on Rabaul where most were soon released. The largest number of prisoners was among those taken by the Japanese in the siege of Qingdao. Some 4,600 German prisoners of war were held in 12 (later 8) Japanese camps in Japan, where they were well treated and received assistance from the Japanese YMCA.

Throughout the war, conditions for prisoners of war varied substantially, depending on circumstance. While there were certainly individual acts of violence against prisoners, the Great War also saw an absence of state policies to deny prisoners the rights accorded to them under international law. They were not intentionally starved or worked to death, or used in medical experiments, as was the practice of some governments during World War II.

Spencer C. Tucker

See also: Armenian Genocide; Deir ez Zor; Holzminden; Ruhleben.

Further Reading

Burdick, Charles, and Ursula Moessner. *The German Prisoners of War in Japan, 1914–1920*. Lanham, MD: University Press of America, 1984.

Dennett, Carl P. *Prisoners of the Great War*. Boston: Houghton Mifflin, 1919.

Farwell, Byron. *The Great War in Africa, 1914–1918*. New York: Norton, 1986.

Fischer, Gerhard. *Enemy Aliens: Internment and the Homefront Experience in Australia, 1914–1920*. St. Lucia: University of Queensland Press, 1989.

Hoffman, Conrad. *In the Prison Camps of Germany: A Narrative of "Y" Service among Prisoners of War*. New York: Association Press, 1920.

Jackson, Robert. *The Prisoners, 1914–18*. London: Routledge, 1989.

Ketchum, J. Davidson. *Ruhleben: A Prison Camp Society*. Toronto: University of Toronto Press, 1965.

Speed, Richard B. *Prisoners, Diplomats, and the Great War: A Study in the Diplomacy of Captivity*. New York: Greenwood, 1990.

Vance, Jonathan F., ed. *Encyclopedia of Prisoners of War and Internment*. Santa Barbara, CA: ABC-CLIO, 2000.

World War II Prisoners of War

In 1929, the Geneva Convention Relative to the Treatment of Prisoners of War replaced the Hague Convention of 1907 regarding protection of POWs. The Hague Convention had dealt primarily with the means of war (for example, it prohibited the use of exploding bullets), whereas the Geneva Convention dealt exclusively with the protection of victims of war. It held that POWs should be considered on a par with the detaining power's garrison troops as far as rations, living space, clothing, and access to medical care were concerned. It also addressed such issues as permissible work and punishment, and access to letters and packages. Forty powers signed the convention, but the Soviet Union did not, meaning that prisoners taken by its forces were not subject to Geneva Convention protection. Although the Japanese delegates at Geneva signed the POW convention, the Tokyo government never ratified it. Its military leaders assumed no Japanese would be taken prisoner and that the convention would thus be applied unilaterally. Cultural attitudes also played an important role, and authorized punishments for POWs were much milder than those the Japanese meted out to their own soldiers. Although in 1942 the Japanese government pledged to live up to the spirit of the convention, its treatment of Allied POWs during the war clearly ran counter to its assurance.

EUROPE, EASTERN FRONT

On September 1, 1939, German forces invaded Poland; two days later Britain and France declared war on Germany, igniting World War II. Two weeks later, Soviet forces invaded Eastern Poland in accordance with the secret provisions of the August 1939 German-Soviet Non-aggression Pact. In 1940, Soviet authorities executed perhaps 15,000 Polish officers in the Katyń Forest of eastern Poland. Prisoners taken by the Germans were sent to slave-labor camps. The Poles thus did not benefit from the Geneva Convention.

In June 1941, German forces invaded the Soviet Union. In response to inquiries by the U.S. government, Moscow had stated that the Soviet Union would observe the Hague Convention of 1907 regarding land warfare, the Geneva Protocol of 1925 regarding chemical and bacteriological warfare, and the Geneva Convention of 1929 regarding care for the wounded and sick of warring armies. However, the Soviets said they would observe the agreements on POWs only as "they were observed by the Germans."

The German government was as obstinate on the issue as the Soviets, and the cost was ultimately very high for the POWs captured in the fighting. Both German and Soviet POWs suffered conditions that were approached only by treatment accorded prisoners of the Japanese. Of some 5.7 million Soviet soldiers taken prisoner by the Germans, at least 3.3 million died in captivity, a mortality rate of 57 percent. This compares with a mortality rate of only 3.5 to 5.1 percent for British and American POWs in German hands.

Many Soviet prisoners taken early in the fighting were simply starved to death. According to Adolf Hitler's notorious Commissar Order, political officers were to be shot on capture. Jewish soldiers taken prisoner were handed over to the SS to be executed. Conditions were horrendous for the others. The Germans marched the prisoners long distances to the rear, and there were no prepared lodging or sanitary facilities and little food for them when they reached the camp locations. As a result, POWs died by the hundreds of thousands. The leaders of the Reich regarded the prisoners as subhuman and treated them accordingly. Of 3.2 million Soviet soldiers taken prisoner by December 1941, 2 million were dead by February 1942.

As the German advance came to a halt and it became impossible to demobilize German soldiers, the Reich's leaders sought to make more effective use of the Soviet POWs by putting them to work in difficult conditions in road building, mining, and agriculture. Not until mid-1944, however, did food rations for Soviet POWs approach those of other Allied POWs in German captivity. So difficult was it for Soviet prisoners of war that at least a quarter million volunteered to serve as auxiliaries to the German army, working as cooks, drivers, and the like, in an effort simply to stay alive. Tens of thousands of others also agreed to serve in a German-sponsored Russian Liberation Army led by former Soviet lieutenant general Andrei A. Vlasov. Hitler, however, refused it any combat role and it became simply a means to encourage desertions.

The plight of Soviet POWs in German hands did not end with the defeat of Germany. Soviet leader Joseph Stalin's infamous Order 270 of August 1941 had branded as traitors all Red Army personnel who allowed themselves to be taken prisoner, regardless of circumstances. It also ordered rations cut off to their families. Of some 1.8 million Soviet POWs repatriated at the end of the war, at least 150,000 were sentenced to long prison terms of forced labor for having "aided the enemy."

On the other side, about a third of the nearly 3 million German and Austrian soldiers taken by the Soviets in the war died in captivity. Of some 91,000 Germans taken prisoner in the Battle of Stalingrad, fewer than 5,000 survived Soviet captivity. Death rates were comparable for the 2 million Axis soldiers taken prisoner by the Soviets.

The only difference in German and Soviet treatment of POWs was that, for the Germans, it was systematic government policy to work the prisoners to death, whereas POWs in Soviet hands fell victim to the general inefficiency and indifference of the Soviet POW camp system (GUPVI), lack of resources in a country ravaged by war, and individual acts of reprisal. Rising numbers of German POWs after 1942 simply overwhelmed available Soviet means to care for them. The Soviets did not begin major repatriation of its POWs until 1947, and the last were not released until 1956.

WESTERN EUROPE

During World War II in Europe and North Africa, the Axis powers captured some 8.5 to 9 million enemy soldiers, of whom 6 million—the vast majority—were Soviets. In turn, the Allies took some 8.25 million Axis soldiers captive, 3.4 million of whom surrendered with the end of hostilities on the Western Front.

Few problems were reported for prisoners held by the Italian government. Experiences for POWs held by the Germans varied according to their citizenship. Treatment was decidedly better for western Europeans and North Americans than for those from eastern or southern Europe. The Germans did not expend scarce resources on the prisoners, however. Thus, in consequence of the high number of parcels sent to western Allied POWs, the German government decided to cut food rations to U.S. and British Commonwealth POWs by one-third, forcing these Allied governments to subsidize German Geneva Convention obligations. The Germans did, however, employ many of its French and Belgian POWs in labor activities (such as the armaments industry) that directly benefited the German war effort.

The Germans organized their POW camps quite methodically. Internally, the camps were run by the prisoners. Generally there was an SAO—Senior Allied Officer or Senior American Officer, depending on the mix of prisoners. Officers were segregated from enlisted men. Stalags were camps that held enlisted personnel, as well as noncommissioned officers. Oflags were camps with only officers and some noncommissioned officers. In stalags, there was generally a "man of confidence" who was usually elected by his fellow POWs, although on occasion he was appointed by the Germans.

Camps usually contained more than one compound, and prisoners were segregated among the compounds by uniform, not by claimed citizenship. Hence, U.S. personnel who flew with the RAF and were captured in RAF uniform were considered to be British and housed with British flyers. Compounds held French, Russians, British, Commonwealth, and various other nationalities. Some camps held only one nationality; some held many different nationalities.

There were also prisoner of war camps located in areas that held concentration camps. Auschwitz, which is known for being an extermination center, was actually a complex of camps comprising more than just the extermination center. French, Soviet, and other nationalities of POWs were held there. Two exceptions to the generally satisfactory German treatment of western POWs came in Hitler's Commando Order of October 1942, which allowed the killing out-of-hand of Allied commandoes, and Berga, a Buchenwald sub-camp that held 352 U.S. "Jewish" POWs. Of that number, only 70 were actually Jewish, but the others were chosen by the Germans because they "appeared" Jewish. Prisoners were regularly beaten and starved, and several were murdered.

There have been unsubstantiated charges in recent years of British and U.S. mistreatment of German POWs in the months immediately following the end of the war in Europe. There is, however, no proof of this, nor of any widespread mistreatment of Axis prisoners of war by British and U.S. authorities during the war itself.

FAR EAST

Japanese cultural attitudes played an overwhelming role in Japanese treatment of its POWs. The Japanese believed that soldiers should die in battle rather than surrender and that those who allowed themselves to be taken prisoner had dishonored themselves. Japanese treatment of POWs was atrocious. Prisoners were subject to torture, starvation, beatings, and denial of medical care. Most were required to perform slave labor, from building railroads to working in coal mines and factories, all of which were forbidden by the Geneva Convention. Mistreatment was rampant, as were disease and starvation, not only among military prisoners, but with civilian internees. Nor would the Japanese allow humanitarian aid to reach the prisoners.

The generally accepted figure for Allied POWs in Japanese hands is 320,000: 140,000 Europeans and North Americans and 180,000 Chinese, Filipino, Indian, and other Asian troops. Most of Japan's prisoners were taken in the Japanese successes of late 1941 and early 1942, especially in the Netherlands East Indies. Although the Japanese soon released many of the nonwhite prisoners, they held their white captives until the surrender in 1945. The Japanese captured some 25,600 U.S. prisoners. Of these, 8,288 died, a rate of 35.6 percent. This was appreciably higher than the rate for all prisoners who died in Japanese hands: 37,800 or

26.9 percent. Part of this disparity was the result of the many American and Filipino POWs who died in the Bataan Death March. Prisoners of the Japanese received
no medical care and little food, and they were seldom allowed to contact their families. Many of the prisoners were transferred from the Philippines and other places
to Japan or Manchuria to prison camps. Sent by ship, the prisoners were entombed
below decks with little or no access to fresh air or water. Many hundreds of men
died in these "Hell Ships" of the conditions, but the exact total is unknown. Several of the ships, unmarked by the Japanese as transporting POWs, were sunk by
Allied planes or submarines. In addition, many POWs who ended up in Manchuria were subjected to the horrors of biological warfare and vivisection experiments
carried out by the infamous Japanese Unit 731. Japanese military codes forbade
surrender, and in consequence, the western Allies took very few Japanese prisoners. On Iwo Jima, U.S. Marines took fewer than 300 prisoners from the 21,000-
man Japanese garrison, and only about 7,400 of nearly 115,000 Japanese soldiers
on Okinawa surrendered. It is also true that once Allied soldiers learned of the barbaric treatment accorded by the Japanese to their prisoners, there was a tendency
to decline to take prisoners, although this was never official policy.

Some 633,000 Japanese personnel were taken prisoner in Southeast Asia, and
most of them surrendered to the British at the end of the war. Many of these were
held well after the war and worked as laborers without pay. Only in October 1947
were Japanese released from Singapore. Some Japanese POWs were also rearmed
and forced to serve with Dutch forces in the Netherlands East Indies in violation
of international law, and nearly 1,000 died.

It is unclear how many Japanese were taken prisoner by the Soviet Union, which
entered the war in the Pacific on August 9, 1945. The Soviets claimed to have captured 594,000 Japanese and claimed that upward of 71,000 of these were immediately freed. Japanese scholars, however, insist that the number was much higher.
Sent to Siberia, the Japanese worked there for several years before they were
released. Because of the dishonor associated with being captured, few Japanese ex-
POWs have left memoirs of their experiences. The record of Americans and Europeans held by the Japanese is, however, well documented.

NORTH AMERICA

When the United States entered World War II, little thought had been given to the
establishment of POW facilities. In March 1942, President Franklin D. Roosevelt
authorized the evacuation of Japanese Americans from "military areas," especially
on the West Coast of the United States. Ultimately some 120,000 Japanese Americans were affected. Although they were not called prisoners of war, they were interned
in camps in Wyoming, California, Colorado, Arizona, Idaho, and Arkansas.

Following the Axis defeat in North Africa, large numbers of German and Ital-
ian POWs were brought to camps in the United States. Ultimately, some 425,000
Axis prisoners of war were held in the United States. By the end of the war, the
United States had established 141 permanent base camps and 319 branch camps,
each holding an average of about 2,500 prisoners. Given the labor shortage in the
United States because of the demands of the war, many of the POWs went to work,

but they were paid for their labor according to rank. Officers were not required to work, although several did accept supervisory positions. Contractors who hired the POWs paid the U.S. government some $22 million for their services, so that the program was nearly self-sufficient. By the end of the war, of 370,000 POWs in the United States, nearly 200,000 were employed in nonmilitary jobs, most of them in agriculture. Conditions in the U.S. camps were generally excellent. The major problem came from die-hard Nazi fellow prisoners, who had to be segregated in special camps.

Following the war, several U.S.-held POWs were turned over to France and Britain to work in mines and help clear bombed roads and cities. Most of these POWs were repatriated to Germany in late 1947 and early 1948, embittered over their postwar treatment.

Spencer C. Tucker and Patricia Wadley

See also: Bataan Death March (1942); Britain; Canada; Denmark; Finland; Germany; Hitler, Adolf; Japan; Katyń Forest Massacre; Sandakan Death Marches; Soviet Union, POW Camps (1941–1956); Stalag; Stalin, Joseph; Switzerland; Unit 731; Zamperini, Louis.

Further Reading

Beattie, Edward J., Jr. *Diary of a Kriegie.* New York: Thomas Y. Crowell, 1946.

Durand, Arthur A. *Stalag Luft III: The Secret Story.* Baton Rouge: Louisiana State University Press, 1988.

Foy, David A. *For You the War Is Over: American Prisoners of War in Nazi Germany.* New York: Stein and Day, 1984.

Hirschfeld, Gerhard, ed. *The Politics of Genocide: Jewish and Soviet Prisoners of War in Nazi Germany.* Boston: Allen and Unwin, 1986.

Hubbard, Preston John. *Apocalypse Undone: My Survival of Japanese Imprisonment during World War II.* Nashville, TN: Vanderbilt University Press, 1990.

Knox, Donald. *Death March: The Survivors of Bataan.* New York: Harcourt Brace Jovanovich, 1981.

Kochan, Miriam. *Prisoners of England.* London: Macmillan Press, 1980.

MacKenzie, S. P. "The Treatment of Prisoners of War in World War II," *Journal of Modern History* 66 (1994): 487–520.

Roland, Charles G. "Allied POWs, Japanese Captures, and the Geneva Convention," *War and Society* 9 (1991): 83–101.

Thompson, Kyle. *A Thousand Cups of Rice: Surviving the Death Railway.* Austin, TX: Easkin Press, 1994.

Vance, Jonathan F., ed. *Encyclopedia of Prisoners of War and Internment.* Santa Barbara, CA: ABC-CLIO, 2000.

Y

Yokohama Trials (1946–1951)

At the end of World War II, the Allied powers conducted war crimes trials involving Japanese defendants, primarily through International Military Tribunal for the Far East (IMTFE), as 'class A" defendants. Other Japanese officials—5,700 in total—were tried as "class B and C" defendants for wartime offences before Allied military courts throughout Asia-Pacific. There were more than 2,000 regional trials, held before 50 tribunals. One ran between 1946 and 1951 in Yokohama, Japan before commissions of the U.S. 8th Army.

One of Japan's largest cities, a major port, and just 30 miles from Tokyo, Yokohama saw much of the war. It was a target of the famous Doolittle raids in April 1942. In May 1945, nearly half the city was destroyed in incendiary bombing. That August, the Supreme Commander of Allied forces in the Pacific, American general Douglas MacArthur, set up his command headquarters there. Yet in some respects, Yokohama saw even more of the war with the parade of Japanese officials tried before it. Among the accused were military men from all services and ranks, but also medical personnel and bureaucrats. Most crimes involved the abuse of prisoners of war, who endured severe malnutrition, torture, and even summary execution. Whereas only 4 percent of American, British, or Commonwealth prisoners held by the Germans and Italians died in captivity, 27 percent died in Japanese camps. With this in mind it is not surprising that many class B defendants at Yokohama were prison guards. Class C defendants were predominantly senior military officers who ordered or failed to prevent such crimes.

Also in class B at Yokohama were members of Japan's notorious Kempei-tai, or secret police. Over 1,500 men in this service were tried at regional trials, representing about one-quarter of all Japanese war criminals. Yokohama trials also saw doctors, scientists, and technicians who took part in barbaric experiments on Allied personnel. Many of the accused worked for the Japanese Imperial Army's Unit 731, which developed biological and chemical weapons. In March 1948, 30 members of Unit 731 were tried at Yokohama for unlawful vivisection and the removal of body parts. Charges of cannibalism against some defendants were also laid. Twenty-three were convicted, 5 were sentenced to death, 4 received life sentences, and 14 were given prison terms. However, in September 1950, with the Korean War underway, General MacArthur commuted most of the sentences. By 1958 all were released. Facing increasing Cold War tensions, some believe that senior U.S. officials quietly intervened to free the accused, anxious to use the Unit's research for similar American programs.

Also tried at Yokohama were Japanese sailors charged in the deaths of more than 1,300 men aboard the ill-fated *Oryoku Maru*. One of the infamous "Hell

Ships"—unmarked freighters used to transport prisoners—the *Oryoku Maru* was packed with 1,619 men in abysmal conditions. En route from Manila to Japan in December 1944, the ship was attacked by American planes, unaware of the captives onboard. In the ensuing chaos, Japanese guards killed 286 prisoners. The survivors were re-boarded on the *Enoura Maru*, which was also hit by an American attack, with the loss of several hundred more. Only 490 reached Japan in late January 1945; 161 more died shortly thereafter of disease and malnutrition. In total, only 271 men survived the affair. At Yokohama, the captain of the guards and an interpreter on the *Oryoku Maru* were sentenced to death, while four others drew prison sentences.

Arraigned as class B criminals, employees of prominent Japanese businesses were also tried at Yokohama. Best known was Kajima Corporation—today one of the largest construction companies in the world—which during the war used thousands of Chinese slave-laborers. In June 1945, at its copper mine facility in Hanaoka, Japan, about 1,000 starving Chinese revolted. Nearly all were savagely hunted down, tortured, and killed. Only three Kajima executives were implicated, all found guilty and sentenced to death. However, in 1956 all three were released. The Japanese government even compensated the corporation for the loss of its slaves.

As was the case with most regional trials, at Yokohama many of the accused were tried conjointly on charges stemming from specific incidents. The hearings at Yokohama were also noted for large amounts of documentary evidence submitted by the prosecution, chiefly eye-witness affidavits. The trials, however, may be best remembered for the relatively lenient treatment of many accused. Anxious to rebuild Japan and count it as an ally in the Cold War, American officials were evidently willing to forget some of the worst war crimes in history, just as occurred in Germany.

Arne Kislenko

See also: Far East, British Military Trials; Nuremberg Trials.

Further Reading

Buruma, Ian. *Wages of Guilt: Memories of War in Germany and Japan.* New York: Farrar, Straus and Giroux, 1994.

Dower, John W. *Embracing Defeat: Japan in the Wake of World War II.* New York: W.W. Norton, 1999.

Hosoya, Chihiro, ed. *The Tokyo War Crimes Trials: An International Symposium.* Tokyo: Kodansha, 1986.

Minnear, Richard. *Victor's Justice: The Tokyo War Crimes Trial.* Princeton, NJ: Princeton University Press, 1971.

Piccigallo, P.R. *The Japanese on Trial: Allied War Crimes Operations in the Far East 1945–1951.* Austin: University of Texas Press, 1979.

Yugoslavia

During World War II, the Kingdom of Yugoslavia fell to the German and Italian invasions in 1941. The kingdom was partitioned between Germany, Italy, Hungary, and Bulgaria and client regimes were set up: Independent State of Croatia, led by

Ante Pavelić, emerged in the north and the Serbian Government of National Salvation, under the leadership of Milan Nedić, existed in the south. Between 1941 and 1944, as many as 70 concentration and extermination camps were set up in Yugoslavia, some maintained by the German authorities, other by their local collaborators, such as the Croatian Ustaša. It has been estimated that almost 2 million people had been detained and killed at these camps, including at Sajmište, Sremska Mitrovica, Sisak, Gospić, and Jasenovac; most victims were ethnic Serbs, Jews, and Romanis, as well as political opponents of the regimes.

After the end of World War II, the National Liberation Army and Partisan Detachments of Yugoslavia, the Communist-led resistance to the Axis powers in occupied Yugoslavia, exacted a measure of ruthless vengeance on collaborators, as well as German minorities. The Communist-run camps at Bački Jarak, Gakovo, Kruševlje, Molin, and Knićanin interned hundreds of thousands of people, who had been subjected to abuse and mistreatment; almost 50,000 of the Danube Swabians, a German minority, perished in these camps before they were disbanded in 1948–1949.

Concentration camps made a comeback after the collapse of Yugoslavia and the start of the Yugoslavian Civil Wars in 1991. Numerous abuses and crimes had been committed at the detention camps at Omarska, Keraterm, Manjača, Trnopolje, Uzamnica, and Vilina Vlas, with some key perpetrators later prosecuted and convicted by the International Criminal Tribunal for the former Yugoslavia.

Alexander Mikaberidze

See also: Bosnian War; Germany; Jasenovac; Sajmište, Sisak; Sremska Mitrovica; Ustaše.

Further Reading

Baker, Catherine. *The Yugoslav Wars of the 1990s.* New York: Macmillian Education Palgrave, 2015.

Faber, Marion, Roy Gutman, and Alexandra Stiglmayer. *Mass Rape: The War against Women in Bosnia-Herzegovina.* Lincoln: University of Nebraska Press, 1994.

Gallagher, Tom. *The Balkans after the Cold War: From Tyranny to Tragedy.* London: Routledge, 2005.

Z

Zamperini, Louis (1917–2014)

American prisoner of war and survivor of Japanese captivity during World War II. Born in Olean, New York, Zamperini discovered his passion for running while still in high school and quickly excelled at it. By 1930s, he was one of the top American runners and qualified for the 5000m race for the 1936 Berlin Olympics; he finished 8th in the event.

When Japan attacked the United States in December 1941, Zamperini joined U.S. Army Air Forces and served as a bombardier in B-24 Liberators in the Pacific Ocean. In April 1943, during a bombing mission against the Japanese-held island of Nauru, Zamperini's aircraft was badly damaged and crashed in the ocean. Zamperini and two other survivors managed to inflate a raft and drifted at sea for over a month; on the 47th day, they landed on the Japanese-occupied Marshall Islands and were captured.

Initially held at Kwajalein Atoll, Zamperini was moved to various Japanese prisoner of war camps (including at Ofuna, Omori, and Naoetsu), where he was subjected to abuse and torture, but stoically endured two and a half years of captivity. He was liberated at the end of the war. In later years, Zamperini wrote memoirs about his experiences and became subject of the best-selling book *Unbroken: A World War II Story of Survival, Resilience, and Redemption* (2010), which was adapted into a feature film, *Unbroken* (2014).

Alexander Mikaberidze

See also: Japan; World War II Prisoners of War.

Further Reading

Hillenbrand, Laura. *Unbroken: A World War II Story of Survival, Resilience, and Redemption.* New York: Random House, 2010.

Zamperini, Louis, with David Rensin. *Devil at My Heels: A World War II Hero's Epic Saga of Torment, Survival, and Forgiveness.* New York: HarperCollins Publishers, 2003.

Zyklon B Case (1946)

In the Trial of Bruno Tesch and Two Others (March 1–March 8, 1946), the British Military Court in Hamburg tried Tesch, Karl Weinbacher, and Joachim Drosihn of Tesch & Stabenow (Testa), for complicity in the murder of Allied internees. The indictment charged that the defendants had supplied the Nazi Schutzstaffel (SS) with Zyklon B (prussic acid), in full knowledge of its use against human beings. Arguing that private individuals who knowingly provide state institutions with the

Canisters contain the Zyklon B gas that was used for human extermination during the Holocaust. (Corbis via Getty Images)

means to commit mass murder are themselves guilty of war crimes, the prosecution charged that the defendants had violated Article 46 of the Hague Regulations of 1907, by abetting the extermination of citizens in territory under military occupation. The court convicted Tesch and Weinbacher and sentenced them to death, but acquitted Drosihn. The British executed Tesch and Weinbacher on May 16, 1946.

Testa was one among several firms involved in Zyklon B distribution. In the interwar years, Deutsche Gold- und Silber-Scheideanstalt (Degussa, German Gold- and Silver-Separation Society), I.G. Farbenindustrie AG (I.G. Farben, Community of Interests, Dye Industry), and Thomas Goldschmidt AG, formed a holding company for insecticides, Deutsche Gesellschaft für Schädlingsbekämpfung (Degesch, German Society for Pest Control). Degesch furnished gas-absorbent pellets, canisters, and other materials to manufacturers Dessauer Werke and Kali Werke. Heerdt-Lingler (Heli) monopolized sales in southern and western Germany. Founded as a partnership by Tesch and Paul Stabenow in 1923, Testa's territory north and east of the Elbe eventually included Auschwitz, where it sold 12 tons of the fumigant in 1943. Until June 1942, Degesch had a controlling interest in Testa, after which Tesch became sole owner. Except when training personnel in fumigation or the use of Degesch delousing chambers, Testa's employees did not directly handle the product.

Convened under the Royal Warrant of June 14, 1945, the British Military Court of Hamburg consisted of Brigadier R.B.L. Persse (president), Lieutenant Colonel Sir Geoffrey Palmer, Major S.M. Johnstone, and Captain H.S. Marshall (alternate). C.L. Stirling, Esq., was Judge Advocate and Major G.I.D. Draper was the prosecutor. Counsel for Tesch, Weinbacher, and Drosihn were respectively Dr. O. Zippel, Dr. C. Stumme, and Dr. A. Stegemann. The Royal Warrant provided for admission of limited hearsay evidence, but confined jurisdiction to war crimes, not crimes against humanity, committed by Germany or Japan against Allied nationals after September 2, 1939. The Royal Warrant also provided for the accused to testify in their own defense, a right availed by each defendant in this case. The indictment excluded German gas victims and, as was then customary, subsumed the Jewish victims' identity under the rubric of Allied nationalities. The British Military Court asserted jurisdiction over the Tesch Case because Testa was headquartered in Hamburg and the charges involved many nationalities.

Hearsay testimony and circumstantial evidence played crucial roles in the conviction of Tesch and Weinbacher. Bookkeeper Eric Sehm described a company travel report (*Reisebericht*) from late 1942, which summarized Tesch's interview with German officers, allegedly from the Wehrmacht (armed forces), not the SS. After mentioning the shooting of Jews on the Eastern Front, the officials solicited Tesch's advice concerning the use of Zyklon B for the enhancement of killing efficiency. Tesch offered technical assistance on the spot. Sehm took notes about the report, but later destroyed them on the advice of Wilhelm Pook, another witness who partly endorsed his account. Two former stenographers, Erna Biagini and Anna Uenzelmann, confirmed their chief's knowledge of mass murder by Zyklon B. The court determined that Tesch had visited Sachsenhausen, Neuengamme, and Gross-Rosen concentration camps, but never Auschwitz. By emphasizing Tesch's meticulousness, counselor Zippel inadvertently aided the case against his client, because the Judge Advocate subsequently cited that characteristic as proof that Tesch must have known how the SS used his product.

Unable to adduce direct evidence against Weinbacher, the prosecution stressed his position as Prokurist, the deputy empowered to transact business in Tesch's absence. Denying that he had seen the damning travel reports, Weinbacher claimed that his heavy workload prevented his reading every document. For 200 days per year, however, Weinbacher directed the firm while Tesch traveled on business. The prosecution argued that Weinbacher was in a circumstantial position to know how the firm's customers used Zyklon B.

As first gassing technician, Drosihn visited several concentration camps in while servicing Degesch chambers. The prosecution was unable to prove that he knew of any illegitimate purpose for Zyklon B before the end of the war, or that he was in a position to influence company policy.

Like the Nuremberg industrialist cases, the Zyklon B case established the precedent that private persons could be held accountable for the commission of war crimes. The specific findings contrasted with the I.G. Farben Case, however, in which the defendants who had supervisory roles in Degesch were acquitted of complicity in genocide, because the prosecution was unable to establish their direct knowledge of criminal activities.

Joseph Robert White

See also: Auschwitz; Bełżec; Bergen-Belsen; Birkenau; Buchenwald; Chełmno; Concentration Camps; Dachau; Death Camps; Dora-Mittelbau; Eichmann, Adolf; Extermination Centers; Gas Chambers; Gestapo; Hitler, Adolf; Holocaust, The; I.G. Farben Case (1947); J.A. Topf & Söhne; Koch Trial (1951); Kramer, Josef; Krupp Case (1948); Mauthausen-Gusen; Monowitz; Natzweiler-Struthof; Neuengamme; Niederhagen; Nuremberg Trials; Ravensbrück; Sachsenhausen; Sobibór; Treblinka.

Further Reading

Allen, Michael Thad. "The Devil in the Details: The Gas Chambers of Birkenau, October 1941," *Holocaust and Genocide Studies* 16:2 (Fall 2002): 189–202.

Hayes, Peter. *Industry and Ideology: I.G. Farben in the Nazi Era.* Cambridge: Cambridge University Press, 1987.

United Nations War Crimes Commission. Law Reports of Trials of War Criminals. Vol. I. London: HMSO, 1949.

United States. Nuremberg Military Tribunals. Trials of War Criminals Before the Nuremberg Military Tribunals Under Control Council Law No. 10. Vol. VIII. Washington: GPO, 1950–1953.

PRIMARY DOCUMENTS

Instructions for the Government of Armies of the United States in the Field (Lieber Code) (1863)

Written by Francis Lieber and distributed to the Union Army in April 1863, Lieber's Code (General Order No. 100) was a set of rules of conduct for the military that attempted to anticipate every possible combative and non-combative situation. The code had a tremendous impact worldwide, particularly shaping the training of the Prussian Army after 1870. Lieber's Code served as the foundation for the rules of warfare established and accepted by all major Western nations in the late nineteenth century. Sections III–VII of the code contain provisions on the treatment of the captured enemy combatants, deserters, and hostages.

Section III: Deserters—Prisoners of War—Hostages—Booty on the Battle-field

Art. 49. A prisoner of war is a public enemy armed or attached to the hostile army for active aid, who has fallen into the hands of the captor, either fighting or wounded, on the field or in the hospital, by individual surrender or by capitulation.

All soldiers, of whatever species of arms; all men who belong to the rising en masse of the hostile country; all those who are attached to the army for its efficiency and promote directly the object of the war, except such as are hereinafter provided for; all disabled men or officers on the field or elsewhere, if captured; all enemies who have thrown away their arms and ask for quarter, are prisoners of war, and as such exposed to the inconveniences as well as entitled to the privileges of a prisoner of war.

Art. 50. Moreover, citizens who accompany an army for whatever purpose, such as sutlers, editors, or reporters of journals, or contractors, if captured, may be made prisoners of war, and be detained as such.

The monarch and members of the hostile reigning family, male or female, the chief, and chief officers of the hostile government, its diplomatic agents, and all persons who are of particular and singular use and benefit to the hostile army or its government, are, if captured on belligerent ground, and if unprovided with a safe conduct granted by the captor's government, prisoners of war.

Art. 51. If the people of that portion of an invaded country which is not yet occupied by the enemy, or of the whole country, at the approach of a hostile army, rise, under a duly authorized levy, en masse to resist the invader, they are now treated as public enemies, and, if captured, are prisoners of war.

Art. 52. No belligerent has the right to declare that he will treat every captured man in arms of a levy en masse as a brigand or bandit.

If, however, the people of a country, or any portion of the same, already occupied by an army, rise against it, they are violators of the laws of war, and are not entitled to their protection.

Art. 53. The enemy's chaplains, officers of the medical staff, apothecaries, hospital nurses, and servants, if they fall into the hands of the American Army, are not prisoners of war, unless the commander has reasons to retain them. In this latter case, or if, at their own desire, they are allowed to remain with their captured companions, they are treated as prisoners of war, and may be exchanged if the commander sees fit.

Art. 56. A prisoner of war is subject to no punishment for being a public enemy, nor is any revenge wreaked upon him by the intentional infliction of any suffering, or disgrace, by cruel imprisonment, want of food, by mutilation, death, or any other barbarity.

Art. 57. So soon as a man is armed by a sovereign government and takes the soldier's oath of fidelity, he is a belligerent; his killing, wounding, or other warlike acts are not individual crimes or offenses. No belligerent has a right to declare that enemies of a certain class, color, or condition, when properly organized as soldiers, will not be treated by him as public enemies.

Art. 58. The law of nations knows of no distinction of color, and if an enemy of the United States should enslave and sell any captured persons of their army, it would be a case for the severest retaliation, if not redressed upon complaint.

The United States cannot retaliate by enslavement; therefore death must be the retaliation for this crime against the law of nations.

Art. 59. A prisoner of war remains answerable for his crimes committed against the captor's army or people, committed before he was captured, and for which he has not been punished by his own authorities.

All prisoners of war are liable to the infliction of retaliatory measures.

Art. 60. It is against the usage of modern war to resolve, in hatred and revenge, to give no quarter. No body of troops has the right to declare that it will not give, and therefore will not expect, quarter; but a commander is permitted to direct his troops to give no quarter, in great straits, when his own salvation makes it impossible to cumber himself with prisoners.

Art. 61. Troops that give no quarter have no right to kill enemies already disabled on the ground, or prisoners captured by other troops.

Art. 62. All troops of the enemy known or discovered to give no quarter in general, or to any portion of the army, receive none.

Art. 63. Troops who fight in the uniform of their enemies, without any plain, striking, and uniform mark of distinction of their own, can expect no quarter.

Art. 72. Money and other valuables on the person of a prisoner, such as watches or jewelry, as well as extra clothing, are regarded by the American Army as the private property of the prisoner, and the appropriation of such valuables or money is considered dishonorable, and is prohibited.

Nevertheless, if large sums are found upon the persons of prisoners, or in their possession, they shall be taken from them, and the surplus, after providing for their own support, appropriated for the use of the army, under the direction of the commander, unless otherwise ordered by the government. Nor can prisoners claim, as private property, large sums found and captured in their train, although they have been placed in the private luggage of the prisoners.

Art. 73. All officers, when captured, must surrender their side arms to the captor. They may be restored to the prisoner in marked cases, by the commander, to signalize admiration of his distinguished bravery or approbation of his humane treatment of prisoners before his capture. The captured officer to whom they may be restored cannot wear them during captivity.

Art. 74. A prisoner of war, being a public enemy, is the prisoner of the government, and not of the captor. No ransom cam be paid by a prisoner of war to his individual captor or to any officer in command. The government alone releases captives, according to rules prescribed by itself.

Art. 75. Prisoners of war are subject to confinement or imprisonment such as may be deemed necessary on account of safety, but they are to be subjected to no other intentional suffering or indignity. The confinement and mode of treating a prisoner may be varied during his captivity according to the demands of safety.

Art. 76. Prisoners of war shall be fed upon plain and wholesome food, whenever practicable, and treated with humanity.

They may be required to work for the benefit of the captor's government, according to their rank and condition.

Art. 77. A prisoner of war who escapes may be shot or otherwise killed in his flight; but neither death nor any other punishment shall be inflicted upon him simply for his attempt to escape, which the law of war does not consider a crime. Stricter means of security shall be used after an unsuccessful attempt at escape.

If, however, a conspiracy is discovered, the purpose of which is a united or general escape, the conspirators may be rigorously punished, even with death; and capital punishment may also be inflicted upon prisoners of war discovered to have plotted rebellion against the authorities of the captors, whether in union with fellow prisoners or other persons.

Art. 78. If prisoners of war having given no pledge nor made any promise on their honor, forcibly or otherwise escape, and are captured again in battle after having rejoined their own army, they shall not be punished for their escape, but shall be treated as simple prisoners of war, although they will be subjected to stricter confinement.

Art. 79. Every captured wounded enemy shall be medically treated, according to the ability of the medical staff.

Art. 80. Honorable men, when captured, will abstain from giving to the enemy information concerning their own army, and the modern law of war permits no longer the use of any violence against prisoners in order to extort the desired information or to punish them for having given false information.

Section VI: Exchange of Prisoners—Flags of Truce—Flags of Protection

Art. 105. Exchanges of prisoners take place—number for number—rank for rank—wounded for wounded—with added condition for added condition—such, for instance, as not to serve for a certain period.

Art. 106. In exchanging prisoners of war, such numbers of persons of inferior rank may be substituted as an equivalent for one of superior rank as may be agreed upon by cartel, which requires the sanction of the government, or of the commander of the army in the field.

Art. 107. A prisoner of war is in honor bound truly to state to the captor his rank; and he is not to assume a lower rank than belongs to him, in order to cause a more advantageous exchange, nor a higher rank, for the purpose of obtaining better treatment.

Offenses to the contrary have been justly punished by the commanders of released prisoners, and may be good cause for refusing to release such prisoners.

Art. 108. The surplus number of prisoners of war remaining after an exchange has taken place is sometimes released either for the payment of a stipulated sum of money, or, in urgent cases, of provision, clothing, or other necessaries.

Such arrangement, however, requires the sanction of the highest authority.

Art. 109. The exchange of prisoners of war is an act of convenience to both belligerents. If no general cartel has been concluded, it cannot be demanded by either of them. No belligerent is obliged to exchange prisoners of war.

A cartel is voidable as soon as either party has violated it.

Art. 110. No exchange of prisoners shall be made except after complete capture, and after an accurate account of them, and a list of the captured officers, has been taken.

Section VII: Parole

Art. 119. Prisoners of war may be released from captivity by exchange, and, under certain circumstances, also by parole.

Art. 120. The term Parole designates the pledge of individual good faith and honor to do, or to omit doing, certain acts after he who gives his parole shall have been dismissed, wholly or partially, from the power of the captor.

Art. 121. The pledge of the parole is always an individual, but not a private act.

Art. 122. The parole applies chiefly to prisoners of war whom the captor allows to return to their country, or to live in greater freedom within the captor's country or territory, on conditions stated in the parole.

Art. 123. Release of prisoners of war by exchange is the general rule; release by parole is the exception.

Art. 124. Breaking the parole is punished with death when the person breaking the parole is captured again.

Accurate lists, therefore, of the paroled persons must be kept by the belligerents.

Art. 125. When paroles are given and received there must be an exchange of two written documents, in which the name and rank of the paroled individuals are accurately and truthfully stated.

Art. 126. Commissioned officers only are allowed to give their parole, and they can give it only with the permission of their superior, as long as a superior in rank is within reach.

Art. 127. No noncommissioned officer or private can give his parole except through an officer. Individual paroles not given through an officer are not only void, but subject the individuals giving them to the punishment of death as deserters. The only admissible exception is where individuals, properly separated from their commands, have suffered long confinement without the possibility of being paroled through an officer.

Art. 128. No paroling on the battlefield; no paroling of entire bodies of troops after a battle; and no dismissal of large numbers of prisoners, with a general declaration that they are paroled, is permitted, or of any value.

Art. 129. In capitulations for the surrender of strong places or fortified camps the commanding officer, in cases of urgent necessity, may agree that the troops under his command shall not fight again during the war unless exchanged.

Art. 130. The usual pledge given in the parole is not to serve during the existing war unless exchanged.

This pledge refers only to the active service in the field, against the paroling belligerent or his allies actively engaged in the same war. These cases of breaking the parole are patent acts, and can be visited with the punishment of death; but the pledge does not refer to internal service, such as recruiting or drilling the recruits, fortifying places not besieged, quelling civil commotions, fighting against belligerents unconnected with the paroling belligerents, or to civil or diplomatic service for which the paroled officer may be employed.

Art. 131. If the government does not approve of the parole, the paroled officer must return into captivity, and should the enemy refuse to receive him, he is free of his parole.

Art. 132. A belligerent government may declare, by a general order, whether it will allow paroling, and on what conditions it will allow it. Such order is communicated to the enemy.

Art. 133. No prisoner of war can be forced by the hostile government to parole himself, and no government is obliged to parole prisoners of war, or to parole all captured officers, if it paroles any. As the pledging of the parole is an individual act, so is paroling, on the other hand, an act of choice on the part of the belligerent.

Art. 146. Prisoners taken in the act of breaking an armistice must be treated as prisoners of war, the officer alone being responsible who gives the order for such a violation of an armistice. The highest authority of the belligerent aggrieved may demand redress for the infraction of an armistice.

Source: U.S. House of Representatives, *Executive Documents, First Session, Forty-Third Congress, 1873–1874* (Washington: Government Printing Office, 1874), IX, 2–17.

Private Prescott Tracy on the Conditions at the Andersonville Prison Camp (1864)

The Confederate prison at Andersonville, Georgia, was the most infamous prisoner-of-war camp of the American Civil War. The prison held 45,000 men during the course of the war, who suffered from disease, overcrowding, and lack of food and water; some 13,000 men who had died at the camps became emblematic of the sufferings of captured soldiers during the war. This account by soldier Prescott Tracy of his experience at Andersonville was part of an attempt by the United States Sanitary Commission to record the conditions faced by Union prisoners during the Civil War.

Deposition of Private Prescott Tracy, August 16, 1864.

I am a private in the 82nd New York Regiment of Volunteers, Company G. I was captured with about eight hundred Federal troops, in front of Petersburg, on the 22nd of June, 1864. We were kept at Petersburg two days, at Richmond, Belle Isle, three days, then conveyed by rail to Lynchburg. Marched seventy-five miles to Danville, thence by rail to Andersonville, Georgia. At Petersburg we were treated fairly, being under the guard of old soldiers of an Alabama regiment; at Richmond we came under the authority of the notorious and inhuman Major Turner, and the equally notorious Home Guard. Our ration was a pint of beans, four ounces of bread, and three ounces of meat a day. Another batch of prisoners joining us, we left Richmond sixteen hundred strong.

All blankets, haversacks, canteens, money, valuables of every kind, extra clothing, and in some cases, the last shirt and drawers had been previously taken from us.

At Lynchburg we were placed under the Home Guard, officered by Major and Captain Moffett. The march to Danville was a weary and painful one of five days, under a torrid sun; many of us falling helpless by the way, and soon filling the empty wagons of our train. On the first day we received a little meat, but the sum of our rations for the five days was thirteen crackers. During the six days by rail to Andersonville, meat was given us twice, and the daily ration was four crackers.

On entering the Stockade Prison, we found it crowded with twenty-eight thousand of our fellow-soldiers. By crowded, I mean that it was difficult to move in any direction without jostling and being jostled. This prison is an open space, sloping on both sides, originally seventeen acres, now twenty-five acres, in the shape of a parallelogram, without trees or shelter of any kind. The soil is sand over a bottom of clay. The fence is made of upright trunks of trees, about twenty feet high, near the top of which are small platforms, where the guards are stationed. Twenty feet inside and parallel to the fence is a light railing, forming the "dead line," beyond which the projection of a foot or finger is sure to bring the deadly bullet of the sentinel.

Through the grounds, at nearly right-angles with the longer sides, runs or rather creeps a stream through an artificial channel, varying from five to six feet in width, the water about ankle deep, and near the middle of the enclosure, spreading out into a swamp of about six acres, filled with refuse wood, stumps, and debris of the camp. Before entering this enclosure, the stream, or more properly sewer, passes through the camp of the guards, receiving from this source, and others farther up, a large amount of the vilest material, even the contents of the sink. The water is of a dark color, and an ordinary glass would collect a thick sediment. This was our only drinking and cooking water. It was our custom to filter it as best we could, through our remnants of haversacks, shirts, and blouses. Wells had been dug, but the water either proved so productive of diarrhea, or so limited in quantity that they were of no general use. The cookhouse was situated on the stream just outside the stockade, and its refuse of decaying offal was thrown into the water, a greasy coating covering much of the surface. To these was added the daily large amount of base matter from the camp itself. There was a system of policing, but the means was so limited, and so large a number of the men were rendered irresolute and depressed by imprisonment, that the work was very imperfectly done. One side of the swamp was naturally used as a sink, the men usually going out some distance into the water. Under the summer sun this place early became corruption too vile for description, the men breeding disgusting life, so that the surface of the water moved as with a gentle breeze.

The newcomers, on reaching this, would exclaim: "Is this hell?" yet they soon would become callous, and enter unmoved the horrible rottenness. The rebel authorities never removed any filth. There was seldom any visitation by the officers in charge. Two surgeons were at one time sent by President Davis to inspect the camp, but a walk through a small section gave them all the information they desired, and we never saw them again.

The guards usually numbered about sixty-four—eight at each end, and twenty-four on a side. On the outside, within three hundred yards, were fortifications, on high ground overlooking and perfectly commanding us, mounting twenty-four twelve-pound Napoleon Parrotts. We were never permitted to go outside, except at times, in small squads, to gather our firewood. During the building of the cookhouse, a few, who were carpenters, were ordered out to assist.

Our only shelter from the sun and rain and night dews was what we could make by stretching over us our coats of scraps of blankets, which a few had, but generally there was no attempt by day or night to protect ourselves.

The rations consisted of eight ounces of corn bread (the cob being ground with the kernel), and generally sour; two ounces of condemned pork, offensive in appearance and smell. Occasionally, about twice a week, two tablespoonfuls of rice, and in place of the pork the same amount (two tablespoonfuls) of molasses was given us about twice a month. This ration was brought into camp about four o'clock p. m., and thrown from the wagons to the ground, the men being arranged in divisions of two hundred and seventy, subdivided into squads of nineties and thirties. It was the custom to consume the whole ration at once, rather than save any for the next day. The distribution being often unequal some would lose the rations altogether. We were allowed no dish or cooking utensil of any kind. On opening the camp in the winter, the first two thousand prisoners were allowed skillets, one to fifty men, but these were soon taken away. To the best of my knowledge, information, and belief, our ration was in quality a starving one, it being either too foul to be touched or too raw to be digested.

The cookhouse went into operation about May 10, prior to which we cooked our own rations. It did not prove at all adequate to the work (thirty thousand is a large town), so that a large proportion were still obliged to prepare their own food. In addition to the utter inability of many to do this, through debility and sickness, we never had a supply of wood. I have often seen men with a little bag of meal in hand, gathered from several rations, starving to death for want of wood, and in desperation would mix the raw material with water and try to eat it.

The clothing of the men was miserable in the extreme. Very few had shoes of any kind, not two thousand had coats and pants, and those were latecomers. More than one-half were indecently exposed, and many were naked.

The usual punishment was to place the men in the stocks, outside, near the Captain's quarters. If a man was missing at roll call, the squad of ninety to which he belonged was deprived of the ration. The "dead-line" bullet, already referred to, spared no offender. One poor fellow, just from Sherman's army, his name was Roberts, was trying to wash his face near the "dead-line" railing, when he slipped on the clayey bottom, and fell with his head just outside the fatal border. We shouted to him, but it was too late. "Another guard would have a furlough," the men said. It was a common belief among our men, arising from statements made by the guard, that General Winder, in command, issued an order that any one of the guard who should shoot a Yankee outside of the "dead-line" should have a month's furlough, but there probably was no truth in this. About two a day were thus shot, some being cases of suicide, brought on by mental depression or physical misery, the poor fellows throwing themselves, or madly rushing outside the "line."

The mental condition of a large portion of the men was melancholy, beginning in despondency and tending to a kind of stolid and idiotic indifference. Many spent much time in arousing and encouraging their fellows, but hundreds were lying about motionless, or stalking vacantly to and fro, quite beyond any help which could be given them within their prison walls. These cases were frequent among those who had been imprisoned but a short time. There were those who were captured at the first Bull Run, July 1861, and had known Belle Isle from the first, yet had preserved their physical and mental health to a wonderful degree. Many were wise and resolute enough to keep themselves occupied, some in cutting bone and wood ornaments, making their knives out of iron hoops, others in manufacturing ink from the rust from these same hoops, and with rude pens sketching or imitating bank notes or any sample that would involve long and patient execution.

Letters from home very seldom reached us, and few had any means of writing. In the early summer, a large batch of letters, five thousand we were told, arrived, having been accumulating somewhere for many months. These were brought into camp by an officer, under orders to collect ten cents on each. Of course most were returned, and we heard no more of them. One of my companions saw among them three from his parents, but he was unable to pay the charge. According to the rules of transmission of letters over the lines, these letters must have already paid ten cents each to the rebel government.

As far as we saw General Winder and Captain Wirtz, the former was kind and considerate in his manners, the latter harsh, though not without kindly feelings.

It is a melancholy and mortifying fact, that some of our trials came from our own men. At Belle Isle and Andersonville there were among us a gang of desperate men, ready to prey on their fellows. Not only thefts and robberies, but even murders were committed. Affairs became so serious at Camp Sumter that an appeal was made to General Winder, who authorized an arrest and trial by a criminal court. Eighty-six were arrested, and six were hung, beside others who were severely punished. These proceedings effected a marked change for the better.

Some few weeks before being released, I was ordered to act as clerk in the hospital. This consists simply of a few scattered trees and fly tents, and is in charge of Dr. White, an excellent and considerate man, with very limited means, but doing all in his power for his patients. He has twenty-five assistants, besides those detailed to examine for admittance to the hospital. This examination was made in a small stockade attached to the main one, to the inside door of which the sick came or were brought by their comrades, the number to be removed being limited. Lately, in consideration of the rapidly increasing sickness, it was extended to one hundred and fifty daily. That this was too small an allowance is shown by the fact that the deaths within our stockade were from thirty to forty a day. I have seen one hundred and fifty bodies waiting passage to the "dead house," to be buried with those who died in hospital. The average of deaths through the earlier months was thirty a day; at the time I left, the average was over one hundred and thirty, and one day the record showed one hundred and forty-six.

The proportion of deaths from starvation, not including those consequent on the diseases originating in the character and limited quantity of food, such as diarrhea, dysentery, and scurvy, I cannot state; but, to the best of my knowledge, information, and belief, there were scores every month. We could, at any time, point out many for whom such a fate was inevitable, as they lay or feebly walked, mere skeletons, whose emaciation exceeded the examples given in Leslie's Illustrated for June 18, 1864. For example: in some cases the inner edges of the two bones of the arms, between the elbow and the wrist, with the intermediate blood vessels, were plainly visible when held toward the light. The ration, in quantity, was perhaps barely sufficient to sustain life, and the cases of starvation were generally those whose stomachs could not retain what had become entirely indigestible.

For a man to find, on waking, that his comrade by his side was dead, was an occurrence too common to be noted. I have seen death in almost all the forms of the hospital and battlefield, but the daily scenes in Camp exceeded in the extremity of misery all my previous experience.

The work of burial is performed by our own men, under guard and orders, twenty-five bodies being placed in a single pit, without headboards, and the sad duty performed with indecent haste. Sometimes our men were rewarded for this work with a few sticks of firewood, and I have known them to quarrel over a dead body for the job.

Dr. White is able to give the patients a diet but little better than the prison rations a little flour porridge, arrowroot, whiskey, and wild or hog tomatoes. In the way of medicine, I saw nothing but camphor, whiskey, and a decoction of some kind of bark-white oak, I think. He often expressed his regret that he had not more medicines. The limitation of military orders, under which the surgeon in charge was placed, is shown by the following occurrence: A supposed private, wounded in the thigh, was under treatment in the hospital, when it was discovered that he was a major of a colored regiment. The assistant-surgeon, under whose immediate charge he was, proceeded at once, not only to remove him, but to kick him out, and he was returned to the stockade, to shift for himself as well as he could. Dr. White could not or did not attempt to restore him.

After entering on my duties at the hospital, I was occasionally favored with double rations and some wild tomatoes. A few of our men succeeded, in spite of the closest examination of our clothes, in secreting some greenbacks, and with these were able to buy useful articles at exorbitant prices: a tea-cup of flour at one dollar; eggs, three to six dollars a dozen; salt, four dollars a pound; molasses, thirty dollars a gallon; nigger beans, a small, inferior article (diet of the slaves and pigs, but highly relished by us), fifty cents a pint. These figures, multiplied by ten, will give very nearly the price in Confederate currency. Though the country abounded in pine and oak, sticks were sold to us at various prices, according to size.

Our men, especially the mechanics, were tempted with the offer of liberty and large wages to take the oath of allegiance to the Confederacy, but it was very rare that their patriotism, even under such a fiery trial, ever gave way. I carry this message from one of my companions to his mother: "My treatment here is killing me, mother, but I die cheerfully for my country."

Some attempts were made to escape, but wholly in vain, for if the prison walls and guards were passed and the protecting woods reached, the bloodhounds were sure to find us out.

Tunneling was once attempted on a large scale, but on the afternoon preceding the night fixed on for escape, an officer rode in and announced to us that the plot was discovered, and from our huge pen we could see on the hill above us the regiments just arriving to strengthen the guard. We had been betrayed. It was our belief that spies were kept in the camp, which could very easily be done.

The number in camp when I left was nearly thirty-five thousand, and daily increasing. The number in hospital was about five thousand. I was exchanged at Port Royal Ferry, August 16th.

Source: *Narrative of Privations and Sufferings of United States Officers and Soldiers in the Hands of the Rebel Authorities* (Philadelphia: King & Baird, 1864)

Emily Hobhouse on the Conditions at the British Concentration Camps in South Africa (1901)

Emily Hobhouse (1860–1926) was secretary to the South African Conciliation Committee (formed in November 1899). She visited South Africa in 1900 and reported on the atrocities against the Boers held in British concentration camps. Her reports caused a political scandal and outraged political opinion in England so much that she was forcibly prevented from entering South Africa when she attempted to visit again in 1901.

January 22nd.

'I had a splendid truck given me at Capetown, through the kind cooperation of Sir Alfred Milner—a large double-covered one, capable of holding 12 tons.

I took £200 worth of groceries, besides all the bales of clothing I could muster. The truck left Capetown the day before myself, was hitched on to my train at De Aar, and so arrived when I did. The first thing next day was to go down to the goods station, claim the truck, and arrange for its unloading. This morning I have spent arranging all my stores—unpacking and sorting them. It is very hot. I think the essence of delightful work is when you quite forget you have a body, but here the heat keeps you in constant recollection that you are still in the flesh, and it's a great hindrance. I did not have a bad journey from Capetown, though it was rather a lonely one. Going through the Karoo it was very hot, and the second day there were horrible dust-storms, varied by thunderstorms. The sand penetrated through closed windows and doors, filled eyes and ears, turned my hair red and covered everything like a tablecloth.

As far as extent and sweep of land and sky go the Karoo is delightful, but it's a vast solitude, and in many parts the very plants grow two or three yards apart, as if they shunned society. From Colesberg on it was a desolate outlook. The land seemed dead and silent as far as eye could reach, absolutely without life, only carcasses of horses, mules, and cattle, with a sort of acute anguish in their look, and bleached bones and refuse of many kinds. I saw a few burnt farms, but those unburnt seemed still and lifeless also, and no work is going on in the fields. Really, the line the whole way up is a string of Tommies [British soldiers], yawning at their posts, and these always crowded to the carriage windows to beg for newspapers, or anything, they said, to pass the time. I gave them all I had, and all my novels. . . . But I must pass on to tell you about the Women's Camp, which, after all, is the central point of interest.'

The Bloemfontein Camp.

January 26th.

The exile camp here is a good two miles from the town, dumped down on the southern slope of a kopje, right out on to the bare brown veldt, not a vestige of a tree in any direction, nor shade of any description. It was about four o'clock of a scorching afternoon when I set foot in the camp, and I can't tell you what I felt like, so I won't try.

I began by finding a woman whose sister I had met in Capetown. It is such a puzzle to find your way in a village of bell tents, no streets or names or numbers. There are nearly 2,000 people in this one camp, of which some few are men—they call them "hands up" men—and over 900 children.

Imagine the heat outside the tents, and the suffocation inside! We sat on their khaki blankets, rolled up, inside Mrs. B.'s tent; and the sun blazed through the single canvas, and the flies lay thick and black on everything; no chair, no table, nor any room for such; only a deal box, standing on its end, served as a wee pantry. In this tiny tent live Mrs. B.'s five children (three quite grown up) and a little Kaffir servant girl. Many tents have more occupants.

Mrs. P. came in, and Mrs. R. and others, and they told me their stories, and we cried together, and even laughed together, and chatted bad Dutch and bad English all the afternoon. On wet nights the water streams down through the canvas and comes flowing in, as it knows how to do in this country, under the flap of the tent, and wets their blanket as they lie on the ground. While we sat there a snake came in. They said it was a puff adder, very poisonous, so they all ran out, and I attacked the creature with my parasol. I could not bear to think the thing should be at large in a community mostly sleeping on the ground. After a struggle I wounded it, and then a man came with a mallet and finished it off.

Mrs. P. is very brave and calm. She has six children, ranging from fifteen down to two years, and she does not know where any one of them is. She was taken right away from them; her husband is in detention of some kind at Bloemfontein, but not allowed to see her. She expects her confinement in about three weeks, and yet has to lie on the bare ground till she is still and sore, and she has had nothing to sit on for over two months, but must squat on a rolled-up blanket. I felt quite sure you would like her to have a mattress, and I asked her if she would accept one. She did so very gratefully, and I did not rest yesterday till I got one out to her. All her baby linen was in readiness at home, but all is lost. This is but one case, quite ordinary, among hundreds and hundreds. The women are wonderful. They cry very little and never complain. The very magnitude of their sufferings, indignities, loss, and anxiety seems to lift them beyond tears. These people, who have had comfortable, even luxurious homes, just set themselves to quiet endurance and to make the best of their bare and terrible lot; only when it cuts afresh at them through their children do their feelings flash out. Mrs. M., for instance. She has six children in camp, all ill, two in the tin hospital with typhoid, and four sick in the tent. She also expects her confinement soon. Her husband is in Ceylon. She has means, and would gladly provide for herself either in town or in the Colony, where she has relations, or by going back to her farm. It was not burnt, only the furniture was destroyed; yet here she has to stay, watching her children droop and sicken. For their sakes she did plead with tears that she might go and fend for herself.

I call this camp system a wholesale cruelty. It can never be wiped out of the memories of the people. It presses hardest on the children. They droop in the terrible heat, and with the insufficient, unsuitable food; whatever you do, whatever the authorities do, and they are, I believe, doing their best with very limited means, it is all only a miserable patch upon a great ill. Thousands, physically unfit, are placed in conditions of life which they have not strength to endure. In front of them is blank ruin. There are cases, too, in which whole families are severed and scattered, they don't know where. Will you try, somehow, to make the British public understand the position, and force it to ask itself what is going to be done with these people? There must be full 15,000 of them; I should not wonder if there are not more. Some few have means, but more are ruined, and have not a present penny. In one of two ways must the British public support them, either by taxation through the authorities, or else by voluntary charity.

If the people at home want to save their purses (you see, I appeal to low motives), why not allow those who can maintain themselves to go to friends and relatives in the Colony? Many wish ardently to do so. That would be some relief. If only the English people would try to exercise a little imagination—picture the whole miserable scene. Entire villages and districts rooted up and dumped in a strange, bare place. To keep these Camps going is murder to the children. Still, of course, by more judicious management they could be improved; but, do what you will, you can't undo the thing itself.

To-day is Sunday; and all the day I have been toiling and moiling over the bales of clothes—unpacking, sorting, and putting up in bundles. We were so glad of such odd things, such as stays and little boys' braces! I found some baby linen for Mrs. P. I do not think that there is a single superfluous article. But what a family to clothe!

[. . .]

We have much typhoid, and are dreading an outbreak, so I am directing my energies to getting the water of the Modder River boiled. As well swallow typhoid germs whole as drink that water—so say doctors. Yet they cannot boil it all; for—first, fuel is very scarce; that which is supplied weekly would not cook a meal a day, and they have to search the already bare kopjes for a supply. There is hardly a bit to be had. Second, they have no extra utensil to hold the water when boiled. I propose, therefore, to give each tent another pail or crock, and get a proclamation issued that all drinking water must be boiled. It will cost nearly £50 to do this, even if utensils are procurable.

In spite of small water supply, and it is very spare, all the tents I have been in are exquisitely neat and clean, except two, and they were ordinary, and such limitations!

January 31st.

I suggested a big railway boiler to boil every drop of water before it is served out. This would economize fuel, and be cheaper in the long run, besides ensuring the end desired, for many could not be trusted to boil their own. Next we want forage for the cows. Fifty have been secured, but they only get four buckets of milk out of the poor starved things.

What is needed is a wash-house with water laid on from the town, but I see no chance of it. Some people in town still assert that the Camp is a haven of bliss. Well, there are eyes and no eyes. I was at the camp to-day, and just in one little corner this is the sort of thing I found. The nurse, underfed and overworked, just sinking on to her bed, hardly able to hold herself up, after coping with some thirty typhoid and other patients, with only the untrained help of two Boer girls—cooking as well as nursing to do herself. Next, I was called to see a woman panting in the heat, just sickening for her confinement. Fortunately, I had a night-dress in my bundle to give her, and two tiny baby gowns.

Next tent, a six months' baby gasping its life out on its mother's knee. The doctor had given it powders in the morning, but it had taken nothing since. Two or three others drooping and sick in that tent. Next, child recovering from measles, sent back from hospital before it could walk, stretched on the ground, white and wan; three or four others lying about. Next, a girl of twenty-one lay dying on a stretcher. The father, a big, gentle Boer, kneeling beside her; while, next tent, his wife was watching a child of six, also dying, and one of about five drooping. Already this couple had lost three children in the hospital and so would not let these go, though I begged hard to take them out of the hot tent. "We must watch these ourselves," he said. I sent———to find brandy, and got some down the girl's throat, but for the most part you must stand and look on, helpless to do anything, because there is nothing to do anything with.

Then a man came up and said: "Sister" (they call me "Sister," or "Di Meisie van England"), "come and see my child, sick for nearly three months." It was a dear little chap of four, and nothing left of him but his great brown eyes and white teeth, from which the lips were drawn back, too thin to close. His body was emaciated. The little fellow had craved for fresh milk; but, of course, there had been none till these last two days, and now the fifty cows only give four buckets, so you can imagine what feed there is for them. I sent———for some of this, and made him lay the child outside on a pillow to get the breeze that comes up at sunset. I can't describe what it is to see these children lying about in a state of collapse. It's just exactly like faded flowers thrown away. And one has to stand and look on at such misery, and be able to do almost nothing.

Source: Emily Hobhouse, *Report of a Visit to the Camps of Women and Children in the Cape and Orange River Colonies* (London: Friars Printing Association, 1901), 3–5.

Peter Moor's Account of the Herero Genocide (1904–1905)

Peter Moor was a German naval infantryman from Kiel who served as a foot soldier during the Herero war in German South West Africa in 1904–1905. As one of the first of the reinforcements sent from Germany after the outbreak of the rebellion, he was in the thick of the initial phases of the conflict and the subsequent pursuit of the Herero into the Kalahari Desert. He related the account of his experiences to a well-known writer of patriotic novels, Gustav Frenssen, in 1906. The book was translated into English by Margaret May Ward in 1908, and sections of it were later incorporated into the British government's Report on the Natives of South West Africa and Their Treatment by Germany (1918).

The next morning we ventured to pursue the enemy. We left our unmounted men with the sick and wounded in camp and set out towards the east, two hundred horsemen in number. But our horses were weak, half-starved, or sick, and the region into which we were advancing was a waterless land and little explored. The ground was trodden down into a floor for a width of about a hundred yards; for in such a broad, thickly crowded horde had the enemy and their herds of cattle stormed along. In the path of their flight lay blankets, skins, ostrich feathers, household utensils, women's ornaments, cattle, and men dead and dying and staring blankly. A shocking smell of old manure and of decaying bodies filled the hot, still air oppressively.

The further we went in the burning sun, the more disheartening became our journey. How deeply the wild, proud, sorrowful people had humbled themselves in the terror of death! Wherever I turned my eyes lay their goods in quantities; oxen and horses, goats and dogs, blankets and skins. And there lay the wounded and the old, women and children. A number of babies lay helplessly languishing by mothers whose breasts hung down long and flabby. Others were lying alone, still living, with eyes and noses full of flies. Somebody sent out our black drivers and I think they helped them to die. All this life lay scattered there, both man and beast, broken in the knees, helpless, still in agony or already motionless; it looked as if it had all been thrown down out of the air.

At noon we halted by water-holes which were filled to the very brim with corpses. We pulled them out by means of the ox-teams from the field pieces, but there was only a little stinking, bloody water in the depths. We tried to dig deeper, but no water came. There was no pasturage, either. The sun blazed down so hot on the sand that we could not even lie down. On our thirsting, starving horses, we thirsting and starving men rode on. At some distance crouched a crowd of old women, who stared in apathy in front of them. Here and there were oxen, bellowing. In the last frenzy of despair man and beast will plunge madly into the bush somewhere, anywhere, to find water, and in the bush they will die of thirst.

We rode on till evening. . . .

Toward evening, when I was ordered to ride in the bush with four men as a flank protection,—for we were shot at now and then,—we chanced to see a Cape wagon behind some high bushes, and we heard human voices. Dismounting, we sneaked up and discovered six of the enemy sitting in animated conversation around a little camp-fire. I indicated, by signs, at which one of them each of us was to shoot. Four lay still immediately; one escaped; the sixth stood half erect, severely wounded. I sprang forward swinging my club; he looked at me indifferently. I wiped my club clean in the sand and threw the weapon on its strap over my shoulder, but I did not like to touch it all that day.

The ground was everywhere bare, yellowish brown and stony; the sparse grass had been eaten, burned, or trodden down. Dead cattle lay about everywhere. The hoarse bellowing of dying oxen quavered horribly through the air. The bush got thinner, often opening into a great clearing.

Entirely forsaken in the scorching sun lay a two-year-old child. When it caught sight of us, it sat up straight and stared at us. I got down from my horse, picked the child up and carried it back where there was a deserted fireplace near a bush. It found at once the remainder of a root or a bone, and began to eat. It did not cry; it did not show fear, either; it was entirely indifferent. I believe it had grown there in the bush without human help. . . .

When it came to my turn to watch and I went outside, the night was so bitter cold that I made all sorts of motions to keep a little warmth in my body. I even climbed twice on a low, tumble-down anthill and watched the fires which here and there in the distance shone through the darkness. While I was thus gazing, however, I was struck by the fact that one fire was burning not far from us in the thick bush. I remembered when I was relieved, and told the lieutenant, who was sitting on the ground by our burned-out fire.

Before dawn we got up, discovered the exact place in the bush, and stealthily surrounded it. Five men and eight or ten women and children, all in rags, were squatting benumbed about their dismal little fire. Telling them with threats not to move, we looked through the bundles which were lying near them and found two guns and some underclothing, probably stolen from our dead. One of the men was wearing a German tunic which bore the name of one of our officers who had been killed. We then led the men away to one side and shot them. The women and children, who looked pitiably starved, we hunted into the bush. . . .

We rode on. The guardsman pointed once or twice into the bushes; I looked over there. Then we reached the summit and then looked attentively out over the plain, which lay in boundless extent an absolute stillness, like a yellowish grey sea. The long rays of the setting sun lay upon it like strips of thin, bright shining cloth.

We sprang off our horses, loosened the girths, and lay down on the ground. The guard's horse began to sniff at his face, but he did not notice it; he was already asleep. The lieutenant stood up again and said to me: "Get up! If we fall asleep, we shall sleep all night and then we are lost." I rose, and we both stood awhile with benumbed senses in a state between sleeping and waking. The sun sank in a dull glow; the air grew cooler, and the horses got somewhat more lively and began with weary steps to nibble a few little bushes.

After a while the Africander woke and asked in a woe-begone voice if I had a drop of water. I said: "No." He said "The lieutenant has some, then." Again I said, "No." Then he said he could hold out no longer without water—he had trusted too much to his strength, he should have to die here. The lieutenant, who had dozed standing by his horse and holding onto the saddle, woke and said consolingly: "Cheer up! We shall start at once. Then we are off for home, for the war is now really over." "Yes," said the guardsman, "it is over; forty thousand of them are dead; all their land belongs to us. But what good does all that do to me? I must die here." He begged mournfully: "Have you not a single drop of water?" The lieutenant shook his head: "You know I have none. Rest a little longer; it is night, and that will refresh us." The guardsman got up with difficulty and went with bent back down the slope to one side where there were some bushes. I said "What does he want? I believe he is out of his senses and wants to search for water."

At that moment there came from the bushes into which he had vanished a noise of cursing, running, and leaping. Immediately he reappeared, holding by the hip a tall thin negro dressed in European clothing. He tore the negro's gun from his hand and, swearing at him in a strange language, dragged him up to us and said: "The wretch has a German gun, but no more cartridges." The guardsman had now become quite lively, and began to talk to his captive, threatening him and kicking him in the knees. The negro crouched, and answered every question with a great flow of words and with quick, very agile and remarkable gestures of the arms and hands. "He says he has not taken part in the war." Then he asked him some more questions, pointing towards the east; and the negro also pointed towards the east, answering all sorts of things of which I understood nothing. The guardsman said: "He is stuffing me with lies." This went on for some time. I can still hear the two dry, shrill voices of the German and the native. Apparently the guardsman at last learned enough, for he said: "The missionary said to me, 'Beloved, don't forget that the blacks are our brothers.' Now I will give my brother his reward." He pushed the black man off and said: "Run away!" The man sprang up and tried to get down across the clearing in long, zigzag jumps, but he had not taken five leaps before the ball hit him and he pitched forward at full length and lay still.

I grumbled a little; I thought the shot might attract to us the attention of hostile tribes who had perhaps stayed behind. But the lieutenant thought I meant it was not right for the guardsman to shoot the negro, and said in his thoughtful, scholarly way: "Safe is safe. He can't raise a gun against us any more, nor beget any children to fight against us. The struggle for South Africa will be a hard one, whether it is to belong to the Germans or to the blacks."

Source: Gustav Frenssen, *Peter Moor's Journey to Southwest Africa: A Narrative of the German Campaign* (London: Constable, 1908)

Excerpts from the 1907 Hague Convention IV with Respect to the Laws and Customs of War on Land (1907)

The Hague Conventions of 1899 and 1907 were the first formal attempts to create an international legal framework for the rules war. They were drafted at two international peace conferences at The Hague in the Netherlands; a third conference was planned for 1914 but it did not take place due to the start of World War I. Although many of the rules laid down at the Hague Conventions were violated in the subsequent conflicts of the twentieth century, they continued to stand as symbols of the need for restrictions on war and humane treatment of prisoners of wars and internees.

Preamble

Until a more complete code of the laws of war has been issued, the High Contracting Parties deem it expedient to declare that, in cases not included in the Regulations adopted by them, the inhabitants and the belligerents remain under the protection and the rule of the principles of the law of nations, as they result from the usages established among civilized peoples, from the laws of humanity, and the dictates of the public conscience.

Article 1. The Contracting Powers shall issue instructions to their armed land forces which shall be in conformity with the Regulations respecting the laws and customs of war on land, annexed to the present Convention.

Article 3. A belligerent party which violates the provisions of the said Regulations shall, if the case demands, be liable to pay compensation. It shall be responsible for all acts committed by persons forming part of its armed forces.

Regulations:

Regulations respecting the laws and customs of war on land.
Section I.—On Belligerents.
Chapter I.—The Qualifications of Belligerents.

Article 1. The laws, rights, and duties of war apply not only to armies, but also to militia and volunteer corps fulfilling the following conditions:

1. To be commanded by a person responsible for his subordinates;
2. To have a fixed distinctive emblem recognizable at a distance;
3. To carry arms openly; and
4. To conduct their operations in accordance with the laws and customs of war.

In countries where militia or volunteer corps constitute the army, or form part of it, they are included under the denomination "army."

Art. 2. The inhabitants of a territory which has not been occupied, who, on the approach of the enemy, spontaneously take up arms to resist the invading troops without having had time to organize themselves in accordance with Article 1 [Link], shall be regarded as belligerents if they carry arms openly and if they respect the laws and customs of war.

Art. 3. The armed forces of the belligerent parties may consist of combatants and non-combatants. In the case of capture by the enemy, both have a right to be treated as prisoners of war.

Chapter II

Prisoners of war

Art. 4. Prisoners of war are in the power of the hostile Government, but not of the individuals or corps who capture them.

They must be humanely treated.

All their personal belongings, except arms, horses, and military papers, remain their property.

Art. 5. Prisoners of war may be interned in a town, fortress, camp, or other place, and bound not to go beyond certain fixed limits; but they cannot be confined except as in indispensable measure of safety and only while the circumstances which necessitate the measure continue to exist.

Art. 6. The State may utilize the labour of prisoners of war according to their rank and aptitude, officers excepted. The tasks shall not be excessive and shall have no connection with the operations of the war.

Prisoners may be authorized to work for the public service, for private persons, or on their own account.

Work done for the State is paid for at the rates in force for work of a similar kind done by soldiers of the national army, or, if there are none in force, at a rate according to the work executed.

When the work is for other branches of the public service or for private persons the conditions are settled in agreement with the military authorities.

The wages of the prisoners shall go towards improving their position, and the balance shall be paid them on their release, after deducting the cost of their maintenance.

Art. 7. The Government into whose hands prisoners of war have fallen is charged with their maintenance.

In the absence of a special agreement between the belligerents, prisoners of war shall be treated as regards board, lodging, and clothing on the same footing as the troops of the Government who captured them.

Art. 8. Prisoners of war shall be subject to the laws, regulations, and orders in force in the army of the State in whose power they are. Any act of insubordination justifies the adoption towards them of such measures of severity as may be considered necessary.

Escaped prisoners who are retaken before being able to rejoin their own army or before leaving the territory occupied by the army which captured them are liable to disciplinary punishment.

Prisoners who, after succeeding in escaping, are again taken prisoners, are not liable to any punishment on account of the previous flight.

Art. 9. Every prisoner of war is bound to give, if he is questioned on the subject, his true name and rank, and if he infringes this rule, he is liable to have the advantages given to prisoners of his class curtailed.

Art. 10. Prisoners of war may be set at liberty on parole if the laws of their country allow, and, in such cases, they are bound, on their personal honour, scrupulously to fulfil, both towards their own Government and the Government by whom they were made prisoners, the engagements they have contracted.

In such cases their own Government is bound neither to require of nor accept from them any service incompatible with the parole given.

Art. 11. A prisoner of war cannot be compelled to accept his liberty on parole; similarly the hostile Government is not obliged to accede to the request of the prisoner to be set at liberty on parole.

Art. 12. Prisoners of war liberated on parole and recaptured bearing arms against the Government to whom they had pledged their honour, or against the allies of that Government, forfeit their right to be treated as prisoners of war, and can be brought before the courts.

Art. 13. Individuals who follow an army without directly belonging to it, such as newspaper correspondents and reporters, sutlers and contractors, who fall into the enemy's hands and whom the latter thinks expedient to detain, are entitled to be treated as prisoners of war, provided they are in possession of a certificate from the military authorities of the army which they were accompanying.

Art. 14. An inquiry office for prisoners of war is instituted on the commencement of hostilities in each of the belligerent States, and, when necessary, in neutral countries which have received belligerents in their territory. It is the function of this office to reply to all inquiries about the prisoners. It receives from the various services concerned full information respecting internments arid transfers, releases on parole, exchanges, escapes, admissions into hospital, deaths, as well as other information necessary to enable it to make out and keep up to date an individual return for each prisoner of war. The office must state in this return the regimental number, name and surname, age, place of origin, rank, unit, wounds, date and place of capture, internment, wounding, and death, as well as any observations of a special character. The individual return shall be sent to the Government of the other belligerent after the conclusion of peace.

It is likewise the function of the inquiry office to receive and collect all objects of personal use, valuables, letters, etc., found on the field of battle or left by prisoners who have been released on parole, or exchanged, or who have escaped, or died in hospitals or ambulances, and to forward them to those concerned.

Art. 15. Relief societies for prisoners of war, which are properly constituted in accordance with the laws of their country and with the object of serving as the channel for charitable effort shall receive from the belligerents, for themselves and their duly accredited agents every facility for the efficient performance of their humane task within the bounds imposed by military necessities and administrative regulations. Agents of these societies may be admitted to the places of internment for the purpose of distributing relief, as also to the halting places of repatriated prisoners, if furnished with a personal permit by the military authorities, and on giving an undertaking in writing to comply with all measures of order and police which the latter may issue.

Art. 16. Inquiry offices enjoy the privilege of free postage. Letters, money orders, and valuables, as well as parcels by post, intended for prisoners of war, or dispatched by them, shall be exempt from all postal duties in the countries of origin and destination, as well as in the countries they pass through.

Presents and relief in kind for prisoners of war shall be admitted free of all import or other duties, as well as of payments for carriage by the State railways.

Art. 17. Officers taken prisoners shall receive the same rate of pay as officers of corresponding rank in the country where they are detained, the amount to be ultimately refunded by their own Government.

Art. 18. Prisoners of war shall enjoy complete liberty in the exercise of their religion, including attendance at the services of whatever church they may belong to, on the sole condition that they comply with the measures of order and police issued by the military authorities.

Art. 19. The wills of prisoners of war are received or drawn up in the same way as for soldiers of the national army.

The same rules shall be observed regarding death certificates as well as for the burial of prisoners of war, due regard being paid to their grade and rank.

Art. 20. After the conclusion of peace, the repatriation of prisoners of war shall be carried out as quickly as possible.

Chapter III

The sick and wounded

Art. 21. The obligations of belligerents with regard to the sick and wounded are governed by the Geneva Convention.

Source: Bevans, Charles I. *United States Treaties and International Agreements. Volume 1 Multilateral 1776–1917.* Laws and Customs of War on Land (Hague IV); October 18, 1907. Department of State Publication 8407, Washington, DC: Government Printing Office, 1968, 631–653.

Rudolf Hoess's Testimony on the Activities at the Auschwitz Concentration Camp (1946)

Rudolf Hoess, the German commandant of the notorious Auschwitz concentration camp, orchestrated the deaths of hundreds of thousands of people during World War II. Below is an excerpt of his signed testimony regarding the activities of the camp, which he delivered on April 5, 1946, at the Nuremberg Trials held to prosecute Nazi war criminals. Hoess was later executed for his role in the Holocaust.

I, RUDOLF FRANZ FERDINAND HOESS, being first duly sworn, depose and say as follows:

1. I am forty-six years old, and have been a member of the NSDAPI since 1922; a member of the SS since 1934; a member of the Waffen-SS since 1939. I was a member from 1 December 1934 of the SS Guard Unit, the so-called Deathshead Formation (Totenkopf Verband).

2. I have been constantly associated with the administration of concentration camps since 1934, serving at Dachau until 1938; then as Adjutant in Sachsenhausen from 1938 to 1 May, 1940, when I was appointed Commandant of Auschwitz. I commanded Auschwitz until 1 December, 1943, and estimate that at least 2,500,000 victims were executed and exterminated there by gassing and burning, and at least another half million succumbed to starvation and disease, making a total dead of about 3,000,000. This figure represents about 70% or 80% of all persons sent to Auschwitz as prisoners, the remainder having been selected and used for slave labor in the concentration camp industries. Included among the executed and burnt were approximately 20,000 Russian prisoners of war (previously screened out of Prisoner of War cages by the Gestapo) who were delivered at Auschwitz in Wehrmacht transports operated by regular Wehrmacht officers and men. The remainder of the total number of victims included about 100,000 German Jews, and great numbers of citizens (mostly Jewish) from Holland, France, Belgium, Poland, Hungary, Czechoslovakia, Greece, or other countries. We executed about 400,000 Hungarian Jews alone at Auschwitz in the summer of 1944 . . .

4. Mass executions by gassing commenced during the summer 1941 and continued until fall 1944. I personally supervised executions at Auschwitz until the first of December 1943 and know by reason of my continued duties in the Inspectorate of Concentration Camps WVHA2 that these mass executions continued as stated above. All mass executions by gassing took place under the direct order, supervision and responsibility of RSHA.31 received all orders for carrying out these mass executions directly from RSHA . . .

6. The "final solution" of the Jewish question meant the complete extermination of all Jews in Europe. I was ordered to establish extermination facilities at Auschwitz in June 1941. At that time there were already in the general government three

other extermination camps; BELZEK, TREBLINKA and WOLZEK. These camps were under the Einsatzkommando of the Security Police and SD. I visited Treblinka to find out how they carried out their exterminations. The Camp Commandant at Treblinka told me that he had liquidated 80,000 in the course of one-half year. He was principally concerned with liquidating all the Jews from the Warsaw Ghetto. He used monoxide gas and I did not think that his methods were very efficient. So when I set up the extermination building at Auschwitz, I used Cyclon B, which was a crystallized Prussic Acid which we dropped into the death chamber from a small opening. It took from 3 to 15 minutes to kill the people in the death chamber depending upon climatic conditions. We knew when the people were dead because their screaming stopped. We usually waited about one-half hour before we opened the doors and removed the bodies. After the bodies were removed our special commandos took off the rings and extracted the gold from the teeth of the corpses.

7. Another improvement we made over Treblinka was that we built our gas chambers to accommodate 2,000 people at one time, whereas at Treblinka their 10 gas chambers only accommodated 200 people each. The way we selected our victims was as follows: we had two SS doctors on duty at Auschwitz to examine the incoming transports of prisoners. The prisoners would be marched by one of the doctors who would make spot decisions as they walked by. Those who were fit for work were sent into the Camp. Others were sent immediately to the extermination plants. Children of tender years were invariably exterminated since by reason of their youth they were unable to work. Still another improvement we made over Treblinka was that at Treblinka the victims almost always knew that they were to be exterminated and at Auschwitz we endeavored to fool the victims into thinking that they were to go through a delousing process. Of course, frequently they realized our true intentions and we sometimes had riots and difficulties due to that fact. Very frequently women would hide their children under the clothes but of course when we found them we would send the children in to be exterminated. We were required to carry out these exterminations in secrecy but of course the foul and nauseating stench from the continuous burning of bodies permeated the entire area and all of the people living in the surrounding communities knew that exterminations were going on at Auschwitz.

8. We received from time to time special prisoners from the local Gestapo office. The SS doctors killed such prisoners by injections of benzine. Doctors had orders to write ordinary death certificates and could put down any reason at all for the cause of death.

9. From time to time we conducted medical experiments on women inmates, including sterilization and experiments relating to cancer. Most of the people who died under these experiments had been already condemned to death by the Gestapo.

10. Rudolf Mildner was the chief of the Gestapo at Kattowicz and as such was head of the political department at Auschwitz which conducted third degree methods of interrogation from approximately March 1941 until September 1943. As such, he frequently sent prisoners to Auschwitz for incarceration or execution. He visited Auschwitz on several occasions. The Gestapo Court, the SS Standgericht, which tried persons accused of various crimes, such as escaping Prisoners of War, etc., frequently met within Auschwitz, and Mildner often attended the trial of such

persons, who usually were executed in Auschwitz following their sentence. I showed Mildner throughout the extermination plant at Auschwitz and he was directly interested in it since he had to send the Jews from his territory for execution at Auschwitz.

I understand English as it is written above. The above statements are true; this declaration is made by me voluntarily and without compulsion; after reading over the statement, I have signed and executed the same at Nuremberg, Germany on the fifth day of April 1946.

> **Source:** Trial of the Major War Criminals Before the International Tribunal, Nuremberg, 14 November 1945–1 October 1946 (Nuremberg: Secretariat of the International Military Tribunal, 1949), Doc. 3868-PS, vol. 33, 275–79.

Excerpts from the Geneva Convention Relative to the Treatment of Prisoners of War (1949)

The First Geneva Convention for the Amelioration of the Condition of the Wounded in Armies in the Field, held on August 22, 1864, is the first of four treaties of the Geneva Conventions. It is inextricably linked to Swiss relief activist Henry Dunant and the International Committee of the Red Cross, which led the effort to create an international mechanism for the protection of the wounded and prisoners of war. In 1859 Dunant witnessed the Battle of Solferino, fought between French-Piedmontese and Austrian armies in Northern Italy, and was horrified by the sight of tens of thousands of wounded soldiers left on the field due to lack of facilities and personnel. Upon return to Switzerland, Dunant published his account and, through his membership in the Geneva Society for Public Welfare, he helped organize an international conference that established the International Committee of the Red Cross in 1863. A year later, delegates from several European states met in Geneva, Switzerland, and signed the Geneva Convention for the Amelioration of the Condition of the Wounded and Sick in Armed Forces in the Field. The treaty was significantly revised in 1906, 1929, and 1949, and remains a cornerstone of modern international framework for the protection of POWs.

Part I. General Provisions

ARTICLE 4

A. Prisoners of war, in the sense of the present Convention, are persons belonging to one of the following categories, who have fallen into the power of the enemy:

(1) Members of the armed forces of a Party to the conflict as well as members of militias or volunteer corps forming part of such armed forces.

(2) Members of other militias and members of other volunteer corps, including those of organized resistance movements, belonging to a Party to the conflict and operating in or outside their own territory, even if this territory is occupied, provided that such militias or volunteer corps, including such organized resistance movements, fulfil the following conditions:

(a) that of being commanded by a person responsible for his subordinates;
(b) that of having a fixed distinctive sign recognizable at a distance;

(c) that of carrying arms openly;

(d) that of conducting their operations in accordance with the laws and customs of war.

(3) Members of regular armed forces who profess allegiance to a government or an authority not recognized by the Detaining Power.

(4) Persons who accompany the armed forces without actually being members thereof, such as civilian members of military aircraft crews, war correspondents, supply contractors, members of labour units or of services responsible for the welfare of the armed forces, provided that they have received authorization from the armed forces which they accompany, who shall provide them for that purpose with an identity card similar to the annexed model.

(5) Members of crews, including masters, pilots and apprentices, of the merchant marine and the crews of civil aircraft of the Parties to the conflict, who do not benefit by more favourable treatment under any other provisions of international law.

(6) Inhabitants of a non-occupied territory, who on the approach of the enemy spontaneously take up arms to resist the invading forces, without having had time to form themselves into regular armed units, provided they carry arms openly and respect the laws and customs of war.

B. The following shall likewise be treated as prisoners of war under the present Convention:

(1) Persons belonging, or having belonged, to the armed forces of the occupied country, if the occupying Power considers it necessary by reason of such allegiance to intern them, even though it has originally liberated them while hostilities were going on outside the territory it occupies, in particular where such persons have made an unsuccessful attempt to rejoin the armed forces to which they belong and which are engaged in combat, or where they fail to comply with a summons made to them with a view to internment.

(2) The persons belonging to one of the categories enumerated in the present Article, who have been received by neutral or non-belligerent Powers on their territory and whom these Powers are required to intern under international law, without prejudice to any more favourable treatment which these Powers may choose to give and with the exception of Articles 8, 10, 15, 30, fifth paragraph, 58–67, 92, 126 and, where diplomatic relations exist between the Parties to the conflict and the neutral or non-belligerent Power concerned, those Articles concerning the Protecting Power. Where such diplomatic relations exist, the Parties to a conflict on whom these persons depend shall be allowed to perform towards them the functions of a Protecting Power as provided in the present Convention, without prejudice to the functions which these Parties normally exercise in conformity with diplomatic and consular usage and treaties.

C. This Article shall in no way affect the status of medical personnel and chaplains as provided for in Article 33 of the present Convention.

Part II. General Protection of Prisoners of War

ARTICLE 13. Prisoners of war must at all times be humanely treated. Any unlawful act or omission by the Detaining Power causing death or seriously endangering the health of a prisoner of war in its custody is prohibited, and will be regarded as a serious breach of the present Convention. In particular, no prisoner of war may be subjected to physical mutilation or to medical or scientific experiments of any kind which are not justified by the medical, dental or hospital treatment of the prisoner concerned and carried out in his interest.

Likewise, prisoners of war must at all times be protected, particularly against acts of violence or intimidation and against insults and public curiosity.

Measures of reprisal against prisoners of war are prohibited.

ARTICLE 14. Prisoners of war are entitled in all circumstances to respect for their persons and their honour.

Women shall be treated with all the regard due to their sex and shall in all cases benefit by treatment as favourable as that granted to men.

Prisoners of war shall retain the full civil capacity which they enjoyed at the time of their capture. The Detaining Power may not restrict the exercise, either within or without its own territory, of the rights such capacity confers except in so far as the captivity requires.

ARTICLE 15. The Power detaining prisoners of war shall be bound to provide free of charge for their maintenance and for the medical attention required by their state of health.

ARTICLE 16. Taking into consideration the provisions of the present Convention relating to rank and sex, and subject to any privileged treatment which may be accorded to them by reason of their state of health, age or professional qualifications, all prisoners of war shall be treated alike by the Detaining Power, without any adverse distinction based on race, nationality, religious belief or political opinions, or any other distinction founded on similar criteria.

Section II. Internment of Prisoners of War

Chapter I. General Observations

ARTICLE 21. The Detaining Power may subject prisoners of war to internment. It may impose on them the obligation of not leaving, beyond certain limits, the camp where they are interned, or if the said camp is fenced in, of not going outside its perimeter. Subject to the provisions of the present Convention relative to penal and disciplinary sanctions, prisoners of war may not be held in close confinement except where necessary to safeguard their health and then only during the continuation of the circumstances which make such confinement necessary.

Prisoners of war may be partially or wholly released on parole or promise, in so far as is allowed by the laws of the Power on which they depend. Such measures shall be taken particularly in cases where this may contribute to the improvement of their state of health. No prisoner of war shall be compelled to accept liberty on parole or promise.

Upon the outbreak of hostilities, each Party to the conflict shall notify the adverse Party of the laws and regulations allowing or forbidding its own nationals to accept liberty on parole or promise. Prisoners of war who are paroled or who have given their promise in conformity with the laws and regulations so notified, are bound on their personal honour scrupulously to fulfil, both towards the Power on which they depend and towards the Power which has captured them, the engagements of their paroles or promises. In such cases, the Power on which they depend is bound neither to require nor to accept from them any service incompatible with the parole or promise given.

ARTICLE 22. Prisoners of war may be interned only in premises located on land and affording every guarantee of hygiene and healthfulness. Except in particular cases which are justified by the interest of the prisoners themselves, they shall not be interned in penitentiaries.

Prisoners of war interned in unhealthy areas, or where the climate is injurious for them, shall be removed as soon as possible to a more favourable climate.

The Detaining Power shall assemble prisoners of war in camps or camp compounds according to their nationality, language and customs, provided that such prisoners shall not be separated from prisoners of war belonging to the armed forces with which they were serving at the time of their capture, except with their consent.

ARTICLE 23. No prisoner of war may at any time be sent to, or detained in areas where he may be exposed to the fire of the combat zone, nor may his presence be used to render certain points or areas immune from military operations.

Prisoners of war shall have shelters against air bombardment and other hazards of war, to the same extent as the local civilian population. With the exception of those engaged in the protection of their quarters against the aforesaid hazards, they may enter such shelters as soon as possible after the giving of the alarm. Any other protective measure taken in favour of the population shall also apply to them.

Detaining Powers shall give the Powers concerned, through the intermediary of the Protecting Powers, all useful information regarding the geographical location of prisoner of war camps.

Whenever military considerations permit, prisoner of war camps shall be indicated in the day-time by the letters PW or PG, placed so as to be clearly visible from the air. The Powers concerned may, however, agree upon any other system of marking. Only prisoner of war camps shall be marked as such.

ARTICLE 24. Transit or screening camps of a permanent kind shall be fitted out under conditions similar to those described in the present Section, and the prisoners therein shall have the same treatment as in other camps.

Chapter II. Quarters, Food and Clothing of Prisoners of War

ARTICLE 25. Prisoners of war shall be quartered under conditions as favourable as those for the forces of the Detaining Power who are billeted in the same area. The said conditions shall make allowance for the habits and customs of the prisoners and shall in no case be prejudicial to their health.

The foregoing provisions shall apply in particular to the dormitories of prisoners of war as regards both total surface and minimum cubic space, and the general installations, bedding and blankets.

The premises provided for the use of prisoners of war individually or collectively, shall be entirely protected from dampness and adequately heated and lighted, in particular between dusk and lights out. All precautions must be taken against the danger of fire.

In any camps in which women prisoners of war, as well as men, are accommodated, separate dormitories shall be provided for them.

ARTICLE 26. The basic daily food rations shall be sufficient in quantity, quality and variety to keep prisoners of war in good health and to prevent loss of weight or the development of nutritional deficiencies. Account shall also be taken of the habitual diet of the prisoners.

The Detaining Power shall supply prisoners of war who work with such additional rations as are necessary for the labour on which they are employed.

Sufficient drinking water shall be supplied to prisoners of war. The use of tobacco shall be permitted.

Prisoners of war shall, as far as possible, be associated with the preparation of their meals; they may be employed for that purpose in the kitchens. Furthermore, they shall be given the means of preparing, themselves, the additional food in their possession.

Adequate premises shall be provided for messing.

Collective disciplinary measures affecting food are prohibited.

ARTICLE 27. Clothing, underwear and footwear shall be supplied to prisoners of war in sufficient quantities by the Detaining Power, which shall make allowance for the climate of the region where the prisoners are detained. Uniforms of enemy armed forces captured by the Detaining Power should, if suitable for the climate, be made available to clothe prisoners of war.

The regular replacement and repair of the above articles shall be assured by the Detaining Power. In addition, prisoners of war who work shall receive appropriate clothing, wherever the nature of the work demands.

ARTICLE 28. Canteens shall be installed in all camps, where prisoners of war may procure foodstuffs, soap and tobacco and ordinary articles in daily use. The tariff shall never be in excess of local market prices.

The profits made by camp canteens shall be used for the benefit of the prisoners; a special fund shall be created for this purpose. The prisoners' representative shall have the right to collaborate in the management of the canteen and of this fund.

When a camp is closed down, the credit balance of the special fund shall be handed to an international welfare organization, to be employed for the benefit of prisoners of war of the same nationality as those who have contributed to the fund. In case of a general repatriation, such profits shall be kept by the Detaining Power, subject to any agreement to the contrary between the Powers concerned.

Chapter III. Hygene and Medical Attention

ARTICLE 29. The Detaining Power shall be bound to take all sanitary measures necessary to ensure the cleanliness and healthfulness of camps and to prevent epidemics.

Prisoners of war shall have for their use, day and night, conveniences which conform to the rules of hygiene and are maintained in a constant state of cleanliness. In any camps in which women prisoners of war are accommodated, separate conveniences shall be provided for them.

Also, apart from the baths and showers with which the camps shall be furnished prisoners of war shall be provided with sufficient water and soap for their personal toilet and for washing their personal laundry; the necessary installations, facilities and time shall be granted them for that purpose.

ARTICLE 30. Every camp shall have an adequate infirmary where prisoners of war may have the attention they require, as well as appropriate diet. Isolation wards shall, if necessary, be set aside for cases of contagious or mental disease.

Prisoners of war suffering from serious disease, or whose condition necessitates special treatment, a surgical operation or hospital care, must be admitted to any military or civilian medical unit where such treatment can be given, even if their repatriation is contemplated in the near future. Special facilities shall be afforded for the care to be given to the disabled, in particular to the blind, and for their. rehabilitation, pending repatriation.

Prisoners of war shall have the attention, preferably, of medical personnel of the Power on which they depend and, if possible, of their nationality.

Prisoners of war may not be prevented from presenting themselves to the medical authorities for examination. The detaining authorities shall, upon request, issue to every prisoner who has undergone treatment, an official certificate indicating the nature of his illness or injury, and the duration and kind of treatment received. A duplicate of this certificate shall be forwarded to the Central Prisoners of War Agency.

The costs of treatment, including those of any apparatus necessary for the maintenance of prisoners of war in good health, particularly dentures and other artificial appliances, and spectacles, shall be borne by the Detaining Power.

ARTICLE 31. Medical inspections of prisoners of war shall be held at least once a month. They shall include the checking and the recording of the weight of each prisoner of war.

Their purpose shall be, in particular, to supervise the general state of health, nutrition and cleanliness of prisoners and to detect contagious diseases, especially tuberculosis, malaria and venereal disease. For this purpose the most efficient methods available shall be employed, e.g. periodic mass miniature radiography for the early detection of tuberculosis.

ARTICLE 32. Prisoners of war who, though not attached to the medical service of their armed forces, are physicians, surgeons, dentists, nurses or medical orderlies, may be required by the Detaining Power to exercise their medical functions in the interests of prisoners of war dependent on the same Power. In that case they shall continue to be prisoners of war, but shall receive the same treatment as corresponding medical personnel retained by the Detaining Power. They shall be exempted from any other work under Article 49.

Chapter VI. Discipline

ARTICLE 39. Every prisoner of war camp shall be put under the immediate authority of a responsible commissioned officer belonging to the regular armed forces of the Detaining Power. Such officer shall have in his possession a copy of the present Convention; he shall ensure that its provisions are known to the camp staff and the guard and shall be responsible, under the direction of his government, for its application.

Prisoners of war, with the exception of officers, must salute and show to all officers of the Detaining Power the external marks of respect provided for by the regulations applying in their own forces.

Officer prisoners of war are bound to salute only officers of a higher rank of the Detaining Power; they must, however, salute the camp commander regardless of his rank.

ARTICLE 40. The wearing of badges of rank and nationality, as well as of decorations, shall be permitted.

ARTICLE 41. In every camp the text of the present Convention and its Annexes and the contents of any special agreement provided for in Article 6, shall be posted, in the prisoners' own language, in places where all may read them. Copies shall be supplied, on request, to the prisoners who cannot have access to the copy which has been posted.

Regulations, orders, notices and publications of every kind relating to the conduct of prisoners of war shall be issued to them in a language which they understand. Such regulations, orders and publications shall be posted in the manner described above and copies shall be handed to the prisoners' representative. Every order and command addressed to prisoners of war individually must likewise be given in a language which they understand.

ARTICLE 42. The use of weapons against prisoners of war, especially against those who are escaping or attempting to escape, shall constitute an extreme measure, which shall always be preceded by warnings appropriate to the circumstances.

Source: Geneva Convention III: Relative to the Treatment of Prisoners of War. Available online at http://www.un-documents.net/gc-3.htm

---

Excerpts from Protocol Additional to the Geneva Conventions Relating to the Protection of Victims of International Armed Conflicts (1977)

In 1977, the Geneva Convention of 1949 was amended with the Protocol I relating to the protection of victims of international conflicts. It reaffirmed the international laws of the original convention and added further clarifications and restrictions on the conduct of modern warfare. As of June 2018, the Protocol had been ratified by 174 states, with the United States, Iran, and Pakistan being notable exceptions.

Article 10 Protection and care

1. All the wounded, sick and shipwrecked, to whichever Party they belong, shall be respected and protected.

2. In all circumstances they shall be treated humanely and shall receive, to the fullest extent practicable and with the least possible delay, the medical care and attention required by their condition. There shall be no distinction among them founded on any grounds other than medical ones.

Article 11 - Protection of persons

1. The physical or mental health and integrity of persons who are in the power of the adverse Party or who are interned, detained or otherwise deprived of liberty

as a result of a situation referred to in Article 1 shall not be endangered by any unjustified act or omission. Accordingly, it is prohibited to subject the persons described in this Article to any medical procedure which is not indicated by the state of health of the person concerned and which is not consistent with generally accepted medical standards which would be applied under similar medical circumstances to persons who are nationals of the Party conducting the procedure and who are in no way deprived of liberty.

2. It is, in particular, prohibited to carry out on such persons, even with their consent:

(a) physical mutilations;
(b) medical or scientific experiments;
(c) removal of tissue or organs for transplantation, except where these acts are justified in conformity with the conditions provided for in paragraph 1.

3. Exceptions to the prohibition in paragraph 2 (c) may be made only in the case of donations of blood for transfusion or of skin for grafting, provided that they are given voluntarily and without any coercion or inducement, and then only for therapeutic purposes, under conditions consistent with generally accepted medical standards and controls designed for the benefit of both the donor and the recipient.

4. Any willful act or omission which seriously endangers the physical or mental health or integrity of any person who is in the power of a Party other than the one on which he depends and which either violates any of the prohibitions in paragraphs 1 and 2 or fails to comply with the requirements of paragraph 3 shall be a grave breach of this Protocol.

5. The persons described in paragraph 1 have the right to refuse any surgical operation. In case of refusal, medical personnel shall endeavour to obtain a written statement to that effect, signed or acknowledged by the patient.

6. Each Party to the conflict shall keep a medical record for every donation of blood for transfusion or skin for grafting by persons referred to in paragraph 1, if that donation is made under the responsibility of that Party. In addition, each Party to the conflict shall endeavour to keep a record of all medical procedures undertaken with respect to any person who is interned, detained or otherwise deprived of liberty as a result of a situation referred to in Article 1. These records shall be available at all times for inspection by the Protecting Power.

Art 15. Protection of civilian medical and religious personnel

1. Civilian medical personnel shall be respected and protected.

2. If needed, all available help shall be afforded to civilian medical personnel in an area where civilian medical services are disrupted by reason of combat activity.

3. The Occupying Power shall afford civilian medical personnel in occupied territories every assistance to enable them to perform, to the best of their ability, their humanitarian functions. The Occupying Power may not require that, in the performance of those functions, such personnel shall give priority to the treatment of any person except on medical grounds. They shall not be compelled to carry out tasks which are not compatible with their humanitarian mission.

4. Civilian medical personnel shall have access to any place where their services are essential, subject to such supervisory and safety measures as the relevant Party to the conflict may deem necessary.

5. Civilian religious personnel shall be respected and protected. The provisions of the Conventions and of this Protocol concerning the protection and identification of medical personnel shall apply equally to such persons.

Art 45. Protection of persons who have taken part in hostilities

1. A person who takes part in hostilities and falls into the power of an adverse Party shall be presumed to be a prisoner of war, and therefore shall be protected by the Third Convention, if he claims the status of prisoner of war, or if he appears to be entitled to such status, or if the Party on which he depends claims such status on his behalf by notification to the detaining Power or to the Protecting Power. Should any doubt arise as to whether any such person is entitled to the status of prisoner of war, he shall continue to have such status and, therefore, to be protected by the Third Convention and this Protocol until such time as his status has been determined by a competent tribunal.

2. If a person who has fallen into the power of an adverse Party is not held as a prisoner of war and is to be tried by that Party for an offence arising out of the hostilities, he shall have the right to assert his entitlement to prisoner-of-war status before a judicial tribunal and to have that question adjudicated. Whenever possible under the applicable procedure, this adjudication shall occur before the trial for the offence. The representatives of the Protecting Power shall be entitled to attend the proceedings in which that question is adjudicated, unless, exceptionally, the proceedings are held in camera in the interest of State security. In such a case the detaining Power shall advise the Protecting Power accordingly.

3. Any person who has taken part in hostilities, who is not entitled to prisoner-of-war status and who does not benefit from more favourable treatment in accordance with the Fourth Convention shall have the right at all times to the protection of Article 75 of this Protocol. In occupied territory, any such person, unless he is held as a spy, shall also be entitled, notwithstanding Article 5 of the Fourth Convention, to his rights of communication under that Convention.

Art 47. Mercenaries

1. A mercenary shall not have the right to be a combatant or a prisoner of war.

2. A mercenary is any person who:

(a) is specially recruited locally or abroad in order to fight in an armed conflict;

(b) does, in fact, take a direct part in the hostilities;

(c) is motivated to take part in the hostilities essentially by the desire for private gain and, in fact, is promised, by or on behalf of a Party to the conflict, material compensation substantially in excess of that promised or paid to combatants of similar ranks and functions in the armed forces of that Party;

(d) is neither a national of a Party to the conflict nor a resident of territory controlled by a Party to the conflict;

(e) is not a member of the armed forces of a Party to the conflict; and

(f) has not been sent by a State which is not a Party to the conflict on official duty as a member of its armed forces.

Part IV. Civilian Population

Section I. General Protection Against Effects of Hostilities

Chapter I. Basic rule and field of application

Art 48. Basic rule

In order to ensure respect for and protection of the civilian population and civilian objects, the Parties to the conflict shall at all times distinguish between the civilian population and combatants and between civilian objects and military objectives and accordingly shall direct their operations only against military objectives.

Art 51.—Protection of the civilian population

1. The civilian population and individual civilians shall enjoy general protection against dangers arising from military operations. To give effect to this protection, the following rules, which are additional to other applicable rules of international law, shall be observed in all circumstances.

2. The civilian population as such, as well as individual civilians, shall not be the object of attack. Acts or threats of violence the primary purpose of which is to spread terror among the civilian population are prohibited.

3. Civilians shall enjoy the protection afforded by this section, unless and for such time as they take a direct part in hostilities.

4. Indiscriminate attacks are prohibited. Indiscriminate attacks are:

(a) those which are not directed at a specific military objective;
(b) those which employ a method or means of combat which cannot be directed at a specific military objective; or
(c) those which employ a method or means of combat the effects of which cannot be limited as required by this Protocol;

and consequently, in each such case, are of a nature to strike military objectives and civilians or civilian objects without distinction.

5. Among others, the following types of attacks are to be considered as indiscriminate:

(a) an attack by bombardment by any methods or means which treats as a single military objective a number of clearly separated and distinct military objectives located in a city, town, village or other area containing a similar concentration of civilians or civilian objects;

and

(b) an attack which may be expected to cause incidental loss of civilian life, injury to civilians, damage to civilian objects, or a combination thereof, which would be excessive in relation to the concrete and direct military advantage anticipated.

6. Attacks against the civilian population or civilians by way of reprisals are prohibited.

7. The presence or movements of the civilian population or individual civilians shall not be used to render certain points or areas immune from military operations, in particular in attempts to shield military objectives from attacks or to shield, favour or impede military operations. The Parties to the conflict shall not direct the movement of the civilian population or individual civilians in order to attempt to shield military objectives from attacks or to shield military operations.

8. Any violation of these prohibitions shall not release the Parties to the conflict from their legal obligations with respect to the civilian population and civilians, including the obligation to take the precautionary measures provided for in Article 57.

Section III. Treatment of Persons in the Power of a Party to the Conflict

Art 75. Fundamental guarantees

1. In so far as they are affected by a situation referred to in Article 1 of this Protocol, persons who are in the power of a Party to the conflict and who do not benefit from more favourable treatment under the Conventions or under this Protocol shall be treated humanely in all circumstances and shall enjoy, as a minimum, the protection provided by this Article without any adverse distinction based upon race, colour, sex, language, religion or belief, political or other opinion, national or social origin, wealth, birth or other status, or on any other similar criteria. Each Party shall respect the person, honour, convictions and religious practices of all such persons.

2. The following acts are and shall remain prohibited at any time and in any place whatsoever, whether committed by civilian or by military agents:

    (a) violence to the life, health, or physical or mental well-being of persons, in particular:
       (i) murder;
       (ii) torture of all kinds, whether physical or mental;
       (iii) corporal punishment; and
       (iv) mutilation;
    (b) outrages upon personal dignity, in particular humiliating and degrading treatment, enforced prostitution and any form of indecent assault;
    (c) the taking of hostages;
    (d) collective punishments; and
    (e) threats to commit any of the foregoing acts.

3. Any person arrested, detained or interned for actions related to the armed conflict shall be informed promptly, in a language he understands, of the reasons why these measures have been taken. Except in cases of arrest or detention for penal offences, such persons shall be released with the minimum delay possible and in any event as soon as the circumstances justifying the arrest, detention or internment have ceased to exist.

4. No sentence may be passed and no penalty may be executed on a person found guilty of a penal offence related to the armed conflict except pursuant to a

conviction pronounced by an impartial and regularly constituted court respecting the generally recognized principles of regular judicial procedure, which include the following:

(a) the procedure shall provide for an accused to be informed without delay of the particulars of the offence alleged against him and shall afford the accused before and during his trial all necessary rights and means of defence;

(b) no one shall be convicted of an offence except on the basis of individual penal responsibility;

(c) no one shall be accused or convicted of a criminal offence on account or any act or omission which did not constitute a criminal offence under the national or international law to which he was subject at the time when it was committed; nor shall a heavier penalty be imposed than that which was applicable at the time when the criminal offence was committed; if, after the commission of the offence, provision is made by law for the imposition of a lighter penalty, the offender shall benefit thereby;

(d) anyone charged with an offence is presumed innocent until proved guilty according to law;

(e) anyone charged with an offence shall have the right to be tried in his presence;

(f) no one shall be compelled to testify against himself or to confess guilt;

(g) anyone charged with an offence shall have the right to examine, or have examined, the witnesses against him and to obtain the attendance and examination of witnesses on his behalf under the same conditions as witnesses against him;

(h) no one shall be prosecuted or punished by the same Party for an offence in respect of which a final judgement acquitting or convicting that person has been previously pronounced under the same law and judicial procedure;

(i) anyone prosecuted for an offence shall have the right to have the judgement pronounced publicly; and

(j) a convicted person shall be advised on conviction of his judicial and other remedies and of the time-limits within which they may be exercised.

5. Women whose liberty has been restricted for reasons related to the armed conflict shall be held in quarters separated from men's quarters. They shall be under the immediate supervision of women. Nevertheless, in cases where families are detained or interned, they shall, whenever possible, be held in the same place and accommodated as family units.

6. Persons who are arrested, detained or interned for reasons related to the armed conflict shall enjoy the protection provided by this Article until their final release, repatriation or re-establishment, even after the end of the armed conflict.

7. In order to avoid any doubt concerning the prosecution and trial of persons accused of war crimes or crimes against humanity, the following principles shall apply:

(a) persons who are accused of such crimes should be submitted for the purpose of prosecution and trial in accordance with the applicable rules of international law; and

(b) any such persons who do not benefit from more favourable treatment under the Conventions or this Protocol shall be accorded the treatment provided by this Article, whether or not the crimes of which they are accused constitute grave breaches of the Conventions or of this Protocol.

8. No provision of this Article may be construed as limiting or infringing any other more favourable provision granting greater protection, under any applicable rules of international law, to persons covered by paragraph 1

Source: Protocol I Additional to the Geneva Conventions of 12 August 1949, and Relating to the Protection of Victims of International Armed Conflicts. Available online at http://www.un-documents.net/gc-p1.htm

Taguba Report on Treatment of Abu Ghraib Prisoners in Iraq (2004)

In the spring of 2004, repeated reports of widespread abuse and torture of civilian detainees in the Iraqi prison camp of Abu Ghraib began circulating in the international media. Credible reports, supported by graphic photographs, appeared on television and in the New Yorker *magazine in late April and early May 2004. U.S. Defense Department officials were already aware of these allegations and in early 2004 had instructed Lt. Gen. Ricardo S. Sanchez to investigate them. The task ultimately fell to Maj. Gen. Antonio M. Taguba, whose report appeared in early May. The Taguba Report drew on the testimony of numerous witnesses to describe pervasive physical, psychological, and sexual abuse of prisoners at the prison camp in October and November 2003, mistreatment that amounted to torture and contravened the Geneva Conventions governing behavior toward prisoners. The report also depicted an understaffed prison camp manned by poorly trained and ignorant U.S. military personnel, whom the military police and intelligence officers deliberately encouraged to abuse prisoners as a means of softening up such captives for subsequent interrogation.*

Findings and Recommendations

Regarding part one of the investigation, I make the following specific findings of fact:

1. (U) That Forward Operating Base (FOB) Abu Ghraib (BCCF) provides security of both criminal and security detainees at the Baghdad Central Correctional Facility, facilitates the conducting of interrogations for CJTF-7, supports other CPA operations at the prison, and enhances the force protection/quality of life of Soldiers assigned in order to ensure the success of ongoing operations to secure a free Iraq. (Annex 31)

5. (S) That between October and December 2003, at the Abu Ghraib Confinement Facility (BCCF), numerous incidents of sadistic, blatant, and wanton criminal abuses were inflicted on several detainees. This systemic and illegal abuse of detainees was intentionally perpetrated by several members of the military police

guard force (372nd Military Police Company, 320th Military Police Battalion, 800th MP Brigade), in Tier (section) 1-A of the Abu Ghraib Prison (BCCF). The allegations of abuse were substantiated by detailed witness statements (ANNEX 26) and the discovery of extremely graphic photographic evidence. Due to the extremely sensitive nature of these photographs and videos, the ongoing CID investigation, and the potential for the criminal prosecution of several suspects, the photographic evidence is not included in the body of my investigation. The pictures and videos are available from the Criminal Investigative Command and the CTJF-7 prosecution team. In addition to the aforementioned crimes, there were also abuses committed by members of the 325th MI Battalion, 205th MI Brigade, and Joint Interrogation and Debriefing Center (JIDC). Specifically, on 24 November 2003, SPC Luciana Spencer, 205th MI Brigade, sought to degrade a detainee by having him strip and returned to cell naked. (ANNEXES 26 and 53)

6. (S) I find that the intentional abuse of detainees by military police personnel included the following acts:

1. (S) Punching, slapping, and kicking detainees; jumping on their naked feet;
2. (S) Videotaping and photographing naked male and female detainees;
3. (S) Forcibly arranging detainees in various sexually explicit positions for photographing;
4. (S) Forcing detainees to remove their clothing and keeping them naked for several days at a time;
5. (S) Forcing naked male detainees to wear women's underwear;
6. (S) Forcing groups of male detainees to masturbate themselves while being photographed and videotaped;
7. (S) Arranging naked male detainees in a pile and then jumping on them;
8. (S) Positioning a naked detainee on a MRE Box, with a sandbag on his head, and attaching wires to his fingers, toes, and penis to simulate electric torture;
9. (S) Writing "I am a Rapest" (sic) on the leg of a detainee alleged to have forcibly raped a 15-year old fellow detainee, and then photographing him naked;
10. (S) Placing a dog chain or strap around a naked detainee's neck and having a female Soldier pose for a picture;
11. (S) A male MP guard having sex with a female detainee;
12. (S) Using military working dogs (without muzzles) to intimidate and frighten detainees, and in at least one case biting and severely injuring a detainee;
13. (S) Taking photographs of dead Iraqi detainees. (ANNEXES 26 and 26)

8. (U) In addition, several detainees also described the following acts of abuse, which under the circumstances, I find credible based on the clarity of their statements and supporting evidence provided by other witnesses (ANNEX 26):

1. (U) Breaking chemical lights and pouring the phosphoric liquid on detainees;
2. (U) Threatening detainees with a charged 9mm pistol;

3.   (U) Pouring cold water on naked detainees;
4.   (U) Beating detainees with a broom handle and a chair;
5.   (U) Threatening male detainees with rape;
6.   (U) Allowing a military police guard to stitch the wound of a detainee who was injured after being slammed against the wall in his cell;
7.   (U) Sodomizing a detainee with a chemical light and perhaps a broom stick.
8.   (U) Using military working dogs to frighten and intimidate detainees with threats of attack, and in one instance actually biting a detainee.

Source: The 'Taguba Report' on Treatment of Abu Ghraib Prisoners in Iraq. Available online at http://news.findlaw.com/hdocs/docs/iraq/tagubarpt.html

The Guantanamo Executive Order (2018)

The prison on the American military base at Guantanamo Bay has been used for years to detain accused terrorists and enemy combatants. The facility has been criticized for its grim conditions, and the U.S. policy of trying detainees. Although U.S. president Barack H. Obama pledged to close the base, he was unable to overcome political opposition within the U.S. Congress. In 2018, the new U.S. president Donald J. Trump signed an executive order justifying continued imprisonment of the detainees and keeping open the controversial prison.

Protecting America through Lawful Detention of Terrorists

By the authority vested in me as President by the Constitution and the laws of the United States of America, it is hereby ordered as follows:

Section 1. Findings. (a) Consistent with long-standing law of war principles and applicable law, the United States may detain certain persons captured in connection with an armed conflict for the duration of the conflict.

(b) Following the terrorist attacks of September 11, 2001, the 2001 Authorization for Use of Military Force (AUMF) and other authorities authorized the United States to detain certain persons who were a part of or substantially supported al-Qa'ida, the Taliban, or associated forces engaged in hostilities against the United States or its coalition partners. Today, the United States remains engaged in an armed conflict with al Qa'ida, the Taliban, and associated forces, including with the Islamic State of Iraq and Syria.

(c) The detention operations at the U.S. Naval Station Guantánamo Bay are legal, safe, humane, and conducted consistent with United States and international law.

(d) Those operations are continuing given that a number of the remaining individuals at the detention facility are being prosecuted in military commissions, while others must be detained to protect against continuing, significant threats to the security of the United States, as determined by periodic reviews.

(e) Given that some of the current detainee population represent the most difficult and dangerous cases from among those historically detained at the facility, there is significant reason for concern regarding their reengagement in hostilities should they have the opportunity.

Sec. 2. Status of Detention Facilities at U.S. Naval Station Guantánamo Bay. (a) Section 3 of Executive Order 13492 of January 22, 2009 (Review and Disposition of Individuals Detained at the Guantánamo Bay Naval Base and Closure of Detention Facilities), ordering the closure of detention facilities at U.S. Naval Station Guantánamo Bay, is hereby revoked.

(b) Detention operations at U.S. Naval Station Guantánamo Bay shall continue to be conducted consistent with all applicable United States and international law, including the Detainee Treatment Act of 2005.

(c) In addition, the United States may transport additional detainees to U.S. Naval Station Guantánamo Bay when lawful and necessary to protect the Nation.

(d) Within 90 days of the date of this order, the Secretary of Defense shall, in consultation with the Secretary of State, the Attorney General, the Secretary of Homeland Security, the Director of National Intelligence, and the heads of any other appropriate executive departments and agencies as determined by the Secretary of Defense, recommend policies to the President regarding the disposition of individuals captured in connection with an armed conflict, including policies governing transfer of individuals to U.S. Naval Station Guantánamo Bay.

(e) Unless charged in or subject to a judgment of conviction by a military commission, any detainees transferred to U.S. Naval Station Guantánamo Bay after the date of this order shall be subject to the procedures for periodic review established in Executive Order 13567 of March 7, 2011 (Periodic Review of Individuals Detained at Guantánamo Bay Naval Station Pursuant to the Authorization for Use of Military Force), to determine whether continued law of war detention is necessary to protect against a significant threat to the security of the United States.

Sec. 3. Rules of Construction. (a) Nothing in this order shall prevent the Secretary of Defense from transferring any individual away from the U.S. Naval Station Guantánamo Bay when appropriate, including to effectuate an order affecting the disposition of that individual issued by a court or competent tribunal of the United States having lawful jurisdiction.

(b) Nothing in this order shall be construed to affect existing law or authorities relating to the detention of United States citizens, lawful permanent residents of the United States, or any persons who are captured or arrested in the United States.

(c) Nothing in this order shall prevent the Attorney General from, as appropriate, investigating, detaining, and prosecuting a terrorist subject to the criminal laws and jurisdiction of the United States.

Sec. 4. General Provisions. (a) Nothing in this order shall be construed to impair or otherwise affect:

(i)   the authority granted by law to an executive department or agency, or the head thereof; or

(ii) the functions of the Director of the Office of Management and Budget relating to budgetary, administrative, or legislative proposals.

(b) This order shall be implemented consistent with applicable law and subject to the availability of appropriations.

(c) This order is not intended to, and does not, create any right or benefit, substantive or procedural, enforceable at law or in equity by any party against the

United States, its departments, agencies, or entities, its officers, employees, or agents, or any other person.

Donald J. Trump

The White House

Source: Trump, Donald. Executive Order 13823. Protecting America Through Lawful Detention of Terrorists. January 30, 2018. 83 Federal Register 4831, Document Number 2018-02261, published February 2, 2018. Available online at https://www .federalregister.gov/documents/2018/02/02/2018-02261/protecting-america-through -lawful-detention-of-terrorists

Bibliography

Abell, Francis. *Prisoners of War in Britain, 1756–1815*. Oxford: Oxford University Press, 1914.

Abzug, Robert. *Inside the Vicious Heart: Americans and the Liberation of Nazi Concentration Camps*. New York: Oxford University Press, 1985.

Akcam, Taner. *The Young Turks' Crime against Humanity: The Armenian Genocide and Ethnic Cleansing in the Ottoman Empire*. Princeton, NJ: Princeton University Press, 2012.

Alexander, Irvin and Dominic J. Caraccilo. *Surviving Bataan and Beyond: Colonel Irvin Alexander's Odyssey as a Japanese Prisoner of War*. London: Greenhill, 2005.

Allen, Beverly. *Rape Warfare: The Hidden Genocide in Bosnia-Hercegovina and Croatia*. Minneapolis: University of Minnesota Press, 1996.

Allen, Michael Thad. *The Business of Genocide: The SS, Slave Labor, and the Concentration Camps*. Chapel Hill: University of North Carolina Press, 2005.

Angell, Ami. *Terrorist Rehabilitation: The U.S. Experience in Iraq*. Boca Raton, FL: CRC Press, 2012.

Applebaum, Anne. *Gulag: A History of the Soviet Camps*. London: Allen Lane, 2003.

Arad, Yitzhak. *Belzec, Sobibor, Treblinka: The Operation Reinhard Death Camps*. Bloomington: Indiana University Press, 1987.

Baev, Jordan. "De-Stalinisation and Political Rehabilitations in Bulgaria," in Kevin McDermott and Matthew Stibbe, eds. *De-Stalinising Eastern Europe: The Rehabilitation of Stalin's Victims after 1953*, 150–169. New York: Palgrave Macmillan, 2015.

Bakirov, E., and V. Shantsev. *Butovskii polygon, 1937–1938*. Moscow: Panorama, 2002.

Ball, Eve. *In the Days of Victorio*. Tucson: University of Arizona Press, 1970.

Barthorp, Michael. *The Anglo-Boer Wars: The British and the Afrikaners, 1815–1902*. Poole, UK: Blandford, 1987.

Bauer, Yehuda. *A History of the Holocaust*. New York: Franklin Watts, 2001.

Benlow, Colin. *Boer Prisoners of War in Bermuda*. Bermuda: Island Press, 1994.

Berry, William A. *Prisoner of the Rising Sun*. Norman: University of Oklahoma Press, 1993.

Best, Geoffrey. *Humanity in Warfare: The Modern History of the International Law of Armed Conflict*. London: Weidenfeld and Nicolson, 1980.

Blatt, Thomas Toivi. *From the Ashes of Sobibor: A Story of Survival*. Evanston, IL: Northwestern University Press, 1997.

Bolton, Charles Knowles. *The Private Soldier under Washington*. New York: Barnes & Noble, 2011.

Bose, Romen. *The End of the War. Singapore's Liberation and the Aftermath of the Second World War*. Singapore: Marshall Cavendish, 2010.

Bowman, Larry G. *Captive Americans: Prisoners during the American Revolution*. Athens: Ohio University Press, 1976.

Braithwaite, Rodric. *Afgantsy: The Russians in Afghanistan, 1979–89*. New York: Oxford University Press, 2013.

Brändström, Elsa. *Among the Prisoners of War in Russia and Siberia*. London: Hutchinson, 1929.

Breuer, William B. *The Great Raid on Cabanatuan: Rescuing the Doomed Ghosts of Bataan and Corregidor*. New York: John Wiley & Sons, Inc., 1994.

Brickhill, Paul. *The Great Escape*. London: Cassell, 2000.

Brown, Daniel P. *The Tragedy of Libby and Andersonville Prison Camps*. Ventura, CA: Golden West Historical Publications, 1991.

Buggeln, Mark. *Slave Labor in Nazi Concentration Camps*. Oxford: Oxford University Press, 2014.

Campbell, Joan. *Joy in Work, German Work: The National Debate, 1800–1945*. Princeton: Princeton University Press, 2014.

Carr-Gregg, Charlotte. *Japanese Prisoners of War in Revolt: The Outbreaks at Featherston and Cowra during World War II*. New York: St. Martin's Press, 1978.

Carson, Andrew D. *My Time in Hell: Memoir of an American Soldier Imprisoned by the Japanese in World War II*. New York: McFarland & Company, 1997.

Carter, David. *Behind Canadian Barbed Wire: Alien, Refugee and Prisoner of War Camps in Canada, 1914–1946*. Elkwater, AB: Eagle Butte Press, 1998.

Chalker, Jack. *Burma Railway: Images of War, the Original War Drawings of Japanese POW Jack Chalker*. London: Macer Books, 2007.

Cook, Haruko Taya, and Theodore Failor Cook. *Japan at War: An Oral History*. New York: New Press, 1992.

Dandridge, Danske. *American Prisoners of the Revolution*. Baltimore, MD: Genealogical Publishing Co., 1967.

Danner, Mark. *Torture and Truth: America, Abu Ghraib, and the War on Terror*. New York: New York Review Books, 2004.

Doyle, Robert. *The Enemy in Our Hands: America's Treatment of Enemy Prisoners of War From The Revolution to the War on Terror*. Lexington: University Press of Kentucky, 2011.

Dundar, Fuat. *Crime of Numbers: The Role of Statistics in the Armenian Question, 1878–1918*. New Brunswick, NJ: Transaction Publishers, 2010.

Dunlop, Nic. *The Lost Executioner: A Journey into the Heart of the Killing Fields*. New York: Walker and Company, 2005.

Durnford, Hugh. *The Tunnellers of Holzminden*. Cambridge: Cambridge University Press, 1920.

Dwork, Debórah, and Robert Jan van Pelt. *Auschwitz: 1270 to the Present*. New York: Norton, 1996.

Falk, Stanley Lawrence. *Bataan: The March of Death*. New York: Norton, 1962.

Ferencz, Benjamin B. *Enforcing International Law—A Way to World Peace: A Documentary History and Analysis.* London: Oceana Publications, 1983.

Fischer, Gerhard. *Enemy Aliens: Internment and the Homefront Experience in Australia, 1914–1920.* St. Lucia, QLD: University of Queensland Press, 1989.

Fogg, Shannon L. *The Politics of Everyday Life in Vichy France: Foreigners, Undesirables and Strangers.* Cambridge: Cambridge University Press, 2009.

Forsythe, David P. *The Politics of Prisoner Abuse: The United States and Enemy Prisoners after 9/11.* Cambridge: Cambridge University Press, 2011.

Fujita, Frank. *Foo: A Japanese-American Prisoner of the Rising Sun*. Denton: University of North Texas Press, 1993.

Futch, Ovid L. *History of Andersonville Prison*. Gainesville: University of Florida Press, 1977.

Gargus, John. *The Son Tay Raid: American POWs in Vietnam Were Not Forgotten*. College Station: Texas A&M University Press, 2007.

Gordon, Harry. *Die like the Carp: The Story of the Greatest Prison Escape Ever.* Melbourne: Transworld, 1980.

Greenberg, Karen J., and Joshua L. Dratel, eds. *The Torture Papers: The Road to Abu Ghraib.* Cambridge: Cambridge University Press, 2005.

Gutman, Israel, ed. *Encyclopedia of the Holocaust*. 4 vols. New York: Macmillan, 1990.

Gutman, Israel, and Michael Berenbaum, eds. *Anatomy of the Auschwitz Death Camp.* Bloomington: Indiana University Press, 1994.

Gutman, Roy. *A Witness to Genocide: The 1993 Pulitzer Prize-Winning Dispatches on the "Ethnic Cleansing" of Bosnia.* New York: Macmillan, 1993.

Hackett, David A. *The Buchenwald Report*. Boulder, CO: Westview Press, 1997.

Hardee, David L. and Frank A. Blazich. *Bataan Survivor: A POW's Account of Japanese Captivity in World War II.* Columbia: University of Missouri Press, 2016.

Havers, R.P.W. *Reassessing the Japanese Prisoner of War Experience: The Changi POW Camp, Singapore, 1942–1945.* London: Routledge, 2012.

Hayes, Peter. *Industry and Ideology: IG Farben in the Nazi Era*. Cambridge: Cambridge University Press, 2001.

Herbert, Ulrich, and William Templer. *Hitler's Foreign Workers: Enforced Foreign Labor in Germany under the Third Reich.* Cambridge: Cambridge University Press, 2006.

Herzberg, Abel Jacob. *Between Two Streams: A Diary from Bergen-Belsen*. London: Tauris Parke, 2009.

Heyningen, E. van. "Women and Disease. The Clash of Medical Cultures in the Concentration Camps of the South African War," in *Writing a Wider War. Rethinking Gender, Race, and Identity in the South African War, 1899–1902.* Edited by G. Cuthbertson et al., 186–212. Athens: Ohio University Press, 2002.

Heyningen, Elizabeth van. *British Concentration Camps of the South African War, 1900–1902, Boer Concentration Camp Project,* http://www2.lib.uct.ac.za/mss/bccd/

Hobhouse, Emily. *The Brunt of the War and Where it Fell*. London: Methuen, 1902.

Howes, Craig. *Voices of the Vietnam POWs: Witnesses to Their Fight*. New York: Oxford University Press, 1993.

Hubbard, Preston. *Apocalypse Undone: My Survival of Japanese Imprisonment during World War II*. Nashville, TN: Vanderbilt University Press, 1990.

Hubbell, John G., et al. *P.O.W.: A Definitive History of the American Prisoner of War Experience in Vietnam, 1964–1973*. New York: Reader's Digest Press, 1976.

Ivanova, Galina, Carol Apollonio Flath, and Donald J. Raleigh. *Labor Camp Socialism: The Gulag in the Soviet Totalitarian System*. New York: M.E. Sharpe, 2000.

Jakobson, Michael. *Origins of the Gulag: The Soviet Prison Camp System, 1917–1934*. Lexington: The University Press of Kentucky, 2015.

Jensen, Steven and Mette Bastholm Jensen. *Denmark and the Holocaust*. Copenhagen: Danish Center for Holocaust and Genocide Studies, 2003

Jones, Heather. *Violence against Prisoners of War in the First World War: Britain, France and German, 1914–1920*. Cambridge: Cambridge University Press, 2011.

Kakar, M. Hasan. *Afghanistan: The Soviet Invasion and the Afghan Response, 1979–1982*. Berkeley: University of California Press, 1997.

Kevorkian, Raymond. *The Armenian Genocide: A Complete History*. London: I.B. Tauris, 2011.

Khlevniuk, Oleg V. *The History of the Gulag. From Collectivization to the Great Terror*. New Haven, CT: Yale University Press, 2004.

Kiernan, Ben. *The Pol Pot Regime: Race, Power and Genocide in Cambodia under the Khmer Rouge, 1975–1979*. New Haven, CT: Yale University Press, 2008.

Kinvig, Clifford. *River Kwai Railway: The Story of the Burma-Siam Railroad*. London: Brasseys, 1998

Knight, Amy. *Beria: Stalin's First Lieutenant*. Princeton, NJ: Princeton University Press, 1993.

Kogon, Eugen. *The Theory and Practice of Hell: The German Concentration Camps and the System behind Them*. New York: Farrar, Straus and Giroux, 2006.

Kordan, Bohdan. *Enemy Aliens: Prisoners of War: Internment in Canada during the Great War*. Kingston, ON: McGill-Queen's University Press, 2002.

Kuromiya, Hiroaki. *The Voices of the Dead: Stalin's Great Terror in the 1930s*. New Haven, CT: Yale University Press, 2007.

Lawrence, F. Lee, and Robert W. Glover. *Camp Ford CSA: The Story of Union Prisoners in Texas*. Austin: Texas Civil War Centennial Advisory Committee, 1964.

Lett, Brian. *An Extraordinary Italian Imprisonment: The Brutal Truth of Campo 21, 1942–1943*. Barnsley, South Yorkshire: Pen & Sword Military, 2014.

Levene, Mark. *The Crisis of Genocide: Volume 2: Annihilation: The European Rimlands, 1939–1953*. Oxford: Oxford University Press, 2013.

Levi, Primo. *Survival in Auschwitz: The Nazi Assault on Humanity.* Austin, TX: Touchstone, 1995.

Levy, George. *To Die in Chicago: Confederate Prisoners at Camp Douglas, 1862–1865.* Gretna, LA: Pelican, 1994.

Lewis, Paul. *Guerrillas and Generals.* Westport, CT: Praeger, 2002.

Lifton, Robert Jay. *The Nazi Doctors: Medical Killing and the Psychology of Genocide.* New York: Basic Books, 2000.

Lukacs, John D. *Escape from Davao: The Forgotten Story of the Most Daring Prison Escape of the Pacific War.* New York: NAL Caliber, 2010.

Marrus, Michael, and Robert Paxton. *Vichy France and the Jews.* Stanford, CA: Stanford University Press, 1981.

Marrus, Michael R., ed. *The Nazi Holocaust: Historical Articles on the Destruction of European Jews.* 9 vols. Westport, CT: Meckler, 1989.

Marrus, Michael R. *The Nazi Holocaust. Volume 6: The Victims of the Holocaust.* London: Meckler, 1989.

Martin, Michael. *The Iraqi Prisoner Abuse Scandal.* Farmington Hills, MI: Lucent Books, 2005.

McCormack, Gavan, and Nelson, Hank, eds. *The Burma-Thailand Railway: Memory and History.* Crows Nest, NSW: Allen & Unwin, 1993.

Miller, Donald Earl, and Lorna Touryan Miller. *Survivors: An Oral History of the Armenian Genocide.* Berkeley: University of California Press, 1999

Mojzes, Paul. *Balkan Genocides: Holocaust and Ethnic Cleansing in the 20th Century.* Lanham, MD: Rowman & Littlefield, 2011.

Moore, Bob, and Kent Fedorovich. *The British Empire and its Italian Prisoners of War, 1940–1947.* New York: Palgrave Macmillan, 2002.

Moorhead, Max L. *The Apache Frontier.* Norman: University of Oklahoma Press, 1968.

Neimeyer, Charles P. *American Soldiers' Lives: The Revolutionary War.* Westport, CT: Greenwood Press, 2007.

Nordin, Carl. S. *We Were Next to Nothing: An American POW's Account of Japanese Prison Camps and Deliverance in World War II.* London: McFarland, 1997.

Ooi, Keat Gin, ed. *Japanese Empire in the Tropics: Selected Documents and Reports of the Japanese Period in Sarawak, Northwest Borneo, 1941–1945.* Athens: Ohio University Center for International Studies, 1998.

Pakenham, Thomas. *The Boer War.* New York: Random House, 1979.

Perdue, Theda, and Michael D. Green. *The Cherokee Nation and the Trail of Tears.* New York: Viking, 2007.

Philpott, Tom. *Glory Denied: The Saga of Jim Thompson, America's Longest-Held Prisoner of War.* New York: W. W. Norton, 2001.

Pohl, J. Otto. *Ethnic Cleansing in the USSR, 1937–1949.* Westport, CT: Greenwood, 1999.

Pohl, J. Otto. *The Stalinist Penal System.* Jefferson, NC: McFarland, 1997.

Polian, Pavel. *Against Their Will: The History and Geography of Forced Migrations in the USSR.* Budapest, HU: Central European Press, 2004.

Posner, Gerald L. and John Ware. *Mengele: The Complete Story.* New York: Cooper Square, 2000.

Prelinger, Catherine M. "Benjamin Franklin and the American Prisoners of War in England During the American Revolution." *William and Mary Quarterly* 33 (1975): 261–294.

Proctor, Robert. *Racial Hygiene: Medicine under the Nazis.* Cambridge, MA: Harvard University Press, 1988.

Reilly, Joanne. *Belsen: The Liberation of a Concentration Camp.* New York: Routledge, 1998.

Ride, Edwin. *BAAG: Hong Kong Resistance, 1942–1945.* Hong Kong: Oxford University Press, 1981.

Rivett, Rohan D. *Behind Bamboo: An Inside Story of the Japanese Prison Camps.* Sydney, AU: Angus and Robertson, 1946.

Robson, Roy P. *Solovki: The Story of Russia Told Through its Most Remarkable Islands.* New Haven, CT: Yale University Press, 2004.

Rock, David. *Authoritarian Argentina.* Berkeley: University of California Press, 1993.

Rowan, Stephan A. *They Wouldn't Let Us Die: The Prisoners of War Tell Their Story.* Middle Village, NY: Jonathan David, 1973.

Ruder, Cynthia A. *Making History for Stalin: The Story of the Belomor Canal.* Gainesville: University Press of Florida, 1998.

Rüdiger Overmans, "German Policy on Prisoners of War, 1939–1945," in Jörg Echternhamp, ed. *Germany and the Second World War. Volume IX/II: German Wartime Society 1939–1945,* 733–881. Oxford: Clarendon Press, 2014.

Sanders, Charles W. *While in the Hands of the Enemy: Military Prisons of the Civil War.* Baton Rouge: Louisiana State University Press, 2005.

Schaft, Gretchen, and Gerhard Zeidler. *Commemorating Hell: The Public Memory of Mittelbau-Dora.* Urbana: University of Illinois Press, 2011.

Seymour, James D., Richard Anderson and Sidong Fan. *New Ghosts, Old Ghosts: Prisons and Labor Reform Camps in China.* New York: Routledge, 2015.

Smith, Denis. *The Prisoners of Cabrera: Napoleon's Forgotten Soldiers, 1809–1814.* New York: Four Walls, Eight Windows. 2001.

Speer, Lonnie R. *Portals to Hell: Military Prisons of the Civil War.* Mechanicsburg, PA: Stackpole Books, 1997.

Springer, Paul J. *America's Captives: Treatment of POWs from the Revolutionary War to the War on Terror.* Lawrence: University Press of Kansas, 2010.

Stover, Eric. *The Witnesses War Crimes and the Promise of Justice in The Hague.* Philadelphia: University of Pennsylvania Press, 2005.

Strasser, Steven, ed. *The Abu Ghraib Investigations: The Official Independent Panel and Pentagon Reports on the Shocking Prisoner Abuse in Iraq.* New York: PublicAffairs, 2004.

"A Summer Vacation in China's Muslim Gulag." *Foreign Policy,* 28 February, 2018, https://foreignpolicy.com/2018/02/28/a-summer-vacation-in-chinas-muslim-gulag/

Tampke, Jurgen, and Colin Doxford. *Australia, Willkommen: A History of Germans in Australia.* Kensington: New South Wales University Press, 1990.

Thrapp, Dan L. *The Conquest of Apacheria.* Norman: University of Oklahoma Press, 1967.

Thum, Rian. "China's Mass Internment Camps Have No Clear End in Sight." *Foreign Policy*, 22 August, 2018, https://foreignpolicy.com/2018/08/22/chinas-mass-internment-camps-have-no-clear-end-in-sight/

Todorov, Tzvetan. *Voices from the Gulag: Life and Death in Communist Bulgaria.* University Park: Pennsylvania State University Press, 1999.

Tomasevich, Jozo. *War and Revolution in Yugoslavia, 1941–1945: Occupation and Collaboration.* Stanford, CA: Stanford University Press, 2001.

Tone, John Lawrence. *War and Genocide in Cuba, 1895–1898.* Chapel Hill: University of North Carolina Press, 2008.

United Nations War Crimes Commission. *Law Reports of Trials of War Criminals.* London: HMSO, 1949.

United States. Nuremberg Military Tribunals. *Trials of War Criminals before the Nuernberg Military Tribunals under Control Council Law No. 10. Vols. VII & VIII.* Washington: GPO, 1950–1953.

U.S. Senate Select Committee on Intelligence. *The Official Senate Report on CIA Torture. Committee Study of the Central Intelligence Agency's Detention and Interrogation Program.* New York: Skyhorse Publishing, 2015.

Utley, Robert M. *The Indian Frontier of the American West, 1846–1890.* Albuquerque: University of New Mexico Press, 1984.

Van Pelt, Robert Jan. *The Case for Auschwitz: Evidence from the Irving Trial.* Bloomington: Indiana University Press, 2002.

Von Plato, Alexander, Almut Leh, and Christoph Thonfeld, eds. *Hitler's Slaves: Life Stories of Forced Labourers in Nazi-Occupied Europe.* New York: Berghahn, 2010.

Vulliamy, Ed. *Seasons in Hell: Understanding Bosnia's War.* London: Simon & Schuster, 1994.

Wachsmann, Nikolaus. *KL: A History of the Nazi Concentration Camps.* New York: Farrar, Straus and Giroux, 2015.

Wallace, Anthony C. *The Long, Bitter Trail: Andrew Jackson and the Indians.* New York: Hill and Wang, 1993.

Walters, Guy. *The Real Great Escape.* London: Bantam, 2013.

Weale, Adrian. *The SS: A New History.* London: Little, Brown, 2010.

Webb, Simon. *British Concentration Camps: A Brief History from 1900–1975.* London: Pen & Sword Books, 2016.

Williams, Philip F., and Yenna Wu. *The Great Wall of Confinement: The Chinese Prison Camp through Contemporary Fiction and Reportage.* Berkeley: University of California Press, 2004.

Winter, Jay, ed. *The Cambridge History of the First World War. Volume III: Civil Society.* Cambridge: Cambridge University Press, 2014.

Wylie, Neville. *Barbed Wire Diplomacy: Britain, Germany, and the Politics of Prisoners of War, 1939–1945.* Oxford: Oxford University Press, 2010.

Young, James. *The Texture of Memory: Holocaust Memorials and Meaning.* New Haven, CT: Yale University Press, 1994.

Zinsstag, Estelle. "Sexual Violence against Women in Armed Conflicts: Standard Responses and New Ideas," *Social Policy & Society* 5:1 (2005), 137–148.

Contributor List

Lee Baker
Independent Scholar

Ralph Baker
Independent Scholar

Paul R. Bartrop
Director of the Center for Judaic,
  Holocaust, and Genocide Studies
Florida Gulf Coast University

Waitman W. Beorn
University of North Carolina- Chapel
  Hill

Frank Beyersdorf
University of Heidelberg, Germany

Jessica Britt
Independent Scholar

Norbert C. Brockman
Professor Emeritus of International
  Relations
St. Mary's University, San Antonio

Dewey A. Browder
Austin Peay State University

Bernard A. Cook
Loyola University

Jeffery B. Cook
North Greenville University

Paul S. Daum
Independent Scholar

Michael Dickerman
Stockton University

Danielle Jean Drew
University of Alabama

Joe P. Dunn
Converse College

Casper W. Erichsen
Positive Vibes, Namibia

Jessica Evers
Florida Gulf Coast University

W.J. Fenrick
International Criminal Tribunal for the
  former Yugoslavia

Glenn E. Helm
Director, Navy Department Library

Alexis Herr
Strassler Center for Holocaust and
  Genocide Studies
Clark University

Steven Leonard Jacobs
Aaron Aronov Endowed Chair of
  Judaic Studies
University of Alabama

Robert Jiggins
University of Bradford, United
 Kingdom

Heather Jones
Independent Scholar

Kotani Ken
The National Institute for Defense
 Studies
Japan Defense Agency

Gary Kerley
North Hall High School, Gainesville,
 Georgia

Jinwung Kim
Kyungpook National University,
 South Korea

Arne Kislenko
Ryerson University

Nobuko Margaret Kosuge
Yamanashi Gakuin University, Japan

Matthew J. Krogman
Independent Scholar

Fred Krome
University of Cincinnati

Claudia Kuretsidis-Haider
Austrian Research Center for Post-War
 Trials, Austria

Lyman H. Legters
Retired, University of Washington

Daniel Lewis
Independent Scholar

Massimiliano Livi
University of Munster, Germany

Robert W. Malick
Harrisburg Area Community College

Martin Moll
University of Graz, Austria

Khatchig Mouradian
Strassler Center for Holocaust and
 Genocide Studies
Clark University

Gene Mueller
Texas A&M University, Texarkana

Charlene T. Overturf
Armstrong Atlantic State
 University

Paul G. Pierpaoli, Jr.
Fellow of Military History,
 ABC-CLIO

J. Otto Pohl
University of Ghana (Legon)

Joseph Ratner
Independent Scholar

Harold E. Raugh, Jr.
Defense Language Institute

John David Rausch, Jr.
West Texas A&M University

Junius P. Rodriguez
Eureka College

Kellie Searle
Independent Scholar

T. Jason Soderstrum
Iowa State University

Paul J. Springer
United States Military
 Academy

Nancy Stockdale
University of North Texas

Pascal Trees
University of Bonn, Germany

Spencer C. Tucker
Retired, Virginia Military Institute

Patricia Wadley
Independent Scholar

Douglas B. Warner
Independent Scholar

Duane L. Wesolick
Harrisburg Area Community
College

Joseph Robert White
University of Maryland University
College

Anna M. Wittmann
University of Alberta,
Canada

Index

Note: Page numbers in **bold** indicate the location of main entries.

About the Editor

Alexander Mikaberidze is Professor of History and Ruth Herring Noel Endowed Chair for the Curatorship of the James Smith Noel Collection. He is an award-winning author and editor of over a dozen books on military history of Europe and the Middle East. His publications include *Conflict and Conquest in the Islamic World: A Historical Encyclopedia* (2011), *Atrocities, Massacres, and War Crimes: An Encyclopedia* (2013), as well as multiple titles on the history of the Napoleonic Wars. He currently serves as the editor of the *Cambridge History of the Napoleonic Wars* and has contributed to the critically acclaimed *West Point History of Warfare*, the official military history textbook of the U.S. Military Academy.